I0885091

Educational Applications of Natural Language Processing, Chatbots, and AI

Suha Khalil Assayed
The British University in Dubai, UAE

IGI Global
Scientific Publishing
Publishing Tomorrow's Research Today

Vice President of Editorial	Melissa Wagner
Director of Acquisitions	Mikaela Felty
Director of Book Development	Jocelynn Hessler
Production Manager	Mike Brehm
Cover Design	Jose Rosado

Published in the United States of America by
IGI Global Scientific Publishing
701 East Chocolate Avenue
Hershey, PA, 17033, USA
Tel: 717-533-8845
Fax: 717-533-7115
Website: https://www.igi-global.com E-mail: cust@igi-global.com

Copyright © 2026 by IGI Global Scientific Publishing. All rights reserved. No part of this publication may be reproduced, stored or distributed in any form or by any means, electronic or mechanical, including photocopying, without written permission from the publisher.

Product or company names used in this set are for identification purposes only. Inclusion of the names of the products or companies does not indicate a claim of ownership by IGI Global Scientific Publishing of the trademark or registered trademark.

Library of Congress Cataloging-in-Publication Data

LCCN: 2025041632 (CIP Data Pending)
ISBN13: 9798337367910
Isbn13Softcover: 9798337367927
EISBN13: 9798337367934

British Cataloguing in Publication Data
A Cataloguing in Publication record for this book is available from the British Library.

All work contributed to this book is new, previously-unpublished material.
The views expressed in this book are those of the authors, but not necessarily of the publisher.
This book contains information sourced from authentic and highly regarded references, with reasonable efforts made to ensure the reliability of the data and information presented. The authors, editors, and publisher believe the information in this book to be accurate and true as of the date of publication. Every effort has been made to trace and credit the copyright holders of all materials included. However, the authors, editors, and publisher cannot assume responsibility for the validity of all materials or the consequences of their use. Should any copyright material be found unacknowledged, please inform the publisher so that corrections may be made in future reprints.

Table of Contents

Detailed Table of Contents

mechanisms, and more adaptive, interactive learning environments. However, the integration of NLP in education must be approached with a balance of enthusiasm and caution. Pedagogical alignment, ethical oversight, and technical limitations must be carefully managed to ensure NLP tools supplement rather than replace human instruction. Future directions include multilingual and multimodal systems, low-resource language support, and bias mitigation strategies to ensure inclusion, transparency, and data privacy.

The chapter provides a comprehensive analysis of the intersection between generative artificial intelligence (GenAI) and andragogy, exploring how emerging AI technologies can transform adult learning. It begins by grounding the discussion in adult learning theories, notably Knowles' model, before unpacking the fundamentals of GenAI. The chapter critically examines how GenAI aligns with adult learners' self-directed, experiential, and problem-centred approaches, offering practical examples and global case studies. It also addresses pedagogical strategies for integrating GenAI, emphasising learner engagement, ethical considerations, and digital readiness. Challenges such as technical, pedagogical, and societal barriers are explored alongside future research and innovation pathways. This work ultimately offers educators, researchers, and policymakers evidence-based insights and recommendations for harnessing GenAI to enhance adult education worldwide.

This survey chapter examines how Natural Language Processing (NLP) and Machine Learning (ML) are transforming the modern education. It shows ways in which AI technologies are transforming learning experience with intelligent tutoring systems, automated feedback, adaptive learning platforms, and personalized recommendations. The chapter reviews baseline concepts, major applications, and

The purpose of this study is to examine the performance of the artificial intelligence-based Gemini chatbot (CB) in answering chemistry questions from the national exam held annually. In this context, seven chemistry questions from the 2021 Basic Competency Test (TYT) prepared by the Measurement, Selection, and Placement Center (ÖSYM) were examined. The TYT chemistry questions were divided into two categories—multiple-choice and open-ended questions—without altering the question order or format from the original textbook, and were then posed to the CB. CB's answers were reviewed by three experts. According to the findings of the study, CB answered 85.71% of the multiple-choice questions correctly, which required reading comprehension and interpretation, but made significant errors in solving one question. In the open-ended questions, it provided detailed and clear explanations and answered all the questions. While providing clear explanations for all the open-ended questions, it answered 85.71% correctly. As a result, CB provided consistent answers to scientific concepts.

The objective of this research is to evaluate the effectiveness of artificial intelligence (AI) in supporting the development of Mandarin language acquisition, specifically focusing on the improvement of reading proficiency in Mandarin for non-native Mandarin learners. The methodology employed an extensive comparative analysis of the audio data spectrum among the three distinct cohorts: individuals who are Malaysian native speakers of Mandarin; recipients of text-to-speech systems facilitated by artificial intelligence; and Mandarin learners who enrolled in a Mandarin program as a non-native language learner at Universiti Malaysia Sabah (UMS). Through a spectrum analysis of the data collected from these cohorts, this study seeks to generate significant discovery delving with the efficacy of artificial intelligence in the domain of Mandarin reading comprehension. Moreover, this

Natural Language Processing (NLP) and Machine Learning (ML) are transforming education by enhancing personalized learning, automating assessments, and improving content generation. Key innovations include AI-powered tutoring systems, adaptive learning platforms, and language acquisition tools that cater to individual student needs. NLP applications, such as sentiment analysis and language modeling, alongside ML algorithms for predictive analytics, are enabling more efficient and inclusive learning experiences. However, challenges such as data privacy concerns, bias in AI models, and technological barriers remain. The future of education lies in integrating these technologies with immersive tools like AR/VR, fostering lifelong learning, and supporting educators as co-teachers. With continuous research and development, NLP and ML hold the potential to reshape educational landscapes, offering both opportunities and ethical considerations.

Natural Language Processing (NLP) and Machine Learning (ML) are transforming education by making learning interactive, adaptive, and personalized. Conversational AI enables AI-driven tools to enhance student support, automate administrative tasks, and improve teaching methods. Innovations in NLP power chatbots, virtual tutors, and automated grading, making them more responsive. ML uses predictive analytics to identify at-risk students and tailor personalized learning paths, fostering inclusivity. This chapter explores NLP and ML applications in K-12 and higher education, highlighting case studies on student engagement, knowledge retention, and teaching efficacy. Key challenges include AI integration, ethical concerns like data privacy, and biases in AI models. The chapter examines policy discussions and the need for regulatory frameworks that balance innovation and ethics. As AI-driven education expands globally, collaboration among researchers, educators, and policymakers is vital to shaping its future for improved learning outcomes.

Preface

Natural language processing (NLP) and natural language understanding (NLU) are essential for any advanced chatbot because they enable the system to interpret natural language in both text and speech in a human-like manner (Rajendran & Chitrarasu, 2024). NLP focuses on the tools and techniques that help the chatbot to read and process human language. This includes breaking down sentences into tokens, identifying keywords, recognizing parts of speech, and structuring the information so it can be analyzed and understood by the system. While, NLU takes this a step further by understanding the intention behind a question or conversation, identifying context, and capturing the meaning behind the text. Together, NLP and NLU allow chatbots to interpret, process, and respond to human language effectively (Han et al., 2024). When combined, the advanced capabilities of both NLP and NLU allow chatbots to introduce a novelty in understanding complex language, managing multiple languages, and responding in a way that feels natural and human-like.

In the era of globalization, universities are becoming increasingly diverse, bringing together students from different linguistic and cultural backgrounds (Oubkkou, 2025; Assayed & Alsayed, 2025). This diversity not only enriches the educational environment but also poses unique challenges for communication and student support services. Researchers and developers worldwide have continuously tested and challenged chatbots by using different languages, dialects, and cultural contexts. This has driven advancements in NLP techniques capable of processing multilingual inputs. For example, tokenization breaks down sentences into meaningful units, part-of-speech tagging identifies the grammatical role of each word, and named entity recognition detects important entities such as names, dates, or locations. Morphological analysis is particularly valuable for languages with rich word forms, like Arabic, Russian, Turkish and more, which are common among international students. Furthermore, the development of transformers and neural networks has greatly enhanced NLU capabilities, enabling chatbots to understand the intent and context behind a user's input. In a university setting, this means a chatbot can correctly interpret a student's query, whether expressed in English, Arabic, Mandarin, using different regional dialect while ensuring everyone has fair access to the information and support they need. This capability promotes equality and fairness by removing language barriers that could limit access to academic guidance and resources. By accurately understanding different languages, the chatbot enables all students to participate fully in their learning journey regardless of their background.

According to a study conducted by Assayed et al. (2023), developing an affordable chatbot can promote equality in education among high school students by providing 24/7 guidance on university and college admission requirements.

However, using chatbots in universities also presents several challenges. These include ensuring the interface is user-friendly for students (Reddy et al., 2024; Assayed et al., 2024) with varying levels of digital literacy, handling multiple languages and regional dialects accurately as well as data privacy, ethical concerns, academic integrity, and over-reliance on technology must be addressed (Davar et al.,2025).

This book, *Educational Applications of Natural Language Processing, Chatbots, and AI,* presents multiple real-world case studies on the use of NLP and chatbots from different regions around the world. It highlights the challenges and opportunities associated with using chatbots in education and explores the evolution of chatbot technology, from early rule-based systems to advanced AI-driven models, including generative AI (GenAI) and transformer architectures. The book also examines other transformer-based technologies such as Gemini and ChatGPT, demonstrating how these tools enhance natural language understanding, enable adaptive learning, and provide personalized student support, by analyzing real-world applications across diverse educational settings. It highlights how AI chatbots can break down language barriers, improve access to resources, and create a more inclusive learning environment, while also covering important topics like ethics, data privacy, and the challenges of using these tools effectively. With real-world examples, the book gives a clear picture of how chatbots and AI are developed, implemented, and used in education, showing how they can make learning more engaging, supportive, and accessible for all students.

The book offers a comprehensive look at the technical development, implementation, and deployment of chatbots and AI in educational settings. It explores how these technologies are designed, the challenges encountered during their integration into learning environments, and the strategies used to ensure they effectively meet the diverse needs of students. Through real-world examples, the book highlights both the practical and theoretical aspects of leveraging AI and NLP, showing how these tools can enhance learning, engagement, and equitable access to educational resources. NLP in education, offering readers a deeper understanding of how these tools can enhance learning, engagement, and equitable access to educational resources.

ORGANIZATION OF THE BOOK

The book is structured into eleven chapters, each exploring an important dimension of artificial intelligence integration in education, it emphasizes the role of chatbots and natural language processing (NLP) in enhancing both learning and teaching experiences. From leveraging AI for innovative educational practices to applying technology to improve student learning and engagement, each chapter explores how these tools can enhance the learning process and support educators in creating more effective and inclusive learning environments. Below is a brief overview of each chapter:

Chapter 1 examines students' and advisers' choices of trusted and effective chatbots among various types and tools of conversational and dialogue systems. The authors conducted interviews with eight high school students from different curricula to compare responses from the domain-specific chatbot "HSGAdviser," developed using RNN architectures such as encoder-decoder models with BiLSTM (Bidirectional Long Short-Term Memory), and ChatGPT-3.5 on advising topics like university applications and admission tests. The results showed that students generally preferred HSGAdviser for quick, simple answers but appreciated ChatGPT-3.5's detailed responses for more complex decisions, highlighting each chatbot's strengths depending on the question type.

Chapter 2 This chapter bridges the gap between theoretical NLP concepts and their practical application in education. It introduces key techniques including the tokenization, text classification, named entity recognition, syntactic parsing, and language modeling. The authors explore both the potential and limitations of these methods, highlighting their pedagogical value for engagement, assessment, and instructional support. Ethical considerations and future directions are also addressed, enabling readers to apply NLP effectively and responsibly in learning environments.

Chapter 3 analyzes the intersection of generative artificial intelligence (GenAI) and adult learning (andragogy), exploring how GenAI can transform adult education. It connects adult learning theories, especially Knowles' model, with GenAI's capabilities, highlighting alignment with self-directed, experiential, and problem-centered learning through practical examples and case studies. The author in this chapter also discusses pedagogical strategies, ethical concerns, and digital readiness, while addressing technical and societal challenges, offering evidence-based recommendations for educators, researchers, and policymakers to effectively integrate GenAI in adult education.

Chapter 4 highlights how core NLP tasks, such as tokenization, syntactic parsing, and transformer-based modeling, are increasingly embedded in tools that support both learners and educators. These innovations offer significant benefits, including workload reduction for teachers, enhanced feedback mechanisms, and more adaptive, interactive learning environments. The chapter also highlights that pedagogical alignment, ethical oversight, and technical limitations must be carefully managed to ensure that NLP tools supplement rather than replace human instruction.

Chapter 5 examines how deep learning and transformer models have transformed educational chatbots and intelligent tutoring systems (ITS). It covers key technologies like RNNs, LSTMs, CNNs, reinforcement learning, and advanced natural language understanding that enable personalized tutoring, automated grading, and multilingual support. While highlighting challenges such as data bias and privacy, the chapter also discusses future directions including few-shot learning, sentiment-aware tutoring, and AI-human collaboration to further advance AI-powered education.

Chapter 6 examines the performance of the AI-based Gemini chatbot (CB) in answering chemistry questions from the 2021 national Basic Competency Test (TYT). Seven questions, both multiple-choice and open-ended, were posed to the CB without changes to their original format, and its answers were evaluated by experts. The chatbot correctly answered 85.71% of multiple-choice questions and provided clear, detailed explanations for all open-ended questions, demonstrating consistent understanding of scientific concepts.

Chapter 7 evaluates the effectiveness of artificial intelligence (AI) in supporting Mandarin language acquisition, focusing on improving reading proficiency for non-native learners. It compares audio data from three groups: native Malaysian Mandarin speakers, users of AI-powered text-to-speech systems, and non-native Mandarin learners at Universiti Malaysia Sabah (UMS). Through this comparative analysis, the study examines AI's role in enhancing Mandarin reading comprehension. Additionally, it explores the implications of AI use in language teaching, especially concerning native speakers' involvement in instruction.

Chapter 8 explores the use of a standalone AI-powered chatbot to support student learning in a 15-week Marketplace Simulations business course. Analysis of student interactions, surveys, and focus groups showed the chatbot reduced anxiety, boosted self-efficacy, and improved performance, especially for strategic users who engaged iteratively. Despite technical challenges, the authors highlight the conversational AI's potential as flexible, effective support in simulation-based learning by combining generative AI with structured teaching methods.

Chapter 9 explores Lynqsphere, an innovative educational platform that integrates AI, data science, and VR to provide personalized, immersive, and collaborative learning experiences across all education levels. Key features include AI-driven personalized content, VR-enabled interactive lessons, an AI chatbot for instant support, and real-time collaborative coding tools. The platform also offers adaptive assessments, progress tracking, and tailored recommendations, emphasizing accessibility and inclusivity to support diverse learner needs and lifelong education.

Chapter 10 explores how Natural Language Processing (NLP) and Machine Learning (ML) are transforming education by enabling interactive, adaptive, and personalized learning experiences. It highlights applications such as conversational AI tools for student support, automated grading, and predictive analytics to identify at-risk students, promoting inclusivity across K-12 and higher education. The chapter also addresses challenges like ethical concerns, data privacy, and AI biases, emphasizing the importance of collaboration among researchers, educators, and policymakers to ensure responsible and effective AI integration in education.

Chapter 11 This chapter looks toward the future of education, highlighting how Natural Language Processing (NLP) and Machine Learning (ML) are set to transform learning environments by enhancing personalized instruction, automating assessments, and improving content creation. It explores key innovations such as AI-driven tutoring systems, adaptive learning platforms, and language tools that address individual student needs through techniques like sentiment analysis and predictive analytics. While these advancements promise more efficient, inclusive, and engaging learning experiences, the chapter also examines challenges such as data privacy, AI bias, and technological limitations. Ultimately, it envisions a future where NLP and ML seamlessly integrate with immersive technologies to foster lifelong learning, strengthen educator collaboration, and redefine educational practices.

Suha Khalil Assayed
The British University in Dubai, UAE

REFERENCES

Assayed, S. K., Alkhatib, M., & Shaalan, K. (2023, May). Artificial intelligence based chatbot for promoting equality in high school advising. In *2023 4th International Conference on Intelligent Engineering and Management (ICIEM)* (pp. 1-4). IEEE.

Assayed, S. K., Alkhatib, M., & Shaalan, K. (2024). The key challenges in educational advising chatbot dialogue system. In *Innovation in the University 4.0 System based on Smart Technologies* (pp. 74–82). Chapman and Hall/CRC.

Assayed, S. K., & Alsayed, S. (2025). The impact of high school curriculum on college readiness: A case study of international students in USA universities. In *Issues and Trends in International School Leadership* (pp. 457–478). IGI Global Scientific Publishing.

Davar, N. F., Dewan, M. A. A., & Zhang, X. (2025). AI Chatbots in Education: Challenges and Opportunities. *Information (Basel)*, *16*(3), 235. DOI: 10.3390/info16030235

Han, S. C., Weld, H., Li, Y., Lee, J., & Poon, J. (2025). *Natural Language Understanding in Conversational AI with Deep Learning*. Springer.

Oubkkou, A. (2025). Building Global Bridges and Fostering Global Competence: The Role of Multicultural Education in Higher Education Institutions. In *Internationalization of Higher Education and Digital Transformation: Insights from Morocco and Beyond* (pp. 69–87). Springer Nature Switzerland.

Rajendran, R. K., & Chitrarasu, K. (2024). Natural Language Processing (NLP) in chatbot design: NLP's impact on chatbot architecture. In *Design and Development of Emerging Chatbot Technology* (pp. 102-113). IGI Global Scientific Publishing.

Reddy, N. S., Chaitanya, N. P., Varshitha, P. S., Varma, R. C., Reddy, P. K., & Dandu, J. (2024, August). Intelligent Chatbot For Educational Institutions. In *2024 7th International Conference on Circuit Power and Computing Technologies (ICCPCT)* (Vol. 1, pp. 1337-1343). IEEE.

Acknowledgment

I'm deeply thankful to my family and friends, especially my parents, my husband, and my children, for their love, support, and encouragement throughout the journey of this book. Your belief in me has made this work possible.

I also sincerely thank all the authors and reviewers who contributed to this book. Your dedication, hard work, and insights have been invaluable, and this book wouldn't exist without your contributions.

Chapter 1
Evaluating the Effectiveness of Generative AI Models as Tutoring Systems:
Domain-Specific Approaches vs. ChatGPT-3.5

Suha Khalil Assayed
https://orcid.org/0000-0002-9924-0324
The British University in Dubai, UAE

Manar Alkhatib
The British University in Dubai, UAE

Khaled Shaalan
https://orcid.org/0000-0003-0823-8390
The British University in Dubai, UAE

Sana' Alsayed
https://orcid.org/0009-0002-1419-219X
Philadelphia University, Jordan

ABSTRACT

Due to the variety of chatbot types and classifications, students and advisers may struggle to select a trusted and effective chatbot. Chatbot classification depends on various factors, including task complexity, response style, and domain specificity. To explore the most suitable option for high school advising, this study employed

DOI: 10.4018/979-8-3373-6791-0.ch001

ght © 2026, IGI Global Scientific Publishing. Copying or distributing in print or electronic forms without written permission of IGI Global Scientific Publishing is prohibited. Use of this chapter to generative artificial intelligence (AI) technologies is expressly prohibited. The publisher reserves all rights to license its use for generative AI training and machine learning model development.

semi-structured interviews with eight high school students to assess their perspectives on seven generative responses from a domain-specific chatbot, HSGAdviser, in comparison with ChatGPT-3.5. The advising-related questions covered topics such as university applications, admission tests, and academic majors. Transcribed data were analyzed using thematic analysis. Findings indicate that most students preferred HSGAdviser for its ease, brevity, and speed, especially for Yes/No questions. However, when dealing with complex or high-impact decisions, some students favored ChatGPT-3.5 for its detailed responses. A key limitation of the study is the small sample size.

INTRODUCTION

Chatbots and conversational agents play an essential role in motivating students toward education and learning (Assayed et al., 2023; Yin et al., 2021) particularly considering the increased stress levels among high school students toward their future career, because of the academic demands and schoolwork. Both students and academic institutions face challenges in supporting students effectively and equally, as most schools have a limited number of advisers compared to the total numbers of students. Additionally, some schools may not be able to afford to hire advisers (Felten & Lambert, 2020).

However, due to the variety of chatbot types and classifications, students and counselors may experience confusion when trying to select the most suitable chatbot. In fact, the classification of chatbots depends on different factors (Assayed et al., 2024a), including the complexity of the task, the response-based approach, and the type of the domain. If the task is limited to basic and simple scenarios, then a rule-based chatbot can be an option. If the task requires a conversational function in natural human language, then natural language processing (NLP) and deep learning approaches are essential to be applied into the chatbot. Furthermore, if the chatbot designed for specific domain with a specific purpose, developers can easily customize it to enhance the performance. For instance, factors such as the feature extraction and the size of the dataset can significantly affect the performance of chatbots powered by neural network models (Shaker et al., 2022). However, several studies (Kapočiūtė-Dzikienė, 2020; Calonge et al., 2023; Lim et al., 2023; Assayed et al., 2024b) have been conducted to examine the accuracy of specific domain chatbots compared to other chatbots. The results vary depending on factors such as the purpose of chatbot, the complexity of the model, the feature extraction and the size of the dataset. Interestingly, due to the advancements in the transformer model (Vaswani et al., 2017) the GPT has played an essential role in the development of the new versions such as GPT-3, GPT-4 and GPT-5 that developed by OpenAI.

These developments aim to enhance the power of ChatGPT by using 175 billion of parameters in GPT-3 and 1.76 trillion parameters in GPT-4 as the large number of parameters can help more to understand the context as human-like. However, ChatGPT is trained in an open domain on different datasets, enabling it to handle different queries from diverse industries. Accordingly, researchers and developers conducted numerous studies to evaluate its accuracy of ChatGPT into different sectors, including the health sector (Biswas, 2023; Frosolini et al., 2023; Khan, 2023) business and banking (Skandali et al., 2023; Ali & Aysan, 2023) customer service (Lakhani, 2023; Subagja et al., 2023) as well as educational industry (Baidoo-Anu & Ansah, 2023; Lo, 2023; Halaweh, 2023). Interestingly, in education, ChatGPT plays various roles, including language learning (Baskara, 2023; Kohnke et al., 2023), serving as a researching tool (Aithal& Aithal, 2023), academic advising (Akiba & Fraboni, 2023; Assayed et al., 2024c) and more.

In general, the accuracy of any model depends on the training dataset and the architecture of the model. Choosing the most accurate and effective chatbot is crucial for schools and students. Therefore, a semi-structured interviews are conducted to address this concern by investigating the students' satisfaction in terms of ease to use of our proposed domain-specific deep learning based chatbot, named HSGAdviser that developed by assayed [2023] in comparison to ChatGPT-3.5. The study focuses on answering to the high school student' inquiries, guiding them successfully toward their colleges and careers. In this study seven questions about guiding the high school students are asked to both the domain-specific chatbot and ChatGPT-3.5. Subsequently, eight students from different high schools were interviewed to explain their perspectives on satisfaction with the provided answers, by identifying the most important factors in predicting technology acceptance, as specified in the Technology acceptance model (TAM), including the perceived ease of use and perceived usefulness (Davis, 1989) Accordingly, this study provides answers to the following two research questions:

> **RQ1:** To what extent do high school students prefer the domain-specific seq2seq chatbot named HSGAdviser over ChatGPT-3.5 to address their inquiries?
> **RQ2:** Which chatbot do high school students prefer, and why?

The next sections of this paper are organized as follows. Section 2 provides the related works. Section 3 describes the research methodology for comparing the generative answers between the HSGAdviser chatbot and ChatGPT-3.5. Section 4 presents the results. Finally, Section 5 and Section 6 cover the discussions and the conclusion, respectively.

RELATED WORK

The comparative study of chatbot is motivated by different researchers, as ChatGPT became the most popular chatbot after its released by OpenAI in 2022. Some studies compared ChatGPT with traditional machine learning based chatbots. For example, Caruccio et al. (2024) conducted a comparative study to evaluate the accuracy of a machine learning predictive model and ChatGPT in making diagnoses of diseases based on the symptoms. On the other hand, other authors compared ChatGPT with other generative LLM such as Bard and BERT. For example, Zhong et al. (2023) conducted an empirical study to evaluate and compare ChatGPT with BERT, and the results show that there is still a gap between both models in some of NLU tasks. Moreover, Ahmed et al. (2023) conducted a survey study comparing the capabilities and features between ChatGPT and Bard. In the field of academic advising, an exploratory study is conducted by Akiba & Fraboni (2023) to investigate the utility of ChatGPT in providing academic advising for current and prospective students who are interested to study BA in education. Seven questions were selected from advising records between 2019 and 2023 which are among the frequently asked questions by students. The results revealed that ChatGPT performs very well, however; it would not replace the human academic adviser. While various studies have compared educational chatbots in different models including ChatGPT, there is a limited focus on advising for high school students. To bridge this gap, this study aims to investigate the high school students' thought and experiences regarding their satisfaction with AI based generative chatbots in responding to their enquiries that are related to their future majors and universities.

METHODOLOGY

In this study, the authors adopted a qualitative research approach by conducting semi-structured interviews with high school students to compare two chatbots. The study focused on factors such as ease of use and the usability within the framework of Technology Acceptance Model (TAM). As mentioned earlier, this study compares two different chatbots: the encoder-decoder Seq2Seq chatbot named HSGAdviser, developed by Assayed [2023] with the most popular generative model, ChatGPT-3.5. In general, the sequence-to-sequence (Seq2Seq) model includes the following main components: encoder, decoder and the context vector, each specific section has specific tasks. The main task of the encoder is to process each single token in the sequential input and then summarize it into a fixed-length vector called the "context vector", which is a numerical representation of fixed-length data. It summarizes and encapsulates all the information from the input sequences. Even when input sequences vary in the length, the context vector ensures that eventually that all sequences have fixed-length vector. The decoder uses the context-vector as an input to predict the new value. The proposed chatbot HSGAdviser adopted the Bidirectional Long Short-Term Memory (BiLSTM) with 400 units in the encoder section. The model is trained on dataset of 10,318 pairs of samples collected from frequently asked questions (FAQ) from schools and universities websites, as well as from students and schools counselors. Interestingly, students in high schools have varying levels of satisfaction regarding their use of both the chatbot and ChatGPT, particularly in the context of student advising.

Experiment Setting

A semi-structured interviews were conducted to solicit the feedback from high school students using both HSGAdviser (Seq2Seq Chatbot) and ChatGPT-3.5 as college guidance adviser. Eight students were provided with seven different questions related to high school and university enquiries for both chatbots. Subsequently, we analyzed and investigated the students' feedback regarding their satisfaction with the responses generated from both chatbots.

Data Collection

High school students in UAE come from divers nationalities and cultures. They attend schools with different academic curricula, such as the American curriculum (HSD), British Curriculum (GCE), International Baccalaureate (IB), and so on. In this study, we selected eight high school students from various high school curricula, as shown in Table 1.

Table 1. The main characteristics of the selected students

Student Code	Gender	Grade	HS Curriculum
Student-01	M	12	British System
Student-02	F	11	Canadian System
Student-03	M	12	American System
Student-04	M	12	IB
Student-05	M	12	American System
Student-06	M	11	American System
Student-07	M	11	British System
Student-08	M	11	IB

All participants had experience in using different chatbots, including ChatGPT-3.5. Nevertheless, 50% of the students were in Grade 11, while the remaining 50% were in grade 12. The majority of participants come from American curriculum (38%) as depicted in Table 2 and Figure 1.

Table 2. The number of selected students in each curriculum

Curriculum	Number of Students
American System	3
British System	2
Canadian System	1
IB	2
Total	**8**

Figure 1. The chart depicts the distribution of students according to their curriculum, indicating that the majority of participants belong to the American System (HSD)

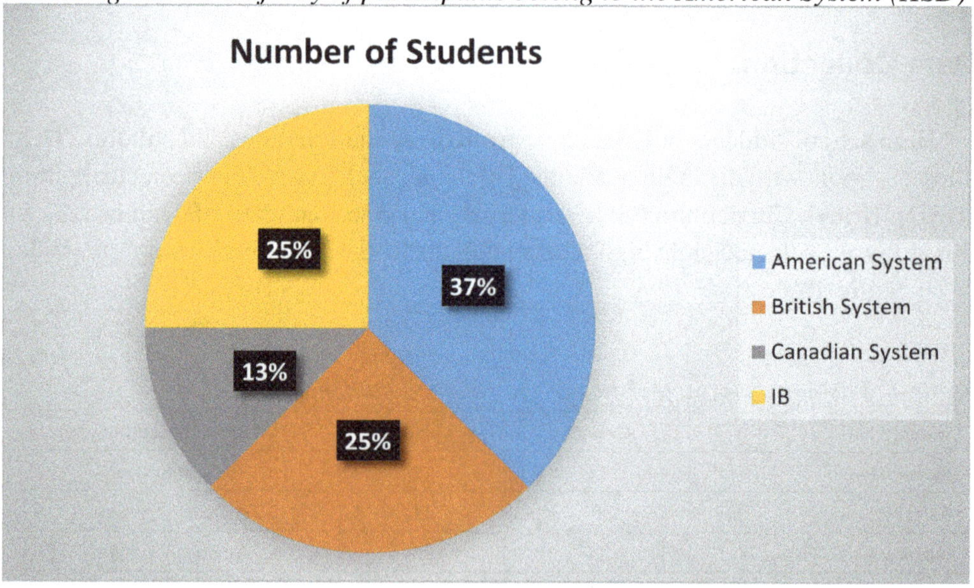

Before starting this study, we conducted a pre-discussion session with the students to understand the most important questions and inquiries. Interestingly, students raised 30 questions related to their areas of interests. We categorized them into the following five main topics:

1- University admission
2- Major/ Career choice
3- Standardized tests
4- Scholarships and Financial Aids
5- Study Abroad

However, after reviewing 30 questions, we removed the duplicate, finalizing the list to the seven questions as depicted in Table 3.

Table 3. The final list of questions that provided to HSGAdviser Chatbot & ChatGPT-3.5

Student Inquiry
1. Why should I take AP exam
2. How can I select my major
3. Should I take IELT test or TOEFL
4. I am confused what to study in university
5. Should I take EMSAT Math
6. Where can I apply to scholarships from UAE
7. Is EMSAT required in all universities

Conducting the Interview

In this study, we selected semi-structured interviews that provide various open-ended questions related to the students' experiences and perceptions of using both chatbots. As explained in the previous section, the questions are designed to address the students' interests in high school. We started the interview as follows:

"Thank you for participating in this interview. We are conducting a study to compare a proposed chatbot named HSGAdviser with ChatGPT 3.5 in order to understand your experiences with the answers generated by both chatbots. Your feedback will help us improve the technology and make our model more user-friendly and useful to high school students".

Accordingly, we focused on comparing the ease of use and complexity of both chatbots in answering the student's enquiries and questions that shown in Table 3, since in the Technology Acceptance Model (TAM), the perceived ease of use (Davis, 1989) plays an important role in influencing users intentions towards adopting and using the technology such as the chatbots.

Data Analysis

We reviewed and examined the transcribed data using the thematic analysis, which is the most important process for encoding the qualitative data (Boyatzis, 1998). Next, we identified the common themes behind the students' transcripts. Then, each section from students' experiences and satisfactions with each chatbot in the transcript was mapped to the corresponding common theme.

RESULTS

The students provided different feedback on the responses that generated by both chatbots HSGAdviser and ChatGPT-3.5, for seven questions related to high school guidance advising. The questions varied in complexity. Therefore, in this section we analyze the results based on each question.

Why Should I Take AP Exam?

Most of students who preferred responses generated by the HSGAdviser chatbot, for this particular question described the answers as effective, shorter and time-consuming. For instance, Student 01 stated "*I'd like the HSGAdviser chatbot because it provides shorter and summarized answers*". In addition, Student 07 and Student 08 justified their preference of using the HSGAdviser chatbot because it's easy and time-consuming. Student 07 described as, "*I preferred the HSAdviser chatbot model over ChatGPT, because it's more time-efficient*". Whereas Student 08 said "*The chatbot gave me a straightforward explanation that is easy to digest*".

How Can I Select my Major?

This question is considered one of the most important enquiries that high school students asked about it because it can shape their future career. However, more than 50% of the selected students preferred the answers that generated from ChatGPT since they need more information about it. For instance, Student 03 described the generative response of ChatGPT as "*wealth of information*" and Student 04 characterized the answer as "*A step by step guide*". Moreover, the perspective of Student 05 from this question is "*I'd rather follow a step by step guide in choosing my major, since it is a big effect on my life, I prefer chatgpt*". Additionally, Student 07 mentioned, "*I favored ChatGPT model as it gave answers that were more in depth*".

Should I Take IELT Test or TOEFL?

"Despite ChatGPT providing a more detailed answer by explaining the differences between both exams in terms of sections and scoring, all students stated that they preferred the HSGAdviser chatbot, which answered in one short sentence as follows: "*It depends on the colleges you are applying to*". However, students justified their preference by using different descriptions such as "it's a straightforward", "it's easier", "shorter answer", "quick answer" and "simplified answer".

I am Confused What to Study in University

This question is somehow related to question in 4.2, as most students preferred the answers that generated from ChatGPT, since it's an opened question and students might need more details about majors that can shape their future. However, the following answer is generated by the HSGAdviser chatbot: *Advising center provides guidance to students' interests."* Whereas the ChatGPT generated an answer in long paragraph with more than 20 lines.

Should I Take EMSAT Math?

In this question, students' perspectives are similar to those in question 4.3. They preferred the HSGAdviser chatbot, because it provides an effective concise answer in one brief sentence without generating extra and unnecessary information.

Where Can I Apply to Scholarships from UAE?

Most students preferred the HSGAdviser chatbot with justifying their preference by using some key words such as "quick", "to the point ", "straightforward"," direct answer", "not time consuming", and "simplified answer". For example, Student 01 explained the reason behind selecting the answer from HSGAdviser chatbot over ChatGPT "*The ChatGPTt gave a more universal answer which I did not like, it treated me not as a student residing in the UAE, but just as a student. While the chatbot gave answers relating to my current residency which in this case is the UAE*". Additionally, Student 07, explained his feedback as "*HSGAdviser chatbot gave simplified answers that were not time consuming*".

Is Emirates Standardized Test (EMSAT) Required in all Universities in UAE?

The majority of students show higher satisfaction with the answers generated by the HSGAdviser chatbot. Some students justified their feedback by explaining that they expected a straightforward and quick answer (yes or no). For instance, the Student 03' feedback is *"Since it's a straightforward yes-or-no question, I like the chatbot response"*. Moreover, Students 04 explained the generated response as "*A shorter answer is what I am looking for here, a quick yes or no answer would be satisfactionary, so the chatbot is perfect in this situation*".

DISCUSSIONS

Since the perceived usefulness and ease of use are the most important factors on users' perspectives toward adopting successfully the technologies,the authors highlighted in this study the most popular indicators that can impact both the ease of use and the usefulness, such as response-time, understandably, ease of use, accuracy, and clarity of information. Accordingly, most students found the developed HSGAdviser chatbot is easier, quicker and more time-saving compared to ChatGPT-3.5, especially for Yes/No questions. Students expect short answers and show more comfort with short and concise responses. Table 4 presents the quantitative measures of the number of students who preferred the HSGAdviser chatbot over ChatGPT-3.5 for yes/ no questions. However, the result shows that 75% of the responses to four different types of yes/no questions indicate a preference for using the HSGAdviser chatbot compared to ChatGPT-3.5 due to its quick and prompt answers.

Table 4. Number of students who preferred the HSGAdviser over the ChatGPT in yes/no questions

Yes/No Question	# of students prefer HSGAdviser Chatbot	# of students prefer ChatGPT
Should I take IELT test or TOEFL	5	3
Should I take EMSAT Math	6	2
Is Emirates Standardized Test (EMSAT) required in all universities in UAE	7	1
The preference percentage (%)	75%	25%

Interestingly, this is aligned with the previous of studies on the impact of having advising chatbot in students advising, emphasizing the importance of providing effective answers. Therefore, the following Research Question1 (RQ1): "To what extent do high school students prefer the domain-specific seq2seq chatbot named HSGAdviser over ChatGPT-3.5 to address their inquiries?" is addressed in this study with a focus on quick answers. Despite the fact that, some students explained that ChatGPT generates long answer with unnecessary information and even though it's not asked for. But other high school students found that some crucial questions that can have a significance impact in their future they would prefer ChatGPT for more details information. For instance, inquiries about selecting majors or courses at universities, such as, "How can I select my major" and "I am confused what to study in university". Student 03 for example, explained the reason behind selecting ChatGPT in such kind of questions: *"I like ChatGPT's response because it provides a wealth of information regarding career exploration, allows you to self-evaluate, and much more"*. As a result, RQ2 is answered by indicating the selection of a generative advising chatbot for high school students depends on the type of inquiries and the significant impacts they may have on their future. However, Figure 2 illustrates the word cloud which represents the frequency of words that students mentioned during the interviews. For example, it shows some words that are repeated multiple times by students such as response, simplified, response, straightforward, details, etc.

Figure 2. Displays the word cloud representing the frequency of words mentioned by students during the interviews, indicating some key words such as major, quick, time, and short

CONCLUSION

This study demonstrates the high school students 'perspectives on the responses of the proposed domain-specific chatbot named HSGAdviser compared it with ChatGPT-3.5, particularly in the context of college guidance advising. However, eight students from different high schools' curricula were interviewed to explain their perspectives on satisfaction from the generative answers to seven of students' inquiries from both chatbots. The results reveal that most students found that HSGAdviser chatbot is easier, shorter, faster and more concise compared to ChatGPT-3.5, especially for Yes/No questions as students expect brief answers. However, others found that some crucial questions that can have a significance impacts on their future, they would prefer ChatGPT for more detailed information.

The limited size of the participants is considered the main limitation in this study. However, in the future research, other high school students from different regions can participate in the study. Since, high school students from different regions could participate in the study. Students from various regions might have different perspectives due to diverse educational systems (Assayed & Alsayed, 2025) and policies, which could influence their use of the chatbot (Gai, 2024) besides their cultural attitudes towards technology and education may influence the student's perspectives. Moreover, regions that depend heavily in technology might have different answers than others. This expansion can enhance the students advising through effective and generative advising chatbot.

AUTHOR CONTRIBUTIONS

S. A. wrote the main manuscript & conducted the research methodology.

S.A., K.S. and M.A. reviewed and analyzed the results. K.S. and M.A. reviewed the final study.

They have all read and approved the final manuscript.

ETHICAL APPROVAL AND GUIDELINES STATEMENTS

Ethical approval: The present study was approved by Research Ethics Committee (REC) at British University in Dubai (BUiD).

Ethical Guidelines: The study was performed in accordance with the principles of Declaration of the Helsinki. Approval was granted by the Ethics Committee of Research Ethics Committee (REC) at British University in Dubai (BUiD).

REFERENCES

Ahmed, I., Kajol, M., Hasan, U., Datta, P. P., Roy, A., & Reza, M. R. (2023). *ChatGPT vs. Bard: a comparative study*. UMBC Student Collection.

Aithal, P. S., & Aithal, S. (2023). Application of ChatGPT in Higher Education and Research–A Futuristic Analysis. [IJAEML]. *International Journal of Applied Engineering and Management Letters*, *7*(3), 168–194.

Akiba, D., & Fraboni, M. C. (2023). AI-Supported Academic Advising: Exploring ChatGPT's Current State and Future Potential toward Student Empowerment. *Education Sciences*, *13*(9), 885.

Ali, H., & Aysan, A. F. (2023). What will ChatGPT Revolutionize in Financial Industry? *Available at* SSRN *4403372*. sassayed. (2023). *GitHub - sassayed/HSGAdviser-BiLSTM-Chatbot: HSGAdviser-Text-Based Chatbot for Student Guidance Advising*. GitHub. https://github.com/sassayed/HSGAdviser-BiLSTM-Chatbot

Assayed, S. K., Alkhatib, M., & Shaalan, K. (2023, June). Advising chatbot for high school in smart cities. In *2023 8th International Conference on Smart and Sustainable Technologies (SpliTech)* (pp. 1-6). IEEE.

Assayed, S. K., Alkhatib, M., & Shaalan, K. (2024a). A Systematic Review of Conversational AI Chatbots in Academic Advising. In *BUiD Doctoral Research Conference 2023* (pp. 346-359). Springer, Cham.

Assayed, S. K., Alkhatib, M., & Shaalan, K. (2024b, March). Enhancing Student Services: Machine Learning Chatbot Intent Recognition for High School Inquiries. In *BUiD Doctoral Research Conference 2023: Multidisciplinary Studies* (pp. 243-254). Cham: Springer Nature Switzerland.

Assayed, S. K., Alkhatib, M., & Shaalan, K. (2024c). A Comparative Study of ChatGPT and Seq2Seq Chatbot for Effective Students Advising. *ChatGPT and Global Higher Education: Using Artificial Intelligence in Teaching and Learning*, 148.

Assayed, S. K., & Alsayed, S. (2025). The Impact of High School Curriculum on College Readiness: A Case Study of international Students in USA Universities. In *Issues and Trends in International School Leadership* (pp. 457–478). IGI Global Scientific Publishing.

Baidoo-Anu, D., & Ansah, L. O. (2023). Education in the era of generative artificial intelligence (AI): Understanding the potential benefits of ChatGPT in promoting teaching and learning. *Journal of AI*, *7*(1), 52–62.

Baskara, R. (2023). Exploring the implications of ChatGPT for language learning in higher education. *Indonesian Journal of English Language Teaching and Applied Linguistics*, *7*(2), 343–358.

Biswas, S. S. (2023). Role of chat gpt in public health. *Annals of Biomedical Engineering*, *51*(5), 868–869. PMID: 36920578

Boyatzis, R. E. (1998). *Transforming Qualitative information: Thematic Analysis and Code Development*. Sage Publications.

Calonge, D. S., Smail, L., & Kamalov, F. (2023). Enough of the chit-chat: A comparative analysis of four AI chatbots for calculus and statistics. *Journal of Applied Learning and Teaching*, *6*(2).

Caruccio, L., Cirillo, S., Polese, G., Solimando, G., Sundaramurthy, S., & Tortora, G. (2024). Can ChatGPT provide intelligent diagnoses? A comparative study between predictive models and ChatGPT to define a new medical diagnostic bot. *Expert Systems with Applications*, *235*, 121186.

Davis, F. D. (1989). Perceived usefulness, perceived ease of use, and user acceptance of information technology. *Management Information Systems Quarterly*, *13*(3), 319–339.

Felten, P., & Lambert, L. M. (2020). *Relationship-rich education: How human connections drive success in college*. Jhu Press.

Frosolini, A., Gennaro, P., Cascino, F., & Gabriele, G. (2023). *Reference to "Role of Chat GPT in Public Health", to Highlight the AI's Incorrect Reference Generation. Annals of Biomedical Engineering*.

Gai, Y. (2024). *Factors that impact intention to continue using ai-based chatbots in different countries* (Doctoral dissertation, Vilniaus universitetas.).

Halaweh, M. (2023). ChatGPT in Education: Strategies for Responsible Implementation. *Contemporary Educational Technology*, *15*(2). https://eric.ed.gov/?id=EJ1385551

Kapočiūtė-Dzikienė, J. (2020). A domain-specific generative chatbot trained from little data. *Applied Sciences (Basel, Switzerland)*, *10*(7), 2221.

Khan, U. (2023). Revolutionizing Personalized Protein Energy Malnutrition Treatment: Harnessing the Power of Chat GPT. *Annals of Biomedical Engineering*, •••, 1–3. PMID: 37728811

Kohnke, L., Moorhouse, B. L., & Zou, D. (2023). ChatGPT for language teaching and learning. *RELC Journal*, •••, 00336882231162768.

Lakhani, A. (2023). *Enhancing Customer Service with ChatGPT Transforming the Way Businesses Interact with Customers*. https://doi.org/DOI: 10.31219/osf.io/7hf4c

Lim, Z. W., Pushpanathan, K., Yew, S. M. E., Lai, Y., Sun, C. H., Lam, J. S. H., & Tham, Y. C. (2023). Benchmarking large language models' performances for myopia care: A comparative analysis of ChatGPT-3.5, ChatGPT-4.0, and Google Bard. *EBioMedicine*, •••, 95. PMID: 37625267

Lo, C. K. (2023). What is the impact of ChatGPT on education? A rapid review of the literature. *Education Sciences*, *13*(4), 410.

Shaker, S. S., Alhajim, D., Al-Khazaali, A. A. T., Hussein, H. A., & Athab, A. F. (2022). Feature Extraction based Text Classification: A review. *Journal of Algebraic Statistics*, *13*(1), 646–653.

Skandali, D., Magoutas, A., & Tsourvakas, G. (2023). Artificial Intelligent Applications in Enabled Banking Services: The Next Frontier of Customer Engagement in the Era of ChatGPT. *Theoretical Economics Letters*, *13*(5), 1203–1223.

Subagja, A. D., Ausat, A. M. A., Sari, A. R., Wanof, M. I., & Suherlan, S. (2023). Improving customer service quality in MSMEs through the use of ChatGPT. *Jurnal Minfo Polgan*, *12*(1), 380–386.

Vaswani, A., Shazeer, N., Parmar, N., Uszkoreit, J., Jones, L., Gomez, A. N., & Polosukhin, I. (2017). Attention is all you need. *Advances in Neural Information Processing Systems*, •••, 30.

Yin, J., Goh, T. T., Yang, B., & Xiaobin, Y. (2021). Conversation technology with micro-learning: The impact of chatbot-based learning on students' learning motivation and performance. *Journal of Educational Computing Research*, *59*(1), 154–177.

Zhong, Q., Ding, L., Liu, J., Du, B., & Tao, D. (2023). Can chatgpt understand too? a comparative study on chatgpt and fine-tuned bert. *arXiv preprint arXiv:2302.10198*.

Chapter 2

Natural Language Processing Core Concepts for Educational Applications

Maida Maqsood
Shenzhen University, China

Shahid Iqbal Rai
https://orcid.org/0009-0006-1868-8407
University of Rome Tor Vergata, Italy

Munir Ahmad
https://orcid.org/0000-0003-4836-6151
Survey of Pakistan, Pakistan

ABSTRACT

Natural Language Processing (NLP) is rapidly transforming the educational landscape by enabling automated assessments, intelligent tutoring systems, and personalized language support. This chapter highlights how core NLP tasks, such as tokenization, syntactic parsing, and transformer-based modeling, are increasingly embedded in tools that support both learners and educators. These innovations offer significant benefits, including workload reduction for teachers, enhanced feedback mechanisms, and more adaptive, interactive learning environments. However, the integration of NLP in education must be approached with a balance of enthusiasm and caution. Pedagogical alignment, ethical oversight, and technical limitations must be carefully managed to ensure NLP tools supplement rather than replace

DOI: 10.4018/979-8-3373-6791-0.ch002

Copyright © 2026, IGI Global Scientific Publishing. Copying or distributing in print or electronic forms without written permission of IGI Global Scientific Publishing is prohibited.

human instruction. Future directions include multilingual and multimodal systems, low-resource language support, and bias mitigation strategies to ensure inclusion, transparency, and data privacy.

INTRODUCTION

Natural Language Processing (NLP), as a branch of artificial intelligence and linguistics, has developed tremendously during the last several decades and has been changing the way machines comprehend and relate to human speech. Since its initial development in the 1950s and 60s, with rule-based models of linguistics, to the introduction of statistical methods in the 1990s and subsequent explosion of neural network models such as transformers and large language models, NLP has radically changed in both how it is completed and its capabilities. It is these developments that have enabled computers to not just process text, but also produce sensible language, read context, as well as simulate elements of human conversations, all on scale and with growing accuracy (Ahammad et al., 2024; Francis & Subha, 2024; Supriyono et al., 2024).

These advancements have implications, to say the least, in the context of modern-day education. Increasing digitization of educational material, the trend to move to online and mixed-mode teaching and learning, and the avalanche of language-based data being created on one hand by students and on the other hand by educators, urgently requires the tools able to analyze and interpret language effectively. NLP provides potent techniques to deal with this requirement. It can be used to run automated grading systems, to allow real-time feedback with intelligent tutoring systems, to aid with learning languages on an interactive basis, and to assist educators in deriving insights into the classroom discourse and writings of students, and it is quickly turning into a pillar of data-driven education. Its capacities to facilitate scalable, targeted, and context-sensitive learning interventions have made it an innovative influence on teaching practice and assessment practices (Campino, 2025; Salem, 2025; Wu et al., 2024; Yu & Chauhan, 2024).

The chapter is meant to fill the gap between theoretical NLP concepts and their application to educational practice. It starts with introducing TSTW-related main techniques of NLP, including tokenization, text classification, named entity recognition, syntactic parsing, and language modeling, described in an understandable way and related to education in a reasonable manner. These approaches and the ways in which they are used in educational technologies are examined below; each of them has its limitations and possibilities. There is a particular emphasis that is given to the pedagogical value of NLP, i.e., how it can engage individuals, contribute to formative assessment, and what educators can do with it. The final section of the chapter is about ethical concerns and some future orientations, and it helps the reader gain a complete idea about how NLP can be efficiently and ethically incorporated into a learning setting. The reader will not only understand the basics of NLP but also develop a critical eye in order to assess and adopt NLP in practical learning situations by the time he or she finishes reading this chapter.

CORE NLP TECHNIQUES

In order to learn how the process of Natural Language Processing (NLP) is applicable in educational use, one should first know the basis of the existing techniques that make up the discipline. These methods can make machines work on, analyze, and produce human language in a manner that aids technology education, such as intelligent tutors, automatic grading instruments, and adaptive learning. This part gives an in-depth look at the most crucial fundamental NLP techniques and demonstrates each one of them by way of instructive examples to exhibit their applicability and practicability.

Tokenization

Tokenization is the method of dividing a constant flow of textual information into segments called tokens. Typically, such tokens will be words, but may be punctuation marks or symbols, or meaningful strings of characters, whatever the application. Tokenization is a commonly unknown initial process in an NLP pipeline, as it breaks up unstructured data that includes natural language into pieces that are easily processed and analyzed (Vayadande, Kale, et al., 2024; Vayadande, Kulkarni, et al., 2024).

For example, the sentence:

"Students enjoy learning through interactive tools."

would be tokenized into the following list:

["Students", "enjoy", "learning", "through", "interactive", "tools", "."]

Whereas it is fairly easy to implement the tokenization task in English, things get trickier when a language uses a different script, such as Chinese, or when it has no specific word boundaries, like Thai. Moreover, high-quality tokenization capabilities should be able to deal with edge conditions, like contraction (e.g., don't → do + not), hyphenation (e.g., email-address), or industry-specific jargon encountered in the case of educational materials.

In educational uses, tokenization is a vital pre-processing step before textual analysis in systems like automatic essay tagging equipment, as well as reading evaluation and plagiarism recognition.

Lemmatization

Lemmatization is the process of reducing a word to its lemma, or dictionary base form, considering the word's part of speech and its context. Unlike stemming, which crudely removes affixes (e.g., turning "running" into "run" or even "runn"), lemmatization uses linguistic knowledge to ensure that the resulting word is meaningful and grammatically correct (Islam et al., 2025; Pant et al., 2024).

For instance, the words:

"studied", "studies", "studying"

would all be lemmatized to:

"study"

Lemmatization helps NLP systems generalize across different forms of the same word, improving the accuracy of various analyses such as frequency counts, semantic similarity, and machine translation. It also reduces vocabulary size when training machine learning models, making them more efficient and less prone to overfitting.

In the educational context, lemmatization is especially valuable in language learning platforms. It helps learners grasp core vocabulary by exposing them to root forms rather than overloading them with every morphological variant. It is also instrumental in simplifying texts to match different reading levels.

Part-of-Speech (POS) Tagging

POS tagging assigns a grammatical category, such as noun, verb, adjective, or adverb, to each token in a sentence. Advanced POS taggers also identify more nuanced tags like modal verbs, gerunds, or past participles, based on context and syntactic roles (Lee, 2025b; Ullah et al., 2024).

Returning to our earlier example:

"Students enjoy learning through interactive tools."

The POS tags are shown in Table 1.

Table 1. POS Tags

Token	POS Tag
Students	Noun
enjoy	Verb
learning	Verb/Noun (depends on context)
through	Preposition

continued on following page

Table 1. Continued

Token	POS Tag
interactive	Adjective
tools	Noun
.	Punctuation

POS tagging is a critical process in most NLP projects. It facilitates syntactic analysis, makes a rule-based grammar check possible, and leaves a trace of how words are used in the context of a sentence and supplied to the assistant in the future. Contemporary POS taggers address the issue of tagging ambiguity with probabilistic models (e.g., generalizations of HMMs) or neural nets, which can be used to decide when one word has a context-dependent category.

For educational purposes, POS tagging is significant in intelligent tutoring systems as well as writing assistants. Such systems employ tags to identify a grammatical error, make correction recommendations, and offer explanations that assist a student to enhance the utilization of the language. As an example, a system may mark a misuse of adjectives when an adverb should be used, and improve the quality of feedback given to students on their written content.

Text Classification

Text classification is where a predetermined set of categories is assigned to a piece of textual material the meaning and form of the material (Vayadande, Kale, et al., 2024). As an example, in an online learning management system, students are inclined to post questions or discussion posts without answering which area the question belongs to. These inputs can be automatically assigned to subjects such as mathematics, biology, or literature that are already fed through a text classification model to make sure that they are directed to the corresponding digital tutor or content repository. Such does not only conserve teaching time, but it also improves education support systems' responsiveness. A second excellent use is in grading open-ended written answers in formative tests. Assume that the students are expected to describe a process in science, such as photosynthesis. Their responses may be analyzed by a classification model that may classify them as either being accurate, partially correct, or a misconception, based on the similarity of their answering patterns to the expected ones. This enables fast, scalable assessment, and teachers can concentrate on more meaningful pedagogical interaction instead of automated marking. The model of these classification systems is usually based on features like term frequency inverse document frequency (TF-IDF), word embeddings, or transformer-based encoding to determine the textual patterns with each type. In that way, text classification is used in the sphere not only to simplify the processes of educational work but also to allow a more individualized and data-based style of teaching.

Sentiment Analysis

A type of text classification is sentiment analysis, which is the domain-specific process of identifying the emotional polarity expressed in the written word (Sayeed et al., 2023; Shen et al., 2024; Tasneem & Hemalatha, 2025; Yu & Chauhan, 2024). The method is getting utilized more and more in learning contexts to measure and address the affective characteristics of student learning. As an example, students usually post their sentiments regarding lessons, assignments, or teaching techniques in discussion forums, surveys, or reflection journals. A sentiment analysis system, which is integrated into an e-learning system, can analyze such responses and reflect the overall mood in a positive/negative/neutral manner. Imagine that you have a group of students who went through a learning module, and they are asked to provide feedback. Examples of such comments as below will be perceived as positive, meaning that the method of teaching was a success, i.e., I enjoyed the interactive quiz- it helped me finally get a grasp of the subject. A negative answer, on the contrary, saying something like This lesson was very confusing and frustrating will be regarded as negative and the instructor will know that something needs to be done. Such analysis, when collected at the level of a course, an entire course, or even across a course, can serve to identify trends in student engagement, satisfaction, or stress level, and allow instructors to change their pedagogy accordingly. More sophisticated models of sentiment analysis could even identify certain emotional states, e.g., confusion or boredom, that can be especially utilized in adaptive learning systems and chatbot tutors that seek to integrate real-time emotional support. Sentiment analysis makes educational systems more intelligent by converting student feelings into meaningful data that can be used as the basis of decisions.

Named Entity Recognition (NER)

NER is one of the most basic NLP methods applied to extract and label certain kinds of information called named entities in a text. These entities are normally names of people, geographical entities, organizations, dates, time expressions, and numerical values, among other types of entities that are important in the field. The way NER works is as follows: it accepts unstructured text as a sentence and labels words or phrases relevant to a particular entity, thereby converting unstructured text to machine-readable structured data. It is a very important feature of comprehending content, searching, and text to knowledge graphs or databases (Kaur et al., 2024; P. Liu et al., 2022; Qu et al., 2024).

The NER is a very useful feature in the educational context of dividing and understanding materials, automatic grading, and intelligent search. An example is the scenario of a student writing a history paper on historic events of the 20th century. With the NER, an NLP system will be able to automatically recognize and pick out the most important entities discussed in the text- e.g., World War II, Winston Churchill, Nazi Germany, and 1945. Such entities would subsequently be compared to what is expected in a grading rubric, allowing a more accurate and objective scores. In addition, NER can be used to index the student submissions in topics and therefore enable the instructors to retrieve, group, and review responses based on the topics. NER can also enhance search by labeling important concepts in articles or books in a digital library or educational resource site, providing better usage to the student in locating useful material. Besides, NER, when used in language classrooms, may enable students to identify and learn proper nouns and cultural allusions in the authentic reading task, which can also contribute to vocabulary retention and understanding.

The NER models are getting context-sensitive and can include ambiguous entities or overlapping entities as they transfer to the machine learning and deep learning NER approaches, and from being rule-based. Nevertheless, NER has remained crucial in organizing textual data in order to streamline intelligent educational systems, which only enhances the effectiveness, accuracy, and relevance of learning and evaluation instruments.

Syntactic Parsing

Syntactic parsing is the process that involves an analysis of the grammatical structure of a sentence to find out the relationship and the grouping of words relating to each other. It allows computers to do more than read the superficiality of text and instead recognize deeper grammatical structures that bear meaning (Jiang & Cai, 2024; Kantor & Morzy, 2024; Kyle & Eguchi, 2024). There are two most widespread syntactic parsing types: constituency and dependency parsing. Constituency parsing is used to divide a sentence into nested phrasings, e.g. noun phrase (NP) and a verb phrase (VP), and the phrasings are recursively grouped to form a hierarchical tree structure that defines how the sentence is constructed. It is especially convenient when it comes to sentence complexity analysis, clause gestures identification, and grasping modifier attachment to the particular parts of a sentence.

In learning applications, syntactic parsing is used so that the student can improve the way the student writes in terms of sentence structure by making it transparent. An example should be the language learning app, which promotes the work in English grammar: constituency parsing can display the sentence structure to the students. The students who finished the project early were then praised by the teacher and composed of a first clause and one relative clause. This assists learners in differentiating between independent and dependent clauses, which enhances their syntactic control and makes them fluent writers. This kind of visualization also helps the teachers to diagnose the structural problems in the student's writing and to advise them on sentence restructuring tasks.

Dependency Trees

Dependency parsers (or simply dependency) are more concerned with these immediate grammatical relations between words and so produce a dependency tree in which each word is added to one word called a head, and the verb usually forms the root. Syntactic roles like subject, object, modifier, and auxiliary can be plotted on these trees to provide a decipherable skeleton to the sentence grammar (Y. Liu et al., 2024; Park & Kim, 2024). To take an example, in the sentence, the teacher explained the concept clearly, the parser would recognize the root verb, which, in this case, is explained, the subject which in this case is the teacher, the subject has a linkage to the verb through a nominal subject link, the object, which is the concept, as well as the adverb that modifies the verb, that is.

Dependency trees: Evaluation of sentence well-formedness, clarity, and syntactic complexity in intelligent writing assistants and grammar feedback systems. Technically, some dependencies can be identified in an essay submitted by a student using the dependency parsing because the system would know that there is an absence of a subject, improper use of verb agreement, or an inappropriate word construction. Visual representation of dependency trees in the classroom used to ESL (English as a Second Language) learners makes them understand how a word is grammatically used in a sentence- a gross error in usage, like wrong use of preposition or their placement effect, can be explained by a representation using tree dependency. This takes the edge off grammar and helps in the understanding of it in a deeper manner as compared to a rule-based instruction per se. Through the valuation of the knowledge brought by dependency structures, educators and tools can provide personalized feedback and be more conscious of the grammar, and direct students through the prism of better understood and more efficient expression.

Language Modeling (Transformers, GPT)

The core of Natural Language Processing is language modeling, which is the task of predicting the probability of a piece of text (i.e., a sequence of words). Language models are basically an estimation of the probability that one word follows another, thus allowing machines to generate, complete text, or interpret it in an appropriate context. In the course of time, language modeling has become advanced not only in basic statistical methods but also reached the realms of the most advanced neural models, which can comprehend and produce human-like text. The following section considers traditional and recent theories of language modeling in their application in language education.

N-Gram Models

One of the first types of language modeling is realized in the form of n-gram models. Such statistical models estimate the following word in a sequence given the prior n-1 words (Dasgupta et al., 2025; Lee, 2025a). As an example, a bigram model (n = 2) considers only the preceding word to come up with its prediction. Though n-gram models are easy to use and computationally efficient, they do not elicit long-term dependencies or higher complexities of contextual meaning, since they work on a fixed window and do not understand syntax and semantics.

Although limited in capability, the n-gram models formed the basis of earlier educational uses, including the prediction of keywords in language learning applications and the correction of spelling devices. As an example, in a vocabulary-building tool, an n-gram model could be used to give probable next words- e.g. propose a word before a word is searched by a student, e.g. "experiment" after "science", or "book" after the search term "read a". Nevertheless, they also could not deal with ambiguity and long sentences, thus, were not well suited to more complicated tasks of education.

Transformers

The invention of the transformer architecture represented a paradigm change in language modeling. Transformers were first presented by Vaswani et al. in 2017, and they use a process called self-attention, where the model weighs and correlates all words in the sequence at once, no matter where they are. This helps transformers learn language in a more contextual and broader sense, gripping short-term and long-term dependencies much better than older models.

Transformer-based models are used in education and act as the foundation for many EdTech apps. As an illustration, transformers can determine the coherence that stretches over several paragraphs because they know how the flow of ideas changes within a text. Using transformers in reading comprehension sites will produce more accurate answers to student queries by considering the context of a whole passage, as opposed to basic keyword matching. Simplified transformer architecture for language modeling is described in Figure 1.

Figure 1. Simplified Transformer Architecture for Language Modeling

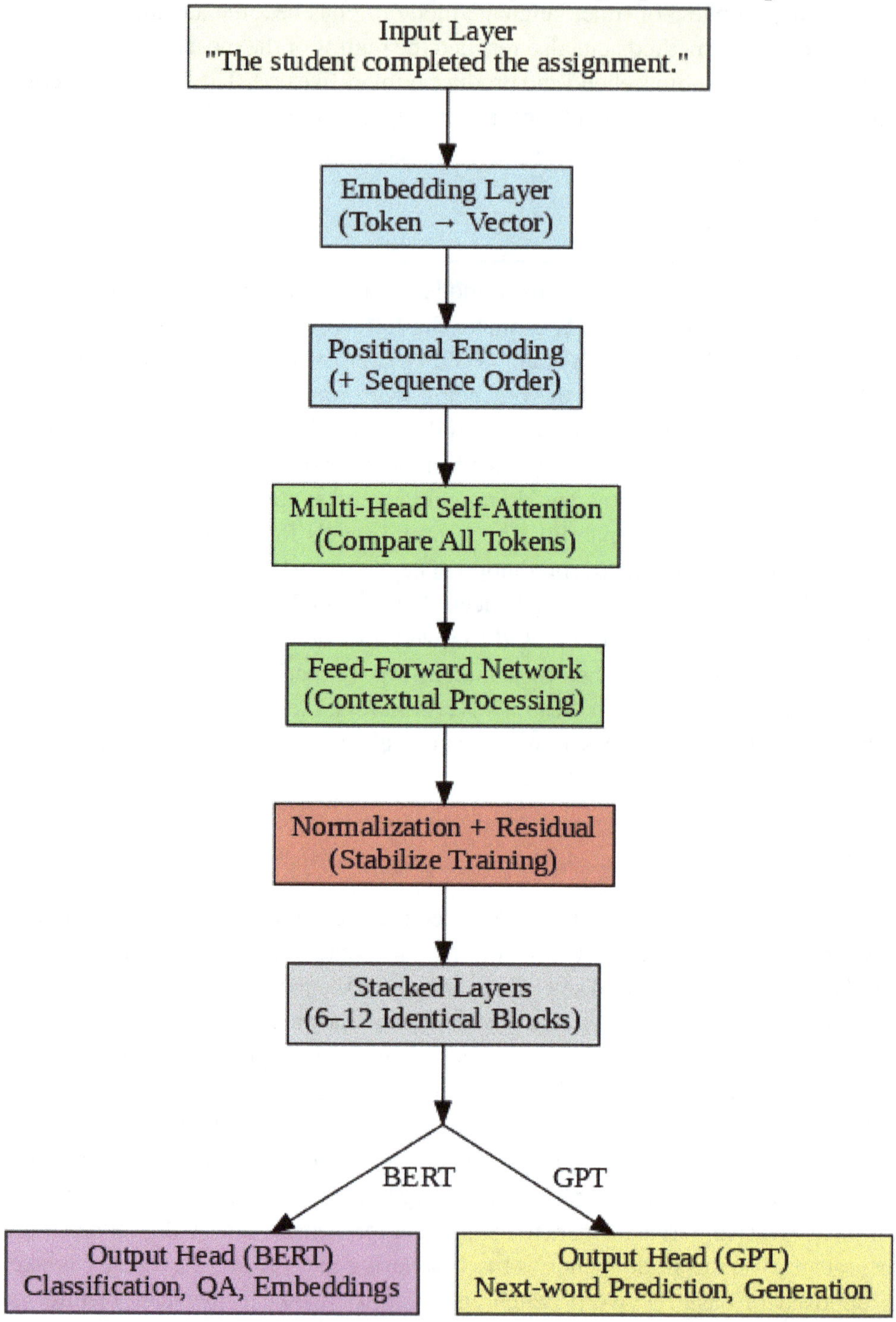

Bidirectional Encoder Representations from Transformers (BERT)

Google BERT is a transformer-generated model that presents the concept of bidirectional contextual understanding. BERT, unlike previous models, which process text left to right or right to left, goes through the context of a word and considers all surrounding words at the same time. Such a substantial, two-way contextualization enables BERT to become good at knowledge about the shades, uncertainties, and indistinct meanings in text (Gardazi et al., 2025; Rana et al., 2025).

BERT is common in educational uses, where it has been used for text classification, question answering, and semantic search. As an example, an intelligent search engine that is driven by BERT can be used in a school-based digital library to more intuitively understand the questions that students ask. When a student types in, Books about climate change in middle schools, BERT will enable the system to comprehend the level of education, the topic, and purpose of the search so that it can produce searches with more apposite results. The same can be done under tutoring systems with just-in-time assistance, where BERT is capable of aligning the natural-language queries of the students with the most appropriate explanations or videos in the context in which they are trying to understand.

Generative Pretrained Transformer (GPT)

GPT is a generative model that was developed by OpenAI and extends the transformer architecture in that it is unidirectional, i.e., makes predictions in left-to-right order. Therefore, GPT models, which were pretrained with vast internet data and later fine-tuned to specific tasks, are very efficient at language generation. In contrast to BERT, trained to understand and classify, GPT is trained to generate coherent and fluent text, having found applications in the creative, conversational domains (Kalyan, 2024; Sufi, 2024).

GPT-based models have also been very influential in education. The models are able to offer custom responses to student writing, develop quiz questions out of lecture notes, summarize long texts, and even simulate the tutoring conversation. To give an example, GPT can analyze a piece of writing in progress and offer sharpened vocabulary options, rewrite clumsy language in real time, or offer corrections of grammatical errors. GPT can also be used as a conversation partner in language learning as it reacts in the most natural way to prompts given by the students, teaching them sentence construction and vocabulary in the process. Magic naming capabilities like the capacity to produce human-like answers and respond to various inputs help GPT-powered tools to sustainably and non-stagnant form of learning: both formative and summative learning. Table 2 shows the comparison of BERT and GPT models.

Table 2. Comparison of BERT and GPT

Feature	BERT	GPT
Architecture	Transformer encoder only	Transformer decoder only
Directionality	Bidirectional (looks at both left and right context)	Unidirectional (left-to-right prediction)
Pretraining Objective	Masked Language Modeling (MLM) and Next Sentence Prediction (NSP)	Causal Language Modeling (predict next word)
Primary Strength	Understanding of text (context, semantics, relationships)	Generation of coherent, fluent text
Fine-tuning Use Cases	Text classification, QA, sentiment analysis, and semantic search	Text completion, summarization, and conversation generation
Output Type	Typically, classification scores or contextual embeddings	Typically, text sequences (generated responses)
Educational Use Examples	- Answering student questions- Improving search relevance- Content tagging & classification	- Writing support- Generating feedback- Tutoring dialogues
Interactivity Level	More analytic, ideal for backend understanding tasks	More conversational; suited for front-end student-facing tools
Notable Versions	BERT, RoBERTa, DistilBERT	GPT-2, GPT-3, GPT-4 (e.g., ChatGPT)

Modern language models, particularly those based on transformers, have significantly expanded the scope of what NLP can achieve in education. From simple completion tasks to advanced interactive tutoring, these models enable systems that are not only linguistically competent but also responsive to the context, intention, and goals of learners. As such, language modeling represents one of the most transformative technologies in the evolution of educational NLP tools. Table 3 provides examples of some of the educational use cases in the context of NLP techniques.

Table 3. Educational Use Cases for Core NLP Techniques

NLP Technique	Primary Educational Applications
Tokenization	Breaks down text into analyzable units, enabling grammar correction tools and language structure analyzers.
Part-of-Speech (POS) Tagging	Identifies grammatical roles (e.g., noun, verb), aiding vocabulary trainers and syntactic feedback systems.
Lemmatization	Supports vocabulary acquisition and synonym mapping in language learning platforms.
Text Classification	Automatically organizes student responses or queries for targeted feedback and content routing.
Sentiment Analysis	Detects student emotions in reflections or feedback to inform adaptive instruction and wellbeing support.

continued on following page

Table 3. Continued

NLP Technique	Primary Educational Applications
Named Entity Recognition	Extracts key terms for content tagging and ensures factual correctness in assessments and essays.
Syntactic Parsing	Visualizes sentence structures to support writing clarity and second-language syntax understanding.
Language Modeling (GPT, BERT)	Powers intelligent tutors, generates feedback and quiz content, and enables interactive writing support.

NLP APPLICATIONS IN EDUCATIONAL TECHNOLOGY

Modern educational technology is incomplete without NLP, upon which a broad range of educational environments is based, including learning, assessment, and instruction. NLP methods enable systems to interpret human language in a manner that is beneficial to teachers and students through the automation of grading and the creation of talking conversational learning partners and tutors. In this section, we shall look at some of the most significant uses of NLP in educational technology, focusing on how the technology finds its way into real-world systems to generate smart, versatile, and adaptable solutions.

Automated Feedback and Grading Systems

One of the most revolutionary NLP applications in the contemporary educational world is automated systems of feedback and grading. These systems use a combination of the fundamentals of NLP, such as the tokenization of text, the tagging of text with part-of-speech (POS) information, syntactic parsing, and classification of text coupled with more modern language modeling (e.g., BERT, RoBERTa) to evaluate the writing of the student, and produce data-driven outputs based on them. These systems include written assignments and study the grammar, comprehensibility, richness of vocabulary, content alignment, and geometry of arguments more consistently and faster than human markers because they process them in large quantities (Ayaan & Ng, 2025; Messer et al., 2024; Nikhil et al., 2025).

Familiar examples like the e-rater application developed by ETS or Revision Assistant, which is produced at Turnitin, show that NLP goes deep into the back-end of educational solutions. Student essays that are submitted in these platforms are automatically parsed, and linguistic and semantic features are extracted and thereafter compared to an ideal response or rubrics. Newer designs combine transformer-based architectures in order to derive meaning, identify conceptual gaps, and deliver targeted suggestions. By using NLP-based pipelines, such processes can take place in real-time to provide students with feedback (as well as save teachers a lot of time and effort associated with monotonous grading). Figure 2 describes the NLP pipeline for automated feedback and grading.

The teaching gains of feedback systems based on NLP are significant, and extend both to the cognitive as well as to the teaching plane:

- NLP algorithms have the potential to provide immediate feedback on the quality of writing, and this would promote progressive learning. As an example, applications, such as Write & Improve by Cambridge University, are implemented with the help of NLP and can give feedback to a student on grammar, structure, and vocabulary. This aids in independent learning of revision and boosts active language practice.
- NLP enables thousands of students to get personalized comments in big classes like MOOCs or even in university LMS settings. Coursera- or edX-embedded systems, to give one example, analyze student answers against answer patterns expected and dole out rubric-based help minus any human input.
- NLP guarantees fairer evaluation by doing away with the inconsistency that accompanies human grading. Tools such as the Revision Assistant in Turnitin employ the rule-based and machine learning methods to conform to scoring rubrics and ensure that bias in grading is reduced in grading subjective assignments such as essays.
- Using NLP-based tools (e.g., identifying trends in the writing samples of students), students can consider their strengths and weaknesses. This develops metacognitive awareness, where the students have ownership and control over their learning process.
- NLP-based tools can identify the non-native use patterns and scaffold English Language Learners (ELLs). As an example, Grammarly EDU employs syntactic parsing and error type to offer language-specific suggestions, which aim at both enhancing fluency and correctness in learners.
- NLP systems, when integrated into daily classroom processes, enable teachers to shift focus away from normative grading to high-stakes teaching processes: curriculum development and focused intervention. Educators who employ such devices as Google Classroom combined with NLP-based extensions can easily evaluate the overall writing pattern in a group of students and adjust the educational process to such results.

Figure 2. NLP Pipeline for Automated Feedback and Grading

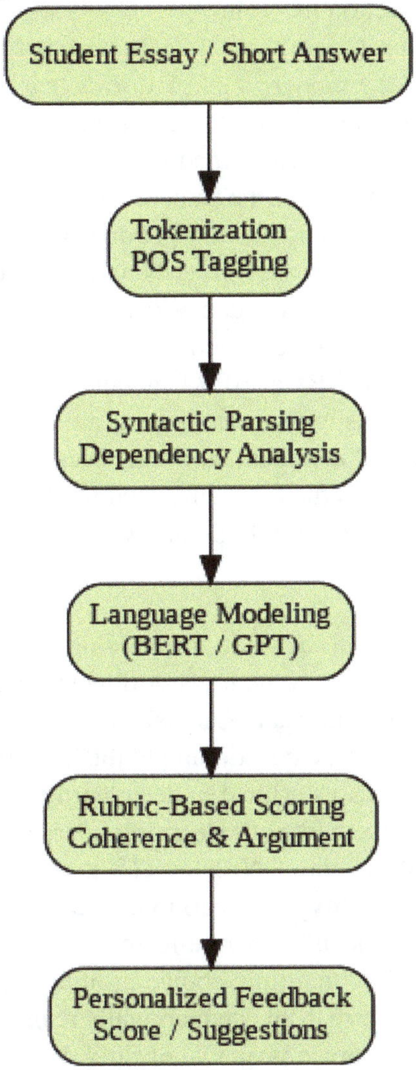

Intelligent Tutoring Systems (ITS)

ITS is one of the most advanced combinations of Artificial Intelligence and education and is capable of giving relatively immediate instructional guidance, according to the needs of the learners. As opposed to conventional e-learning systems that utilize fixed content, ITS adapts to the contribution of the learner and provides feedback, scaffolding, and problem-solving techniques individually. The key to this flexibility lies in the Natural Language Processing (NLP) that would allow ITS to understand, analyze, and act on the written or spoken words of students in a pedagogically significant context (Alam et al., 2024; Bode & Satpute, 2024; Wang, 2025).

In the architecture of the modern ITS platforms, e.g., the Carnegie Learning MATHia, AutoTutor, or Wayang Outpost integrations, the use of NLP is injected at numerous levels. These systems include modules of natural language understanding (NLU) to understand the meaning of the student responses and dialog management systems to identify proper instructional replies. Some of the most notable techniques to be used are semantic similarity analysis (when the student input should be compared to the correct concepts), dependency parsing (when the grammatical and logical structure should be evaluated), and transformer-based language modeling (e.g., we can use a fine-tuned GPT or BERT model) to provide contextualized and coherent feedback. Such tools ensure the system can identify misconceptions and determine the motive behind a student, and introduce a corrective or elaborative conversation. Figure 3 outlines the NLP-enhanced intelligent tutoring system. The teaching advantages of ITS are both high and wide-ranging on the cognitive and instructional level:

- NLP-enabled ITS has the capability of noticing if a student has not grasped a concept and producing specific hints or directed inquiries. As an example, AutoTutor employs semantic analysis to identify incomplete or wrong mental models and applies Socratic questioning to the learner. This fosters cognitive repair, one of the processes critical in deep learning, and enables learners to fix their mistakes on the part of the learning interaction.
- Among the greatest effects of NLP on ITS is the fact that NLP facilitates a conversational, natural type of learning. Because students are allowed to engage with the system through free-form textual interactions, rather than following predetermined multiple-choice prompts, students will be capable of dealing with the system in an occupationally realistic manner. As an example, the GPT-driven tutors are capable of fluid dialogs with learners that are content contextualized and simulate the presence of a human tutor. This increases motivation and, in addition, offers a chance at self-explanation; self-explanation is a well-tested approach to enhance retention and transfer.
- NLP will allow ITS to construct learner models based on linguistic signs of knowledge, confidence, and interest. Engines such as MATHia differentiate practice activities based upon representations of how learners convey their explanations, rather than simply whether the answer is correct. In this way, ITS enables difficulty, tempo, and feedback plan changes, based on the shifting needs of learners, and the specific approach in this respect can help to support differentiated instruction and equity in performance.

- In addition to academic skills, NLP-based ITS has the potential to examine emotional tone and metacognitive indicators of the student's language. Another example is when a student constantly applies phrases of confusion or frustration (“I do not understand this,” “This is difficult”), sentiment analysis can cause the supportive text or change the feedback tone. This ability helps develop affective involvement as well as learner endurance, which are vital aspects in long-term academic achievement.
- One-on-one tutoring can be offered at scale by the integration of NLP into ITS. In remote or other under-resourced settings, in particular, ITS may serve to provide rich, individualized instruction to a student population who otherwise would have no access to human tutors. In a multilingual environment, another use of NLP tools is to allow ITS to reply to language learners in various languages, being more inclusive and accessible.

Figure 3. NLP-Enhanced Intelligent Tutoring System

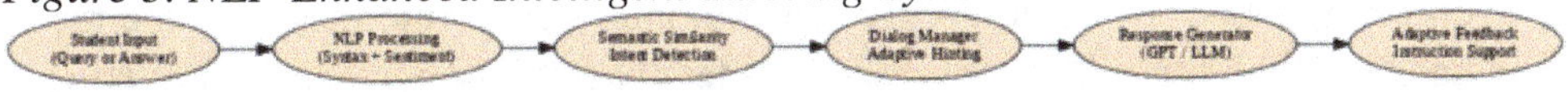

Language Learning Platforms and Chatbots

One of the effective and natural areas in the implementation of Natural Language Processing (NLP) is language learning. Language learning platforms that have been available in the modern market, like Duolingo, Babbel, Rosetta Stone, and Google Read Along, are based on NLPs to facilitate important learning processes like pronunciation, correction of grammar errors, vocabulary, and translating contextual information (Davar et al., 2025; Dhivvya & Karnati, 2024; Jeon et al., 2024). Most recently, chatbots and conversational agents, usually with the support of large language models (LLMs) such as GPT, BERT, or Dialogflow, brought innovations to language learning practice with a human-like, interactive communication in a scalable form.

Such platforms incorporate NLP throughout different functionalities. Speech-to-text models take the form of learner speech and convert it into tokens used to provide pronunciation feedback, whereas named entity recognition (NER) and semantic parsing models read meaning out of learner input. With the help of language modeling and especially transformers, it is quite possible to reach real-time dialogue generation, content adaptation, and error detection. Sentiment analysis is a feature of NLP that enables platforms to measure learner frustration or confusion to gauge the need to adjust the level or tone accordingly. These systems allow learners to develop not only fluency in language use but also culturally related knowledge and pragmatic competence, components that have been harder to achieve in formal training programs. Figure 4 shows the use of NLP in language learning platforms and chatbots.

The pedagogical values of the Language Learning Platforms and Chatbots are so high and have a cognitive and instructional scope:

- Chatbots based on NLP enable learners to have realistic conversations, and this gives the illusion of being in a target-language environment. Applications such as Duolingo Max, powered by GPT-4, make two-way communication possible when the learner might explain something, request an explanation, or even get their answer wrong, but are not put to shame. This improves fluency, confidence, and spontaneity of the language.
- These platforms are built on NLP to interpret not only individual errors made by a learner but also the context of their sentence and therefore provide specific corrections or hints. To give an example, the AI tutor assesses the feedback of Babbel and gives phrase-level feedback that does not ignore the idiomatic use, which can help to establish natural and native-like expression.
- NLP models with speech recognition (e.g., Whisper by OpenAI or Wav2Vec2 by Google) allow learners to get feedback about the correctness of their pronunciation and intonation. The example is the Google Read Along app; it is based on a real-time voice interaction, correcting the mistakes in achieving reading fluency required to enhance the phonological awareness and listening comprehension of young learners.
- NLP enables platforms to examine learning histories and conversational patterns to manipulate the veracity of vocabulary, pace, and type of feedback. Sentiment analysis in ELSA Speak and ELSA Speak-like tool can adjust exercises depending on learners and their sentiments and engagement, encouraging intrinsic motivation and concentration.
- The use of NLP also allows real-time translation, support of code switching, and a multilingual interface, increasing the inclusivity of platforms. An example would be in saying that through the use of NER and translation APIs, SayHi and Replika assist in clarifying meaning to the learner without interrupting the flow of speech, especially useful to a new learner or a self-directed multilingual audience.
- In the environments in which there may be limited availability of fluent language tutors, such as geography, cost, or resource access in institutions, NLP-driven platforms provide democratized access to quality, personalized lan-

guage practice. This can be of greatest use in rural schools, refugee learning, or adult literacy, where the ratio of teacher to students is not optimal.

Figure 4. NLP in Language Learning Platforms and Chatbots

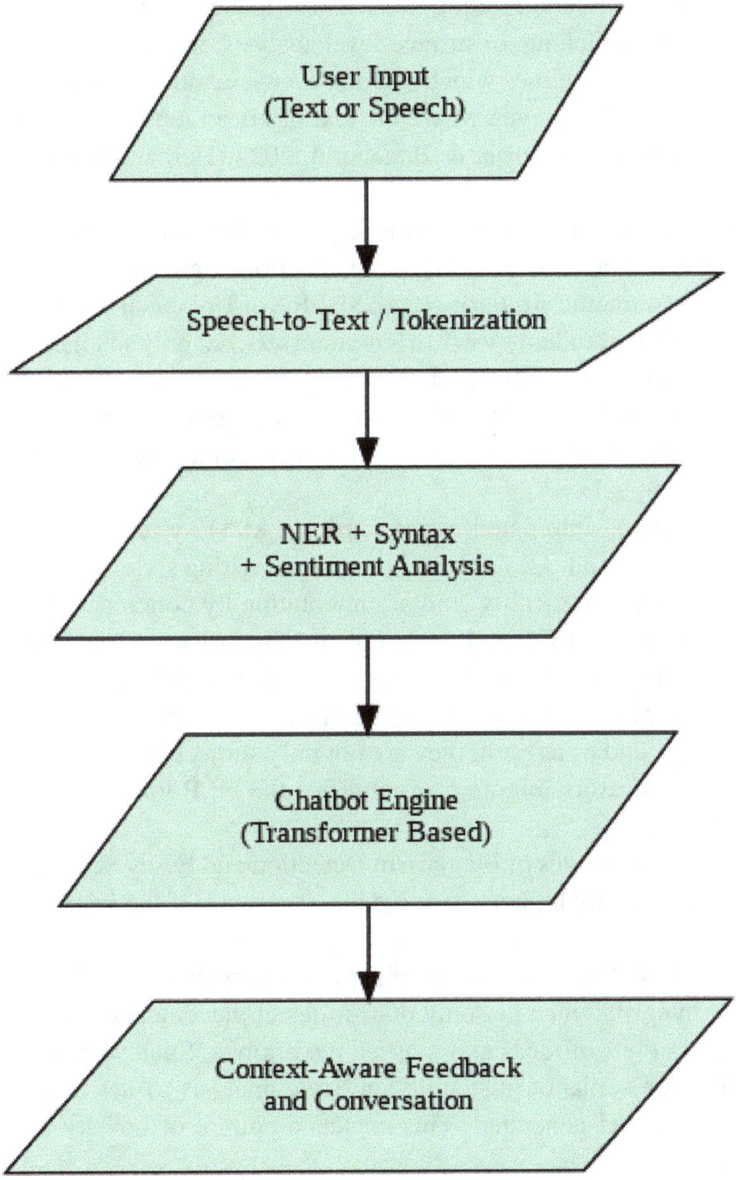

Plagiarism Detection and Essay Scoring

The digital era has created the importance of establishing academic integrity and delivering fair and scalable assessment in education, which were considered essential concerns in the academic sector. NLP is an effective tool that enables the detection of plagiarism and grading tools. These technologies are not simply used to find basic string matching, or surface-level analysis; they are now equipped with more advanced NLP pipelines which can discover semantic overlaps, restatements, and semantic similarities- even where the text has been rephrased in an attempt to slip through undetected (Berqia & Benaboud, 2024; Hemandkumar et al., 2024; Patil et al., 2024; Sajid et al., 2025).

In the plagiarism detection programs, e.g., Turnitin, Unicheck, Copyleaks, the NLP is performed as text tokenization, lemmatization, n-gram comparison, sentence embedding, and semantic similarity (e.g., SBERT or Universal Sentence Encoder). These tools match the student's work to huge data sets, not only scholarly repositories and websites, but also to institutional document stores. The modern systems are also able to check and analyze the lexical features, syntax, and rhetorical organization to identify inconsistencies in writing styles, pointing to content stitching, ghostwriting, or writing aided by AI.

In the meantime, automated essay scoring (AES) systems incorporate NLP methodologies to compute several axes of student writing style: syntactic intricacy, term variety, material topicality, and argumentation by coherence. E-rater (ETS), Project Essay Grade (PEG), and more recent transformer models (like OpenAIs GPT, or RobERTa) present more subtle scores that match human scoring criteria. The systems offer the same type of continuous assessment even on large numbers of student essays, and as a result, they are not only subjective but also less work on the part of the educators. Figure 5 exemplifies the NLP for plagiarism detection and essay scoring.

Pedagogical advantages of Plagiarism Detection and Essay Scoring are so great and encompass not only higher cognitive but also those of the instructional plane:

- The use of NLP in detecting plagiarism ensures that institutions impose academic integrity since not only does it detect piecemeal copying, but it also establishes theft of ideas and masked reworkings. Such websites as Turnitin employ deep semantic matching and style analysis to detect advanced plagiarism, e.g., AI-generated. This creates a culture of novelty and academic integrity.
- Automated essay scoring systems will demystify grading as they can give out criterion-based scoring and explanations to the students. The current platforms, such as Criterion by ETS, provide feedback on coherence, grammar,

word choice, and organization, so that the learners can know the basis of their specific score on the grading and improve it.

- NLP enables the upscaling of essay assessment in the absence of a fairness compromise. AES systems are standard to cover raters and distortions across locations in standardized testing situations, such as TOEFL, SAT, or IELTS. This minimizes human bias and contributes to equality irrespective of socio-economic conditions and language.
- Most of the contemporary scoring systems now entail the assistive feed-forward feedback that aids the learner in correcting their essays and resubmission. By way of example, such tools as SAGe (Scoring and Assessment for Generation) evaluate the level of argumentation and its logic and provide recommendations to revise reasoning skills.
- NLP models can process the length of a sentence, punctuation patterns, and lexical variation to identify style breakouts that can be signs of non-human authorship by outsourcing or artificial intelligence. It is especially convenient to use in cases with academic integrity checks or even thesis monitoring procedures, where the unified writing voice is important.
- Coined scoring and plagiarism NLP data may be used in curriculum analysis to show weak points among students (e.g., in writing a thesis, in cohesiveness). Teachers may rely on this information to tailor lessons and focus on particular writing skills in the next lesson.

Figure 5. NLP for Plagiarism Detection and Essay Scoring

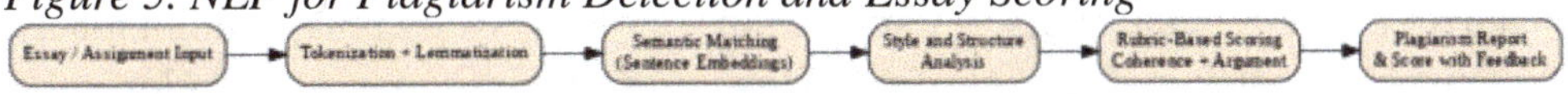

CHALLENGES IN APPLYING NLP IN EDUCATION

Technical Challenges

Although Natural Language Processing systems are robust, various technical constraints somehow undermine their applications in learning. A primary limitation is that the modern-day NLP models are computationally demanding. Model architectures based on transformers such as BERT or GPT are also more uploading, involving high hardware requirements when training, and real-time inference. This can have the drawbacks of being challenging to implement within a low-resource setting, which would include a public school in an underfunded area or an institution that does not have a well-developed IT infrastructure.

Domain adaptation is another important technical obstacle. The performance of NLP models that were trained on general web data could be low when these models are used on education-focused text, e.g., student essays, homework questions, or classroom conversation. These contexts may contain incomplete sentences, imaginative wordings, or fallacies characterizing language-learners ' effects that have not been shaped into optimal language models. Also, problems such as multilingual input, code-switching, and non-standard language usage are constantly a matter of concern, especially in pluralistic educational systems, such as in South Asia or Africa.

Latency and scalability are also important. In the case that NLP tools are integrated on interactive platforms (e.g., chatbots or tutoring systems), they should be able to provide correct answers in real time. Channeling delays or intermittent outputs may worsen the learning process and decrease the user's confidence. Although more efficient, live, classroom-driven, low-latency, high-accuracy performance is a challenging technical goal, despite increased efficiency.

Pedagogical Challenges

Pedagogically, the inclusion of NLP in the learning contexts must be managed as closely as possible to instructional intentions and educational practices that happen in the classrooms. Of importance is the over-automatization of feedback and evaluation. Although the NLP-based tools are fast and capable of grading short answers or even essays and offering linguistic corrections, they can ignore deeper cognitive or conceptual errors. As an example, an NLP system may extol a nicely written essay that is not thought-provoking or original as long as it follows the pattern of what is expected.

Moreover, due to the way they transform the language, NLP tools may influence the behavior of the students without their intention. When learners are made aware that a system rewards preset or keyword-based writing, they could make it a priority to learn to perform well superficially, rather than to write genuinely, or to learn to think. This is very problematic, especially about learning a language where creativity, risk-taking, and the use of nuance are paramount to learning it. With time, the excess use of algorithmic feedback can make students less broad in their expression instead of being more expansive.

Integration in the classroom is also not easy. Most of the teachers are not trained to know how to critique NLP outputs and how to solve the problem in the event of the tools becoming faulty. In case teachers accept machine-based scores or recommendations as authoritative, they final easily ignore personal education needs or system bias without even intending to. Therefore, both technical literacy and a sensitivity to pedagogy are important when pedagogical integration is to be effective, and do not necessarily find support in the existing professional development programs.

Ethical Challenges

Ethical issues surrounding the use of NLP in schools are a broad subject and one that should be viewed seriously. Algorithmic bias is considered one of the most severe issues. The tendency of the NLP model to reproduce and even enhance existing societal biases (connected to race, gender, low or high socioeconomic status, or culture) is since many NLP models are trained on large publicly available corpora, called the internet, but many in fact are. This is because when these models are applied in grading, feedback, or recommendation, they can even be systematically skewed against some categories of students, despite the lack of intention.

Privacy is another weighty problem. A wide range of personal data, such as student essays, chat logs, voice recordings, and behavioral metrics, is sometimes necessary for educational applications of NLP. In the absence of robust data governance strategies, this information is liable to abuse or fail to be stored properly, or rather, fall into hacking. When dealing with student data, the ethical treatment of students requires clear policies about consent, how long the information will be kept, who can share it out and how any student can demand deletion.

Such ethical issues as interpretability and transparency are also urgent. Predominant examples of state-of-the-art NLP models are "black boxes": they provide essentially no explanation on how a specific prediction or suggestion was made. When applied at the school, this explainability can reduce trust and accountability. In case the work of a student should be handed back unfairly or be flagged as plagiarism, the teachers, as well as the students, can find it difficult to refute or interpret the ruling due to the lack of transparency. NLP tools become the authority that cannot be held accountable without human control and explainable rationalizations in educational activities.

Lastly is the case of digital equity. NLP devices are almost always commercial products that must either be paid for as a subscription or on a device or require an internet connection, which disenfranchises learners in underserved populations. The development of technologies and NLP products must be ethically accompanied by the guarantee of their inclusive, fair access to learning experiences. Figure 6 shows the challenges in NLP for Education.

Figure 6. Challenges in NLP for Education

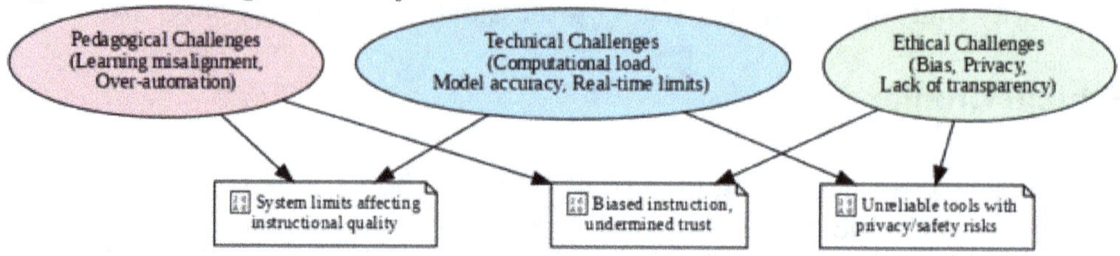

CONCLUSION

NLP is quickly reshaping the educational environment by making automated evaluations, smart tutoring, individual language preparation, and dynamic learning in educational ethics. Most fundamental NLP tasks, as shown in this chapter, such as tokenization, syntactic parsing, and transformer-based language modeling, are entering the realm of teaching technologies used by learners and educators alike. The innovations can have a lot of potential to decrease the workload of teachers, increase opportunities to get high-quality feedback, and enhance more interactive and adaptive environments of learning.

Nevertheless, the combination of NLP with education should be a mixture of an eager and pessimistic approach. Although the technological improvements are spectacular, technical constraints, pedagogical issues, and ethical hazards should be evaluated critically, implemented openly, and should be monitored constantly by human people. The most promising application of NLP systems is when they are applied to supplement, rather than substitute, educational interactions, and their output must be accessed in the educational context so that there is a chance of misjudging or disadvantaging the student.

In the future, a number of new developments are going to increase the scope and applicability of NLP in education. Multilingual NLP will become a strong diversity inclusion resource, support various linguistic backgrounds, and promote barrier-breaking in classrooms that are becoming more and more international. Technological developments of the recent years enable systems to understand and react to an increasing range of language data and multi-lingual expressions, such as those underrepresented or mixed-language expressions used by bilingual and multi-lingual students. In like manner, text, sound, and video multimodal systems are coming up with a more realistic and immersive learning environment. Such systems are capable of interpreting aural feedback, visual feedback, and combining multiple similar data inputs to facilitate a more natural and comprehensive form of instruction.

The necessity to expand opportunities for NLP to low-resource languages and underdeveloped communities is also an essential question. It is crucial that the NLP technologies that may not increase educational disparities are developed, which means that it is necessary to develop models that work with insufficiently labeled datasets, use less computing power, or can operate offline. The adaptations will go a long way in delivering quality, AI-enhanced learning access to communities that were not part of digital innovation.

NLP is an evolving system; therefore, the responsible utilization of NLP in education is all the more crucial nowadays. Developers and educators need to make sure that NLP systems are not black boxes and are explainable, returning results that can be queried by teachers and learners. Counters to the algorithmic bias are extremely important and involve the attentive study of training information and a corrective pattern against the discriminatory mechanism. It is also worth protecting the privacy of students by ensuring privacy, protection during data handling, open informed consent, and well-established policies regarding data use. Moreover, human control will always be in focus; whereas NLP may help to give more customized feedback, at the end, the pedagogical decisions should be made by educated professionals. Lastly, these tools need to be designed with an eye toward inclusivity and accessibility to accommodate the needs of learners regardless of their origins in terms of language, culture, and mental abilities.

Through its ethical and pedagogical responsibility, which majors in aligning innovation, NLP can be an effective enhancer of equity, engagement, and effectiveness in contemporary learning. It can not only automate rote tasks and scale training, but can itself be used to improve the very quality of learning experiences, given it is built or deployed with caution, foresight, and appreciation of the many needs of the diverse learner and educator populations.

REFERENCES

Ahammad, S. H., Kalangi, R. R., Nagendram, S., Inthiyaz, S., Priya, P. P., Faragallah, O. S., Mohammad, A., Eid, M. M. A., & Rashed, A. N. Z. (2024). Improved neural machine translation using Natural Language Processing (NLP). *Multimedia Tools and Applications*, *83*(13), 39335–39348. DOI: 10.1007/S11042-023-17207-7

Alam, S., Kumar, S., Khursheed, Z., Mahato, H. K., Bashar, S., & Suman, A. (2024). Designing an AI-driven intelligent Tutorial System. *5th International Conference on Recent Trends in Computer Science and Technology, ICRTCST 2024 - Proceedings*, 585–588. https://doi.org/DOI: 10.1109/ICRTCST61793.2024.10578476

Ayaan, A., & Ng, K. W. (2025). Automated grading using natural language processing and semantic analysis. *MethodsX*, *14*, 103395. DOI: 10.1016/J.MEX.2025.103395 PMID: 40529512

Berqia, M., & Benaboud, H. (2024). Detecting LLM-Enabled Plagiarism in Student Essays Using Ensemble Learning and NLP. *Lecture Notes in Information Systems and Organisation, 71 LNISO*, 376–382. https://doi.org/DOI: 10.1007/978-3-031-75329-9_42

Bode, S. P., & Satpute, R. S. (2024). Natural Language Processing in Education System. *2024 2nd DMIHER International Conference on Artificial Intelligence in Healthcare, Education and Industry, IDICAIEI 2024*. https://doi.org/DOI: 10.1109/IDICAIEI61867.2024.10842725

Campino, J. (2025). Unleashing the transformers: NLP models detect AI writing in education. *Journal of Computers in Education*, *12*(2), 645–673. DOI: 10.1007/S40692-024-00325-Y

Dasgupta, S., Maity, C., Mukherjee, S., Singh, R., Dutta, D., & Jana, D. (2025). HITgram: A Platform for Experimenting with n-Gram Language Models. *Lecture Notes in Computer Science, 15505 LNCS*, 92–104. https://doi.org/DOI: 10.1007/978-3-031-84543-7_8

Davar, N. F., Dewan, M. A. A., & Zhang, X. (2025). AI Chatbots in Education: Challenges and Opportunities. *Information 2025, Vol. 16, Page 235*, *16*(3), 235. https://doi.org/DOI: 10.3390/INFO16030235

Dhivvya, J. P., & Karnati, S. B. (2024). BuddyBot: AI Powered Chatbot for Enhancing English Language Learning. *2024 IEEE International Conference on Interdisciplinary Approaches in Technology and Management for Social Innovation, IATMSI 2024*. https://doi.org/DOI: 10.1109/IATMSI60426.2024.10502595

Francis, J., & Subha, M. (2024). An Overview of Natural Language Processing (NLP) in Healthcare: Implications for English Language Teaching. *8th International Conference on I-SMAC (IoT in Social, Mobile, Analytics and Cloud), I-SMAC 2024 - Proceedings*, 824–827. https://doi.org/DOI: 10.1109/I-SMAC61858.2024.10714890

Gardazi, N. M., Daud, A., Malik, M. K., Bukhari, A., Alsahfi, T., & Alshemaimri, B. (2025). BERT applications in natural language processing: a review. *Artificial Intelligence Review 2025 58:6, 58*(6), 1–49. https://doi.org/DOI: 10.1007/S10462-025-11162-5

Hemandkumar, E., Varun Kumar, A., & Gracewell, J. (2024). Enhanced Plagiarism Detection in Online Assignments by Natural Language Processing and Machine Learning Techniques. *3rd International Conference on Automation, Computing and Renewable Systems, ICACRS 2024 - Proceedings*, 1281–1286. https://doi.org/DOI: 10.1109/ICACRS62842.2024.10841520

Islam, M. F., Hasan, J., Islam, M. A., Dewan, P., & Rahman, M. S. (2025). BanglaLem: A Transformer-based Bangla Lemmatizer with an Enhanced Dataset. *Systems and Soft Computing, 7*, 200244. DOI: 10.1016/J.SASC.2025.200244

Jeon, J., Lee, S., & Choi, S. (2024). A systematic review of research on speech-recognition chatbots for language learning: Implications for future directions in the era of large language models. *Interactive Learning Environments, 32*(8), 4613–4631. DOI: 10.1080/10494820.2023.2204343

Jiang, P., & Cai, X. (2024). A Survey of Semantic Parsing Techniques. *Symmetry 2024, Vol. 16, Page 1201, 16*(9), 1201. https://doi.org/DOI: 10.3390/SYM16091201

Kalyan, K. S. (2024). A survey of GPT-3 family large language models including ChatGPT and GPT-4. *Natural Language Processing Journal, 6*, 100048. DOI: 10.1016/j.nlp.2023.100048

Kantor, K., & Morzy, M. (2024). Machine learning and natural language processing in clinical trial eligibility criteria parsing: A scoping review. *Drug Discovery Today, 29*(10), 104139. DOI: 10.1016/J.DRUDIS.2024.104139 PMID: 39154773

Kaur, N., Saha, A., Swami, M., Singh, M., & Dalal, R. (2024). Bert-Ner: A Transformer-Based Approach For Named Entity Recognition. *2024 15th International Conference on Computing Communication and Networking Technologies, ICCCNT 2024*. https://doi.org/DOI: 10.1109/ICCCNT61001.2024.10724703

Kyle, K., & Eguchi, M. (2024). Evaluating NLP models with written and spoken L2 samples. *Research Methods in Applied Linguistics, 3*(2), 100120. DOI: 10.1016/J.RMAL.2024.100120

Lee, R. (2025a). N-Gram Language Model. *Natural Language Processing*, 19–43. https://doi.org/DOI: 10.1007/978-981-96-3208-4_2

Lee, R. (2025b). Part-of-Speech (POS) Tagging. *Natural Language Processing*, 45–68. https://doi.org/DOI: 10.1007/978-981-96-3208-4_3

Liu, P., Guo, Y., Wang, F., & Li, G. (2022). Chinese named entity recognition: The state of the art. *Neurocomputing*, *473*. Advance online publication. DOI: 10.1016/j.neucom.2021.10.101

Liu, Y., Han, D., Wu, G., & Qiao, B. (2024). KnowDT: Empathetic dialogue generation with knowledge enhanced dependency tree. *Applied Intelligence*, *54*(17–18), 8059–8072. DOI: 10.1007/s10489-024-05611-x

Messer, M., Brown, N. C. C., Kölling, M., & Shi, M. (2024). Automated Grading and Feedback Tools for Programming Education: A Systematic Review. *ACM Transactions on Computing Education*, *24*(1), 10. DOI: 10.1145/3636515

Nikhil, V., Annamalai, R., & Jayapal, S. (2025). NLP-Driven Approaches to Automated Essay Grading and Feedback. *Adopting Artificial Intelligence Tools in Higher Education: Student Assessment*, 99–117. https://doi.org/DOI: 10.1201/9781003470304-5

Pant, V. K., Sharma, R., & Kundu, S. (2024). An overview of Stemming and Lemmatization Techniques. *Advances in Networks. Intelligent Computing*, •••, 308–321. DOI: 10.1201/9781003430421-31

Park, S., & Kim, H. (2024). Effective sentence-level relation extraction model using entity-centric dependency tree. *PeerJ. Computer Science*, *10*, e2311. DOI: 10.7717/PEERJ-CS.2311/SUPP-2 PMID: 39314697

Patil, R., Kadam, V., Nakate, R., Kadam, S., Pattade, S., & Mitkari, M. (2024). A Novel Natural Language Processing Based Model for Plagiarism Detection. *2024 International Conference on Emerging Smart Computing and Informatics, ESCI 2024*. https://doi.org/DOI: 10.1109/ESCI59607.2024.10497386

Qu, X., Gu, Y., Xia, Q., Li, Z., Wang, Z., & Huai, B. (2024). A Survey on Arabic Named Entity Recognition: Past, Recent Advances, and Future Trends. *IEEE Transactions on Knowledge and Data Engineering*, *36*(3). Advance online publication. DOI: 10.1109/TKDE.2023.3303136

Rana, M. R. R., Nawaz, A., Rehman, S. U., Abid, M. A., Garayevi, M., & Kajanová, J. (2025). BERT-BiGRU-Senti-GCN: An Advanced NLP Framework for Analyzing Customer Sentiments in E-Commerce. *International Journal of Computational Intelligence Systems*, *18*(1), 1–18. DOI: 10.1007/S44196-025-00747-1

Sajid, M., Sanaullah, M., Fuzail, M., Malik, T. S., & Shuhidan, S. M. (2025). Comparative analysis of text-based plagiarism detection techniques. *PLoS One*, *20*(4), e0319551. DOI: 10.1371/JOURNAL.PONE.0319551 PMID: 40198663

Salem, M. A. (2025). Bridging or Burning? Digital Sustainability and PY Students' Intentions to Adopt AI-NLP in Educational Contexts. *Computers 2025, Vol. 14, Page 265, 14*(7), 265. https://doi.org/DOI: 10.3390/COMPUTERS14070265

Sayeed, M. S., Mohan, V., & Muthu, K. S. (2023). BERT: A Review of Applications in Sentiment Analysis. In *HighTech and Innovation Journal* (Vol. 4, Issue 2). https://doi.org/DOI: 10.28991/HIJ-2023-04-02-015

Shen, Y., Yang, L., & Deng, B. (2024). NLP-Driven Sentiment Analysis for Stakeholder Feedback in Sustainable Projects. *2024 6th International Conference on Frontier Technologies of Information and Computer, ICFTIC 2024*, 713–716. https://doi.org/DOI: 10.1109/ICFTIC64248.2024.10913250

Sufi, F. (2024). Generative Pre-Trained Transformer (GPT) in Research: A Systematic Review on Data Augmentation. *Information 2024, Vol. 15, Page 99, 15*(2), 99. https://doi.org/DOI: 10.3390/INFO15020099

Supriyono, , Wibawa, A. P., Suyono, , & Kurniawan, F. (2024). Advancements in natural language processing: Implications, challenges, and future directions. *Telematics and Informatics Reports*, *16*, 100173. DOI: 10.1016/J.TELER.2024.100173

Tasneem, N. S., & Hemalatha, R. (2025). Real-Time Sentiment Analysis of Customer Feedback Using Neural Networks and NLP Methods. *2024 International Conference on IT Innovation and Knowledge Discovery (ITIKD)*, 1–6. https://doi .org/DOI: 10.1109/ITIKD63574.2025.11004792

Ullah, S., Ahmad, R., Namoun, A., Muhammad, S., Ullah, K., Hussain, I., & Ibrahim, I. A. (2024). A Deep Learning-Based Approach for Part of Speech (PoS) Tagging in the Pashto Language. *IEEE Access : Practical Innovations, Open Solutions*, *12*, 86355–86364. DOI: 10.1109/ACCESS.2024.3412175

Vayadande, K., Kale, D. R., Nalavade, J., Kumar, R., & Magar, H. D. (2024). Text Generation & Classification in NLP. *How Machine Learning Is Innovating Today's World: A Concise Technical Guide*, 25–36. https://doi.org/DOI: 10.1002/9781394214167.CH3

Vayadande, K., Kulkarni, A. M., Yadav, G. B., Kumar, R., & Sawant, A. R. (2024). A Comprehensive Analysis of Various Tokenization Techniques and Sequence-to-Sequence Model in Natural Language Processing. *How Machine Learning Is Innovating Today's World: A Concise Technical Guide*, 3–11. https://doi.org/DOI: 10.1002/9781394214167

Wang, W. (2025). Real-Time Feedback and Tutoring of College English Using Artificial Intelligence Algorithms and IoT Sensors. *International Journal of High Speed Electronics and Systems*. Advance online publication. DOI: 10.1142/S0129156425406692

Wu, H., Li, S., Gao, Y., Weng, J., & Ding, G. (2024). Natural language processing in educational research: The evolution of research topics. *Education and Information Technologies*, *29*(17), 23271–23297. DOI: 10.1007/s10639-024-12764-2

Yu, J. H., & Chauhan, D. (2024). Trends in NLP for personalized learning: LDA and sentiment analysis insights. *Education and Information Technologies 2024 30:4*, *30*(4), 4307–4348. https://doi.org/DOI: 10.1007/S10639-024-12988-2

Chapter 3
Generative Artificial Intelligence in Enhancing Andragogy: Future Trends of AI in Education

Mussa Saidi Abubakari
https://orcid.org/0000-0003-3782-281X
Dig Connectivity Research Laboratory (DCRLab), Uganda & Universiti Brunei Darussalam, Brunei

ABSTRACT

The chapter provides a comprehensive analysis of the intersection between generative artificial intelligence (GenAI) and andragogy, exploring how emerging AI technologies can transform adult learning. It begins by grounding the discussion in adult learning theories, notably Knowles' model, before unpacking the fundamentals of GenAI. The chapter critically examines how GenAI aligns with adult learners' self-directed, experiential, and problem-centred approaches, offering practical examples and global case studies. It also addresses pedagogical strategies for integrating GenAI, emphasising learner engagement, ethical considerations, and digital readiness. Challenges such as technical, pedagogical, and societal barriers are explored alongside future research and innovation pathways. This work ultimately offers educators, researchers, and policymakers evidence-based insights and recommendations for harnessing GenAI to enhance adult education worldwide.

DOI: 10.4018/979-8-3373-6791-0.ch003

Copyright © 2026, IGI Global Scientific Publishing. Copying or distributing in print or electronic forms without written permission of IGI Global Scientific Publishing is prohibited.

INTRODUCTION

Background

Generative Artificial Intelligence technologies have shown a tremendous impact on how people acquire and create knowledge. Within adult educational contexts, the role of GenAI is even more significant for empowering Andragogical practices. Andragogy refers to the methods and principles of adult education, a term popularised by Malcolm Knowles to differentiate adult learning from traditional child pedagogy (Knowles, 1975; Knowles et al., 2025). Knowles emphasised that adult learners are self-directed, rich in experience, goal-oriented, relevancy-oriented, and motivated by internal factors (Dockens & Shelton, 2025; Knowles et al., 2025). In essence, andragogy is the art and science of helping adults learn, centring educational design on adults' unique needs and characteristics. Adult learning theories have evolved over time, but they consistently highlight that adults learn best when learning is self-initiated and builds on their prior life experiences. This chapter begins by grounding the discussion in andragogical theory and its core assumptions, providing an overview of how adults approach learning.

Generative Artificial Intelligence (GenAI) broadly describes AI systems capable of creating new content, such as text, images, code, or multimedia, that is often indistinguishable from human-generated content (Hsu & Ching, 2023a). Recent breakthroughs in GAI, notably large language models like OpenAI's GPT series, have brought these tools into mainstream use. ChatGPT, for example, reached 100 million users just two months after its public launch in late 2022, underscoring how rapidly GAI has "taken the world by storm." (Hsu & Ching, 2023a; Lim et al., 2023). The advent of widely accessible GAI tools presents a transformative opportunity in education, including adult learning contexts. Educators and institutions are only beginning to grapple with the disruptive potential of these technologies. Initially, some educational institutions reacted with alarm, even banning tools like ChatGPT due to fears of plagiarism, but the trend has shifted toward developing guidelines and harnessing GAI for constructive use (World Economic Forum, 2023). Indeed, UNESCO released the first global guidance on generative AI in education in 2023 to help policymakers and educators "navigate the potential of AI for the primary interest of learners" (Miao & Holmes, 2023; World Economic Forum, 2023). This reflects a growing consensus that instead of resisting GenAI, educators should learn to integrate it ethically and effectively, both in pedagogical and andragogical settings.

In Andragogy, adult education stands at a crossroads in the face of rapid AI advancements. As Adarkwah (2024) observes, "adult learners are a neglected species in the generative AI era". Traditional adult learning programs often struggle with limited resources and teacher capacity, issues that have been exacerbated by the pandemic and rising demands for upskilling. GenAI offers novel solutions to some of these challenges. For instance, AI-driven tools can automate routine tasks and generate instructional content, freeing educators' time for more personalised mentoring (Adarkwah, 2024; Cacicio & Riggs, 2023). They can also provide on-demand support and feedback to learners, effectively scaling individualised instruction. In contexts where adult learners face barriers such as geographical isolation or incarceration, GenAI can help "support the rapid creation of high-quality, tailored, and engaging materials for instruction and assessment" (Cacicio & Riggs, 2023). Additionally, GenAI can simulate conversational tutors or coaches available 24/7, aligning with adults' need for flexible, self-paced learning opportunities.

At the same time, integrating GenAI into andragogy is not without concerns. Critics point to risks such as algorithmic bias, inaccuracies or "hallucinations" in AI-generated content, privacy issues, and the potential erosion of learners' critical thinking if over-reliant on AI (Cacicio & Riggs, 2023). These concerns underscore the importance of thoughtful implementation. The rationale for exploring GAI in adult learning, therefore, is twofold: to leverage its strengths for enhancing adult learners' experiences, and to proactively address the challenges and ethical considerations it raises. The accelerating pace of workplace change amplifies the importance of this integration – adults must continually learn new skills (lifelong learning) in an AI-transformed economy (Poquet & de Laat, 2021). Bridging the gap between advanced AI technologies and classical adult education practices is crucial to ensure adult learners are not left behind in the AI age.

Chapter Objectives, Organisation, and Methods

This chapter aims to provide a comprehensive analysis of how generative AI can enhance andragogical practices and what future trends may emerge at the intersection of AI and adult education. We begin with the theoretical foundations of andragogy, outlining key principles of adult learning and contemporary developments. We then explain GAI fundamentals – what generative AI is, how it works, and its current capabilities and limitations in education. With these foundations, we explore the alignment between GAI and andragogy, identifying opportunities where GAI can support adult learning principles (such as self-direction, experiential learning, and readiness to learn). Next, we delve into practical applications and case studies of GAI in adult learning contexts, illustrating how these technologies are being implemented to create content, facilitate reflection, provide mentoring, or simulate real-world scenarios. We also propose pedagogical strategies for integrating GAI into adult learning design, including how to prepare educators and learners, and how to address digital literacy and ethical issues. Challenges and limitations – technical, pedagogical, and ethical – are discussed frankly to provide a balanced view. Finally, after we look ahead to future directions and emerging trends, considering innovations on the horizon and their implications for adult educators, policymakers, and researchers worldwide, the chapter ends with key insights and recommendations. Throughout the chapter, a global perspective is maintained, drawing on insights from different regions and international bodies (e.g., UNESCO) to ensure the discussion is inclusive and globally relevant. By the conclusion, readers should have a clear understanding of the transformative potential of generative AI in adult learning, the best practices for implementation, and the precautions needed to use these tools responsibly. In sum, this chapter seeks to chart a path forward for an AI-enhanced andragogy that can empower adult learners in the years to come.

To achieve the chapter's objectives, we deployed conceptual and integrative review methods, drawing on recent scholarly literature, policy documents, and illustrative case studies published mostly in recent years. The chapter selected sources from various reliable databases (e.g., Scopus, Springer Link, Taylor and Francis, and Google Scholar, among others) based on their relevance to core themes of generative AI and andragogy, adult learning, lifelong learning across formal, non-formal, and informal educational contexts. A thematic and narrative synthesis was used to organise themes (sections) to gain comprehensive insights. Even though not a systematic review, this approach enabled a comprehensive examination of current practices while also projecting informed pathways for future developments.

THEORETICAL FOUNDATIONS OF ANDRAGOGY

Key Assumptions of the Andragogy Model

Adult learning theory has been shaped significantly by Malcolm Knowles' model of andragogy, which outlines assumptions about adult learners that inform effective teaching strategies. Knowles' framework identified several key characteristics differentiating adult learners from children, forming the foundation of modern andragogical practice (Knowles et al., 2025). Below, we summarise five key assumptions of Knowles' andragogy model and then consider contemporary perspectives and challenges related to adult learning theory.

Self-Directed Learning

As individuals mature, their self-concept moves from dependent to self-directed. Adults typically prefer to take initiative in their learning, setting their own goals and defining what they need to learn. Knowles argued that adult education should facilitate and encourage learners' independence and autonomy (Knowles et al., 2020).

In practice, this means offering choices in learning activities and empowering adults to plan and evaluate their progress. Self-direction is considered "a central element of adult learning" (B. Li et al., 2024; Z. Li et al., 2024) that supports learning in informal contexts. For example, in an online study context, adults often value having control over pacing and content selection. However, it is also recognised that not every adult immediately embraces self-directed learning; some may need guidance to develop this skill. The self-directed nature of adult learners aligns well with tools like GAI, as we will later discuss (e.g., ChatGPT can assist learners in independently locating resources or brainstorming learning plans, thereby supporting self-direction (Z. Li et al., 2024).

Learner's Experience

Adults bring a rich reservoir of personal and professional experience to any learning situation. This prior experience is a valuable asset – andragogy assumes that adults "build on their experience" as a core part of learning (Dockens & Shelton, 2025; Knowles et al., 2020). Effective adult education strategies, therefore, connect new knowledge to the learners' existing knowledge base, often through discussion, reflection, or problem-solving that draws on real-life experiences. Adults also have a diversity of backgrounds, which means peer learning and sharing experiences can be powerful. A challenge in traditional adult education is leveraging these varied experiences in a meaningful way for all learners. Nonetheless, recognising the adult learner as an experienced individual helps create learning that is relevant and respectful. In technology-mediated learning, for instance, adaptive systems can tailor content based on a learner's prior knowledge, honouring the role of experience. Additionally, experience can sometimes be a double-edged sword – adults may have ingrained habits or outdated knowledge that educators must help them relearn or unlearn.

Readiness to Learn

Adult learners are usually ready to learn things they feel they need to know or do in order to cope effectively with real-life tasks or problems. Knowles posited that adults become ready to learn when they encounter life situations that create a need (job changes, raising children, civic duties, etc.) (Knowles et al., 2020). This readiness is often tied to developmental stages and social roles (for instance, an adult becoming a first-time manager will be eager to learn leadership skills). Therefore, andragogical approaches try to time learning opportunities to moments when adults are most receptive, or to create awareness of why learning something is important *now*. This is sometimes described as adults' "need to know" the reason for learning something before undertaking it. In a traditional classroom, this might mean explaining upfront how a lesson's content will solve a practical problem the adult learners face. A contemporary development is the use of personalised learning paths and analytics to detect when a learner might be ready for the next challenge. AI could play a role here by identifying patterns of readiness or need through data (though doing so raises privacy considerations). Knowles' concept of readiness underscores that adult education is most effective when it is immediately applicable to the learner's context.

Orientation to Learning

Unlike children, who often learn subjects for future use, adults are more problem-centred in their orientation to learning. Their learning is oriented toward solving problems or completing tasks rather than merely acquiring knowledge for its own sake. This means adults prefer applicability – they learn best when new information is presented in a real-life context and can be applied immediately. For example, an adult learning a new software will be more engaged if the training is framed around actual tasks they need to perform at work, rather than abstract theory. Knowles highlighted that adult learning is "life-centred (or task-centred or problem-centred)" rather than subject-centred (Knowles et al., 2025). This principle prompts educators to use case studies, simulations, and problem-solving activities in adult education programs. Contemporary adult learning theories, like experiential learning (Kolb) or transformative learning (Mezirow), also emphasise problem-solving and real-world application. GAI can potentially enhance this orientation by providing realistic simulations or generating context-specific scenarios for adults to work through, aligning learning closely with practical needs. For instance, generative AI could create a scenario for a management trainee to practice handling a difficult employee conversation, making the learning immediately relevant.

Motivation to Learn

Adults are largely driven by internal motivations (personal growth, job satisfaction, quality of life) rather than external ones (grades, rewards, or fear of punishment). While external factors like career advancement or certification can certainly influence adults, Knowles argued that intrinsic motivators – such as the desire for self-esteem, curiosity, or achievement – are paramount. Effective adult learning taps into these internal motivators. For example, providing opportunities for mastery and recognising competence can fuel an adult learner's internal motivation. Additionally, adults want to see progress and results; thus, clear outcomes and feedback are important. One challenge is that adult learners often juggle multiple responsibilities (work, family, etc.), so even a motivated learner may struggle with time and energy, requiring flexible and supportive learning environments. Modern research suggests that motivation in adult learning is also linked to self-efficacy and the value the learner places on the learning task (Dockens & Shelton, 2025; Lim et al., 2023). Ensuring content is relevant and beneficial to the learner's goals is crucial for maintaining motivation. Technologies like GAI might boost motivation by making learning more engaging or reducing tedious aspects of learning (e.g., automating practice tasks or providing instant feedback can keep learners motivated to continue). However, over-reliance on AI could also dampen motivation if not carefully managed (for instance, if learners feel the AI will "do it for them," they might disengage – a dynamic we will revisit in ethical considerations).

These five assumptions – self-direction, experience, readiness, problem-orientation, and intrinsic motivation – form the backbone of andragogical theory (Knowles et al., 2015). They have been widely applied in adult education program design, from corporate training to community college classes. Contemporary perspectives, however, have extended and sometimes critiqued these assumptions. For instance, some scholars note that Knowles' model presumes an idealised autonomous learner and may not account enough for cultural and individual differences (Anyichie & Butler, 2023; Clair, 2024; Roessger et al., 2022). Not all adults have equal capacity or desire for self-direction; factors like previous educational experience, culture, and confidence influence how self-directed a learner can be (J. Li & Wu, 2023; Makmee et al., 2024; Roessger et al., 2018). Thus, modern adult learning approaches often blend andragogy with pedagogical support when needed, especially for adults who are returning to learning after a long gap or who lack content expertise.

Challenges in Traditional Andragogical Approaches

Traditional adult education programs have sometimes struggled to implement andragogical ideals fully. Large class sizes or standardised curricula can make it difficult to personalise learning or honour each learner's experience. Many adult education systems (especially in formal higher education or vocational training) still rely on lecture-centric, instructor-led methods – a pedagogical approach that can clash with adult learners' expectations for autonomy. In some cases, adults encountering such environments become disengaged, as the methods fail to acknowledge their maturity and experience. There are also structural challenges: adult learners often study part-time while working or caregiving, and programs may not be flexible enough to accommodate these demands. The COVID-19 pandemic highlighted that adult educators needed to "build capacity as instructional designers, leveraging digital technologies to enhance learning opportunities" (). Many were unprepared for the rapid switch to online learning, revealing a gap in andragogy when it comes to technology integration.

Furthermore, while adults are ready to learn things that help solve immediate problems, sometimes they are not aware of what they need to learn next (the "unknown unknowns") (McGregor, 2004; Taylor & Hamdy, 2013). Thus, an educator must occasionally persuade adult learners of the need for certain learning (e.g., upskilling in digital literacy) even if it is not yet on the learner's radar. This intersects with motivational challenges—adults may know a learning activity is beneficial, yet still lack the time or energy to pursue it due to external pressures. Maintaining motivation and engagement in long-term learning (like completing a degree later in life or a multi-month training) can be difficult when life intervenes.

Cultural expectations can also challenge andragogy's application. For instance, in some cultures or contexts, adult learners might actually expect a teacher-directed style (perhaps due to prior educational norms) and feel uncomfortable with a suddenly self-directed format. In workplace training, an employee might prefer clear instructions from an expert rather than purely exploratory learning (Reischmann, 2017; Roessger et al., 2018). This means adult educators must sometimes balance between giving structure and promoting autonomy.

Notably, technology has begun to challenge and enhance traditional adult education practices. A recent systematic analysis in China found that AI integration "has been gradually integrated into Chinese adult education through innovations and explorations", with profound influences such as enabling personalised learning and transforming resource development (Kang, 2023). The analysis identified that AI "challenges traditional adult education practices by helping to actualise personalised learning and precision education". In other words, one of the long-standing difficulties in adult education – addressing diverse needs and customising learning – can be tackled with AI tools that adapt content or provide individualised pathways. This presents an opportunity to fulfil andragogy's promise (meeting learners where they are) but requires educators to adapt their strategies and skills.

In summary, the theoretical bedrock of adult learning is built on principles that emphasise autonomy, experience, relevance, and intrinsic motivation. These principles guide the design of effective adult learning experiences. Yet, as we move further into the 21st century, adult learning theory is evolving. It is incorporating insights from newer theories, addressing challenges that arise from digital transformation, and being re-contextualised for a global, technologically-driven society. Andragogy in the age of AI may need to extend its assumptions. Some scholars have suggested that implementing GenAI in adult education "calls for the need to rethink Malcolm Knowles's andragogical model in light of emerging technologies" (Adarkwah, 2024). The fundamentals remain, but we must consider how tools like generative AI can both support and reshape these foundational assumptions. The next sections of this chapter will delve into those tools and their intersection with andragogy, exploring how theory meets practice in the era of generative AI.

Contemporary Perspectives on Andragogy and Developments

In recent decades, additional theories have enriched our understanding of adult learning. Transformative learning, introduced by Mezirow, describes how adults can undergo perspective shifts through critical reflection – an especially relevant concept in contexts like social or community education (C. D. Hoggan, 2016; C. Hoggan & Kloubert, 2020; Mezirow, 1978). Experiential learning (founded by David Kolb) provides a model (concrete experience, reflective observation, abstract conceptualisation, active experimentation) that is frequently used in adult training workshops to ensure learning is iterative and applied (Kolb, 2015; Salinas-Navarro et al., 2024). Self-determination theory (by Deci & Ryan) looks at the conditions (autonomy, competence, relatedness) that foster intrinsic motivation, complementing Knowles' focus on internal motivation (Ryan & Deci, 2022). Additionally, the rise of technology has given birth to frameworks like digital age learning for adults, which incorporate digital literacy and self-directed learning in online environments (Z. Li et al., 2024; Z. Li & Bonk, 2025). A key contemporary idea is that adult learning is lifelong and life-wide – learning doesn't just happen in formal courses, but continually through work, social interactions, and increasingly via online platforms. Some authors argue that in the age of AI, developing the capability for lifelong learning is essential, as adults must constantly adapt to new tools and information (Adarkwah, 2024; Poquet & de Laat, 2021).

Despite these advancements, core andragogical principles remain highly relevant. What has changed is the context in which they are applied. Modern adult learners might be engaging in online courses with peers from around the world, using digital tools that did not exist a decade ago. This brings new challenges to traditional andragogy. For example, facilitating experiential learning and peer sharing in an online environment requires different approaches and technological support. Ensuring self-directed learners do not feel isolated in e-learning contexts has become a concern, which is where AI tutors or chatbots might step in to provide guidance or companionship, effectively supporting self-direction without replacing human contact entirely.

BASIC GENERATIVE ARTIFICIAL INTELLIGENCE CONCEPTS

Generative Artificial Intelligence refers to AI systems designed to produce new content—novel text, images, audio, video, or other data—similar to what a human might create. Unlike traditional AI, which might classify data or make predictions, generative AI creates data. In simple words, GenAI is an emerging technology that can produce entirely new creative works, such as text, pictures, music, or poetry, in response to simple prompts (Cacicio & Riggs, 2023; Muller et al., 2022). In other words, a generative AI system takes an input (often called a *prompt*, which could be natural language instructions, a piece of text, an image, etc.) and generates an output that did not exist before. This output is based on patterns the AI learned from training data, but it isn't a rote copy – it is a synthesis or creation that can often be unique and context-specific.

Generative AI models are trained on large datasets in an unsupervised or self-supervised manner (Zhu et al., 2024). Take an LLM as an example: it might be given a sentence with a missing word and tasked with predicting that word, over and over, on trillions of examples. Through this process, it learns grammar, facts, and some reasoning abilities implicitly. The model consists of layers of artificial neurons that adjust weights during training to minimise prediction errors. After training, what we have is essentially a very powerful next-word predictor (or next-pixel predictor for images, etc.). When you input a prompt, the model processes it and then starts generating an output one step at a time. It uses the statistical relationships it learned. For instance, if the prompt is "Explain the concept of andragogy to a new corporate trainer," the model recognises terms and likely contexts from its training (it knows "andragogy" is associated with adult learning, "corporate trainer" implies a business training context, etc.). It then likely starts the response with something like "Andragogy is the theory and practice of educating adult learners…" because those words have high probability given the question. It continues sentence by sentence. The coherence of the result comes from the model having captured a lot of the structure of language and knowledge during training.

Crucially, the model does not have a database of exact answers it is pulling from; rather, it is synthesising on the fly. That is why it can generate unique paragraphs each time. However, it also means that if the prompt asks for factual knowledge, the model's answer may or may not be correct – it is not retrieving a fact from memory in a reliable way, it is generating what looks like a fact based on patterns. Often it is correct, especially on well-covered topics, but not always. Educators using GAI need to remember this: verification is needed for factual or high-stakes content.

To understand generative AI, it is helpful to know in broad strokes how it works. Most state-of-the-art generative AI models are built on deep learning techniques, especially neural networks with billions of parameters trained on massive datasets. A prominent architecture used in many generative models is the Transformer, which enables handling sequential data (like language) very effectively (Alshammari et al., 2024). Transformer-based models, such as GPT (Generative Pre-trained Transformer), learn to predict the next word (or pixel, etc.) in a sequence, which allows them to generate coherent continuations of prompts. During training, these models are fed huge amounts of data (for example, GPT-4 was trained on hundreds of billions of words from the internet) and they adjust their internal parameters to statistically model that data. The result is that at runtime, given a prompt, the model can produce content that follows the patterns it learned, often exhibiting impressive fluency or creativity.

From a user's perspective, Generative AI systems have a simple interface: you provide a prompt, and the AI provides an output. However, under the hood, these systems rely on complex pattern recognition. For instance, a large language model (LLM) like GPT-4.5 generates text by choosing one word at a time (or even one letter at a time) based on probabilities of what word is likely to come next, given the prompt and everything it has "learned." The remarkable thing is that with sufficient training, this probabilistic process can produce outputs that are contextually appropriate and often indistinguishable from human writing (Hsu & Ching, 2023a). Similarly, image generators like DALL·E 2 or Stable Diffusion have learned from millions of images and can compose new images from textual descriptions (e.g., "a group of adults in a classroom setting, in the style of Van Gogh"). Essentially, generative models work by generalising patterns in the training data and recombining or extending them in response to new inputs. Thus, generative AI works by leveraging learned patterns to create new content in response to prompts. It can handle complex tasks by virtue of the extensive training data it has absorbed, but it lacks genuine understanding or a true accuracy guarantee. It excels at fluency, versatility, and speed, but can falter with truthfulness and reasoning at times. These strengths and weaknesses directly inform how GAI should be integrated into educational contexts, as we will explore.

Finally, it is important to note that generative AI does not "think" or "understand" in the way humans do. It does not have consciousness or intentionality; it operates on statistical correlations. This is why an LLM can sometimes produce incorrect or bizarre answers (known as "hallucinations") – it might statistically assemble an answer that sounds plausible but is not grounded in fact (El Ganadi et al., 2025; Gill et al., 2024). That limitation aside, these models have shown astonishing capabilities in recent years, blurring the line between human and machine-generated content. As Hsu and Ching (2023) remarked, generative AI content is "increasingly difficult to distinguish from content created by human beings". This has spurred both excitement and concern across various sectors, including education, and most especially in andragogy.

INTERSECTION OF GENERATIVE AI AND ANDRAGOGY: GENAI APPLICATIONS

Aligning Generative AI with Adult Learning Principles

There is a strong conceptual alignment between the capabilities of generative AI and the needs of adult learners as described by andragogy. As Dockens and Shelton (2025) note, AI integration can be guided by adult learning principles to ensure ethical and effective use. Key areas of alignment include: enhancing self-direction, leveraging experience through personalisation, providing immediately applicable learning support, and fostering higher-order skills like critical thinking and creativity.

Self-Directed Exploration

Generative AI can act as a catalyst for self-directed learning, giving adults tools to explore topics independently. Recall that a cornerstone of andragogy is that adults are self-directed and learn best when they can control the learning process. GAI can serve as a responsive learning companion that an adult learner can consult at any time. For example, an adult learner curious about a new topic (say, digital marketing) can engage with an AI chatbot to ask questions and get explanations at their own pace. The AI, available 24/7, allows the learner to drive the inquiry based on their interests and needs, effectively putting the learner in control. Recent work found that ChatGPT shows "great potential to address the challenges faced by adult learners, such as the difficulty of locating resources and the lack of a supportive learning environment (Z. Li et al., 2024; Lin, 2024). In a self-directed project, an adult learner might use GAI to quickly gather information or generate examples, reducing dependency on a formal class or instructor for every answer. This immediate access to knowledge resources can increase learners' confidence and willingness to undertake learning projects on their own (Z. Li et al., 2024). In addition, generative AI can help learners set goals and plan learning – for instance, a learner could prompt an AI for a recommended learning plan on mastering a skill, and the AI can outline steps and resources, which the learner can then modify as they see fit. By providing structure on demand, AI supports self-management in learning, which is critical to self-directed learning (Garrison, 1997).

It is important, however, for educators to guide learners in how to use AI effectively for self-directed learning. The goal is a "human-centred andragogy" where technology is tailored to empower the learner, not overshadow them (Adarkwah, 2024). This might involve teaching prompt strategies or critical evaluation of AI output as part of learning how to learn in the modern age. When done right, GAI becomes a flexible extension of the learner's agency. Adult learners can follow tangents of curiosity, test their understanding by querying the AI, or seek alternative explanations if one does not resonate – all without waiting for scheduled class times or teacher availability. This synergy between self-direction and AI support exemplifies a positive intersection of GAI and andragogy. Figure 1 demonstrates the core Andragogical elements and how GenAI can support them.

Figure 1. Generative AI in adult learning

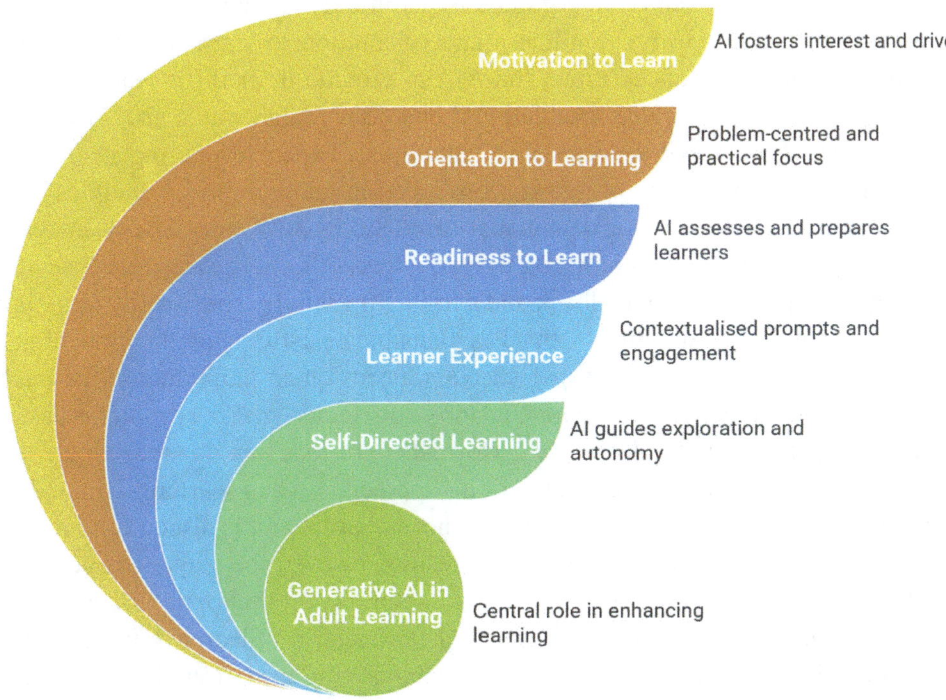

Personalised Learning Experiences

As earlier noted, adults bring diverse experiences and prior knowledge, which andragogy says should be acknowledged in teaching. Generative AI can help personalise content and learning pathways to better connect with each learner's background. Since AI can generate content on-the-fly, it is possible to tailor examples or scenarios to individual learners. For instance, if an adult student in a finance course has a background in healthcare, an AI tutor might adapt its explanations to use healthcare industry examples for financial concepts, making the learning more relatable and grounded in the learner's experience. This kind of personalisation at scale is difficult for human instructors to do with many students, but an AI can handle it if it knows some context about the learner (either provided explicitly or inferred through interaction). According to a recent study, AI in Chinese adult education has "helped actualise personalised learning and precision education", challenging the one-size-fits-all paradigm of traditional practice (Kang, 2023).

Personalisation also means adjusting to the learner's level and progress. GAI can generate remedial explanations for those who are struggling or deeper insights for those who grasp basics quickly. It can transform the pace of learning to suit the individual – a form of self-pacing guided by an intelligent agent. This is in direct harmony with adult learners' readiness and orientation to learn; when a learner is ready for a more advanced topic, the AI can provide it, or if the learner is not yet ready, the AI can provide foundational exercises. Adarkwah's (2024) GenAI adult learning framework suggests that "intelligent LMS" leveraging generative AI could provide individual programs "grounded in andragogical principles", by tracking and analysing learning data in real-time (Storey & Wagner, 2024). Imagine a learning platform that uses an LLM to read a learner's short essay response and then generates personalised feedback and a follow-up activity specifically targeting that learner's misunderstandings – this is a plausible near-future application, aligning feedback with the learner's experience and needs on an individual basis. Such personalisation might also incorporate adaptive difficulty: making problems easier or harder depending on the learner's performance, or focusing on areas where the learner has shown less competence. Adults appreciate when learning is tuned to their level – not so easy that it is boring, but not so hard that it is discouraging. AI's ability to swiftly analyse input (e.g., quiz results, or even the way a learner asks questions) and adjust can keep the learning experience in that optimal zone. This addresses a challenge in adult education: the heterogeneity of learners. In any given adult education class, people often have widely varying backgrounds. AI offers a route to *mass personalisation*, which can significantly enhance engagement and effectiveness for each learner.

Experiential and Problem-Centred Learning

Generative AI can enrich experiential learning opportunities for adults by creating simulations, role-play scenarios, or problem-solving exercises aligned with real-life tasks. Knowles emphasised that adult learning is most effective when it is problem-centred and tied to real-world applications. GAI is well-suited to generate situated learning experiences on demand. For example, consider training for emergency responders (who are adult learners). An AI could generate a variety of emergency scenarios with different parameters for trainees to practice decision-making. Each trainee could get a unique scenario, and the AI could even play the role of people in the scenario, responding to the trainee's actions. This provides realistic practice that is hard to arrange in physical drills frequently. In business training, an AI can simulate a difficult negotiation or a customer service call, allowing the learner to practice communication and problem-solving in a safe environment. After the simulation, the AI can give feedback or prompt reflection, closing the experiential learning loop.

In less formal scenarios, an adult learning a language could have immersive conversations with an AI that acts out different personas or contexts (ordering food, job interview, casual friend chat, etc.). The learner is experiencing the language use rather than just studying it in the abstract. If they make mistakes, the AI can correct them in context or adapt the conversation to address those points (e.g., if the learner struggles with the past tense, the AI might weave more past-tense questions into the dialogue for practice). This is problem-centred in that the "problem" is carrying out a conversation successfully. Generative AI's ability to produce case studies and scenarios spontaneously is a game-changer for problem-based learning. Instead of all learners working on the same pre-written case, which might not resonate with everyone, an AI could tailor a case to each learner's interests or workplace. This relevancy reinforces the adult's readiness and orientation to learn because they see immediate applicability.

Additionally, AI can help with reflective learning by prompting adults after an experience. For instance, after a project or case, the AI might ask the learner to reflect on what went well or what they would do differently, helping the learner abstract lessons. If the learner's reflection misses a key insight, the AI could gently bring it up. This kind of guided reflection is something human facilitators do; an AI could supplement that role, especially in self-study contexts.

It is worth noting that relying on AI for experiential learning requires careful oversight to ensure scenarios remain realistic and useful. If an AI-generated scenario is too far-fetched or the AI "role-player" responds in nonsensical ways, it could break the experiential illusion or even teach the wrong lesson. Thus, while the potential is great, implementing this intersection requires verifying that AI scenarios meet quality standards and probably mixing AI-driven experiences with human debriefings.

Critical Thinking and Creativity Development

Some might fear that using AI, which often provides quick answers, could make learners passive. However, if used intentionally, GAI can actually stimulate critical thinking and creativity among adult learners (Chrostowski, 2024; Gonsalves, 2024). Because AI can generate multiple perspectives or solutions to a problem, learners can be tasked with analysing and evaluating those. For example, an instructor might have an AI generate two or three different approaches to solving a workplace dilemma – some sound, some flawed – and ask adult students to discuss which approach is best and why, identifying any faulty reasoning in the AI-generated ones. This approach leverages AI as a tool to produce material for critical analysis. AI can also simulate multidisciplinary perspectives – a person could ask the AI, "How would an economist view this issue? How about a psychologist?" and it can articulate those viewpoints, which learners can then critically compare. Researchers note that generative AI opens up opportunities and challenges from multiple angles (technology, ethics, application), and engaging with AI on those different angles can sharpen learners' understanding (Adarkwah, 2024; Dwivedi et al., 2023).

For creativity, AI can serve as a brainstorming partner or a source of inspiration. Adult learners in a design course might use an image generator to visualise their concept in different styles and then refine their artistic vision through what they see. Or entrepreneurs in a business course could use an AI to generate dozens of hypothetical business model ideas, then use their judgment to pick viable ones and develop them further. The key is that AI can produce a quantity and variety of ideas quickly, a starting point which the human learner must then apply quality filters to. This process can be very educational: learners practice divergent thinking with the AI's help and then convergent thinking as they evaluate options.

However, educators should coach learners not to accept AI outputs uncritically. One method is to incorporate a step where the AI's answer is intentionally flawed or incomplete, and the learner must improve it. For instance, an AI might generate a draft policy for improving workplace learning, and the adult learner's task is to identify weaknesses or gaps in that draft and rewrite it better. This mirrors real-world situations where initial proposals (perhaps now AI-generated) need human expertise to refine. By doing so, learners practice critical assessment and problem-solving, rather than rote acceptance. Such activities resonate with the concept of "critical reflection" in transformative learning – learners examine assumptions (in this case, the AI's assumptions) and form their own justified conclusions. Some researchers pointed out the importance of "building AI-literate citizens" who understand AI's limits and consider their relationship with GenAI thoughtfully (Adarkwah, 2024; Biagini, 2025; Southworth et al., 2023). Using AI in the classroom to provoke critical discussion about AI's outputs can contribute to this broader digital literacy outcome, making adult learners not just consumers of AI but savvy critics of it.

Motivation and Engagement

Integrating AI in andragogy can potentially boost adult learner motivation if done right. Adults often juggle learning with work and family, so making learning more engaging is key to sustaining their motivation. GAI can introduce elements of interactivity and novelty that capture interest. For example, instead of reading a dry textbook chapter, a learner could engage in a Q&A with an AI that makes the material more conversational. If the AI is programmed to be supportive and positive (somewhat like a coach), it can encourage the learner, which might increase the learner's self-efficacy and willingness to persist. Moreover, for topics that a learner might initially find intimidating, an AI that breaks down the topic and patiently answers "dumb" questions without judgment can reduce anxiety, which in turn improves motivation (Z. Li et al., 2024).

On the flip side, reliance on AI could potentially diminish motivation to learn if, say, a learner feels the AI will always answer, so they do not need to engage deeply. That is why alignment with andragogy's principle of internal motivation is crucial. The integration should be done in a way that *heightens* the learner's intrinsic motivation – for instance, by quickly showing them success or progress through AI-assisted practice, or by enabling them to apply knowledge, which gives a sense of achievement immediately. If an adult learner can solve a realistic problem with the aid of AI, they may feel more motivated to tackle the next problem (with perhaps a bit less aid next time). Also, using AI for more *menial* tasks (like generating flashcards or summarising notes) frees learners to focus on the aspects of learning they find most meaningful, potentially increasing their overall engagement.

In summary, the intersection of generative AI and andragogy is rich with possibilities. GenAI tools, when used intentionally, can operationalise many of the ideals of adult learning theory: empowering self-direction, honouring and building on experience through personalisation, providing just-in-time learning for immediate needs, engaging adults in problem-solving, and creating a responsive, supportive learning environment. As one conceptual piece noted, "the andragogical model advocates for instructional technologists and educators to tailor GenAI tools to adult learning strategies" (Adarkwah, 2024). Rather than adopting AI for its own sake, the goal is to adapt AI's use to fit how adults learn best. Each of the opportunities described also carries a mirror challenge (ensuring accuracy, maintaining engagement, etc.), which underscores that human educators and instructional designers play a critical role in mediating this intersection. The next section will delve into practical applications and implementations where these theoretical alignments come to life, illustrating how adult learning programs are beginning to integrate GAI in concrete ways.

Case Studies of Generative AI Integration in Adult Education

Empirical case studies published since 2023 provide strong evidence that integrating generative AI (primarily large language models such as ChatGPT and GitHub Copilot) into adult formal education—especially in programming/computer science and English as a Foreign Language (EFL) writing—reliably improves short-term learning outcomes and skill acquisition, though these gains are context-dependent and risks related to over-reliance and shallow learning persist (Escalante et al., 2023; S. Li et al., 2025; Nebiu Hyseni & Dermaku, 2025). Some of the recent case studies are presented as follows:

Case 1: The Impact of GenAI-Assisted Programming Education on Self-Efficacy and Learning Outcomes

Recently, researchers have examined the impact of generative AI on adult programming learners' performance and processes (S. Li et al., 2025). Their study used a quasi-experiment with adults in self-directed programming, comparing GenAI vs. alternative tools and analysing learning behaviours. The study provides empirical evidence of improved short-term outcomes but diminished long-term knowledge transfer, meeting key criteria for relevance in adult education contexts.

Case 2: Enhancing EFL Writing Skills With ChatGPT Feedback

In another case, investigators examined the role of ChatGPT in improving the writing abilities of university students learning EFL, most of whom belong to Generation Z (Polakova & Ivenz, 2024). The study adopted a mixed-methods approach, combining quantitative measures and qualitative insights, to assess the impact of AI-driven feedback. Using a quasi-experimental design, 110 EFL students participated in pre- and post-tests, completed questionnaires, and engaged in focus group discussions to evaluate the effectiveness of ChatGPT's feedback. Results showed that after interacting with ChatGPT, learners demonstrated notable gains in writing clarity, grammatical accuracy, the inclusion of essential information, and the appropriate use of passive constructions (Polakova & Ivenz, 2024). Feedback from focus groups reinforced these findings, with many students reporting that ChatGPT significantly supported their writing development and boosted their confidence. The study highlights ChatGPT's promise as an innovative resource in language education, suggesting that integrating AI feedback tools can better address the learning preferences and needs of modern adult learners, particularly within the evolving digital landscape.

Case 3: Leveraging Generative AI to Bridge Programming Skill Gaps in Adult Learners

Another case study highlights an initiative that incorporated Generative AI tools—specifically ChatGPT and GitHub CoPilot—into an application design and development course for Information Systems students. Conducted over five parallel sessions on two different campuses, the study involved 162 learners with diverse levels of programming experience. Findings of the study revealed that GenAI significantly supported students in completing programming tasks, effectively narrowing immediate disparities in coding skills (Bouamor et al., 2025). Learners who depended heavily on AI assistance, however, encountered difficulties with more advanced assessments that required critical thinking and independent problem-solving, such as closed-book examinations. This suggests that while GenAI can be a valuable tool for helping adult learners quickly acquire procedural programming capabilities, it may not sufficiently cultivate the deeper conceptual understanding and transformative learning necessary for sustained success in complex software development contexts.

PEDAGOGICAL AND ETHICAL CONSIDERATIONS FOR INTEGRATING GENAI IN ANDRAGOGY

Integrating generative AI into adult learning requires careful pedagogical planning. It is not just about having the technology available, but about using it in ways that truly enhance learning and respect the needs of adult learners. In this section, we discuss strategies for designing instructional activities with GenAI, methods to engage and motivate adult learners when AI is in the mix, the importance of developing digital competencies for both educators and learners, and crucial ethical considerations for the responsible use of AI in adult education.

Designing Instructional Activities With Generative AI

To effectively leverage generative AI, adult facilitators or educators should design activities where AI's strengths align with learning objectives. Here are some strategies:

AI as a Co-Creator

Involve learners in creating content with the AI. For example, in a professional development workshop, instead of just reading AI-generated case studies, learners can prompt the AI to generate a case relevant to a problem they face at work, then solve it. This gives learners agency and ensures relevance. The educator's role is to guide how to prompt the AI (as observed in the writing course case study) and how to appraise the AI's output critically. By framing the AI as a partner or tool that the learner controls, we adhere to andragogy's principle of self-direction.

Guided AI Exploration

Especially when first introducing AI, structured tasks can help learners explore its capabilities. A strategy could be an assignment where learners must query the AI for specific information or ideas, and then verify or expand on those with real-world data or readings. For instance, "Use an AI (like ChatGPT) to gather three possible solutions to a workplace challenge you face. Then research or reflect on each solution's viability, and write a brief report." This not only engages the AI for idea generation but also practices information literacy, as learners must confirm what the AI says (since AI can sometimes produce incorrect information). It capitalises on AI's breadth (giving multiple perspectives quickly) while reinforcing the learner's role in validating and deciding (World Economic Forum, 2023). Educators can scaffold this by providing a checklist for evaluating AI-generated content, building learners' critical thinking.

Role-play Scenarios

Design activities where learners interact with AI in a role-play context. For example, in a customer service training, one learner plays the customer (via an AI persona) and the other the service rep. Tools or prompts can let the AI adopt certain roles. This requires the educator to set clear parameters. This interactive use makes the learning active and can be more engaging than a static case. The educator should provide guidance afterwards: what could be done differently, connecting to theoretical frameworks (like conflict resolution techniques). By including the AI in role-play, we add variety and spontaneity to class activities, which can maintain motivation for adults who might otherwise find role-play artificial or repetitive.

Reflection and Debrief Integration

Always pair AI-rich activities with reflection. After using an AI tool, adult learners benefit from stepping back and discussing: How did the AI's involvement affect your learning? What did you learn from the AI vs. from your analysis? Do you trust the outcomes? This meta-cognitive element ensures that learners are conscious of the learning process and the role of AI, aligning with principles of adult learning that emphasise self-awareness and the *need to know* why/how learning is happening (Knowles' "need to know" principle). In a strategy, one might dedicate the last 15 minutes of a session to a group debrief on the AI activity, prompting learners with questions like, "What was a surprising suggestion the AI gave? How did you decide whether to use it?" Such a discussion can surface valuable insights and also feedback for the educator on how the AI is fitting into andragogy (Adarkwah, 2024).

Personalisation and Choice

Design activities that give learners choices on how much or in what way to use AI. For instance, an assignment might allow either writing a piece from scratch or using AI for an initial draft and then revising – the learner can choose their mode (with a requirement to document their process). Adult learners value autonomy; not everyone will want to use the AI extensively, and that's fine. The key is offering it as a resource. If one learner is sceptical of AI, they might opt to do more themselves, and another might lean on AI more heavily – both can learn, perhaps differently. Educators can then have those learners compare experiences, fostering peer learning. This strategy respects different learning preferences and comfort levels with technology, which is important since adult classes often have tech-savvy and tech-averse individuals side by side.

In designing with AI, educators should essentially think of AI as a new type of instructional medium, like how one designs differently for group discussion vs. individual reading. One should ask: what part of this learning goal could the AI make more efficient, engaging, or deeper? And conversely, what human elements must I preserve? By answering these, the design will naturally incorporate AI where it helps and avoid using it where it might hinder (e.g., not using AI in a context where the struggle to articulate one's thoughts is itself a valuable learning experience – sometimes doing it the hard way is intentional).

Facilitating Engagement and Motivation With AI

One concern instructors have is whether using AI will affect learners' motivation, either by making things too easy and thus less satisfying, or conversely, by intimidating learners who are less tech-confident. Strategies to keep adult learners engaged and motivated while using generative AI include:

Emphasise Skill Development, Not Just Answers

Learners must understand that the *purpose* of using AI is to improve their skills, not just to get answers faster. Framing matters. For instance, an instructor might say: "We're using this AI tool to practice more and get feedback, which will help you master the skill faster – it is like a gym for your brain." This framing ties into internal motivation by linking AI use to personal improvement (intrinsic goal) rather than extrinsic reward. If learners see AI as a tool that helps them *get better* (and not as a shortcut to avoid effort), they are more likely to use it earnestly. In the earlier writing tutor case, because students had to show their drafts and AI feedback, they knew the goal was to learn from it, not to have ChatGPT do the work for them – such transparency fosters a mastery orientation.

Maintain Challenge

Adults can lose motivation if tasks become too trivial. If AI assistance risks making tasks too easy, educators can raise the complexity of the task to keep the challenge optimal. For example, if a coding class uses Copilot to suggest code, the instructor might give more complex assignments than before, since Copilot eases basic coding. The challenge shifts to higher-level problem-solving or debugging more subtle issues, thus keeping learners in the flow state (not bored, not overwhelmed). Some researcher in their SWOT analyses pointed out that while AI can handle routine tasks (a strength), a challenge is redesigning tasks to ensure critical thinking is still required (Abubakari, Shafik, et al., 2024; Farrokhnia et al., 2024). So, strategy: offload rote parts to AI, and fill the freed time with analysis, extension, or reflection tasks that deepen difficulty appropriately.

Peer Learning With AI

Encourage learners to share and compare experiences of using AI. Adults often learn well from peers and enjoy sharing strategies (this leverages their experience and need for social interaction in learning). For example, after an AI-supported activity, have small groups discuss "How did you use the AI? What did it help with, and what were its limitations for you?" This not only reinforces learning by articulation but might surface tips and tricks (one learner might teach others a useful prompt or warning). It also normalises that everyone is learning how to work with AI together, making the process communal can reduce any stigma or fear. In terms of motivation, it can become a fun, collaborative exploration (some groups might even get a light competitive spirit: who can get the AI to produce the best result, like a friendly contest to refine a prompt for the clearest explanation, etc.). This taps into the social and achievement motivations.

Address Anxiety and Build Confidence

Some adult learners might feel intimidated by AI or fear it will expose their weaknesses. Facilitators should create a supportive climate around AI use. Reassure learners that making mistakes or not knowing something (which might prompt using AI for help) is a normal part of learning. Emphasise that the AI is a tool, not a judge. One could draw parallels: "Using AI in learning is like using a calculator in math – it does not mean you are bad at math; it helps you get to the more interesting parts of the problem." For those hesitant, maybe start them on low-stakes uses (like practising with AI on a simple task) to build comfort, then ramp up. Monitoring and giving positive reinforcement when a learner effectively uses the AI can boost confidence.

Gamification Elements

Some programs have started to gamify AI interactions (e.g., awarding "badges" for effective prompt use, or tracking streaks of practice problems solved with AI hints). Adults respond to gamification when it is done in a respectful, voluntary way (not childish, but as optional challenges or recognition of progress). For instance, an app might have a progress bar showing how many AI-practice sessions one has completed toward a goal. If integrated carefully, this can motivate continued use and practice. But caution: external gamification should not override intrinsic goals; it is just a nudge. A learner might feel a sense of accomplishment seeing that they've completed 10 simulated scenarios (with the AI facilitating them) and earned a "Scenario Master" badge, tying back to the intrinsic reward of skill mastery.

Connect to Real-world Impact

Always loop activities back to how they help in real life. Adults are motivated when they see immediate relevance. After an AI-enhanced task, discuss how the skill or outcome can be applied at work or in personal life. This reinforces the value of the learning and, by extension, the AI's role in it. When learners see that AI use directly contributed to something they care about (like performing better at work, or being able to help their child with homework now that they brushed up on math with the AI), their motivation is bolstered. This touches on Knowles' principle of readiness and orientation, showing that using AI is oriented to solving real problems here and now.

Developing Digital Competencies and Readiness

Integrating GAI means both educators and learners need certain digital competencies. Not everyone comes in ready to effectively use these tools. Here is how to address that:

Educator Training

Instructors themselves must be comfortable with generative AI to facilitate its use. Professional development should be provided, focusing not just on technical how-to, but on pedagogical integration. Instructors could practice designing an AI-inclusive lesson and get feedback. They should also be aware of issues like bias in AI outputs and how to mitigate them so that they can guide learners accordingly. As some have pointed out, there is a need to prepare teachers internationally to create AI-facilitated learning experiences responsibly (Hsu & Ching, 2023b, 2023a). This might involve working through examples of AI failures and how to turn them into teaching moments.

Learner Orientation

Do not assume adult learners (even younger ones) automatically know how to use AI tools effectively for learning. A short orientation session or tutorial can be crucial. Cover basics: where the AI's knowledge comes from, why it might be wrong sometimes, how to phrase questions or prompts, and privacy considerations (e.g., not to input sensitive personal info). It is akin to an information literacy module. Perhaps incorporate a simple, non-threatening activity to let them play with the AI and share an interesting result (like "Ask the AI to tell you about a hobby of yours, and then verify one fact it gives"). This gets them hands-on quickly, demystifying it. People often become more at ease once they try it and see that it is not magical or beyond comprehension.

Digital Literacy as a Goal

Using AI can itself build digital literacy, which is an increasingly important skill. Emphasise to learners that part of what they are learning is how to use digital tools – something valuable in many domains, effectively. Some have highlighted nurturing lifelong learning capabilities, including digital literacy in using GenAI (Abubakari et al., 2025; Abubakari & Kalinaki, 2024; Poquet & de Laat, 2021). Thus, time spent on teaching how to use AI is not time wasted; it is dual-purpose. For older adult learners or those less familiar with tech, this can be empowering: they may start with apprehension but end with a new skill that makes them feel more competent in the modern digital world. That addresses motivation, too, as they see personal growth in tech-savviness.

Infrastructure Readiness and Accessibility

Ensure the learning environment has the needed infrastructure – devices, internet, accounts for AI services, etc. There should be contingency plans (like cached models or offline tools) if the internet fails, especially if the setting is remote or bandwidth-limited. Technical hiccups can kill momentum, so a strategy is to have some backup exercise that doesn't rely on AI if something goes wrong, to keep the class on track.

Over time, investing in stable infrastructure is key; in some workplaces, that might mean negotiating access through IT policies or addressing data security concerns proactively so that using AI is smooth and sanctioned. Furthermore, not all adult learners may be equally able to interact with AI tools (e.g., visual impairments, reading difficulties). Use features like text-to-speech or speech-to-text if needed. Many AI chat interfaces can integrate with screen readers or accept voice input. Ensuring the tools adhere to accessibility standards is part of readiness. If a learner is not comfortable typing, encourage them to dictate if possible. For those with low literacy, using AI via voice can ironically help them get needed assistance (an AI-based assistant could read content out loud to them, for instance).

Cultural Readiness

Particularly in diverse global contexts, some adult learners might have cultural, religious, or language backgrounds that affect how they interact with AI or any digital technology introduced (Abubakari, 2025a; Abubakari, Zakaria, et al., 2024; Alhammadi et al., 2023; Djazilan et al., 2024). Educators should be sensitive to such dynamics. They may need to explicitly encourage a mindset of questioning the AI or emphasise that it is okay to disagree with or correct the AI. In multilingual settings, if the AI supports multiple languages, allow learners to use their preferred language or bilingual approach – this can scaffold learning (like an adult learner could ask for an explanation in their native language if English content is confusing). Being ready for such culturally responsive usage ensures AI is a help, not a hindrance.

GENAI CHALLENGES AND LIMITATIONS IN ADULT LEARNING

While generative AI offers substantial opportunities to enhance adult learning, there are also significant challenges and limitations to consider. These can be broadly categorised into technical barriers, pedagogical constraints, and ethical/social implications. Recognising and addressing these limitations and challenges is crucial for the successful integration of AI in andragogy.

Technical Barriers

Infrastructure and Access

Not all adult learning programs have the necessary infrastructure to support advanced AI tools. High-speed internet, modern computing devices, and access to AI platforms may be limited in some regions (especially in developing countries or rural areas) or underfunded adult education centres. This creates an access gap – a point highlighted by a recent researcher with the concept of a *"GenAI divide"* (Adarkwah, 2024). If only some learners can effectively use the tools due to infrastructure, it can widen educational inequalities. Moreover, even when tools are available, they might be blocked by institutional IT policies or data protection concerns. Thus, stakeholders must invest in upgrading facilities and possibly use offline or locally hosted AI solutions where the internet is an issue. Partnerships with tech companies or government initiatives may be needed to provide access in community centres (like donated hardware or subsidised software access). Bridging this gap is essential to not leaving portions of adult learners behind.

Digital Literacy Gaps

As previous studies on digital competencies (DC) highlight, many adult learners (and some educators) lack advanced digital skills (Abubakari et al., 2023a, 2025; Abubakari & Kalinaki, 2024). Even if the tech is there, users might not know how to use it effectively. This is a barrier that can make the introduction of AI frustrating or underutilised. Some adult learners might find interfaces confusing, or may have low typing skills that hinder effective interaction with chatbots. Incorporating digital skills training as part of the curriculum when introducing AI can be among the mitigation approaches to DC gaps (Abubakari, 2025b; Abubakari et al., 2023b; Musa et al., 2025). This slows initial content coverage, perhaps, but pays off by enabling learners to participate fully. Alternatively, for those truly uncomfortable, provide analogue or human-mediated alternatives so they are not completely excluded. Overcoming this requires patience and instructional design that does not assume tech-savviness.

Reliability of AI Systems

Generative AI systems are not always reliable – they can suffer downtime, usage limits (as often seen with popular tools like ChatGPT being overloaded), or changes in behaviour after updates. If a lesson plan heavily relies on an AI and it is unavailable or acting up, that's a challenge. Even on a smaller scale, response times might vary, which can disrupt class flow if an AI is slow to answer on a given day. Over time, as AI infrastructure improves and dedicated educational AI systems are employed, reliability might improve, but the wise approach is to expect hiccups and plan around them.

Integration With Legacy Systems

Many educational or training programs use specific Learning Management Systems (LMS) or other software. Integrating AI tools into these existing systems might be non-trivial. For example, embedding an AI chatbot into an LMS or connecting an AI-driven assessment with the gradebook requires technical coordination. If not seamless, instructors might have to juggle multiple platforms, which can be burdensome. There is also the issue of data–syncing AI output (like scores or logs) with institutional data systems, which can be a technical project beyond an individual instructor's scope. Institutions should foresee this and allocate resources to doing it securely and efficiently if they plan to scale AI usage.

Cost and Licensing

Many advanced generative AI services have usage costs or subscription fees, especially for premium versions needed for heavy or institutional use. Licenses for enterprise-level AI (with privacy guarantees) can be expensive. This could be a barrier for adult educational programs with tight budgets. On the other hand, using only free versions might come with limitations or ads. Exploring open-source models or those provided through educational partnerships (some companies offer free educational access) can be alternative solutions. If demonstrating success on a small scale, use that evidence to seek funding or make a case for cost-benefit to sponsors (e.g., showing improved outcomes that justify investing in the AI tool). Additionally, manage usage to stay within free tier limits if possible. Thus, this requires some creativity to balance cost and benefit.

Pedagogical Constraints

Individuals' Readiness and Acceptance

Some educators may be resistant or anxious about using AI in their teaching. They might worry it is too complex, that it could threaten their role, or not see its value. Without instructor buy-in, AI tools could be underutilised or misused. Some have noted the ambivalence – AI is here, but whether it is for good depends a lot on our approach (Sætra, 2023). Providing professional development and success stories to show educators the potential can help mitigate this constraint. Further, reassuring them that their expertise is still crucial – AI is a tool that can amplify their teaching, not replace them, can help boost acceptance. It also helps to start with volunteers or early adopters and then have them share their experience with peers (peer influence can be strong in teacher communities). Give instructors time to tinker in low-stakes contexts first, so they gain confidence. Administrators should avoid forcing it abruptly; change management principles apply here.

Curriculum Alignment

Existing curricula might not have obvious slots for AI activities. Teachers are often bound by syllabi, standards, or tight schedules to cover certain content. Introducing AI-based projects or new assessments might feel like an "add-on" that they do not have time for. To mitigate this, stakeholders should identify which existing activities could be replaced or improved by AI, rather than always adding. Align AI tasks with learning objectives explicitly so it is clear they are not just tech demos but legitimate pedagogical methods. It may require some curriculum redesign, which can be slow if approvals are needed. Starting with small pilot modules (like a 2-week AI-enhanced unit within a longer course) can demonstrate alignment and then pave the way for broader curriculum integration.

Learning Efficacy Concerns

There is a pedagogical worry: Does relying on AI hinder certain learning processes? For instance, if learners use AI to solve problems, are they developing their problem-solving skills or just learning to consult AI? If they use AI for writing, are they actually improving writing or just editing AI output? These are open questions being researched (Ifelebuegu, 2023; Luckin, 2025). Thus, the design of activities surrounding GenAI usage should ensure cognitive engagement. One should guard against AI turning learners into passive recipients. Techniques like "AI as stimulus, human as responder" can ensure the human is doing the substantive work (e.g., AI poses a problem, human solves it, not vice versa). If noticing that learners are coasting thanks to AI, the instructor might tweak the tasks to require deeper personal input. It is a balance to keep, and research like that by Lim et al. (2023), asking if AI is "Ragnarök or reformation" in education, suggests that it has to be carefully managed to reform rather than spoil the learner's engagement truly (Lim et al., 2023).

Ethical and Social Implications

Trust and Authenticity

One social implication is trust – if learners know something is AI-generated, do they value it as much as if it came from an instructor or peer? Similarly, the authenticity of work becomes a concern: Is the learner's submission authentically theirs? Overuse of AI can blur authorship. For authenticity, having stages where learners must do tasks without AI (like in-class portions) can ensure they have the skill, even if they use AI elsewhere. If trust issues arise (like a learner feeling an AI feedback is off), the instructor should address it and perhaps involve human judgment (maybe cross-check certain AI-provided info). Preserving a sense of authenticity may also involve personalising tasks (as said, tasks drawing on personal experience ensure an authentic response that AI cannot fabricate believably).

Dependency and Critical Thinking

There is the risk that learners become overly dependent on AI and do not develop their independent critical thinking or problem-solving to the needed degree. If an adult learner learns always asks the AI first, they might not try on their own. To mitigate this, encourage a scaffolded approach – maybe initially allow AI support, but gradually wean off on more advanced tasks. Or institute an "AI-free challenge" where learners intentionally work without AI to test their skills periodically. Teach metacognitive strategies: for example, "Ask yourself first, then confirm with AI" as a rule of thumb. Sætra (2023) questions whether generative AI will be for good – one dimension is making sure it augments rather than atrophies human intellect. By designing learning activities that sometimes deliberately remove AI support, one can guard against over-dependence.

Bias and Fairness in Content

As previously noted, AI can generate biased content. If not addressed, this could propagate stereotypes or misinformation, which is ethically problematic. Furthermore, if AI language or examples inadvertently cater to certain groups more than others (like Western-centric examples) (Abubakari, 2025b; Ferrara, 2023), that could alienate some learners. As a mitigation approach, people should vet AI outputs and correct biases in real time. Encourage learners to analyse AI content for bias as a learning exercise, critically. Use AI from providers that are known to put effort into bias reduction (though none are perfect). From a global perspective, try to use AI that has been trained on diverse data sets. Also, supplement AI with local or culturally relevant material to ensure inclusivity. This aligns with UNESCO's guideline to "Promote inclusion, equity, linguistic and cultural diversity" when using AI (Y. Li et al., 2025; World Economic Forum, 2023).

Accountability and Transparency

Societally, there is the concern of accountability (e.g., if an AI gives wrong advice and a learner uses it at work, who is accountable for the error?) Educationally, hopefully, the stakes are not too high, but it raises an issue of teaching accountability: we should teach learners that using AI does not absolve them of responsibility for the results. Further, being transparent about AI's involvement in work (in some professional settings, it could even be an ethical requirement to note AI involvement if it affects safety or compliance). For mitigation, instil a practice that any AI usage is documented (even in the classroom context) to create a habit of transparency. Discuss professional norms about AI (some industries are drafting guidelines for AI use – if relevant to the learners, bring that in). And ensure learners practice verifying AI-generated work themselves, reinforcing that final accountability lies with the human using the tool.

FUTURE DIRECTIONS AND EMERGING TRENDS

The integration of generative AI into adult education is still in its early stages, and we can expect significant evolution in the coming years. Several emerging trends and future directions are worth noting:

More Advanced and Specialised Generative AI Tools

The generative AI of today (2025) will likely seem rudimentary compared to what is coming. We anticipate more advanced AI models with greater accuracy, multimodality, and domain specialisation. For example, future AI tutors may combine language, vision, IoT technologies, and even sensor data (Abubakari & Mashoedah, 2021) to provide holistic feedback (an AI that watches you perform a physical task via camera and gives tips, for instance). We also expect domain-specific AI trained on the jargon and scenarios of fields like healthcare, law, or engineering. These could provide highly nuanced guidance to adult learners in professional programs. For adult learners, this means AI help will become more accurate and context-aware (Adarkwah, 2024). However, the need for human oversight will remain, as AI gets more powerful, ensuring its advice is pedagogically sound and trustworthy will be an ongoing area of work.

Integration of AI Into Learning Management Systems and Platforms

We can expect generative AI to become a standard feature of educational technology platforms. Learning Management Systems (LMS) are beginning to incorporate AI-driven chatbots for student support and AI-assisted grading tools. In adult education, which often happens online or in blended formats, this could be transformative. Imagine an LMS where each adult learner has a built-in AI study coach that can answer course content questions anytime, help plan their study schedule, or even generate practice quizzes on the fly. Policymakers and institutions will need to create guidelines for such integrations. It also raises questions of data sharing between AI providers and educational institutions, which will need careful governance. Nonetheless, when done responsibly, such integration will make AI support a seamless part of the learning experience rather than an external tool. Adarkwah's (2024) vision of a "GenAI adult learning ecology" includes institutional adoption of GenAI in curriculum and policy – we are likely to see educational institutions formally include AI literacy and usage as part of their offerings.

Lifelong Learning Companions

In the future, adults may have personalised AI "mentors" that accompany them throughout their lifelong learning journey, not just in one course. These AIs could keep a profile of one's skills, learning history, and goals (secured and privacy-protected), and proactively suggest learning opportunities or career advice. The OECD and UNESCO have already mused about generative AI enabling continuous guidance beyond formal schooling (Sekmokas et al., 2024; Stanistreet, 2024). For instance, an adult might consult their AI mentor on whether a new certification or workshop is worth pursuing for their career, and the AI could tailor its advice based on the person's learning profile and the latest job market trends (somewhat like a personalised guidance counsellor). This scenario raises important policy questions: How do we certify or trust advice from AI mentors? What happens if different AI mentors give conflicting guidance? It suggests a future need for standards and possibly "AI counsellor accreditation" in some form. Yet, the potential is empowering – continuous, data-informed support could help adults navigate fast-changing skill demands in the workforce. Policymakers should start considering frameworks for recognising and integrating such AI guidance into public employment and education services.

Global Collaboration and Resource Sharing via AI

Generative AI might facilitate more global exchange of adult education resources. For example, an educator in one country could design an excellent AI-driven simulation, and that "prompt/program" could be shared and adapted worldwide with translation and context adjustments done by the AI. UNESCO emphasises international collaboration on AI in education to ensure it benefits all regions (World Economic Forum, 2023). In the future, we might have international consortia curating AI training data or prompts that ensure cultural diversity and representation, which local adult educators can draw on. This could reduce duplication of effort and raise the quality of AI educational content globally. However, it will require addressing language barriers (though AI translation is improving rapidly) and contextualization (ensuring examples and scenarios make sense locally – something AI can help adapt).

Focus on AI Ethics and Policy in Education

As AI becomes more embedded in adult education, expect stronger policy frameworks at the institutional, national, and international levels. Accreditation bodies might set standards for AI use in curricula (for example, requiring that programs teach AI literacy outcomes, or ensuring assessment integrity in the presence of AI). Issues of data privacy will likely lead to regulations about educational AI tools, perhaps mandating local data storage for student interactions or transparency in AI algorithms used in learning. UNESCO's ethical guidance is an early step in this direction (Miao & Holmes, 2023; Morandín-Ahuerma, 2024). On the flip side, there may be policies to ensure equitable access – perhaps public libraries or community centres will be funded to provide AI learning stations so that all adults, including those outside formal education, can benefit from learning with AI. Policymakers and researchers are already examining these angles; for example, recent studies call for re-examining the concept of originality and assessment policy in the age of GenAI (Luo (Jess), 2024; Weng et al., 2024). We will likely see updated definitions of academic misconduct, new guidelines for citing AI, and perhaps even new pedagogical accreditation criteria.

Research on Efficacy and Best Practices

The next few years should bring a wave of research studying the impact of generative AI on adult learning outcomes. Key questions include: Does AI support improve retention and completion rates in adult education programs? How does AI-tutoring compare to human tutoring for adult learners, or what is the optimal blend? What new pedagogical models emerge (e.g., "flipped AI classroom" where initial teaching is via AI and class time is all discussion)? Also, longitudinal studies might look at how using AI in training affects on-the-job performance for adult learners in professional development contexts. The field of adult education will need theoretical updates too – perhaps expansions of andragogy theory to explicitly incorporate learning in human-AI partnerships. Dockens and Shelton (2025) have begun that conversation, suggesting alignment of AI with andragogical principles. Future research can validate or refine these alignments by observing real classrooms and training sessions with AI. We can imagine new models like "AndrAIgogy" being fleshed out, balancing Knowles' assumptions with the realities of AI-augmented self-directed learning. Researchers will also need to examine the psychological aspects – adult learner trust in AI, changes in self-efficacy, and the metacognitive skills needed to use AI effectively. The findings will inform educators and policy: for example, if studies show that certain groups benefit less from AI, targeted interventions can be developed.

Evolution of the Educator's Role

A notable future trend is the shifting role of adult educators. With AI handling more routine instruction and feedback, instructors will likely spend more time as facilitators, coaches, and content curators. They may focus on higher-order guidance: interpreting AI-provided analytics about student performance, orchestrating collaborative learning experiences, and addressing affective needs like motivation and confidence, which AI is not well-equipped to handle. Some describe this as a reorientation of teacher knowledge frameworks in the age of ChatGPT (Mishra et al., 2023). Professional development for educators will increasingly emphasise skills like prompt engineering for education, analysing AI-generated data, and maintaining human connection in a partially AI-driven classroom. We may also see new specialisations – for example, an "AI in Adult Learning Facilitator" certificate for teachers who excel in blending AI with teaching. This transition might be challenging for some, but many educators will likely find it rewarding to be freed from drudge work (like grading every draft of an essay) to focus on more impactful mentoring. Importantly, the human educator will be the moral and ethical compass of the classroom, ensuring fairness, equity, and values are upheld in ways an AI cannot. That role will only grow in significance.

In sum, the future of generative AI in adult education promises more intelligent, interactive, and personalised learning experiences, but it also comes with the need for thoughtful integration, robust support systems, and policy frameworks. We are likely to see a synergy of global collaboration and local customisation – AI providing scale and breadth, while educators ensure depth and relevance. As Lim et al. (2023) provocatively asked, is this future a "Ragnarök or reformation" for education. The trends suggest it can be a positive reformation if guided by sound pedagogy and ethics. Adult education has always evolved with societal and technological changes, from correspondence courses to e-learning; generative AI is the next evolution, potentially one of the most significant. The coming years will be critical in shaping this evolution through research, innovation, and dialogue among educators, learners, technologists, and policymakers worldwide. The goal on the horizon is a future where AI is a natural, beneficial part of lifelong learning, helping adults everywhere to grow and adapt in a fast-changing world continually.

CONCLUSION AND RECOMMENDATIONS

Chapter's Key Insights

Generative AI stands at the forefront of a new era in adult education. This chapter has explored how GAI can enhance andragogy – the art and science of adult learning – by aligning with core adult learning principles, introducing innovative instructional practices, and offering personalised support at scale. We began with a foundation in andragogy, reaffirming Knowles' assumptions about adult learners and noting contemporary developments. We then delved into the fundamentals of generative AI, identifying its capabilities in creating content, answering questions, and simulating interactions, along with its advantages (like personalised learning and immediate feedback) and limitations (such as occasional inaccuracies and biases) in educational contexts. The intersection of GAI and andragogy revealed myriad opportunities: from self-directed exploration and experiential learning via AI-driven scenarios to the use of conversational agents as always-available mentors. Real-world case studies illustrated these opportunities in practice, showing improved writing skills, better management training, and expanded literacy outreach when AI was thoughtfully integrated. Throughout the discussion, several key insights emerged:

Generative AI Can Significantly Personalise and Enrich Adult Learning

But this works best as a complement to, not a replacement for, human educators and peers. The most successful implementations treated AI as a tool under the learner's and instructor's control, aligning with adults' need for autonomy and relevance.

Alignment With Adult Learning Principles Is Critical

AI usage that reinforced self-direction, leveraged learners' experiences, and stayed problem-oriented tended to be well-received and effective. On the other hand, uses of AI that might reduce engagement or bypass meaningful learner involvement were identified as counterproductive. Thus, pedagogy must lead technology – using andragogical theory as a guide for when and how to employ GAI.

Global and Ethical Perspectives Must Be Integral

Adult learners around the world can benefit from AI, but equity of access, cultural inclusivity, and ethical safeguards are paramount. We saw that international bodies like UNESCO are actively issuing guidance to ensure AI in education promotes inclusion, equity, and human agency. Responsible use is not optional; it is essential for trust and sustainability of AI integration. This includes transparency about AI involvement, data privacy protection, unbiased algorithms, and clear policies on academic integrity.

The Role of the Adult Educator Is Evolving Rather than Diminishing

In a GAI-enhanced learning environment, educators take on roles as facilitators, ethicists, mentors, and designers of learning experiences. Their expertise is needed to design AI-inclusive curricula, to train learners in AI literacy, to intervene when AI falls short, and to provide the human touch of empathy and contextual judgment that AI cannot. In short, the human element remains irreplaceable, but it can focus more on the higher-value aspects of education thanks to AI support.

Key Recommendations

Based on the chapter's insights, several recommendations for effective integration of generative AI into adult learning can be made:

Invest in Educator Training and AI Literacy

Educators and adult learners alike should be given opportunities to develop their understanding and skills in using generative AI. Workshops, courses, or modules on AI literacy (covering how GAI works, how to critically evaluate its output, and how to use it ethically) should become a standard part of professional development and even learner orientation. Equipping adult learners with AI literacy is in itself empowering, as it becomes a valuable 21st-century skill for the workplace and civic life.

Update Andragogical Practice and Curriculum Design

Adult education programs should revisit their curricula and learning activity designs in light of AI capabilities. This means identifying areas where AI can add value (e.g., providing more practice, enabling simulation, offering translation or reading support) and redesigning those learning experiences accordingly. It also means setting learning outcomes related to AI use – for instance, "Learners will be able to effectively use AI tools to research and solve problems in [their domain] and critically appraise the solutions." Including such outcomes legitimises AI use as part of the learning goals rather than an external tool.

Implement Clear Usage Policies and Ethics Guidelines

Institutions and instructors should proactively craft policies about AI usage in learning and assessment and communicate them clearly to learners. These should cover what is considered acceptable assistance (with an emphasis on learning, not cheating), how to cite or acknowledge AI contributions, and the consequences of misuse. Involving learners in discussions about these policies can also raise their ethical awareness (for example, a class could discuss a scenario of AI misuse and collectively decide on a fair policy). This participatory approach echoes adult learners' need to be involved in the process and respect their maturity.

Ensure Infrastructure and Support Systems

Effectively using AI requires a reliable tech infrastructure and support. Adult learning providers should assess their technology readiness – devices, internet bandwidth, software access – and make necessary improvements, potentially seeking funding or partnerships to do so. Additionally, technical support should be available to troubleshoot AI tools, and alternative options should be in place for learners with limited digital access (such as providing on-site access or loaner devices). Without these, the promise of AI can become a source of frustration or inequity.

Continuous Evaluation and Research

Treat the integration of generative AI as an iterative process subject to evaluation. Collect data on learner outcomes, satisfaction, and engagement in AI-augmented activities versus traditional ones. Use surveys, interviews, or learning analytics to gauge what's working and what is not. This evidence-based approach will help refine methods and also contribute to the broader knowledge base. Partnerships between practitioners and researchers can be valuable – for example, an adult education centre might collaborate with a university research team to formally study their AI pilot and publish the results, benefiting the field at large.

In closing, generative AI presents both great potential and significant responsibility for adult education. If we embrace it thoughtfully, it can help us realise long-standing goals in the field: truly learner-centred, self-paced, accessible, and relevant education for adults, supported by resources tailored to individual needs and contexts. We saw glimpses of this in the chapter, from AI enabling a learner to practice workplace scenarios that would be hard to set up otherwise, to an adult literacy student reading about something personally meaningful with AI assistance. These are encouraging signs of AI being leveraged for good, fulfilling the promise of "a synergy between humans and GenAI" in learning. However, achieving this at scale will require concerted effort by all stakeholders. Educators must adapt and guide, learners must stay curious and critical, technologists must design with ethics and education in mind, and policymakers must create conducive frameworks. Generative AI can open doors and furnish the learning environment with rich resources, but human educators and learners must walk through those doors together, hand in hand with AI. The future of adult learning will be built on such collaboration, harnessing the speed and scale of AI while nurturing the wisdom, creativity, and empathy that only come from human experience. With mindful integration, generative AI can indeed become a powerful ally in the mission of lifelong learning, helping adults everywhere to learn, adapt, and thrive in the dynamic future that awaits.

REFERENCES

Abubakari, M. S., & Mashoedah, . (2021). The Internet of Things (IoT) as an Emerging Technological Solution for the Covid-19 Pandemic Mitigation: An Overview. *Journal of Physics: Conference Series*, *1737*(1), 012003. DOI: 10.1088/1742-6596/1737/1/012003

Abubakari, M. S. (2025a). Digital Technologies Adoption in Islamic Education for Fostering Lifelong Learning Culture: Pilot Survey Preliminary Insights. In Anshari, M., Almunawar, M. N., & Ordóñez de Pablos, P. (Eds.), *Multi-Industry Digitalization and Technological Governance in the AI Era* (pp. 103–126). IGI Global., DOI: 10.4018/979-8-3373-1681-9.ch005

Abubakari, M. S. (2025b). Overviewing Biases in Generative AI-Powered Models in the Arabic Language: AI Fairness for Sustainable Future. In Syafrudin, M., Fitriyani, N. L., & Anshari, M. (Eds.), *Achieving Sustainability in Multi-Industry Settings With AI* (pp. 361–390). IGI Global., DOI: 10.4018/979-8-3373-2530-9.ch013

Abubakari, M. S., & Kalinaki, K. (2024). Digital Competence in Islamic Education for Lifelong Learning: Preliminary Analysis Using DigComp 2.1 Framework. In Hawamdeh, M. M. K., & Abdelhafid, F. (Eds.), *Embracing Technological Advancements for Lifelong Learning* (pp. 1–31). IGI Global., DOI: 10.4018/979-8-3693-1410-4.ch001

Abubakari, M. S., Shafik, W., & Hidayatullah, A. F. (2024). Evaluating the Potential of Artificial Intelligence in Islamic Religious Education: A SWOT Analysis Overview. In *AI-Enhanced Teaching Methods* (pp. 216–239). IGI Global. https://doi.org/DOI: 10.4018/979-8-3693-2728-9.ch010

Abubakari, M. S., Zakaria, G. A. N., & Musa, J. (2024). Perceived compatibility and students' intention to adopt digital technologies in Islamic education institutions. *Cogent Education*, *11*(1), 2430869. DOI: 10.1080/2331186X.2024.2430869

Abubakari, M. S., Zakaria, G. A. N., & Musa, J. (2025). Validating the DigComp framework among university students across different educational systems. *Discover Education*, *4*(1), 200. DOI: 10.1007/s44217-025-00652-x

Abubakari, M. S., Zakaria, G. A. N., Musa, J., & Kalinaki, K. (2023a). Assessing Digital Competence in Higher Education: A Gender Analysis of DigComp 2.1 Framework in Uganda. *SAGA: Journal of Technology and Information System*, *1*(4), 114–120. DOI: 10.58905/saga.v1i4.210

Abubakari, M. S., Zakaria, G. A. N., Musa, J., & Kalinaki, K. (2023b). Validating the Digital Competence (Dig-Comp 2.1) Framework in Higher Education Using Confirmatory Factor Analysis: Non-Western Perspective. *Canadian Journal of Educational and Social Studies*, *3*(6), 15–26. DOI: 10.53103/cjess.v6i1.184

Adarkwah, M. A. (2024). GenAI-Infused Adult Learning in the Digital Era: A Conceptual Framework for Higher Education. *Adult Learning*, *0*(0). Advance online publication. DOI: 10.1177/10451595241271161

Alhammadi, K., Marashdeh, H., & Hussain, M. (2023). Assessing the effect of innovation diffusion and technology readiness theories on attitude, behavioral intention and implementation of smart learning. *Cross Cultural & Strategic Management*. Advance online publication. DOI: 10.1108/CCSM-12-2022-0213

Alshammari, H., El-Sayed, A., & Elleithy, K. (2024). AI-Generated Text Detector for Arabic Language Using Encoder-Based Transformer Architecture. *Big Data and Cognitive Computing*, *8*(3), 32. DOI: 10.3390/bdcc8030032

Anyichie, A. C., & Butler, D. L. (2023). Examining culturally diverse learners' motivation and engagement processes as situated in the context of a complex task. *Frontiers in Education*, *8*, 1041946. DOI: 10.3389/feduc.2023.1041946

Biagini, G. (2025). Towards an AI-Literate Future: A Systematic Literature Review Exploring Education, Ethics, and Applications. *International Journal of Artificial Intelligence in Education*. Advance online publication. DOI: 10.1007/s40593-025-00466-w

Bouamor, H., Gongora-Svartzman, G., Heimann, L., & Huang, S. (2025). Evaluating GenAI's Effectiveness for Students with Varied Programming Backgrounds in a Software Development Course. *Proceedings of the 56th ACM Technical Symposium on Computer Science Education* V. 2, 1395–1396. https://doi.org/DOI: 10.1145/3641555.3705175

Cacicio, S., & Riggs, R. (2023). Bridging Resource Gaps in Adult Education: The Role of Generative AI. *Adult Literacy Education: The International Journal of Literacy, Language, and Numeracy*, *5*(3), 80–86. DOI: 10.35847/SCacicio.RRiggs.5.3.80

Chrostowski, M. (2024). Promoting critical thinking through the use of ChatGPT in religious education. *Österreichisches Religionspädagogisches Forum, 32*(2), 166–181. https://doi.org/DOI: 10.25364/10.32:2024.2.10

Djazilan, M. S., Rulyansah, A., & Rihlah, J. (2024). Why AI is Essential for the Future of Islamic Education: A Call for Ethical and Effective Implementation. *EDUKASIA: Jurnal Pendidikan Dan Pembelajaran*, *5*(2), 201–216. DOI: 10.62775/edukasia.v5i2.1373

Dockens, A. L., & Shelton, K. (2025). Andragogy as a Theoretical Framework for AI Integration in Higher Education. In Wang, V. (Ed.), *AI Integration Into Andragogical Education* (pp. 71–108). IGI Global., DOI: 10.4018/979-8-3373-0502-8.ch004

Dwivedi, Y. K., Kshetri, N., Hughes, L., Slade, E. L., Jeyaraj, A., Kar, A. K., Baabdullah, A. M., Koohang, A., Raghavan, V., Ahuja, M., Albanna, H., Albashrawi, M. A., Al-Busaidi, A. S., Balakrishnan, J., Barlette, Y., Basu, S., Bose, I., Brooks, L., Buhalis, D., & Wright, R. (2023). Opinion Paper: "So what if ChatGPT wrote it?" Multidisciplinary perspectives on opportunities, challenges and implications of generative conversational AI for research, practice and policy. *International Journal of Information Management*, *71*(March), 102642. DOI: 10.1016/j.ijinfomgt.2023.102642

El Ganadi, A., Aftar, S., Gagliardelli, L., & Ruozzi, F. (2025). Generative AI for Islamic Texts: The EMAN Framework for Mitigating GPT Hallucinations. *Proceedings of the 17th International Conference on Agents and Artificial Intelligence*, 1221–1228. https://doi.org/DOI: 10.5220/0013312800003890

Escalante, J., Pack, A., & Barrett, A. (2023). AI-generated feedback on writing: Insights into efficacy and ENL student preference. *International Journal of Educational Technology in Higher Education*, *20*(1), 57. DOI: 10.1186/s41239-023-00425-2

Farrokhnia, M., Banihashem, S. K., Noroozi, O., & Wals, A. (2024). A SWOT analysis of ChatGPT: Implications for educational practice and research. *Innovations in Education and Teaching International*, *61*(3), 460–474. DOI: 10.1080/14703297.2023.2195846

Ferrara, E. (2023). Fairness and Bias in Artificial Intelligence: A Brief Survey of Sources, Impacts, and Mitigation Strategies. *Sci*, *6*(1), 3. DOI: 10.3390/sci6010003

Garrison, D. R. (1997). Self-Directed Learning: Toward a Comprehensive Model. *Adult Education Quarterly*, *48*(1), 18–33. DOI: 10.1177/074171369704800103

Gill, S. S., Xu, M., Patros, P., Wu, H., Kaur, R., Kaur, K., Fuller, S., Singh, M., Arora, P., Parlikad, A. K., Stankovski, V., Abraham, A., Ghosh, S. K., Lutfiyya, H., Kanhere, S. S., Bahsoon, R., Rana, O., Dustdar, S., Sakellariou, R., & Buyya, R. (2024). Transformative effects of ChatGPT on modern education: Emerging Era of AI Chatbots. *Internet of Things and Cyber-Physical Systems*, *4*, 19–23. DOI: 10.1016/j.iotcps.2023.06.002

Gonsalves, C. (2024). Generative AI's Impact on Critical Thinking: Revisiting Bloom's Taxonomy. *Journal of Marketing Education*. Advance online publication. DOI: 10.1177/02734753241305980

Hoggan, C., & Kloubert, T. (2020). Transformative Learning in Theory and Practice. *Adult Education Quarterly*, *70*(3), 295–307. DOI: 10.1177/0741713620918510

Hoggan, C. D. (2016). Transformative Learning as a Metatheory: Definition, Criteria, and Typology. *Adult Education Quarterly*, *66*(1), 57–75. DOI: 10.1177/0741713615611216

Hsu, Y.-C., & Ching, Y.-H. (2023a). Generative Artificial Intelligence in Education, Part One: The Dynamic Frontier. *TechTrends*, *67*(4), 603–607. DOI: 10.1007/s11528-023-00863-9

Hsu, Y.-C., & Ching, Y.-H. (2023b). Generative Artificial Intelligence in Education, Part Two: International Perspectives. *TechTrends*, *67*(6), 885–890. DOI: 10.1007/s11528-023-00913-2

Ifelebuegu, A. O. (2023). Rethinking online assessment strategies: Authenticity versus AI chatbot intervention. *Journal of Applied Learning & Teaching*, *6*(2), 385–392. DOI: 10.37074/jalt.2023.6.2.2

Kang, H. (2023). Artificial intelligence and its influence in adult learning in China. *Higher Education. Skills and Work-Based Learning*, *13*(3), 450–464. DOI: 10.1108/HESWBL-01-2023-0017

Knowles, M. S. (1975). *Self-directed Learning: A Guide for Learners and Teachers*. Cambridge Adult Education.

Knowles, M. S., Holton, E. F.III, Robinson, P. A., & Caraccioli, C. (2025). *The Adult Learner: The Definitive Classic in Adult Education and Human Resource Development* (10th ed.). Routledge., DOI: 10.4324/9781003387671

Knowles, M. S., Holton III, E. F., & Swanson, R. A. (2015). *The Adult Learner: The definitive classic in adult education and human resource development* (8th Editio). Routledge. https://doi.org/DOI: 10.4324/9781315816951

Knowles, M. S., Holton III, E. F., Swanson, R. A., & Robinson, P. A. (2020). *The Adult Learner: The Definitive Classic in Adult Education and Human Resource Development* (9th Editio). Routledge. https://doi.org/DOI: 10.4324/9780429299612

Kolb, D. A. (2015). *Experiential Learning: Experience as the source of Learning and Development* (2nd Editio). Pearson Education Inc.

Li, B., Bonk, C. J., Wang, C., & Kou, X. (2024). Reconceptualizing Self-Directed Learning in the Era of Generative AI: An Exploratory Analysis of Language Learning. *IEEE Transactions on Learning Technologies*, *17*, 1489–1503. DOI: 10.1109/TLT.2024.3386098

Li, J., & Wu, C.-H. (2023). Determinants of Learners' Self-Directed Learning and Online Learning Attitudes in Online Learning. *Sustainability*, *15*(12), 9381. DOI: 10.3390/su15129381

Li, S., Liu, J., & Dong, Q. (2025). Generative artificial intelligence-supported programming education: Effects on learning performance, self-efficacy and processes. *Australasian Journal of Educational Technology*, *41*(3), 1–25. DOI: 10.14742/ajet.9932

Li, Y., Tolosa, L., Rivas-Echeverria, F., & Marquez, R. (2025). *Integrating AI in Education: Navigating UNESCO Global Guidelines, Emerging Trends, and Its Intersection with Sustainable Development Goals*. https://doi.org/DOI: 10.26434/chemrxiv-2025-wz4n9

Li, Z., & Bonk, C. J. (2025). Self-directed language learning with Duolingo in an out-of-class context. *Computer Assisted Language Learning*, *38*(3), 569–591. DOI: 10.1080/09588221.2023.2206874

Li, Z., Wang, C., & Bonk, C. (2024). Exploring the Utility of ChatGPT for Self-directed Online Language Learning. *Online Learning : the Official Journal of the Online Learning Consortium*, *28*(3), 157–180. DOI: 10.24059/olj.v28i3.4497

Lim, W. M., Gunasekara, A., Pallant, J. L., Pallant, J. I., & Pechenkina, E. (2023). Generative AI and the future of education: Ragnarök or reformation? A paradoxical perspective from management educators. *International Journal of Management Education*, *21*(2), 100790. DOI: 10.1016/j.ijme.2023.100790

Lin, X. (2024). Exploring the Role of ChatGPT as a Facilitator for Motivating Self-Directed Learning Among Adult Learners. *Adult Learning*, *35*(3), 156–166. DOI: 10.1177/10451595231184928

Luckin, R. (2025). Nurturing human intelligence in the age of AI: Rethinking education for the future. *Development and Learning in Organizations*, *39*(1), 1–4. DOI: 10.1108/DLO-04-2024-0108

Luo (Jess), J. (2024). A critical review of GenAI policies in higher education assessment: A call to reconsider the "originality" of students' work. *Assessment & Evaluation in Higher Education*, *49*(5), 651–664. DOI: 10.1080/02602938.2024.2309963

Makmee, P., Sompaisarnsilp, S., & Krairiksh, T. (2024). Influence factors on self-directed learning behavior of veterinary students on gross anatomy: A multiple group analysis. *Cogent Education, 11*(1), 2378512. DOI: 10.1080/2331186X.2024.2378512

McGregor, S. (2004). Learning with Donald Rumsfeld - flexible learning: The relevance and resonance of multiprofessional learning in primary care. *The British Journal of General Practice, 54*(506), 722–723. https://www.ncbi.nlm.nih.gov/pubmed/15558869

Mezirow, J. (1978). Perspective Transformation. *Adult Education, 28*(2), 100–110. DOI: 10.1177/074171367802800202

Miao, F., & Holmes, W. (2023). *Guidance for generative AI in education and research.* UNESCO., DOI: 10.54675/EWZM9535

Mishra, P., Warr, M., & Islam, R. (2023). TPACK in the age of ChatGPT and Generative AI. *Journal of Digital Learning in Teacher Education, 39*(4), 235–251. DOI: 10.1080/21532974.2023.2247480

Morandín-Ahuerma, F. (2024). UNESCO Proposal for the use of Generative AI in Education: Eight Challenges and Seven Actions (pp. 62–115). https://doi.org/DOI: 10.31219/osf.io/78d3j

Muller, M., Chilton, L. B., Kantosalo, A., Martin, C. P., & Walsh, G. (2022). GenAICHI: Generative AI and HCI. *CHI Conference on Human Factors in Computing Systems Extended Abstracts*, 1–7. https://doi.org/DOI: 10.1145/3491101.3503719

Musa, S., Abubakari, M. S., & Abdulwahab, L. O. (2025). Evaluating the Potential of Adapting Artificial Intelligence (AI) in Small and Medium Enterprises for Competitive Advantage. In Anshari, M., Almunawar, M. N., & Ordóñez de Pablos, P. (Eds.), *Multi-Industry Digitalization and Technological Governance in the AI Era* (pp. 233–266). IGI Global., DOI: 10.4018/979-8-3373-1681-9.ch012

Nebiu Hyseni, L., & Dermaku, A. (2025). Comparative Analysis of GitHub Copilot and ChatGPT in Web Application Development: An Experimental Study. *International Journal of Computational and Experimental Science and Engineering, 11*(2), 3375–3398. DOI: 10.22399/ijcesen.1846

Polakova, P., & Ivenz, P. (2024). The impact of ChatGPT feedback on the development of EFL students' writing skills. *Cogent Education, 11*(1), 2410101. DOI: 10.1080/2331186X.2024.2410101

Poquet, O., & de Laat, M. (2021). Developing capabilities: Lifelong learning in the age of AI. *British Journal of Educational Technology, 52*(4), 1695–1708. DOI: 10.1111/bjet.13123

Reischmann, J. (2017). Lifewide learning – Challenges for Andragogy. *Journal of Adult Learning. Knowledge and Innovation*, *1*(1), 43–50. DOI: 10.1556/2059.01.2017.2

Roessger, K. M., Roumell, E. A., & Weese, J. (2018). Testing Andragogical Assumptions Across Countries Using Multi-Level Analyses of PIAAC Data. *American Institutes for Research PIAAC Research Conference*, 6–7.

Roessger, K. M., Roumell, E. A., & Weese, J. (2022). Rethinking andragogical assumptions in the global age: How preferences for andragogical learning vary across people and cultures. *Studies in Continuing Education*, *44*(1), 14–38. DOI: 10.1080/0158037X.2020.1732335

Ryan, R. M., & Deci, E. L. (2022). Self-Determination Theory. In Maggino, F. (Ed.), *Encyclopedia of Quality of Life and Well-Being Research* (pp. 1–7). Springer International Publishing., DOI: 10.1007/978-3-319-69909-7_2630-2

Sætra, H. S. (2023). Generative AI: Here to stay, but for good? *Technology in Society*, *75*, 102372. DOI: 10.1016/j.techsoc.2023.102372

Salinas-Navarro, D. E., Vilalta-Perdomo, E., Michel-Villarreal, R., & Montesinos, L. (2024). Using Generative Artificial Intelligence Tools to Explain and Enhance Experiential Learning for Authentic Assessment. *Education Sciences*, *14*(1), 83. DOI: 10.3390/educsci14010083

Sekmokas, M., Larsson, L., Roberts, A., von Erlach, E., Guo, Y., & González, G. R. (2024). *Updated Framework for Monitoring Adult Learning: Enhancing Data Identification and Indicator Selection* (No. 317; OECD Education Working Papers, Vol. 317). https://doi.org/DOI: 10.1787/02bbacdc-en

Southworth, J., Migliaccio, K., Glover, J., Glover, J., Reed, D., McCarty, C., Brendemuhl, J., & Thomas, A. (2023). Developing a model for AI Across the curriculum: Transforming the higher education landscape via innovation in AI literacy. *Computers and Education: Artificial Intelligence*, *4*, 100127. DOI: 10.1016/j.caeai.2023.100127

St. Clair, R. (2024). Andragogy: Past and Present Potential. *New Directions for Adult and Continuing Education*, *2024*(184), 7–13. DOI: 10.1002/ace.20546

Stanistreet, P. (2024). Lifelong learning in the age of AI. In *Only Connect: The Lifelong Learning Blog*. UNESCO Institute for Lifelong Learning. https://thelifelonglearningblog.uil.unesco.org/2024/03/19/lifelong-learning-in-the-age-of-ai/#:~:text=The 2023 AI Index Report,bolstering research and development%2C with Storey, V. A., & Wagner, A. (2024). Integrating Artificial Intelligence (AI) Into Adult Education. *International Journal of Adult Education and Technology, 15*(1), 1–15. https://doi.org/DOI: 10.4018/IJAET.345921

Taylor, D. C. M., & Hamdy, H. (2013). Adult learning theories: Implications for learning and teaching in medical education: AMEE Guide No. 83. *Medical Teacher*, *35*(11), e1561–e1572. DOI: 10.3109/0142159X.2013.828153

Weng, X., XIA, Q., Gu, M., Rajaram, K., & Chiu, T. K. F. (2024). Assessment and learning outcomes for generative AI in higher education: A scoping review on current research status and trends. *Australasian Journal of Educational Technology*, *40*(6), 37–55. DOI: 10.14742/ajet.9540

World Economic Forum. (2023). *Generative AI has disrupted education. Here's how it can be used for good – UNESCO*. World Economic Forum.

Zhu, L., Mou, W., Lai, Y., Lin, J., & Luo, P. (2024). Language and cultural bias in AI: Comparing the performance of large language models developed in different countries on Traditional Chinese Medicine highlights the need for localized models. *Journal of Translational Medicine*, *22*(1), 319. DOI: 10.1186/s12967-024-05128-4

Chapter 4
NLP and Machine Learning Innovations in Education: Transforming Learning and Personalization

K. Sahitya Priyadharshini
Panimalar Engineering College, India

B. Yamini
https://orcid.org/0000-0003-3531-108X
SRM Institute of Science and Technology, India

T. P. Anish
https://orcid.org/0000-0002-4308-9645
R.M.K. College of Engineering and Technology, India

T. Thilagam
https://orcid.org/0000-0002-7657-0726
Vel Tech Rangarajan Dr. Sagunthala R&D Institute of Science and Technology, India

A. Adaikkammai
RMD Engineering College, India

Nivas Kumar V.
https://orcid.org/0009-0003-6080-3999
Jawahar Engineering College, India

ABSTRACT

This survey chapter examines how Natural Language Processing (NLP) and Machine Learning (ML) are transforming the modern education. It shows ways in which AI technologies are transforming learning experience with intelligent tutoring systems, automated feedback, adaptive learning platforms, and personalized recommendations. The chapter reviews baseline concepts, major applications, and emerging innovations, including large language models and multimodal analytics. It also tackles some of the major issues such as algorithmic bias, data privacy, and ethical use of AI in education. Interdisciplinary work and responsible design are

DOI: 10.4018/979-8-3373-6791-0.ch004

ight © 2026, IGI Global Scientific Publishing. Copying or distributing in print or electronic forms without written permission of IGI Global Scientific Publishing is prohibited. Use of this chapter to ı generative artificial intelligence (AI) technologies is expressly prohibited. The publisher reserves all rights to license its use for generative AI training and machine learning model development.

highlighted as being critical to making AI-driven education equitable, transparent, and effective. By combining the current trends, the chapter provides an overview of the way NLP and ML are improving personalization and the future of learning.

INTRODUCTION

The Background of the Integration of AI in Education

The adoption of Artificial Intelligence (AI) into education has changed the way learners engage with the content, educators manage classrooms and institutions provide customized experiences. AI technologies have in the last decade been increasingly adopted to mitigate such issues as learner engagement and assessment of knowledge and delivery of curriculum. What previously needed to be done manually is now automated in part or in whole, allowing more scalable and efficient educational environments. The transition to digital and blended learning models further accelerated by global disruptions such as COVID-19 pandemic has brought into focus the need for adaptive and intelligent systems that can support diverse learners' needs. AI tools, and in particular, those based on data-driven approaches, are now a must in developing personalized and inclusive learning settings that break away from the traditional one-size-fits-all education models(Ponnuviji, N. P et al., 2024).

The Significance of NLP and ML in the Contemporary Educational Systems

The most outstanding of the AI branches are Natural Language Processing (NLP) and Machine Learning (ML) and these have had a big impact on educational technology. This is why NLP is so important in automated feedback, content recommendation, grading essays and chatbot based tutoring (Bowman et al., 2021). However, ML enables systems to improve over time, learning from student data to become better – learn patterns, predict outcomes, customize resources based on them (Chowdhary, K., & Chowdhary, K. R., 2020). New paradigms of learning which focus on personalization, engagement and data based teaching have been brought to the fore by these technologies. For example, NLP is used on intelligent tutoring systems to build simulated, real time conversational interactions with learners, while the ML models help in identifying at risk students by analyzing their performance. NLP and ML combined can help build intelligent learning environments that respond dynamically to the pace, preference and progress of the learners ultimately improving learning results.

Objectives and the Scope of the Survey Chapter

In this survey chapter we aim to provide a general description of the innovations in NLP and ML that are changing the educational landscapes, especially the learning personalization and adaptive instruction. The main goal is to synthesize the most recent developments and evaluate the way these technologies are used in different educational settings, ranging from K–12 classrooms to higher learning institutions and online learning systems.

Specifically, the chapter will: Explores about the key NLP and ML techniques in educational tools and platforms. Look at state-of-the-art applications such as intelligent tutoring, automated assessment, and learning analytics. Emphasize on successful implementations and real-world case studies. Deal with critical issues such as bias, privacy of data, and ethical use of AI in education. Investigate new directions and emerging trends of personalized and AI-powered learning. The scope encompasses theoretical contributions and practical systems, thus, presenting a harmonized perspective of fundamental research and applied innovation. Although the emphasis is on educational applications, relevant cross-disciplinary perspectives in the field of cognitive science, human-computer interaction, and data ethics are recognized to situate the overall effect of these technologies.

FOUNDATIONS AND KEY CONCEPTS

Overview of NLP and ML

Artificial Intelligence (AI) has become central to the transformation of educational technologies, but this transformation is due to two closely related but distinct branches of AI: Natural Language Processing (NLP) and Machine Learning (ML). They together form the backbone of modern intelligent educational systems that personalize, enable and enhance the learning experience.

In other words, NLP is all about making machines understand, interpret, generate and respond to human language. This is both written and spoken communication (Fanni et al., 2023). NLP enables computers to process and interpret large amounts of natural language data so that humans can interact with machines without difficulty. Tasks in NLP are common, they include language translation, grammar parsing, sentiment analysis, text summarization and question answering. In an education setting, NLP allows for the understanding of student questions, assessing student written responses and facilitating conversational agents such as chatbots who can tutor or help learners (Mir et al., 2023).

Machine Learning however is the ability of computer systems to learn from data, recognize patterns and make decisions or predictions without being explicitly programmed for what to do for every possible scenario (Hilbert et al., 2021). Algorithms drive ML which allows systems to get better and better over time in response to the data they are exposed to. In particular, this capability is useful in educational settings where adaptive learning, performance prediction and content recommendation are important. NLP is the linguistic side of AI like grammar, context and meaning and ML brings the computational models and learning strategies that make these applications work. Through the integration of NLP and ML advanced educational tools like a computerized grading system, an intelligent tutoring system and an AI powered educational chatbot have been developed. These tools can understand natural language inputs and take intelligent decisions or provide meaningful feedback using learning data (Maheswari et al., 2024). NLP and ML techniques have both evolved a lot, increasing the effectiveness of educational technologies a great deal. Most prior approaches to NLP were rule based or were based on very simple statistical models. However, with deep learning, the field has changed a lot. Deep learning uses artificial neural networks (ANNs) in particular Recurrent Neural Network (RNNs), Long Short Term Memory (LSTM) networks and very recently Transformers (Kotei, E., & Thirunavukarasu, R. 2023). With these architectures, we have significantly improved the capability of NLP systems to comprehend and generate human language, by capturing intricate linguistic patterns and dependencies across long sequences of text. These advances have made applications such as real time translation, automated summarization and intelligent question answering more accurate and context aware.

Figure 1. NLP and ML in education

In Machine Learning domain, techniques are broadly classified as: supervised, unsupervised and reinforcement learning (Luan et al., 2021). Training models on labeled datasets, supervised learning is good for predicting outcome like student exam score, course completion likelihood or learning progression. Unsupervised learning works with unlabeled data and helps us to find hidden patterns or grouping, for example segregating students based on their learning behavior or interaction style. Adaptive learning environments have been dominated by reinforcement learning. The system in this setup learns from interactions with the learner and its decisions (e.g., when to give hints, present a quiz or change the difficulty level of a concept) improve over time, in order to maximize the learner's long term success (Munir et al., 2022).

When you combine the language processing power of NLP with the data driven adaptability of ML, educational systems can be deeply personalized. With these AI based system, they can take large amounts of learning data and find trends and learner needs and provide customized feedback and content in real time. Not only do they automate the tasks such as grading, they enable more engaging and interactive, as well as more responsive, learning environments. These systems enable learning styles of individuals to be catered for, learning gaps to be detected early and educational outcomes to be improved generally.

Finally, NLP and ML in educational technologies can be integrated to provide a great leap forward in how learning is delivered and experienced. These technologies are helping build intelligent education systems, data informed and learner centric, scalable to large sizes, efficient and effective in catering to the varied needs of the modern learners.

Personalization in Education

Educational personalization is the process of adapting learning experiences to meet the particular needs, objectives, choices and rate of learning of individual students. Instead, this approach tries to break away from the traditional one size fits all way of delivering education, whereby all students learn the same content in the same way despite their individual learning differences. It's not about personalization, it is about providing adaptive learning pathways which are dynamically adapted in real time based on each learner's strengths and weaknesses, progress and understanding. The change in emphasis is well suited to contemporary pedagogical theory that stresses student centered learning and formative, ongoing assessment. Educational personalization aims overall to increase student interest and achievement, decrease dropout rates and encourage ownership, autonomy and intrinsic motivation in learning. What motivates students to stay the course is when they feel their journey to learn is all about them. Personal learning can be in in many ways. This could be, for example, offering the learner different ways of accessing the content; videos, interactive simulations or text, depending on the learner's learning style. It could also be about making the content more or less difficult, reordering the topics based on what the learner has learned or giving immediate and personalized feedback and encouragement. The result is that learning becomes meaningful and accessible for the wide range of learners: learners with learning difficulties, advanced learners, learners with various interests in learning. Machine Learning (ML) and Natural Language Processing (NLP) are the two key technologies that are the basis of these personalized and adaptive system. The deployment of ML algorithms in adaptive learning platforms generates dynamic learner models(Ponnuviji, N. P et al., 2023). Bayesian networks and knowledge tracing are used to estimate the current knowledge state of a student in these models. This model is used by the system to select and present learning content or exercises which are appropriate to the current level and learning history of the individual and optimize the learning pathway in real time. NLP is necessary for personalization because without its systems can't understand and respond to a student's natural language input (Mathew et al., 2021).

This allows a more in depth interaction between the learner and the system. Using NLP it interprets student queries, grades open ended answers and provides tailored hints, clarifications or explanations that are appropriate to the learner's needs. This lets the system act as a human tutor, able to understand responses and guide the learner appropriately. This isn't just about academic content. Emotional and behavioral support is also provided using affective computing technologies. Affective computing is about systems that can detect and act on the emotional states of learners, by looking at text, speech, facial expressions or interaction patterns. For example, NLP techniques can pick up if a student has written something confused or frustrated or if they're using a frustrated tone in their voice. This allows the system to then speed up or slow down the pace of the lesson, provide supportive feedback or suggest that the learner takes a break to reset and refocus. Relevance and potential of personalization is increasing as educational environments increasingly become digital and rich in data. Institutions and educators are increasingly realizing AI driven personalization as a major role player in identifying and filling individual learning gaps, providing learning support that meets diverse learning needs and improving the quality and equity of education in general. In that way, educators can get to those students who may fall behind in a classroom and they have resources to push those ahead. Finally, we demonstrate that educational personalization through ML and NLP will shape the future of learning. Being able to adapt to each learner in real time is the promise of more responsive, more inclusive and more effective educational experiences. Despite their infancy, these technologies will allow us to deliver truly personalized education at scale whether to any one type of learner in any one context or background.

NLP APPLICATIONS IN EDUCATION

An important component in modern educational technologies that enable systems to understand and interpret and communicate with students in human language is Natural Language Processing (NLP)(Pajila et al., 2023). This advancement allows digital learning platforms to step away from the rigid interfaces to provide more intuitive and interactive experience of learning. NLP is where we make learning personalized, scalable and rich in linguistic engagement. The second part of the thesis talks about some of the important applications of NLP in educational context.

Intelligent Tutoring Systems

Advanced AI driven educational platforms, Intelligent tutoring systems (ITS), are there to replicate the benefits of one on one tutoring by providing personalized instruction, guidance and feedback for learners. The purpose of these systems is to be able to learn with the individual's learning needs and progress and support the individual as close as possible to the human tutor. Natural Language Processing (NLP) is a large part of most ITS platforms and is the ability to allow the system and the learner to communicate in natural, interactive ways. Intelligent Tutoring Systems and conversational agents are important components of the dialogue system and NLP has a particularly important role in their development. NLP allows these systems to actually hold context aware conversations with students. Unlike static, pre defined content, NLP powered ITSs can understand student inputs in natural language, interpret the student's intent and respond with appropriate explanations, guidance or follow up questions. And that makes the learning experience more interactive and more responsive because students can participate actively rather than passively get information(Kurni M et al., 2023).

An important benefit of NLP based ITS is that they are able to assess the current level of student understanding through dialogue. The system listens to a student ask a question or answer a question and, based on the language it hears, it learns about student misconceptions or gaps in understanding and tailors its response. So, for example if a student is struggling with a particular concept, the system might provide a more basic explanation of the concept or provide an analogy or suggest some practice questions more specific to that concept. In addition, these systems can monitor the learner's progress in time and modify their instructional strategies based on the changing learner model. ITS adjusts itself continually to the student's performance and responses and is capable of offering a very personalized learning experience which is dynamic as a human tutor would. In short, Intelligent Tutoring System has the ability to converse naturally, conversationally and understand the context of the learner input through NLP. This means that education is more engaging, more effective and more personalized. Advancement in technology has enabled NLP to be integrated with ITS, with a better and better accuracy of understanding the need of the student and giving it adaptive and meaningful instruction. As a result, ITS are emerging as strong tools in modern education by helping learners to learn complex concepts with tailored, AI powered support(Stamper, J et al., 2024).

Figure 2. Intelligent tutoring systems

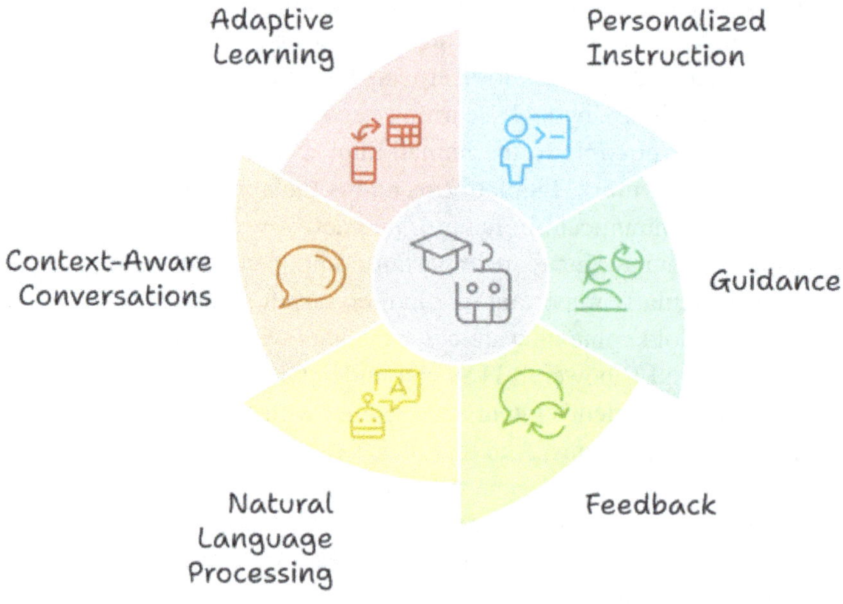

Automated Essay Scoring and Feedback

Automated Essay Scoring and Feedback (AES) systems are powerful tools for modern educational environments that want to assess and provide feedback for student writing with little human involvement. They evaluate all sorts of writing using cutting edge Natural Language Processing (NLP) techniques: grammar, vocabulary, sentence structure, coherence and general quality of argumentation. Traditionally, essay evaluation is a time consuming task for educators in large classrooms or in settings which use standardized testing. AES systems reduce the burden of this scoring process, automate the process and help ensure consistency and objectivity. Modern AES tools are more than just a rule based, grammar check.

And they use very sophisticated machine learning algorithms, specifically models based on transformer architecture that enable the system to understand not only a single sentence, but also a wider context and semantics of the whole essay. The resulting contextual awareness results in more nuanced evaluations of the same which are nearer to human level understanding.

Real time, formative feedback is one of the most valuable features of contemporary AES systems. Unlike just giving a score these systems point out specific areas for improvement in student writing. For example, they may point out excessive use of the passive voice, grammatical inconsistencies, vagueness or ambiguity, unclear argument structure and insufficient evidence to support a claim. The feedback inspires students to make changes, reflect and ultimately learn from their errors as they improve at writing. AES systems are both evaluative and instructional tools in this way. Despite all of their advantages though, AES systems are not without their limitations and challenges. The first big problem is in bias of the scoring. To work, however, these systems need training data, lots of essays that have already been scored. These datasets might then generate assessment models that reproduce the lack of diversity or inherent biases (e.g. favoring some writing styles or some linguistic backgrounds). For instance, it may be to the disadvantage of students from different linguistic and cultural backgrounds or students who may have non-conventional writing styles. Another massive problem is explainability. AES systems can generate accurate scores and even with some amount of detail as feedback, but they are not transparent to explain why a score was given to a specific individual. The problem with this is it can be confusing for students when they don't know why a comment or suggestion was made. However, to close this gap, researchers and developers are now exploring ways to increase explainability such as giving annotated examples, visual feedback or interactive explanations. Automated Essay Scoring and Feedback systems are finally a boon for educational technology, using NLP and machine learning to provide a scalable and personalized writing support. If used thoughtfully and continually refined, these tools can dramatically increase assessment efficiency and student learning outcomes. There is still work to do to ensure these systems are fair, trustworthy and actually support diverse learners, but there is work being done.

Text Simplification and Reading Assistance

The other important NLP application, which advances inclusive education, particularly for language learners, young readers, and students with learning disabilities, is text simplification. NLP algorithms make complex texts easier by rewriting sentences, substituting complex words and reorganizing syntax without changing the meaning. This process makes the academic and technical materials easily accessible.

Question Generation and Answering

NLP techniques are more and more applied for automatic question generation (QG) when questions are automatically generated from the educational content. These tools transform textual materials to multiple-choice, fill-in-the-blank or short-answer questions thereby eliminating the manual task for educators. QG systems usually employ the use of syntactic and semantic analysis or pre-trained models such as GPT to retrieve important details and convert them into assessment items.

On the other hand, the question answering (QA) systems assist students to engage in self-testing by answering queries in natural language. Such systems search and summarize the relevant content from textbooks/lecture notes, and they are like intelligent study aids.

Sentiment Analysis and Engagement Monitoring

Sentiment analysis is a branch of NLP and is now playing a major role in modern educational technology. It means using computer methods to study opinions, emotions and attitudes found in written texts. In schools, sentiment analysis is applied to understand students' feelings and participation by observing their exchanges in discussion forums, texts, feedback and assignments. Sentiment analysis helps educators and learning platforms notice when learners are feeling frustrated, confused, bored or enthusiastic in real time, (Mmbayi et al., 2025). The ability to do this improves how students feel and perform in their studies. Learning is strongly influenced by emotions and feeling negative can decrease your understanding, desire to learn and involvement. When sentiment analysis tools are used, educational platforms can spot when a student is struggling or losing focus. For example, seeing negative words in a student's work or messages might be a warning sign. If this occurs, the system will automatically inform instructors or academic counselors to act promptly. As a result, teachers can help each student individually, tackle the main challenges or change their teaching style to fit the student. Many people connect this technology with emotional AI which is designed to notice, understand and react to human emotions. Through emotional AI, education helps link the mind and feelings which benefits the overall student learning experience. When linked to a Learning Management System (LMS), emotional AI can display information about the emotional state of a whole class or institution. This allows everyone involved in education to observe student interest and change their plans to keep students involved. When affective computing is added to sentiment analysis, the system can react more empathetically and respond to students' moods through their facial expressions, voice tone and physical signals. As an example, a virtual tutor could recognize confusion based on how the student looks and what they write. After that, the system may change the information to make it simpler or give extra materials to help students understand. AI can now respond to each student's needs better because of the teamwork between NLP and affective computing. Online or hybrid classes can benefit from technology's ability to view the engagement of the whole class. Teachers can learn about the students' opinions on a specific topic by reviewing discussion boards, group chats or collaborative documents. If students show signs of frustration, it often suggests that the material is too difficult, unclear or dull, so the curriculum should be changed quickly. All in all, using sentiment analysis and engagement monitoring gives teachers better ways to support their students. If emotional AI and affective computing are used, educational systems can be more caring, customized and active, supporting both a student's emotions and their school performance, (Kumar & Kumar, 2024).

MACHINE LEARNING INNOVATIONS FOR INDIVIDUAL LEARNING

Nowadays, Machine Learning (ML) is crucial for making education adjust to each student's needs and skills. Through analyzing a lot of student information, ML algorithms find out how students learn, predict their grades and personalize lessons for each student. This new approach is different from the old way which frequently used a one-size-fits-all method that didn't work for all students. Adaptive learning systems are one of the most important ways ML is used in education. They keep checking a student's results and adjust the lessons, speed and learning route as needed. If a student has trouble with a certain idea, the system will supply extra support or extra ways to learn it until it's fully understood. Advanced learners can move quickly through information they have already learned, to avoid feeling bored by repeating the same things. ML is used to drive predictive analytics in the field of education. ML models use attendance, involvement, quiz results and work submission information to discover students who might have problems. Because of this, students can receive early help and customized strategies that help them keep up and do well in school. Using ML, recommendation engines can advise students on learning materials, activities or courses that match their past actions and what they care about. Learners are more engaged and also develop the ability to learn by themselves. In addition, ML-based systems can check a student's motivation and introduce games or feedback methods that help students stay interested and achieve more. With machine learning, education becomes smarter, more open to all and more interesting for everyone, (Subramanian et al., 2021).

Adaptive Learning Systems

Adaptive learning systems are meant to change instructional content in real time depending on how the learner performs, learns, and prefers. These systems use an ML-based learner modeling, i.e., algorithms create a dynamic model of a student's knowledge, misconceptions, and learning pattern. The key goal is to provide content adaptation change in the order, level of difficulty, or format of materials for maximizing learning outcomes.

Two of the preferred ML techniques applied to adaptive learning include the Bayesian Knowledge Tracing (BKT) and the Reinforcement Learning (RL). BKT models predict a student's level of mastery of certain skills from his or her responses to tasks in a period of time. These probabilistic models assist the system in inferring, what the student knows and decide which concept should be introduced next. The learning process, on the contrary, is considered to be a problem of decision-making in the reinforcement learning. The system learns an optimal teaching policy by getting rewarded (feedback) according to the performance of the learner. As the students move forward, the system keeps on changing its actions in order to maximize long-term learning gains. Such adaptive algorithms are used by tools to provide personalized math instruction to every student based on their respective knowledge state.

Predictive Analytics in Education

Predictive analytics makes use of ML to predict future learning outcomes and timely interventions. Using historical data (e.g., attendance, quiz scores, engagement metrics, and behavioral logs), ML models can detect students that are at risk and mark them for extra attention. These early warning systems are priceless in avoiding academic failure, increasing the retention rates, and providing individual guidance even before poor performance is evident.

Some of the typical models used in the predictive analytics are decision trees, logistic regression, support vector machines and deep learning networks, (Ganesan et al., 2024). These models are taught to find patterns that are associated with success or struggle, so that institutions can take preventive measures. For instance, a model may advise instructors on which students may drop out of an online course based on their interaction patterns so that they can send a reminder, motivational message, or extra resources to the students.

Besides, ML models are employed to develop performance prediction tools that can calculate the probability of a student understanding the upcoming concepts or passing final tests. These tools help the instructors in personalizing instruction and pace to the learner's trajectory, thus increasing the efficiency and effectiveness, (Subramanian et al., 2022).

Recommender Systems for Learning Resources

The functioning of recommender systems in education is similar to the ones applied in e-commerce or entertainment sites but the task is to individualize the delivery of educational content. ML-based recommenders rely on profiles of learners, history of courses, assessment data, and patterns of behavior to recommend relevant study materials, courses, exercises, or videos.

There are two primary approaches: collaborative filtering, that is recommending content based on similarities between learners, and content-based filtering that recommends resources that align with a learner's preference or skill gaps. More sophisticated systems make use of hybrid models that integrate both methods and use deep learning to improve the accuracy.

Such platforms use recommendation algorithms to create the learning content routes for the learners, thus each individual gets the most beneficial materials according to their individual learning history. These systems do not only increase the engagement but also facilitate autonomous, self-directed learning.

Gamification and Motivation Modeling

Gamification uses game design features, such as points, levels, rewards, or challenges, to drive motivation and engagement in learning spaces. ML improves gamification by learning patterns of engagement and customizing the gamification experience according to the user's behaviour. For instance, if a model identifies the decreasing engagement, it may add a new challenge, reward, or interactive feature to re-engage the learner.

Dynamic difficulty adjustment is perhaps one of the most important developments in this field, where the ML algorithms adjust the level of difficulty of tasks to maintain a learner in his or her optimal engagement zone. Thus, the activities are not monotonous, but are neither too difficult nor too easy, very important for continuous motivation and learning success. Additionally, ML based motivation modelling results in long term persistence with personal feedback and tracking progress. These systems help the learners to set achievable goals, celebrate on success and continue working on their learning process.

EMERGING TRENDS AND TECHNOLOGIES

Artificial intelligence is evolving over time and is bringing a new type of tools and techniques that are changing the way educational systems can customize learning and analyze student behavior. With new inventions, smart education is being rewritten by large language models, multimodal analytics and privacy preserving machine learning(Dhinakaran, D et al., 2025; Ponnuviji, N. P et a., 2025). This section investigates these cutting edge developments with a view to their implication for educational transformation.

LLMs in Education

The Large Language Models (LLMs) have become great revolutionary tools in the educational technology field. These models are trained on huge corpora of human language and can understand, generate, translate and reason in language. They were especially important in the world of personalized learning. They can be these on demand tutors to answer students' questions, explain difficult concepts in simpler ways, make practice questions, even help learn a language. They are models that look like a human tutor, have a natural conversation with a student and provide guidance based on the current understanding and inclinations of the student. Besides, the educators can make quizzes, assignments, summaries and lesson plans faster with LLMs. Because they are flexible, the students and the teachers find them useful tools, particularly in the resource poor environments. Over reliance on AI also has ethical and pedagogical issues. While LLMs can assist in learning, they are not replacements for the knowledge of the human expert and need to be deployed within transparent pedagogical frameworks. But the model transparency and controllability keep on improving and LLMs are a big step forward in scalable, personalized education.

Figure 3. Emerging trends and technologies

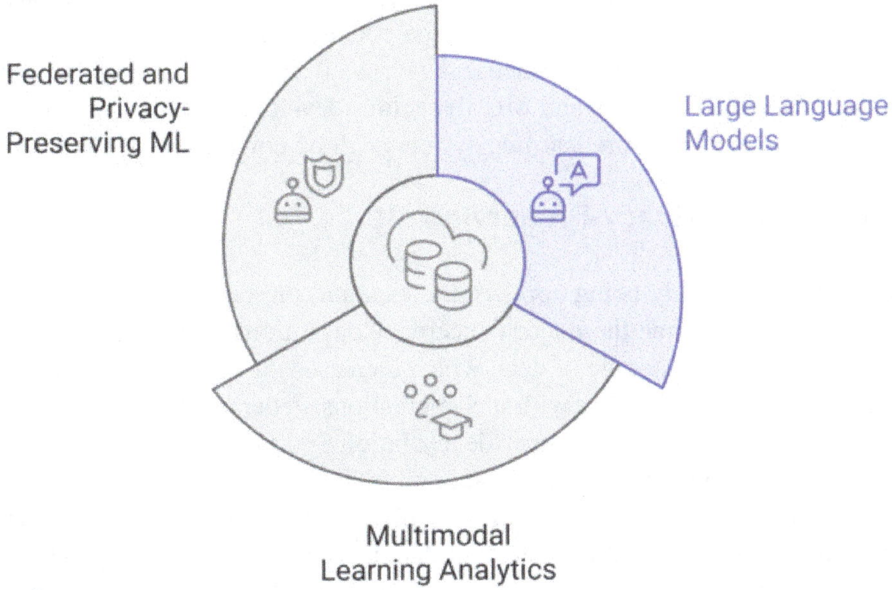

Multimodal Learning Analytics

Multimodal Learning Analytics (MMLA) is an emerging area which combines multiple modal data such as text, speech, facial expressions, gestures and physiological signals to gain more in depth understanding of learner's behavior and cognition.

MMLA takes NLP, computer vision, and sensor data and provides a more comprehensive view of how students interact with content, interfaces, and their emotional response to learning.

For instance, an MMLA system may perform facial expression (webcam) analysis, analyse typing patterns, spoken language, and screen activity for levels of confusion, engagement, or distraction. These understandings can influence adaptive feedback, as a suggestion to a student that he or she may need to take a break, receive a motivational nudge, or receive an alternative explanation.

NLP is at the heart of this integration, especially in the analysis of language that is written or spoken to determine an understanding, sentiment, and intent. In combination with vision-based inputs e.g. eye-tracking or facial emotion recognition, the system can triangulate states of students more accurately than a single mode of data.

MMLA also promises in collaborative learning environments. It can track the discussions in groups, the levels of participation and social dynamics that affect the group learning outcomes. MMLA has the potential to be plagued by issues of data privacy and ethical use of biometric data as well as interpretability. However, as the technologies of sensors and ML algorithms develop, the next generation of intelligent, emotionally-aware learning systems will be powered by MMLA.

Federated and Privacy-Preserving ML

As AI is increasingly being applied in education, the privacy and security of student data have become the major concerns. Conventional ML systems usually necessitate centralized storage of data, which increases the risks of data breaches, misuse, and the non-compliance with such regulations. Federated Learning (FL) and privacy-preserving ML methods provide a solution as it allows training of models on distributed data points without sharing raw data.

In federated learning, model is trained locally on devices or institutional servers, and only model updates and not personal data are aggregated centrally. This approach enables the educational institutions to work together to enhance AI models without violating the privacy of the students. For instance, several schools could train a common predictive model for the risk of dropout while maintaining the confidentiality of their student records and keeping them locally.

Other methods, like differential privacy, add well-tuned noise to data or model results so that no person can be identified, even if data is aggregated. Homomorphic encryption and secure multi-party computation are also being investigated for stronger privacy promises.

In education, pilot projects are appearing in adaptive learning platforms and research partnerships, developing new norms of ethical AI.

As data protection is emerging as a global goal, federated and privacy-preserving ML will be key to scaling the AI-powered education in a responsible and secure way.

CHALLENGES AND ETHICAL CONSIDERATIONS

Although there are so many opportunities for the integration of NLP and Machine Learning in education, this integration also brings along with it some serious challenges and ethical dilemmas. These are the issues that must be resolved to make sure that the AI-driven educational systems are fair, transparent, secure and can support all learners. This section describes the most important issues which are algorithmic bias, data privacy, overreliance on automation and explainability of AI systems.

ML/NLP Models Bias and the Educational Fairness

One of the most important problems in the area of education when implementing ML and NLP technologies is the problem of algorithmic bias. These models are biased because they are built from the training data which likely is biased which can lead to unfair or discriminatory outcomes for some groups of students. For example, if a language model is trained mainly on a particular set of data from a certain region, dialect or socioeconomic setup, it won't be able to interpret input from learners not in that demographic. In a variety of destructive ways, it may come to the fore: automated essay scoring systems penalize students who speak non-standard English; recommendation algorithms may send students down a path to content which perpetuates existing inequalities; and predictive analytics tools may misclassify some students as at risk and cut off opportunities, rather than help them. ML systems need to be stringently tested across different groups to ensure educational fairness which is to achieve equal outcomes.

The developers and institutions have to make bias mitigation methods a priority, including balanced training datasets, fairness-aware algorithms, and continuous auditing for disparities. Consulting educators, ethicists, and students in the development and trials of the AI systems can also ensure that the technologies promote inclusivity instead of reinforcing the existing inequities.

Data Privacy and Security

Educational technologies frequently gather huge sets of personal and behavioral information such as demographic data, patterns of learning, information on the location, and even biometric inputs. Privacy and security of this data are the key. The misuse or inappropriate access to student data may lead to severe consequences, from identity theft to misuse of the sensitive academic information.

However, the AI-driven educational platforms work across jurisdictions and fail to comply with the laws in full. What is more, students and parents are also not aware of how their data is used, stored, or shared.

In order to protect data, institutions need to implement strong encryption protocols, access controls, and clear data practices. The risks can also be mitigated by decentralizing the data processing and limiting the individual data exposure through the use of federated learning and differential privacy. Notably, students and educators should have clear and transparent information on data policies and have the control of their own information.

Over-Reliance on Automation

The efficiency of the AI systems may lead institutions to overuse automation in the areas that need human judgment, like grading, advising, or behavioral intervention. But excessive dependence on automation can result in the unintended consequences. For example, an automated grading system might not appreciate creative or non-traditional student answers, so that it would deter critical thinking and originality.

In the same manner, if AI systems mark students for intervention without adequate human supervision, then they might perpetuate stereotypes or stigmatize students due to wrong predictions. The decision-making in education should continue to be a joint venture in which human educators scrutinize and situate AI-produced findings before making any move.

In order to combine automation and human judgment, AI systems should be used as assistive tools that enhance but do not replace educators. It is important to train teachers so that they can comprehend and apply AI outputs into their pedagogy in a manner that builds trust and responsible use.

Explainability and Transparency for AI Systems

Many modern AI models, particularly the deep learning systems, are commonly referred to as black boxes because their decision-making processes are hard to explain(Priyadharshini, S. et al., 2025). This lack of explainability and transparency is a trust-buster, especially in educational settings where learners and teachers need to know how decisions are made, such as scores, recommendations, or risk flags.

For students, ambiguity in AI systems' feedback may be confusing and discouraging. Opaque models may pose a challenge for educators in terms of verifying or challenging automated suggestions. Further, without transparency, it is hard to tell and correct mistakes or biases.

When possible, developers should focus on interpretable models and include methods of explainable AI (XAI) that would enable users to understand why the system made a particular prediction or decision. Making user-friendly explanations that would include which features contributed to a recommendation or providing comparative student cases can significantly increase trust and usability.

Transparency also includes clear system goals, limitations, data sources, and use cases documentations. This information should empower the educational stakeholders to make informed decisions on the time and the way to apply AI in classrooms.

FUTURE DIRECTIONS

Along with the further development of the educational environment in the context of the advances of Artificial Intelligence in the fields of Natural Language Processing (NLP), Machine Learning (ML), the future of personalized learning is becoming more dynamic and interdisciplinary. Although, the current innovations have already started to redefine how students interact with content, get feedback, and move through learning pathways, the next AI-enabled generation in education is set to take these boundaries to new heights. This section describes the leading trends in personalization research, the increasing popularity of interdisciplinary cooperation, and the vision of the future of intelligent, inclusive, and adaptive education systems.

Trends in Personalization Research

Personalization of education is shifting from the static content adaptation to real-time, multimodal, and context-aware systems. Future research is becoming more and more oriented towards the improvement of how AI understands not only what a learner is doing, but why and how he or she is learning. This change is likely to lead to more detailed learner models, which include cognitive states, emotional clues, social contacts, and long-term learning paths.

One of the major trends is integration of the affective computing with ML models to identify and react to student emotions including confusion, frustration, boredom, or excitement. These emotional signals, correctly detected with the help of NLP, eye-tracking, or facial recognition, can enable systems to change tone, pace or content difficulty dynamically, hence increasing learner engagement and persistence.

The second important trend is the shift towards lifelong and cross-platform personalization. AI systems will more and more be able to follow learning behaviors across devices and across time and bring continuity and coherence to educational support from early schooling through professional development. This will mean that educational platforms will start developing persistent learner profiles that develop and change in contexts, to help scaffold learning with an unprecedented degree of accuracy.

In addition, meta-learning and self-regulation support are the emerging research areas. In the future, personalization engines will also assist the learners in reflecting on their learning strategies, time management, and goal setting. Intelligent systems will provide suggestions for learning how to learn so that the students would be more autonomous and effective learners.

Interdisciplinary Collaborations

In order to create truly transformative educational technologies, researchers, educators, cognitive scientists, ethicists, designers and technologists will have to collaborate in a highly interdisciplinary way. Education is not only a technical issue. it is a very human process which is affected by the social, cultural and psychological factors. Therefore, co-design of AI tools with educators and learners will be more crucial in the future in order to make sure that such systems match pedagogical intentions and realities in classrooms.

Human-computer interaction (HCI) experts and user experience (UX) designers will be instrumental in the making of AI interfaces user-friendly, inclusive, and usable in diverse learner populations. Simultaneously, cognitive scientists will keep providing the insight into the ways people learn, remember things, and react to feedbacks, thus, ensuring that AI models are based on the evidence-based learning theories.

Working with policy makers and legal scholars is also crucial to the process of creating ethical frameworks and data governance structures that can be scaled up in educational systems without compromising privacy and achieving equity. Institutions will have to set clear standards on how data usage, explainability, accountability, and human oversight are to be used in AI-powered educational tools.

Moreover, the ecosystem of the educational innovation will continue to be defined by industry-academic partnerships. Companies such as Google, Microsoft, OpenAI, as well as Duolingo, are already blazing the trail for the use of LLMs and ML in education, and partnerships between these companies and universities, and public education bodies will help close the gap between research and real-world classroom implementation.

Vision for Next-Generation AI-Powered Education

Moving ahead, the vision of next-generation education is that which is highly intelligent, inclusive, ethical and learner-centric. AI systems will not be considered as external tools anymore but as incorporated co-instructors who can adjust to every learner's background, environment, and aspirations. These systems will provide multilingual, multimodal, and culturally responsive education at scale, to help close opportunity gaps in the world.

In the long run, AI will also help collaborative and project-based learning, with the help of NLP and ML, to support group discussions, peer assessment, and collective writing. It will not only be the academic mastery, but also skills of critical thinking, creativity, empathy, and lifelong learning.

In the end, the future of AI in education is not in the substitution of human teachers but in the expansion of their capability insights for the teachers, less administrative burdens, and more individual attention. With careful planning, in-depth research, and cross-disciplinary collaboration, the educational systems of the future can be more attuned, fairer, and empowering to learners of all levels.

CONCLUSION

The combination of NLP and ML in education is a paradigmatic change in the delivery of learning, personalization, and evaluation of learning. This chapter has explored basic ideas, important uses, and emerging trends that have illustrated the increasing role of AI in the creation of intelligent and responsive learning systems. From intelligent tutoring systems and automated assessment tools to multimodal learning analytics and predictive models, such technologies are transforming how learning has been traditionally viewed and providing opportunities for more personalized, data-driven learning. One of the recurring things in the chapter is the possibilities of NLP and ML to meet learners' various needs, enhance engagement and timely interventions. Individualized content recommendation, adaptive learning path and emotionally aware systems become more possible with the development of large language models and deep learning methods. Simultaneously, such innovations are a cause of critical concerns in regard to bias, privacy, explainability, and the role of automation in pedagogical decision-making. The future of AI-powered education is in striking a balance between technological advancement and the ethical responsibility. With research development and interdisciplinary collaboration, the spotlight has to be on inclusivity, transparency, and learner agency. Educators, technologists, policy makers and learners themselves will have to co-create systems that do not only increase academic outcomes, but also uphold human dignity and diversity. In a nutshell, NLP and ML promise to change the face of education and make it more personal, equitable, and intelligent. Through meeting the present challenges and exploiting future opportunities, these technologies can empower educators and learners alike, to create the next generation of global education systems. If properly applied and with the right innovation, AI can be a great ally in the quest of lifelong learning and educational superiority.

REFERENCES

Bowman, S. R., & Dahl, G. E. (2021). What will it take to fix benchmarking in natural language understanding? arXiv preprint arXiv:2104.02145.

Chowdhary, K., & Chowdhary, K. R. (2020). Natural language processing. *Fundamentals of artificial intelligence*, 603-649.

Dhinakaran, D., Kumar, N. J., & Ponnuviji, N. P. (2025). Safeguarding confidentiality and privacy in cloud-enabled healthcare systems with spectrasafe encryption and dynamic k-anonymity algorithm. *Expert Systems with Applications*, *279*, 127584.

Fanni, S. C., Febi, M., Aghakhanyan, G., & Neri, E. (2023). Natural language processing. In *Introduction to artificial intelligence* (pp. 87–99). Springer International Publishing.

Ganesan, I., Ponnuviji, N. P., Kumar, A. S., Nithya, M., Jambulingam, U., & Lalitha, S. D. (2024). Real-Time Event Detection and Predictive Analytics Using IoT and Deep Learning. In *Industry Applications of Thrust Manufacturing: Convergence with Real-Time Data and AI* (pp. 1-41). IGI Global Scientific Publishing.

Hilbert, S., Coors, S., Kraus, E., Bischl, B., Lindl, A., Frei, M., & Stachl, C. (2021). Machine learning for the educational sciences. *Review of Education*, *9*(3), e3310.

Kotei, E., & Thirunavukarasu, R. (2023). A systematic review of transformer-based pre-trained language models through self-supervised learning. *Information (Basel)*, *14*(3), 187.

Kumar, A., & Kumar, S. (2024, May). Sentiment analysis for enhancing student engagement and learning outcomes. In *2024 International Conference on Emerging Innovations and Advanced Computing (INNOCOMP)* (pp. 132-137). IEEE.

Kurni, M., Mohammed, M. S., & Srinivasa, K. G. (2023). Intelligent tutoring systems. In *A beginner's guide to introduce artificial intelligence in teaching and learning* (pp. 29–44). Springer International Publishing.

Luan, H., & Tsai, C. C. (2021). A review of using machine learning approaches for precision education. *Journal of Educational Technology & Society*, *24*(1), 250–266.

Maheswari, B., & Nagarajan, R. (2024). EduChatbot: Implementing educational Chatbot for assisting the teaching-learning process by NLP-based hybrid heuristic adopted deep learning framework. *Kybernetes*.

Mathew, A. N., Rohini, V., & Paulose, J. (2021). NLP-based personal learning assistant for school education. *International Journal of Electrical and Computer Engineering, 11*(5), 4522–4530.

Mir, T. A., Lawaye, A. A., & Khanday, A. M. U. D. (2023). NLP techniques and challenges to process social media data. In *Advanced applications of NLP and deep learning in social media data* (pp. 171–218). IGI Global.

Mmbayi, I. I., Gakii, C., & Musyoka, F. M. (2025). Sentiment Analysis-Based Model for Monitoring User Engagement With Mental Health Chatbots. *Engineering Reports, 7*(6), e70247.

Munir, H., Vogel, B., & Jacobsson, A. (2022). Artificial intelligence and machine learning approaches in digital education: A systematic revision. *Information (Basel), 13*(4), 203.

Pajila, P. B., Sudha, K., Selvi, D. K., Kumar, V. N., Gayathri, S., & Subramanian, R. S. (2023, July). A survey on natural language processing and its applications. In *2023 4th International Conference on Electronics and Sustainable Communication Systems (ICESC)* (pp. 996-1001). IEEE.

Ponnuviji, N. P., Murugan, P., Esakkiammal, S., Kumar, S., Vishal, K. S., & Meenakshi, S. (2024, March). AI-Powered Business Intelligence for Transforming Finance and Education. In *2024 2nd International Conference on Disruptive Technologies (ICDT)* (pp. 1287-1291). IEEE.

Ponnuviji, N. P., Nirmala, G., Kokila, M. S., & Priyadharshini, S. I. (2025). Optimizing Image Retrieval in Cloud Servers with TN-AGW: A Secure and Efficient Approach. *Journal of The Institution of Engineers (India): Series B*, 106(2), 459-473.

Ponnuviji, N. P., Sumaiya Begum, A., Gnanasekaran, T., Rajendiran, M., & Shenbaga Ezhil, S. (2023, April). Leveraging Random Forest for Intelligent IoT Systems in Industrial Environments. In *International Conference on Internet of Things* (pp. 46-57). Cham: Springer Nature Switzerland.

Priyadharshini, S. I., Irene, D. S., Beulah, J. R., & Ponnuviji, N. P. (2025). Enhancing real-time health monitoring with hybrid recurrent long short-term tyrannosaurus search for menstrual cups. *Biomedical Signal Processing and Control, 100*, 107065.

Siva Subramanian, R., Prabha, D., Maheswari, B., & Aswini, J. (2021). Customer analysis using machine learning algorithms: A case study using banking consumer dataset. In *Recent Trends in Intensive Computing* (pp. 689–694). IOS Press.

Stamper, J., Xiao, R., & Hou, X. (2024, July). Enhancing llm-based feedback: Insights from intelligent tutoring systems and the learning sciences. In International Conference on Artificial Intelligence in Education (pp. 32-43). Cham: Springer Nature Switzerland.

Subramanian, R. S., Aswini, J., Bushra, S. N., Nirmala, G., & Maheswari, B. (2022, November). Customer Analysis using Machine Learning with Feature Selection Approaches: A Comparative Study. In *2022 International Conference on Augmented Intelligence and Sustainable Systems (ICAISS)* (pp. 196-202). IEEE.

Chapter 5
Deep Learning and Transformer Models for Educational Chatbots:
Enhancing Intelligent Tutoring Systems

R. Siva Subramanian
https://orcid.org/0000-0002-7509-9223
SRM Institute of Science and Technology, India

G. Anurekha
https://orcid.org/0000-0003-1478-4021
Vel Tech Rangarajan Dr. Sagunthala R&D Institute of Science and Technology, India

C. Gomathi
Panimalar Engineering College, India

Somsubhra Saha
R.M.K. College of Engineering and Technology, India

A. Rajalakshmi
Vel Tech Multi Tech Dr. Rangarajan Dr. Sakunthala Engineering College, India

J. Elavarasi
Vel Tech High Tech Dr. Rangarajan Dr. Sakunthala Engineering College, India

M. Ezhilvendan
https://orcid.org/0009-0003-3213-1304
Panimalar Engineering College, India

ABSTRACT

The integration of deep learning and transformer models has revolutionized educational chatbots, enhancing the capabilities of intelligent tutoring systems (ITS). This chapter explores the evolution of AI-driven chatbots, focusing on Recurrent Neural Networks (RNNs), Long Short-Term Memory (LSTM), Convolutional Neural Networks (CNNs), and reinforcement learning for adaptive learning experiences. Additionally, transformer-based models enable superior natural language under-

DOI: 10.4018/979-8-3373-6791-0.ch005

Copyright © 2026, IGI Global Scientific Publishing. Copying or distributing in print or electronic forms without written permission of IGI Global Scientific Publishing is prohibited.

standing (NLU), improving chatbot interactions in education. Key applications include personalized tutoring, automated grading, multilingual support, and student progress tracking. However, challenges such as data bias, explainability, privacy concerns, and scalability persist. Future advancements in few-shot learning, knowledge graphs, sentiment-aware tutoring, and AI-human collaboration will further enhance AI-powered education. This chapter highlights emerging trends, challenges, and research directions in AI-driven intelligent tutoring systems.

INTRODUCTION

Overview of Educational Chatbots and Their Role in Modern Learning

Introducing educational chatbots in the learning process is a modern trend in education that has become popular due to its effectiveness in enhancing learning for students of all levels, (Kuhail et al., 2023). These virtual assistants are created using AI which incorporates the use of NLP and ML to allow the learners to interact with various platforms in real time. In the process of learning, educational institutions as well as online learning platforms have incorporated chatbots that help in responding to questions or top up a student when he or she is stuck during a course. Unlike conventional approaches to learning that involve tutors, educational chatbots are available to students at all times and one can learn at his or her own pace. Also, they engage the students through the use of features such as quizzes, the use of game elements, and real-time feedback. As a result of this, educators are relieved from the normal teaching burden and this makes education, especially in online learning, cheaper and more efficient. Further, educational chatbots are ITS, which is an intelligent system that adapts to the student's performance and learning preferences. These systems assess the responses of students, monitor the performance indicators and modify the approaches to teaching. For instance, it is possible to use AI-powered chatbots that will be able to point out the gaps in knowledge and offer to watch additional lectures or practice more questions on the subject. Incorporation of deep learning and transformer model have revolutionized the capability of chatbot by making it capable of managing context, conversing like human, and providing user engaging and meaningful conversation. In the current society where learning institutions are adopting the use of technology and AI in learning, chatbots have become essential in determining the future of learning by enhancing accessibility, effectiveness and interest in learning, (Kavipriya et al., 2024; Uma, S 2023).

The Evolution of Intelligent Tutoring Systems (ITS)

The idea of ITS has been there from the early period of AI, and rule-based systems were designed to imitate tutors. The old ITS systems were based on procedural approach where the system played pre-scripted roles and followed the logic based rules for guidance but it lacked flexibility and failed to understand natural language. The first systems were best suited to mathematical, programming and other structured domains in which you can easily apply preexisting knowledge bases. However, with time, changed the educational needs and there was need for more dynamic and context sensitive tutoring systems, (Alrakhawi et al., 2023). ITS have been changing with the enhanced artificial intelligence in machine learning and NLP. Modern ITS use AI and ML algorithms to process large amounts of data about the students in order to provide tailored learning, (Ponmalar et al., 2024). Thus, the modern ITS use deep learning algorithms to create content, answer questions, and track the progress of learning process. It has also helped improve on the previous features of ITS such as speech recognition, sentiment analysis and conversational AI making them smarter (Lin et al., 2023). Among the recent achievements in ITS development, it is possible to note the use of deep learning methods, including RNN, LSTM networks, and transformer models. The above AI approaches have enhanced the NLP of the chatbots, and thus ITS is in a position to have meaningful interactions with the students. Also, the current ITS can adopt the use of texts, images, audio, and video in the learning process to suit the learning styles of learners. Therefore, ITS are not strictly limited to the computer-based training but are integrated within the mobile application, online learning environment, and virtual classrooms.

Importance of Deep Learning and Transformer Models in Educational Chatbots

The recent advancements in deep learning and transformer model have brought a significant change to the educational chatbots as they have become smarter and can understand the context and generate human-like responses. Many of the traditional chatbots came with rule-based systems that needed much coding on the part of the programmer; they were not good with complex questions. However, in current progression with deep learning, the chatbot is now capable of being trained with the data and is able to analyze the large data to produce quality and evolving responses (Maheswari, B., & Nagarajan, R 2024). RNNs and LSTMs have further contributed towards improving the chatbot capabilities by helping the AI to learn and manage sequential data and also have a context of the previous interactions. These models have been particularly beneficial in the contexts of computer aided tutor systems that involve exchanges with the student. However, there are downsides to RNN-based models, and some of them include the long short-term memory problem and scalability. Transformer models are highly effective in handling big amount of text while understanding the context, this is why they are widely used in the development of chatbots. Unlike other models, transformers self-attentive mechanisms to determine how relevant a word is in a given sentence, making it easier to produce coherent answers. This feature is most helpful in the educational chatbots since it helps the chatbot to understand the student's question better, give out the right explanation and keep the conversation going. Also, with the help of transformers, it is possible to create more context-based responses in the type of conversation, which makes the conversation with the chatbot seem more natural and interesting for students. One more significant benefit of the transformer models when implemented in educational chatbots is the multilingual capability to help students from different countries. Through the use of multilingual transformer models, there is the possibility of availing AI tutoring on educational platforms in several languages without the need to translate every content. In addition, transformer-based chatbots can be further trained for certain topics, which means that a student can learn the material that is relevant to his or her class or level of study. The trends in deep learning and transformer technologies will also remain strong and significant in contributing to the improvement of ITS and the development of the new type of education.

Objectives and Scope of the Survey

This study will seek to give a general understanding of how deep learning and transformer models are revolutionizing the educational chatbots and intelligent tutoring systems. Thus, the research questions of this chapter are as follows:

1. To identify and define the basic notions of educational chatbots and their presence in intelligent tutoring systems.
2. To review the use of DL algorithms such as RNNs, LSTMs and CNNs in the improvement of chatbot-based education.
3. To understand how transformer models enhance the interactions of a chatbot and also the adaptive learning process.
4. To focus on the use of the AI-based educational chatbots and the possibilities of using it in the educational system, namely as the tutor, the testing system, and the engagement system.
5. To explain the issues such as privacy, fairness and limitations of the AI tutoring systems.
6. To establish the future research areas of AI-based education or AI-based learning trends in the future including artificial intelligence based emotional learning, multi-modal learning, and federated learning.

The scope of this survey encompasses a wide range of AI-driven approaches for educational chatbots, from foundational deep learning techniques to advanced transformer-based architectures. The chapter will also provide some insights on ethics in AI within the context of education, including bias, transparency, and proper implementation of AI. This survey will present the recent developments in DL and transformers for ITSs to be beneficial for the researchers, educators, and developers in the field of ITSs to design the new generation of ITSs.

FUNDAMENTALS OF EDUCATIONAL CHATBOTS AND INTELLIGENT TUTORING SYSTEMS

Definition and Characteristics of Educational Chatbots

In the context of education, chatbots are intelligent and interactive agents that are programmed to help students as well as educators. They engage the users in text or speech mode, providing information, responding to questions, testing the knowledge, and suggesting learning materials. These are applications that are based on NLP and ML to replicate human-like conversation, which in turn makes education more engaging, affordable, and time-effective (Mageira et al., 2022). Personalization is one of the essential features of the educational chatbots that can be used in the learning process. Unlike conventional teaching methods, chatbots study the students' behaviors and performance, as well as modify their response patterns to the students' learning styles. In this way, they are able to address the needs of each learner and provide each of them with the necessary clarifications and teaching aids. The other advantage is accessibility since the students can get help at any time of the day or night since it is not limited by the time availability of a human tutor. This makes chatbots particularly useful in self-paced online learning environment, because it is easy to get disoriented and give up learning for a while. Furthermore, education oriented chatbots enhance interactivity through use of elements like quizzes, challenges and exercises in their dialogues. These features assist in keeping the students motivated as well as fostering their desire to learn. Another defining characteristic is the multimodal support where the chatbots are capable of incorporating text, image, audio, and video to improve the understanding. In addition, the modern chatbots help in multilingual learning since students from different linguistic backgrounds can learn easily.

Another benefit of educational chatbots is in the assessment and feedback process carried out by the chatbot. From the responses of the students, they are able to immediately give feedback, identify areas where the students require more practice and recommend on where the students can practice more in order to get it right. In addition to that, they help the educators in handling administrative responsibilities like grading assignments, session scheduling, and management of course contents, which in turn lessens the burden on the educators and the efficiency of the learning institutions.

Components and Architecture of Intelligent Tutoring Systems

An ITS is an advanced AI system that imitates human tutors and provides students with targeted learning environments. As for the structure of ITS, it is composed of several elements that are critical for its functioning in the capacity of an adaptive and intelligent tutor.

Student Model

This component reflects the intellectual and behavioral characteristics of the student. It includes the information about the intensity of knowledge, learning rate, preferences, previous communications, and performance of the student. The student model is dynamic in that it is updated each time the learner interacts with the system; this makes the content adaptive.

Domain Model

It will contain all the knowledge and information which is required by the tutoring system. It includes information in a logical manner about what the content is about, what is expected to be learnt, how it is to be taught and how the problems are to be solved. The domain model makes it possible for the chatbot to provide the students with appropriate and relevant answers to their questions.

The Pedagogical Model

The other component is known as instructional model that defines the manner in which the chatbot will be engaging the students and or disseminating information. It has the use of AI to personalize the teaching process, modify the difficulty of the questions, and use instructional approaches to facilitate the learning process of students. The pedagogical model also incorporates reinforcement learning strategies that adapt tutoring according to the feedback received from the student as well as the performance of the student.

NLP Engine

It is the main tool that allows chatbots to decode and produce humanlike interaction. The student inputs are fed to the NLP engine for intent and context analysis and for formulating suitable replies. The latest ITS incorporate deep learning models like transformers to enhance the understanding of contextual clues in the chatbot's dialogues.

User Interface (UI) and Communication Layer

This layer facilitates interaction between the student & the tutoring system. It can cover the text chat applications, voice interfaces, or a combination of the graphical and voice ones. The UI also enables the students to easily interact with the chatbot and find the necessary learning materials.

These components make it possible for ITS to provide personalized, adaptative and scalable learning hence making it an effective tool of learning in this present era.

Role of NLP in Chatbot-Based Education

NLP is the foundation of the chatbot-based education because it is the technique that allows the machines to decipher the human language. NLP also improves educational chatbots by making it easier for the chatbot to understand the student, allowing the chatbot to interact with the student and engage in meaningful conversation (Wong, 2022).

Figure 1. Natural Language Processing (NLP) in chatbot-based education

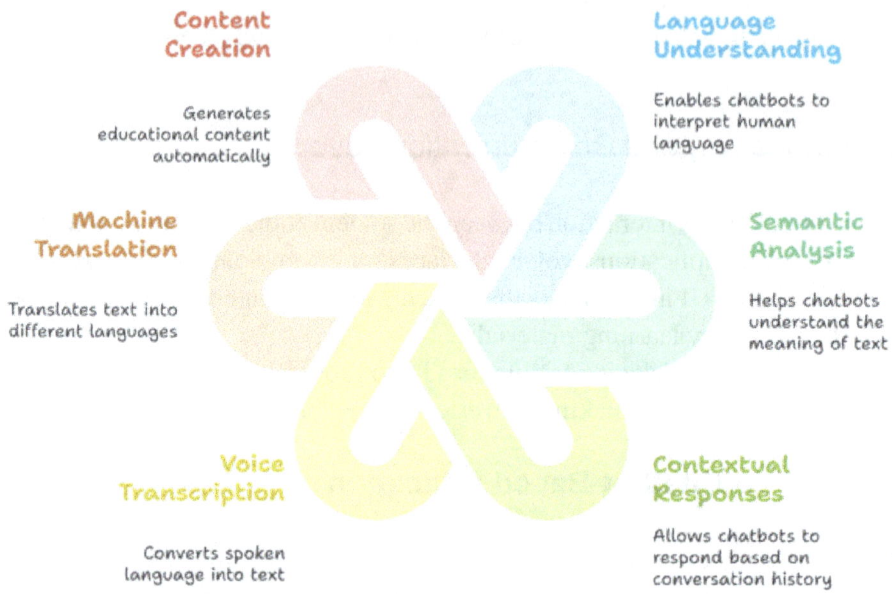

Another significant function of NLP in the context of the educational chatbots is the understanding of the text and semantic analysis. The student queries are then preprocessed by NLP algorithms where the system tries to determine the concepts that are important and the intent of the question. The use of NER, sentiment analysis as well as topic modeling enhances the quality of responses given by the chatbot. Furthermore, with the help of NLP, chatbots are capable of responding based on the context hence making them capable of having multi- turn conversations. NLP-based chatbots do not follow a set of predetermined rules, but rather interact with the user, remember the conversation and adjust to the discussion. This is especially the case in systems that are involved in the tutoring process where there is a sequence of learning steps (Dinh et al., 2023). Yet another application of NLP comprises of the voice transcription and creation. Voice-based educational chatbots use ASR and TTS that allow for spoken communication to enhance the learning process of students with reading problems or other impairments. Additionally, the use of the NLP machine translation makes the chatbots to translate to different languages so that the students in different parts of the world can benefit from education. It also allows for automatic content creation with the help of the modern NLP techniques.

AI models, especially the transformer based architecture can provide explanations, can summarize learning material and even can generate quizzes according to the students' performance. This capability improves the interactivity of the chatbot and makes it possible to offer a form of tutoring to the users.

The Comparison between the Rule-Based Educational Chatbots and AI-based Educational Chatbots

On this basis, the educational chatbots could be classified as the rule-based & the AI-based chatbots with their specific characteristics and drawbacks.

Rule-based Chatbots

These chatbots work with the help of programs that contain a set of rules for interaction. Some of them use decision trees, some of them use pattern matching techniques and some of them use manually programmed responses for answering the queries of the students. However, rule-based chatbots are easy to develop and perfect for answering FAQs, but they are not very versatile in answering new and different questions or addressing changing demands from students. Also, they are not good at handling natural language differences that need frequent manual intervention to enhance the accuracy of the models.

AI Educational Chatbots

These are more advanced than the rule-based ones, as the latter are based on ML, DL and NLP. These are chatbots that can handle all forms of information and learn based on context; these learn through reinforcement. Current advancements in machine learning permitted the use of deep neural networks, transformers, and RL that improve the performance of the AI-based chatbots in terms of conversation (Jain et al., 2024).

Machine Learning-based Chatbots

These chatbots apply the supervised and unsupervised learning approach to analyze the queries made by the students and determine the kind of response that is required to be generated. These chatbots use decision trees and other methods such as SVM and neural networks to make it more accurate with time (Singh et al., 2024; Saravanan, K et al., 2023).

Sophisticated Dialog-based Chatbots

A few of the cutting-edge chatbots apply Deep learning models like RNNs, LSTMs, and transformers. These models improve the contextual awareness, and hence the chatbot is able to respond with relevant and context-specific answers. Out of all the types of chatbots, transformer-based chatbots have significantly impacted the education sector mainly due to real-time tutoring, adaptive learning, and content generation.

An important benefit of chatbots that are based on AI is the possibility of their learning. Contrary to rule-based chatbots that need constant update with human interference, the AI-powered chatbots learn from interaction with the users. Furthermore, AI-based chatbots can identify student's emotions and learning issues through sentiment analysis and affective computing and thus can be friendly to the students.

However, there are some limitations associated with the use of AI chatbots; they include the following; Data privacy, computational unsophistication, and biasness of data fed into the chatbots. However, there are some challenges that are associated with the integration of AI in educational chatbots and which have led to the improvement of the ITS in terms of efficiency, flexibility, and expansiveness in catering for learning difficulties.

Machine learning and in particular deep learning helped to shift educational chatbots from the previously used simple rule based systems to the complex intelligent forms of tutoring(Rajendran, T et al., 2023 ; Subramanian, R et al.,2021). With the help of NLP, deep learning, and the transformer model, the modern chatbots can offer the students the individual approach, immediate feedback, and adaptive learning. The history of Intelligent Tutoring Systems suggests that the AI is becoming an important tool in the process of education delivery, effectiveness and access. In the future, the research will further develop new innovative and intelligent educational chatbots to transform education, increase accessibility, personalize and utilize data strategy for students.

DEEP LEARNING IN EDUCATIONAL CHATBOTS

DL has being the one of the key frontiers of improving the intelligent and context aware chatbots in the field of education. The research established that prior approaches to developing chatbots based on rule-based and machine learning algorithms have been done with certain limitations in the ability to interpret natural language, handle context in conversations, and learn from their experiences(Yamini, B et al., 2024). Nevertheless, with the development of complex neural networks, the chatbots have become more intelligent and adaptive in their features. This section aims to discuss the selected deep learning methods that can be used in developing an educational chatbot, which are RNNs, LSTM, GRUs, CNNs, and reinforcement learning (Davar et al., 2025).

Overview of DL Techniques for Chatbot Development

DL is one of the approaches of artificial intelligence that aims at feeding neural networks with many layers to achieve the underlying features of the given data. One of the important features of educational chatbots is the application of deep learning approaches to improve NLP proficiency, which helps to comprehend the students' questions, generate the adequate answers, and take into consideration students' learning peculiarities (Boopathi, S 2023). Another benefit of deep learning in the development of a chatbot is the capability of processing and understanding the unstructured text data. In contrast to the rule or statistical approaches, deep learning-based chatbots have a powerful ability to process textual information, learn and refine the responses from the dialogue data. Based on the large amounts of data, such as textbooks, online courses, academic papers, and students' conversations, deep learning models can give contextually accurate responses. Deep learning chatbots also use contextual embeddings to capture relationship of words and meaning of the sentence. These embeddings enhance the human-like response of the chatbot and enables the interactions to be more fluid and more like a conversation (Patel, R et al., 2021).

Recurrent Neural Networks (RNNs), Long Short-Term Memory (LSTM), and Gated Recurrent Units (GRUs) in Chatbot Responses

Recurrent Neural Networks (RNNs) is one of the first DL models that have been used for the chatbot development. As opposed to feedforward neural networks, RNNs are employed specifically for sequential data, which is most suitable for text-based tasks. In the educational context, the RNNs' capability helps in understanding student queries, maintaining context, and efficiently providing an appropriate response based on the previous conversations. However, it was found that standard RNNs are not suitable for long term dependencies in conversation because they suffer from vanishing gradient. To overcome this limitation, the LSTM networks were applied. LSTMs are an improved version of RNN that have the capability of learning long-term dependencies and storing information over lengthy sequences. LSTMs in educational chatbots help them remember previous conversations with a particular student, track his/her learning progress, and provide the most suitable responses. For instance, an LSTM-based chatbot can retrieve a student's previous question concerning a specific concept in mathematics and give further clarification in areas the student has struggled with before. Likewise, GRUs are another type of RNNs that improve the performance of the chatbot. Compared with LSTMs, GRUs have less computational requirements while giving similar results in the analysis of sequential information. The GRU-based chatbots are useful in educational institutions since they are expected to produce responses in real-time and are flexible. They allow the chatbots to adapt the teaching process according to the students' activity and achievement level, respectively. LSTMs and GRUs are beneficial in the handling of dialogues within the educational chatbots (Kasthuri & Balaji, 2023). They enable the chatbots to have a conversational flow, ensure that the flow of the conversation is logical and that the responses are coherent. These deep learning models assist the chatbots to perform as tutors and explain the concepts to students in detail.

Figure 2. Deep learning in educational chatbots

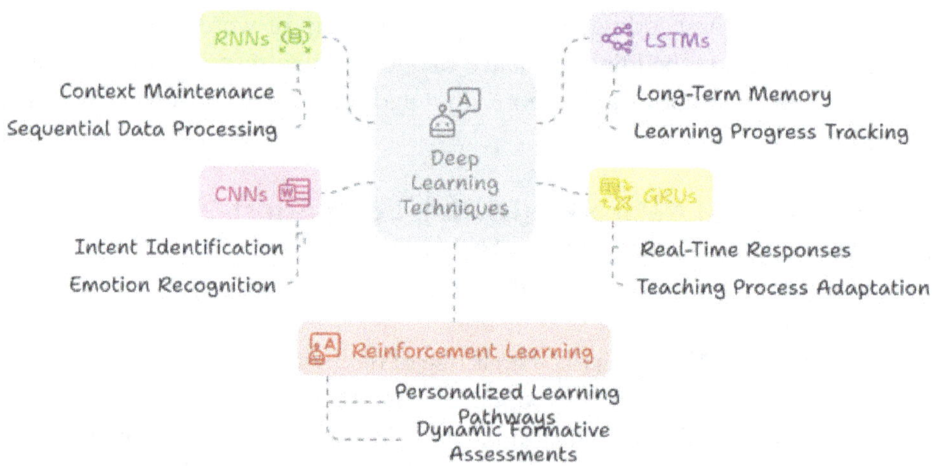

Convolutional Neural Networks (CNNs) for Text Classification and Knowledge Extraction

CNNs are mainly associated with image processing but they have been applied effectively in text-based applications such as educational chatbots. CNNs are especially suitable for text classification, intent identification, and knowledge extraction that are crucial for the chatbot.

In general, CNN-based models in educational chatbots are useful in the following ways:

Identifying the purpose of the student: By categorizing user queries based on certain categories (explaining, practice, assessment), CNNs help chatbots to give correct answers.

Some aspects of student queries: Using CNNs, the patterns from the student queries are extracted to determine the keywords, and thus, the chatbot can provide relevant educational content.

Emotion recognition and sentiment analysis: Depending on the message provided by the student, CNNs can detect whether the student is frustrated or confused, and the chatbot can adapt its response accordingly.

For instance, if a student types, "I don't understand how to solve quadratic equations," a CNN-based chatbot interprets this as a help needed in solving mathematics problems and will thereafter provide the steps to do that.

Also, CNNs can improve the automatic scoring of educational chatbots because the latter is capable of analyzing and scoring student answers. This relieves pressure from the human teachers and makes it possible to provide fast and uniform feedback to the learners.

Reinforcement Learning for Adaptive and Personalized Learning Experiences

RL is an enhanced type of deep learning that helps the chatbot to learn through the interactions with the users. In the context of educational chatbots, RL is used to generate effective and unique learning processes by altering the chatbot's behaviors according to the learners' interactions. Supplementing the information from the previous lesson, let me specify that, unlike other models that use labeled data, chatbots learn through trial and error. The feedback from the user is in the form of a reward or a penalty depending on the response given by the chatbot. In the long run, RL assists the chatbot in refining its tutoring approaches and enhancing its interaction with the learners.

Some of the most important areas where RL has been applied in the case of educational chatbots include:

Personalized Learning Pathways

RL-based chatbots are capable of identifying the performance of a student and offer teaching methods based on the same. In case a student has some misunderstanding, the chatbot offers more information, different examples, or questions to check understanding.

Interactivity

Unlike other forms of formative assessments, which are sequential in nature, RL-based chatbots provide formative assessments in a dynamic manner as per the performance of the student. This makes it possible for the students to get challenges that they are capable of handling.

Fluency

With the help of reinforcement learning, the conversation flow is enhanced so that the chatbot can keep students' conversation going in a meaningful and productive manner.

For example, an RL-based chatbot that is designed to help a learner practice language proficiency can change the level of the exercises it offers depending on the learner's ability. In this case, if a student answers correctly, the chatbot brings in the higher level of difficulty by incorporating hard words and structure in sentences.

Another application of RL in the context of educational chatbots is collaboration of several agents that may work together to give the student comprehensive learning experience. For instance, one of the two may be designed to provide answers to theoretical questions, while the other is for practical problems. These agents are integrated with RL to ensure that their replies are coordinated to provide an efficient learning process. Deep learning has enhanced the intelligence of educational chatbots to be smarter, contextually relevant, and to learn from the students. RNNs, LSTMs, and GRUs help in the management of the chatbot's dialogue so that it can have a conversation that has more than one turn. They enhance the input of text classification, the sentiment analysis, and the intent recognition so that the chatbot will be more effective in the exchanges. Reinforcement learning is the next level in chatbot usage as it allows for individualised and dynamic ways of coaching, flow of conversation and engagement of students (Ramineni et al., 2024 ; Dhyani, M., & Kumar, R. 2021). This is because as the models advance, educational chatbots will improve in their learning, teaching, and assessment to improve student experiences. The future developments in the transformer models and self-supervision learning will also enhance the chatbot experience and make the AI-driven education more effective and accessible to learners in the world.

TRANSFORMER MODELS FOR EDUCATIONAL CHATBOTS

Transformer models have acted as new breakthrough advancements in artificial intelligence and NLP which has helped enhance the functions of educational chatbots. Unlike RNNs or LSTMs, transformer frameworks give better context, modularity, and flexibility, all of which are advantageous in ITS. The transformer models help in giving natural responses, ability to have multi-turn conversations and personalised education chatbots. In addition, there has been an enhancement of multimodal transformers that has adopted interactive learning through text, audio, and video in the chatbot learning. This part describes the main transformer architectures, their adaptation for domain-specific tutoring, and benefits compared to deep learning in the context of educational chatbots (Chopde, A., & Agrawal, M. 2022).

Introduction to Transformer Architectures

Transformers are deep learning models that follow the self-attention mechanism that enables the model to work with the whole text at once rather than in a sequential manner. This leads to the enhancement of the contextual understanding of the model and helps in avoiding the vanishing gradient problem associated with RNNs and LSTMs. Transformers are a type of DL architectures that are different from the usual ones because they use multi-head self-attention and positional encoding mechanisms that allow for dependencies in the text to be learned at a distance. It makes them suitable for educational chatbots that need to provide coherent, contextually relevant, and grammatically correct responses in a multi-turn dialogue.

Fine-Tuning Transformer Models for Domain-Specific Tutoring

Although the pre-trained transformer models are quite powerful, the building blocks need to be trained on the relevant domain of education for the best performance of the tutor system. It is a process that enhances the transformer model's capability to generate and understand content relevant to the subject by training it with domain-specific datasets like subject related textbooks, research papers, and students' interaction. The following are some of the steps that helps to fine-tune transformer models for educational chatbots:

Mathematical Knowledge

Transformers can be trained on large blocks of data covering mathematics, physics, or language learning, as well as in the sphere of medical enlightenment. For instance, a chatbot intended for medical students can be further trained on biomedical texts to enhance the correctness of the answers given.

Supervised Learning with Labeled Data

Only in this case, there will be labeled dataset which contains student queries and expert responses with which the model will be trained. This enhances the computation of the structure of the question, the formulation of an explanation based on the question, and the identification of learning barriers.

Transfer Learning for Adaptive Tutoring

It means that a general transformer model can be adapted to a particular curriculum and the educational content that the chatbot provides is consistent with the lesson plan.

Evaluation and Optimization

Evaluation of the fine-tuned models are based on the assessment of the response quality and the coherence which is measured using the BLEU score, ROUGE score and the perplexity score of the generated responses. It is also important that human educators may analyze the answer given by the chatbot to check its correctness and relevance.

In other words, fine-tuning transformers make sure that the educational chatbots provide subject-specific information, recommendations and further learning paths, and the learning process customized for each learner.

Performance Comparison of Transformers vs. Traditional Deep Learning Models in Educational Chatbots

Transformer models are more effective in the development of chatbots than DL models since they are efficient, contextually aware, and easily scalable. The following are the advantages of transformers over RNNs, LSTMs and CNNs in educational chatbots:

Table 1. Advantages of transformers over RNNs, LSTMs and CNNs in educational chatbots

Feature	RNNs/LSTMs	CNNs	Transformers
Context Retention	Struggles with long-range dependencies	Not applicable	Captures long-range dependencies effectively
Scalability	Limited scalability due to sequential processing	High scalability for text classification	Highly scalable, parallelizable
Response Coherence	May lose context in multi-turn dialogues	Limited to classification tasks	Maintains context over long conversations
Training Efficiency	Slow due to sequential computations	Faster but not ideal for generative tasks	Faster with parallel processing
Personalization	Requires extensive training data	Less adaptable to personalized learning	Easily fine-tuned for personalized tutoring
Multimodal Integration	Not supported	Limited	Supports text, speech, and video integration

Compared to the conventional models like LSTMs and CNNs, transformers yield better accuracy, versatility, and dynamic capability and are the best-suited for the advanced educational chatbots. Transformer models have helped to improve the performance, flexibility, and interactivity of educational chatbots to a great extent. These changes act as building blocks in the productions of the chatbots, as well as the fine-tuning methods that increase domain relevancy. Multimodal transformers in learning takes the education experience to the next level with the addition of text, speech, and video into the learning process. These are the self-supervised learning, federate learning or the quantum computing that is believed to propel in the near future further advancing the educational chatbot system in terms of hyper-personalized, real-time and autonomous tutoring system. The educational institutions and researchers have to keep on working on the transformer-based solutions for building more intelligent, effective, and accessible AI-based learning platforms.

APPLICATIONS OF AI-POWERED EDUCATIONAL CHATBOTS

AI-based educational chatbots uplift the education system by offering tutor's support, grading performance, and intercommunication. These chatbots use NLP, & deep learning and transformer model for providing learning instructions, timely feedback and tutoring at scale. The incorporation of AI in educational chatbots has improved adaptability of learning, automated assessment, translation, monitoring of student's performance and peer tutoring (Solanki et al., 2023 ; Darwish 2024). This section discusses primary areas of utilization of AI-based educational chatbots to understand their significance in the current learning system.

Personalized Learning and Adaptive Tutoring Systems

The most important use of AI educational chatbots is in the category of adaptive learning where chatbots deliver contents in line with the needs of the students. It is especially Illegitimate when in one sitting these broad classes of learners are subjected to a similar learning model since they learn in different ways and pace. This is a limitation that AI-driven chatbots do not have since they are programmed to use machine learning algorithms in analyzing students' interactions, identifying areas of weakness, and modifying lesson plans. To be more specific, intelligent tutoring systems include tailoring of instructional content, recommending resources, and applying changes to the level of material and approach, in the course of operating. For instance, if a student is having difficulties in comprehending some problem in mathematics, the chatbot can offer more examples of such problems, detailed explanations and more problems for practice. In addition, the process of interaction with a chatbot can be more effective since it allows students to get instant feedback and correct their mistakes when answering questions. Unlike traditional face-to-face teaching and learning environment where students are forced to wait for the teacher's feedback on their queries and assignments, the use of AI- tutoring chatbots provide instantaneous feedback. These chatbots also have the capability of recognizing the different categories of learning: visual, auditory, and presenting content in the most preferred way. This flexibility of AI makes the AI tutoring systems more efficient compared to traditional methods. Furthermore, these chatbots are available at any time which makes the education system flexible and more accessible to the students.

Figure 3. Applications of AI-powered educational chatbots

Automated Grading and Feedback Generation

Educational chatbots also have the ability to automate the grading process and provide detailed feedbacks on the performance of the students. In a large class, it is quite tasking for the teacher to go through each student's assignment and write comments on each of them. Automated grading systems are based on NLP and deep learning algorithms where it can grade essays, check the grammar, check the coherence, and assign a grade according to the rubric given. Besides essay grading, the AI chatbots are equally effective in dealing with MCQ assessments as it provides explanations for the answers given by the students. Likewise, the use of AI in grading short-answer responses helps avoid the problem of giving credit only to students who use the exact words as a model answer since semantic similarity is used in grading. In programming classes, chatbots by AI detect whether the code provided is syntactically or logically correct and if it can be optimized. These chatbots also provide performance reports to the students, which display their strong and weak areas. The use of such systems also relieves the educators from the time-consuming process of evaluation so that they can dedicate their time to other important aspects of teaching and appraisal while the students can be given feedback in a timely and constructive manner.

Multilingual Chatbots for Global Education Accessibility

In situations where people speak different languages, language can be a major hindrance in the education process of students. AI-enabled multilingual chatbots proved useful in resolving this dilemma since they offer real-time translation and communication services. Since these chatbots use transformer models they have the capability to process multi-lingual text and thus students can engage in the preferred language. This feature is especially helpful to students who have poor English language proficiency, refugees, and international students. Apart from text translators, AI-enabled chatbots use speech to text (STT) and text to speech (TTS) to make education easily accessible to the disabled students. However, these multilingual chatbots also ensure that the content to be delivered is culturally appropriate & relatable to the learners, thus, improving understanding and interest. Through language translation, the use of chatbots in education ensures that any barriers hindering students from learning due to language differences are eliminated, thus allowing students from different linguistic backgrounds to have access to quality education.

AI-Powered Assessment and Student Progress Tracking

Monitoring the student performance is very important in the process of discovering deficiencies that may affect education and training. Automatic chatbots are useful in the assessment and tracking of the progress of students because they use the performance data to inform the educators. These chatbots develop dynamic and interactive quizzes that change according to the responses made by the students so that the learners are given a suitable challenge. Curriculum learning can be implemented through AI based analytical systems which produces reports of its performance showing activities that involves students' engagement, quiz, scores and mastery of concepts. These findings can help educators to easily notice learner who is lagging behind and then find ways to assist him or her. In the same regard, AI-powered chatbots act as early warning signals of the learner's withdrawal, poor performance, and inconsistent learner study behavior. This enables teachers to be able to follow up on their students and prevent them from lagging behind. Flexible study plans developed by the artificial intelligence keep students more engaged and also help to increase their outcome by considering their abilities and disabilities. Through assessment and tracking of the progress, the AI chatbots improve on the delivery of curriculum as well as the retention rate of the students.

Peer-assisted Tutoring: Building up Collaboration in Learning with Chatbots

Group work is very important in promoting interaction and sharing of ideas among students. AI chatbots help in student to student interaction, monitoring of group discussions, and encourage co-operation. In a similar manner these chatbots help in formation of groups where students of similar academic background can work in groups to complete their assignments and share information and knowledge. Intelligent peer mentoring involves pairing high achieving students with low achievers with the aim of creating an environment that supports peer tutoring as a mode of learning. Additional elements like quizzes, challenges, and leaderboards also help to increase the level of participation and engagement of the students. Moreover, it is also helpful in group work since it can help students with brainstorming and provide them with the necessary resources for the project and immediately give feedback on the group activity. Introducing AI into the concept of peer learning, the educational chatbots build a social learning environment in an engaging manner that enhances the academic performance of the students. The use of AI in education has enhanced the implementation of educational chatbots in the following ways; individualized tutoring, grading, handling learners who speak different languages, keeping track of the students' performance, and improving collaboration. These chatbots utilize deep learning, the transformer models and NLP for the provision of intelligent, interactive and effective learning. With the advancement in AI technology, the use of chatbots in enhancing education practices will improve access, student interaction, and learning, thus improving education.

CHALLENGES AND LIMITATIONS

Although the use of AI in creating educational chatbots has been proved to be effective in enhancing the learning process, there are several pros and cons associated with it. These include the problems pertaining to data quality and its representation, biases, explainability of AI systems, ethical issues, computational constraints and the capability of a chatbot to grasp the context and feelings of a user. It is important to consider all these challenges in order to make AI-based tutoring systems more effective and reliable in terms of fairness.

Data Quality and Bias in AI-Driven Tutoring Systems

The effectiveness of the AI educational chatbots greatly relies on the quality and the variety of the data fed into the program. Inaccurate responses can be obtained from poor quality data and this affects the tutoring process as well as the learning process being offered to the students. In most cases, AI models require big data to identify patterns, anticipate students' requirements, and provide appropriate learning materials. However, the problem is that if the training data is limited, irrelevant, or not very diverse, the chatbot will be able to provide the user with the wrong or rather inaccurate information. Another issue related to AI is the issue of bias in the AI tutoring systems. In this way, the chatbot may contribute to the training data's biases, whether cultural, gender-related, or socioeconomic, in its answers. For instance, if an educational chatbot was trained on English content from Western education systems, it will not be in a position to give suitable responses to students of other languages or cultures. In the same way, if a chatbot has been trained on data, which contains specific stereotype, it may reproduce it. To tackle these problems, it is crucial to develop and use high quality, diverse and inclusive datasets in educational institutions and developers. There is the need to schedule the models for auditing and using bias detection mechanisms to make sure that the models do not create a bias in learning for students. Moreover, when the chatbot is used in the communication process, it is possible to prevent the influence of prejudice and inaccuracy by involving the human factor in the process.

Explainability and Interpretability of DL Models in Education

This creates a major problem of how to handle deep learning models in educational chatbots, as such models are black boxes. Several AI models especially the deep neural network, contain features that make them hard to explain how they arrived at certain decisions. This certainly makes it difficult for educators and students to rely on the recommendations or feedback proffered by AI. This is important especially in the learning process since students and teachers require to know the rationale behind a given AI response, suggestion, or score. For instance, if the chatbot recommends a student to concentrate on a particular area, the student should be able to find a logical reasoning as to why this decision has been made. Lack of transparency makes the students not to believe or act on the information provided by the AI based feedback. To enhance the explainability of models, the following are some of the approaches that have been proposed by researchers such as the use of attention mechanisms in the transformers, feature visualization, and rule-based AI explanations. Also, the use of the hybrid models that combine rule-based systems and deep learning can bring improvement in terms of interpretability. Developers must also focus on the fact that educational chatbots should have interfaces that allow the students and teachers to understand why the bot is making certain decisions to make them comfortable using the AI tutoring system.

Ethical Concerns: Student Privacy, Misinformation, and AI Reliability

The following issues were identified as ethical issues of educational chatbots: privacy, credibility, and reliability of the AI.

This chapter identifies several main concerns: the first one is student data privacy. AI tutoring systems take in large amounts of data regarding students' learning profiles, personal information, and academic achievements. If it is not properly protected then this data may be at risk of being hacked or accessed by unauthorized persons or misused. Any information pertaining to students should therefore be protected through encryption, anonymization and limited access in educational institutions. Various laws exist should also be followed to ensure the protection of data utilized in the development of AI educational systems.

The next ethic that is relevant in this case is the risk of giving inaccurate information. It is common for AI chatbots, particularly those that are based on generative models to give out wrong or even potentially misleading information. When a chatbot gives out wrong information in an educational setting, the students are likely to be fed with wrong information which they will spread out to others. AI-generated responses must be accurate and therefore need to be fine-tuned and checked for facts and where necessary, the involvement of human input is crucial.

Moreover, there is an issue of trustworthiness of the AI used in the learning processes and educational spheres that require higher levels of reliability. Otherwise, if a chatbot gives an unhelpful, slow, or incorrect answer, learners may completely disbelieve in AI systems. These include frequent updates, effective testing, and feedback mechanism to ensure that the chatbot is reliable among developers.

Scalability and Computational Cost of Real-Time AI-Powered Chatbots

Another challenge that has to do with the use and implementation of AI in the educational process is the scalability of the educational chatbots. Albeit the fact that AI chatbots can engage millions of students at once and respond to all of them in real-time, achieving high accuracy and adapting to the needs of different learners is impossible without using a considerable amount of computational resources.

The one that has been identified repeatedly as a major challenge is computational complexity which makes the use of deep learning models time-consuming.

Systems use transformers which consume a lot of computing resources and therefore are costly to scale. Depiction and keeping of the AI models on cloud servers or edge devices has many expenses, which may be even unaffordable to institutions of learning with fewer resources. Also, there should be an ability for a chatbot to handle numerous requests at once, all the while ensuring the quality of the answers. This is because high latency in the response of the chatbot is likely to demoralize the student and repel him/her from continuing to learn from the system. To mitigate this, developers have to redesign the model architectures, use optimal inference strategies such as pruning and quantizing the models, and look for affordable cloud computing services, (Dhinakaran et al., 2025; Ponnuviji et al., 2025). The last factor is related to the ability of the AI models to be applied in different educational systems. The scenario of a high school math chatbot is unadaptable to university physics or language learning. The costs, flexibility of the AI models to the subjects, languages and learning environment, remain a difficult issue that needs to be addressed in future research.

FUTURE TRENDS AND RESEARCH DIRECTIONS

As the technology of educational chatbots based on artificial intelligence is still developing, scientists and software engineers are searching for new approaches to the problem. The future trends will be the enhanced ability to learn context, emotions, privacy, as well as the blending of AI and human teachers. In this section, the current trends include few-shot and zero-shot learning, knowledge graph for reasoning, AI emotional intelligence, federated learning for privacy concerns, as well as human-AI learning systems.

Advances in Few-Shot and Zero-Shot Learning for Educational Chatbots

This chapter identifies the fact that AI tutor systems require large sets of data for training as one of the major issues. Most traditional deep learning models need large amounts of training datasets for them to perform well, which in most cases may take a lot of resources to prepare. FSL and ZSL try to overcome this problem by teaching the AI the ability to learn from a few or no training examples at all. Few-shot learning enables a chatbot to learn from a limited number of examples and is helpful for specific topics or languages. In contrast, zero-shot learning allows the models to deduce information about other topics not seen during training using the learned representations and contextual understanding. This approach proves most effective in education since chatbots must address various curricula, student learning preferences, and changing subject matter. Future work will be aimed at further enhancing the effectiveness and flexibility of FSL and ZSL for the purpose of increasing the response rates of the chatbot in different educational contexts.

Integration of Knowledge Graphs and Reasoning for Better Contextual Understanding

Most of the present day chatbots which incorporate AI are limited in their abilities to remember the context and reason and therefore the conversations can be random or superficial. KGs can be considered as an effective solution to this problem because KGs represent connections between concepts, facts, and entities, which allows chatbots to provide more contextually relevant answers. Introducing knowledge graphs that are composed of concepts and relations in deep learning models can help educational chatbots to enhance their capacity to search for and link related information(Ponnuviji, N. P et al., 2023). For instance, if a student asks a question about a historical event, they will get an answer that not only gives a straight-forward answer but also other topics related to the event, the timeline of the event, and the people involved in the event. This can help improve the conceptual knowledge, critical thinking and individual learning patterns. Further research will be dedicated to the integration of KGs and neural networks for the improvement of the performance of the chatbot in educational context while having better explainability.

AI-Driven Emotional Intelligence and Sentiment-Aware Tutoring Systems

One of the key weaknesses in the present day educational chatbots is that they do not take into consideration the emotional state of the students. They identify that the gap of AI empathy can be filled through the integration of sentiment analysis, multimodal AI, and affective computing to the chatbot technology. In the future, chatbot systems will incorporate the use of NLP, facial recognition and voice intonation to identify frustration, confusion or motivation of the students. This may allow chatbots to adapt their answers, encourage clients or offer additional information depending on the detected emotions. Human-imitative sentiment-aware tutoring systems will generate new and more effective learning environments that reflect the positive emotions of a good teacher. The future research will be directed towards the improvement of the accuracy of the emotion recognition technologies and the assurance of the ethical use of the technology while protecting the privacy of the users.

CONCLUSION

The use of deep learning and transformer models to reinvent ITS has indeed paved the way to providing rich, finely tuned, and highly extended education made possible through interactive chatbots. The survey focused on the development of AI-based educational chatbots and their use in improving adaptability of learning, assessment, and motivation. Algorithms that are used for generating contextually sound and intelligent responses are more advanced than traditional rule-based systems; these are derived from deep learning algorithms which include RNNs, LSTM networks, CNNs as well as reinforcement learning algorithms. In addition, the use of transformer models has enhanced natural language understanding in the processing, comprehension and generation of human-like chats by the chatbots. The meeting on applications of the AI-based educational chatbots evidences the use of educational chatbots in tutoring, marking, translation, monitoring the performance of the students and peer learning. These chatbots use machine learning and NLP to provide immediate feedback and meet the learning requirements of the populace and close learning gaps across classes. In addition, the use of AI in chatbots increases access to education by offering assistive learning solutions for disabled students and learners from different parts of the world with poor English language skills. Nevertheless, a number of issues and limitations can still be identified as follows: This may result in poor quality and inadequate training data that will in turn provide poor or biased responses to the user. The black box nature of DL is a problem that hinders the ability of a tutor to trust an AI tutor and also the effectiveness of the tutoring. Some of the challenges include issues to do with ethical nature such as student data sharing, fake news generated by AI, and dependency on chatbots. Furthermore, the nature of the large-scale AI models in terms of the computational requirements is that they are expensive and not easily scalable to fit institutions with small budgets. The future trends in AI for education will include few-shot and zero-shot learning, integration of knowledge graphs, sentiment-aware tutoring, federated learning, as well as AI and human collaboration. Few-shot and zero-shot learning will enable the chatbots to learn new subjects with little data, while knowledge graphs will help the chatbots remember context and use logic in educational conversations. Emotionally intelligent chatbots will help to increase the level of students' activity by identifying frustration or confusion; federated learning will help to train privacy-preserving models that meet the requirements of the current data protection laws of different countries. Last but not the least, integration of AI in educational system will lead to the development of blended learning environment where AI will act as a complement to teachers and not a replacement. Lastly, deep learning and transformer models are revolutionizing intelligent tutoring systems and delivering the concepts of education on adjustment to the needful students' personalization. However, more research and development of technologies will result in better, more ethical, and more human-oriented AI-based learning solutions in the future.

REFERENCES

Alrakhawi, H. A., Jamiat, Nurullizam., & Abu-Naser, S. S. (2023). Intelligent tutoring systems in education: A systematic review of usage, tools, effects and evaluation. *Journal of Theoretical and Applied Information Technology*, *101*(4), 1205–1226.

Boopathi, S. (2023). Deep learning techniques applied for automatic sentence generation. In *Promoting Diversity, Equity, and Inclusion in Language Learning Environments* (pp. 255-273). IGI Global.

Chopde, A., & Agrawal, M. (2022, June). Chatbot using deep learning. In *Proceedings of the international conference on innovative computing & communication (ICICC)*.

Darwish, D. (Ed.). (2024). *Design and Development of Emerging Chatbot Technology*. IGI Global.

Davar, N. F., Dewan, M. A. A., & Zhang, X. (2025). AI chatbots in education: Challenges and opportunities. *Information (Basel)*, *16*(3), 235.

Dhinakaran, D., Kumar, N. J., & Ponnuviji, N. P. (2025). Safeguarding confidentiality and privacy in cloud-enabled healthcare systems with spectrasafe encryption and dynamic k-anonymity algorithm. *Expert Systems with Applications*, *279*, 127584.

Dhyani, M., & Kumar, R. (2021). An intelligent Chatbot using deep learning with Bidirectional RNN and attention model. *Materials Today: Proceedings*, *34*, 817–824. PMID: 32837917

Dinh, H., & Tran, T. K. (2023). EduChat: An AI-based chatbot for university-related information using a hybrid approach. *Applied Sciences (Basel, Switzerland)*, *13*(22), 12446.

Jain, V., Singh, I., Syed, M., Mondal, S., & Palai, D. R. (2024). Enhancing educational interactions: A comprehensive review of AI chatbots in learning environments. In *2024 11th international conference on reliability, infocom technologies and optimization (trends and future directions)(ICRITO)* (pp. 1-5). IEEE.

Kasthuri, E., & Balaji, S. (2023). Natural language processing and deep learning chatbot using long short term memory algorithm. *Materials Today: Proceedings*, *81*, 690–693.

Kavipriya, P., Jegan, G., Lakshmi, S., & Jebarani, M. E. (2024). Conversational Techniques Using Artificial Intelligence for Customer Support. In *Bio-Inspired Intelligence for Smart Decision-Making* (pp. 115–122). IGI Global.

Kuhail, M. A., Alturki, N., Alramlawi, S., & Alhejori, K. (2023). Interacting with educational chatbots: A systematic review. *Education and Information Technologies*, *28*(1), 973–1018.

Lin, C. C., Huang, A. Y., & Lu, O. H. (2023). Artificial intelligence in intelligent tutoring systems toward sustainable education: A systematic review. *Smart Learning Environments*, *10*(1), 41.

Mageira, K., Pittou, D., Papasalouros, A., Kotis, K., Zangogianni, P., & Daradoumis, A. (2022). Educational AI chatbots for content and language integrated learning. *Applied Sciences (Basel, Switzerland)*, *12*(7), 3239.

Maheswari, B., & Nagarajan, R. (2024). EduChatbot: Implementing educational Chatbot for assisting the teaching-learning process by NLP-based hybrid heuristic adopted deep learning framework. *Kybernetes*.

Patel, R., Patel, P., Bhatt, C. M., & Rahevar, M. L. (2021). Question Answering Chatbot Using Memory Networks. In *Handbook of Research on Applied Data Science and Artificial Intelligence in Business and Industry* (pp. 401–413). IGI Global.

Ponmalar, A., Vijayakumar, K., Lakshmipriya, C., Karthikeyan, M., Gracelin Sheena, B., Beslin Pajila, P. J., & Siva Subramanian, R. (2024). Meta-Heuristics and Machine Learning Applications in Complex Systems. In *Metaheuristic and Machine Learning Optimization Strategies for Complex Systems* (pp. 257–275). IGI Global Scientific Publishing.

Ponnuviji, N. P., Nirmala, G., Kokila, M. S., & Priyadharshini, S. I. (2025). Optimizing Image Retrieval in Cloud Servers with TN-AGW: A Secure and Efficient Approach. *Journal of The Institution of Engineers (India): Series B, 106*(2), 459-473.

Ponnuviji, N. P., Sumaiya Begum, A., Gnanasekaran, T., Rajendiran, M., & Shenbaga Ezhil, S. (2023, April). Leveraging Random Forest for Intelligent IoT Systems in Industrial Environments. In *International Conference on Internet of Things* (pp. 46-57). Cham: Springer Nature Switzerland.

Rajendran, T., Rajathi, S. A., Balakrishnan, C., Aswini, J., Prakash, R. B., & Subramanian, R. S. (2023, December). Risk Prediction Modeling for Breast Cancer using Supervised Machine Learning Approaches. In *2023 2nd International Conference on Automation, Computing and Renewable Systems (ICACRS)* (pp. 702-708). IEEE.

Ramineni, K., Harshith Reddy, K., Sai Thrikoteshwara Chary, L., Nikhil, L., & Akanksha, P. (2024, February). Designing an Intelligent Chatbot with Deep Learning: Leveraging FNN Algorithm for Conversational Agents to Improve the Chatbot Performance. In *World Conference on Artificial Intelligence: Advances and Applications* (pp. 143-151). Singapore: Springer Nature Singapore.

Saravanan, K., Prakash, R. B., Balakrishnan, C., Kumar, G. V. P., Subramanian, R. S., & Anita, M. (2023, December). Support Vector Machines: Unveiling the Power and Versatility of SVMs in Modern Machine Learning. In *2023 3rd International Conference on Innovative Mechanisms for Industry Applications (ICIMIA)* (pp. 680-687). IEEE.

Singh, A., Agarwal, A., Kumar, A., Rastogi, U., & Kumar, S. (2024, June). A Comprehensive Approach to Stress Detection and Management Using Machine Learning, Deep Learning, and Chatbot Integration. In *2024 15th International Conference on Computing Communication and Networking Technologies (ICCCNT)* (pp. 1-5). IEEE.

Solanki, R. K., Rajawat, A. S., Gadekar, A. R., & Patil, M. E. (2023). Building a conversational chatbot using machine learning: Towards a more intelligent healthcare application. In *Handbook of research on instructional technologies in health education and allied disciplines* (pp. 285–309). IGI Global Scientific Publishing.

Subramanian, R. S., Prabha, D., Aswini, J., Maheswari, B., & Anita, M. (2021, February). Alleviating NB conditional independence using multi-stage variable selection (MSVS): Banking customer dataset application. [). IOP Publishing.]. *Journal of Physics: Conference Series*, *1767*(1), 012002.

Uma, S. (2023). Conversational AI Chatbots in digital engagement: Privacy and security concerns. In *Trends, applications, and challenges of Chatbot technology* (pp. 274–317). IGI Global.

Wong, A. (2022). The design of an intelligent chatbot with natural language processing capabilities to support learners. [). IOP Publishing.]. *Journal of Physics: Conference Series*, *2251*(1), 012005.

Yamini, B., Ramana, K. V., Nalini, M., Devi, D. C., Maheswari, B., & Siva, S. R. (2024). Customer churn prediction model in enterprises using machine learning. *International Journal of Advanced Technology and Engineering Exploration*, *11*(110), 94.

Chapter 6

Analyzing the Performance of Artificial Intelligence–Based Chatbot in Answering National Exam Chemistry Questions: Gemini Example

Nagihan Kadıoğlu
https://orcid.org/0000-0003-4911-8985
Hacettepe University, Turkey

Harun Önder
Hacettepe University, Turkey

Özge Özyalçın Oskay
https://orcid.org/0000-0002-9368-5381
Hacettepe University, Turkey

ABSTRACT

The purpose of this study is to examine the performance of the artificial intelligence-based Gemini chatbot (CB) in answering chemistry questions from the national exam held annually. In this context, seven chemistry questions from the 2021 Basic Competency Test (TYT) prepared by the Measurement, Selection, and Placement Center (ÖSYM) were examined. The TYT chemistry questions were divided into two categories—multiple-choice and open-ended questions—without altering the

DOI: 10.4018/979-8-3373-6791-0.ch006

ght © 2026, IGI Global Scientific Publishing. Copying or distributing in print or electronic forms without written permission of IGI Global Scientific Publishing is prohibited. Use of this chapter to generative artificial intelligence (AI) technologies is expressly prohibited. The publisher reserves all rights to license its use for generative AI training and machine learning model development.

question order or format from the original textbook, and were then posed to the CB. CB's answers were reviewed by three experts. According to the findings of the study, CB answered 85.71% of the multiple-choice questions correctly, which required reading comprehension and interpretation, but made significant errors in solving one question. In the open-ended questions, it provided detailed and clear explanations and answered all the questions. While providing clear explanations for all the open-ended questions, it answered 85.71% correctly. As a result, CB provided consistent answers to scientific concepts.

ARTIFICIAL INTELLIGENCE AND ITS HISTORICAL EVOLUTION

Nowadays, with the development of computer-aided technologies, there have been significant developments especially in software innovations. With the rapid and comprehensive digitisation of society, technology products and applications have become an integral part of daily life, and individuals have begun to live within the dynamics of the digital age (Selwyn, 2021). Education is one of the fields most affected by the rapid technological advancements. Education has changed from a passive structure to a more interactive and proactive process through the use of technology, which is assessed in four ways: as a component of the curriculum, as a system for delivering instruction, as a tool to support the teaching process, and as a way to improve the overall learning experience (Raja & Nagasubramani, 2018). One of the technological developments that can help to effectively implement the teaching-learning process is artificial intelligence (AI) (Yildirim & Akcan, 2024). The concept of artificial intelligence was first introduced to the world in 1956 by John McCarthy. It has continued its rapid development over time, and in 2018, the Generative Pre-trained Transformer (GPT), a Large Language Model (LLM) that can imitate human dialogue, was developed by OpenAI (Lund & Wang, 2023). Although there is no common approach to integrating artificial intelligence into educational environments due to the novelty and current uncertainty surrounding the concept, countries such as China, United States, Canada, and South Korea are planning to include artificial intelligence in their educational curricula by investing in this field with the aim of training individuals who are literate in artificial intelligence (Yildirim & Akcan, 2024).

AI systems, which are created by humans to fulfil certain tasks and continuously improve themselves with the knowledge they acquire, imitate humans (Kuleto et al., 2022). Especially with the emergence of AI-based chatbots, many requirements needed in daily life, including the education system, have been affected. The most important impact of chatbots started with ChatGPT and Gemini (Arman & Lamiyar, 2023). Like these chatbots, other AI-based chatbots have been developed and continue to be developed.

Use of Chatbots in Education

In the educational process, chatbots are considered as one of the artificial intelligence-based technologies that are seen as a good solution to analyse the personal needs of each student and create a suitable learning method with personalised educational content. There is evidence that chatbots can change the way students search for information and learn. Nowadays, e-learning and Massive Online Courses can be a supporting tool or alternative to chatbots. In cases where physical classrooms are not possible, as we experienced in the COVID-19 era (Zobel et al., 2023), chatbots can be a solution to provide social distance and continuity in face-to-face classrooms. The use of chatbots in education can help reduce the negative impact on students during pandemic periods (Gaglo et al., 2021).

The most effective aspect of chatbots in education is their ability to simplify the learning process by providing learners with resources previously tailored to their personal learning level. The integration of chatbots into the e-learning system can fill the gap of face-to-face counselling that is not available in offline courses, responding to the personal needs of each learner. The interaction and communication skills of chatbots are categorised using different parameters such as knowledge domain, service offered, goals and effects (Lakshmi et al., 2022). According to Kasthuri and Balaji (2021), the knowledge domain is as much as the knowledge possessed by the chatbot. Moreover, with the use of chatbots in education, students can correct their mistakes at any time without human support.

Efforts are being made for chatbot software to improve individualised education. Developers, researchers and academics are working freely for chatbot applications to enhance education with technology. Researchers such as Hobert (2019), Okonkwo and Ade-Ibijola (2021) and Kuhail et al. (2023) have conducted a systematic review of chatbots in education. Hobert (2019) focused on the methods used to evaluate pedagogical dialogues; Okonkwo and Ade-Ibijola (2021) reviewed 53 articles to examine the benefits and challenges of chatbots in education; Kuhail et al. (2023) analysed 36 articles to understand and compare recent research on the use of chatbots in seven categories, including educational domain, platform, design principles, role of chatbots, interaction styles, evidence, and limitations.

Limitations in the Use of Chatbots

There are criticisms that the answers prepared by artificial intelligence-based chatbots are not always correct, that they make comments based on incorrect/incomplete data, or that they produce incorrect/untrue information (Han et al., 2023). Inaccurate or incomplete answers given by artificial intelligence tools can be an important challenge that prevents meaningful learning for students (Clark, 2023).

LLMs are based on detailed learning and focus on statistics and probabilities without understanding what the world is really like. Reliable answers can be obtained if there is sufficient data and training from a particular discipline. However, if the question is complex and they do not have enough learning about the question, their answer may be wrong and may lead to so-called hallucinations or bias (Kwak & Pardos, 2024; Williams, 2024).

Moreover, training data and models used for machine learning are corrected and evaluated by humans (Murphy, 2019). Since there are no defined guidelines for AI applications in education (Nichols & Holmes, 2018), weaknesses of AI tools may have negative consequences for education due to the increasing interest of AI researchers, product developers, risk managers and educational technology advocates in the education market (Murphy, 2019). The use of AI tools and technological solutions in education raises the question of 'who sets the teaching and learning agenda' (Popenici & Kerr, 2017).

Chatbots and Ethics

It is also not ethically appropriate for artificial intelligence-based chatbots to do homework or answer exams instead of students (Mhlanga, 2023; Susnjak, 2022). In order to minimise such problems, it is suggested that online exams or assignments should be given in the form of questions or assignments that require higher-order thinking skills instead of multiple-choice or short-answer questions (Geerling et al., 2023; Susnjak, 2022). In addition, who trains these software? How is it trained? Such a powerful technology can be manipulated for reasons such as. Algorithms developed to process data can potentially be created by programmers who may have biases (Nichols & Holmes, 2018). Holmes (2018) argues that 'worldwide, virtually no research has been conducted, no guidelines provided, no policies developed, and no regulations enacted to address the specific ethical issues raised by the AI-based education system'. The need for ethical frameworks for AI in education is exacerbated by the potential for research-oriented organisations to experiment on university students. To give an example, an application pseudonymised as Jill Watson (a Virtual Teaching Assistant developed by an academic at Georgia Tech in the computer science module) was implemented disguised as a chatbot. It was observed that it responded late to the answers. Comments posted in response to the article publicising Jill Watson reveal ethical tensions (McFarland, 2016).

The stronger AI-based CBs become and the more they become a standard feature of everyday life, the more critical ethical issues become. It attempts to apply data in objective ways. However, there is no such thing as 'raw data' as the source data is not free from bias (Gitelman & Jackson, 2013). Moreover, algorithms designed to process data according to the preferences set by AI engineers themselves have ethical implications. There are examples where AI systems reflect sexist, racist and other discriminatory behaviours, and where the use of AI systems reinforces and reproduces negative data in a vicious cycle (Crawford, 2016). Furthermore, according to Parker (2018), it is clear that personal data may have the potential to undermine democracy through AI algorithms. AI-based CB utilises data and therefore faces the same ethical issues as analytics (Prinsloo & Slade, 2016). It seems that chatbots inevitably reflect the motivations of their developers and interact with a world where decisions have ethical consequences.

Chatbot Gemini

Gemini is an AI-based chatbot developed by Google and Alphabet, Google's parent company, and contributed to its development by Google Deep Mind. Gemini is able to understand not only text but also content in different formats such as images, audio, video; answer complex problems in mathematics, physics, chemistry and other fields, as well as create and respond to codes in various programming languages. As a basic resource for the preparation of course curricula, teaching materials and evaluation strategies, Gemini can be useful for educators. However, concerns arise about the authenticity of the content it produces, (McIntosh et al., 2023). A potential solution could be to develop educational material specific to any course using the Gemini chatbot. For example, educators can use Gemini as a 'native speaker' to simulate conversations and support students' learning of English, (Yaacoub et al., 2023). Furthermore, Gemini has the potential to enhance active learning methodologies. For example, educators can implement flipped learning approaches where students interact with the course content before class. This model allows for more participatory learning activities such as group discussions during class sessions. However, traditional flipped classrooms have faced challenges during the COVID-19 pandemic, and online education has resulted in reduced class participation and limited peer interaction, (Jones 2023; Perera et al., 2023; Xie 2023). Acting as a virtual instructor, Gemini can help students conduct independent online research by addressing their questions and encouraging collaboration through structured discussion frameworks and immediate feedback. These functionalities underline Gemini's potential to improve learning outcomes and encourage engagement in online learning environments (Venkatesh & Venkatesha 2024). Furthermore, the combination of Gemini and the Internet of Things holds promise in advancing online education by transforming the way educators and students use modern educational platforms to enhance their teaching and learning experiences (Rane, 2024). By establishing the relationship between the Internet of Things and Natural Language Processing, it enables Gemini and educators to engage in natural dialogues instantly using a variety of online collaboration tools such as instant messaging applications and video conferencing systems accessible via tablets, e-readers and smartphones (Venkatesh & Venkatesha 2024).

According to a study examining the success of AI-based chatbots, Clark (2023) ChatGPT was used to answer two final exam questions of the undergraduate general chemistry course; closed-ended and open-ended questions were asked. In closed-ended questions, it was observed that the students were very skilful in defining the concept even if the question heavily involved the symbolic language of chemistry. However, the problem solving success of ChatGPT was 44%, which is well below the class average of 69%. His answers in open-ended questions showed higher performance in questions that can be solved with general knowledge compared to questions that require detailed knowledge, especially in general chemistry topics. Incorrect answers and incomplete explanations may be convincing for those who do not have sufficient domain knowledge. The chatbot is not equipped to provide students with reliable answers or explanations for representative exam questions, but potentially to create assignments where students analyse and improve their answers. In another study, Daher et al. (2023) asked ChatGPT to solve 30 chemistry problems and 43.33% answered the questions correctly without conceptual difficulty. This showed that ChatGPT can accompany students in solving chemistry problems in a promising way. Therefore, it is suggested that ChatGPT should be integrated into the chemistry course to support students' learning. ChatGPT was also asked to answer questions about his ability in topics related to conceptual understanding in chemistry, but it revealed that it could not work with voice expressions.

Based on the above explanations and examples, further research is needed to investigate the performance of CBs and to examine the factors affecting this performance. It is recommended to conduct research on the Gemini chatbot to answer questions related to chemistry education. Because the studies on Gemini are quite few.

Higher Education Institutions Examination (YKS)

In Turkey, students who want to study at university are subjected to a two-stage exam after completing their high school programme. These exams have been prepared and implemented by the Centre for Measurement, Selection and Placement (ÖSYM) since 1974. In 2018, ÖSYM made a change in the exam format and switched to a two-stage exam under the general name of Higher Education Institutions Exam (YKS). The first stage is the Basic Proficiency Test (TYT) and the second stage is the Field Proficiency Test (AYT), which are multiple-choice measurement tools. However, candidates who want to study university departments that provide education in foreign languages are required to take the third stage Foreign Language Test (YDT) exam.

The TYT exam measures the reading comprehension and interpretation skills of prospective students. In addition, the exam questions are prepared according to the 2018 Ministry of National Education (MoNE) Curriculum, taking into account the 9th and 10th grade curriculum. TYT exam consists of Turkish, social sciences, maths and science tests. The Turkish test includes 40 questions on grammar and paragraph topics related to the ability to use Turkish. In the social sciences test, there are 20 questions including History, Geography, Philosophy, Religious Culture and Ethics / Philosophy branches based on thinking with basic concepts and principles in social sciences. The mathematics test consists of 40 skill-based questions about the ability to make use of mathematical relationships and includes mathematics-geometry branches. Science test consists of 20 questions based on thinking with basic concepts and principles in science. It covers physics, chemistry and biology branches. There are 7 chemistry questions. The TYT exam is problematic for all candidates. In order to calculate the TYT score, candidates must have at least 0.5 raw points in the Basic Mathematics Test or Turkish Test. The exam duration is 165 minutes. TYT contribution to the exam score is 40%.

The AYT exam consists of questions that test knowledge and involve numerical calculations. The test questions are prepared in accordance with the 2018 MoNE Teaching Program for the 11th and 12th grade curriculum. There are four different types of scores in the AYT exam: equal weight, numerical, verbal, and foreign language. Candidates must take the exams corresponding to these score types according to the university departments they wish to apply to. For the AYT equal weight score calculation, the Turkish Language and Literature-Social Sciences-1 test must be taken, for the verbal score calculation, the Social Sciences-2 test must be taken, and for the numerical score calculation, the Mathematics and Science test must be taken. Each test consists of 40 questions. The AYT contributes 60% to the exam score. The exam duration is 180 minutes. The YDT consists of 80 questions from German, Arabic, French, English, and Russian tests.

The YKS is a ranking exam. Candidates are ranked nationwide according to their scores. Applications for university preferences are made according to this ranking. Applications are submitted electronically to ÖSYM. Based on data collected nationwide, ÖSYM announces the results, determining whether candidates have been accepted into their preferred universities based on their success rankings. Successful candidates contact the relevant university and complete the registration process electronically.

Purpose of the Study

Today, AI technologies are increasingly being integrated into educational curricula; therefore, teachers need to have a high level of knowledge about these technologies and detailed information about their usage skills. Any deficiencies in this regard are a critical obstacle to fully realizing the potential of technology and optimizing its applications in education (Işler and Kılıç, 2021).

This study aims to analyze the performance of the AI-based Gemini chatbot, introduced on March 21, 2023, by examining its responses to multiple-choice and open-ended questions from the Higher Education Institutions Exam Basic Proficiency Chemistry Test administered in Turkey. This study will examine how the Gemini chatbot responds to assessment tools used in chemistry education, as well as the accuracy, limitations, and shortcomings of these responses. It will serve as a guide for teachers and students who use this chatbot.

Research Questions

1. What is the chatbot's level of success in answering questions?
2. How does the chatbot respond to questions?
3. How understandable are the chatbot's responses?

METHOD

Research Design

In this study, a case study design was used, taking into account the qualitative research method, as it analyzed the answers given by the Gemini chatbot to multiple-choice and open-ended questions from the TYT Chemistry exam. This is because the responses provided in the study will be examined in detail. A case study is a technique used to deeply describe, examine, and interpret a person, event, or situation in a natural environment (Yıldırım and Şimşek, 2018). A case study is a methodological approach that involves the in-depth examination of a limited system using multiple data collection methods to systematically gather information about how that system works and operates (Chmiliar, 2010). A case study is an in-depth description and examination of a limited system (Merriam, 2013). To understand the case study design, the case must be defined. A case is defined as a phenomenon observed at a single point in time or over a specific period of time (Gerring, 2007).

Data Collection Tool

The data set used in the study consisted of multiple-choice questions from the 2021 TYT Chemistry exam and the open-ended versions of these questions. The questions on the scale were asked in the order given in the 2021 TYT basic booklet. It consists of 7 multiple-choice questions and their open-ended versions prepared by us. The questions are based on the achievements of the 9th and 10th grades of the secondary school chemistry course and require the interpretation of information. Care was taken to ensure that the questions did not contain any visuals or symbols that the chatbot could not read. The opinions of two experts in the field of chemistry education were sought to verify that the questions were suitable for the chatbot. Table 1 shows which grade curriculum of the chemistry teaching program the questions belong to.

Table 1. Distribution of questions by grade level and learning outcome

Question	Grade	Learning Outcome
1	9th grade	Matches the formulas of compounds with their names.
2	9th grade	Explains the principles of the arrangement of elements in the periodic table.
3	9th grade	Explains the formation of metallic bonds.
4	9th grade	Explains the concept of equilibrium vapor pressure through the processes of evaporation and condensation in closed containers.
5	10th grade	Performs calculations by relating the concepts of mass, mole number, molecule number, atom number, and volume under normal conditions for gases.
6	10th grade	Explains the properties of solutions using examples from everyday life.
7	10th grade.	Explains the important reactions of acids and bases in everyday life..

On June 26, 2021, 2,592,390 students applied to take the TYT exam. While 2,416,974 candidates took the exam, 175,416 candidates did not take the exam. The number of candidates whose exams were deemed invalid was 226 (ÖSYM 2021).

FINDINGS

In the study, the Gemini chatbot was asked to answer questions from the 2021 TYT Chemistry exam. The exam questions consisted of two different types: 7 multiple-choice questions and 7 open-ended questions. (Prompted)

- When examining the research question, “What is the chatbot's level of success in answering the questions?”

When the Gemini chatbot's answers to the multiple-choice test questions in the 2021 TYT Chemistry exam were examined, it was observed that it answered 6 out of 7 questions correctly and 1 question incorrectly. It answered 85.71% of the questions correctly. There were no questions that it answered by chance without understanding the question. It provided reasonable answers to all questions. It gave an incorrect/wrong answer to one question due to its complexity. The other answers are in line with the chemistry curriculum and the institution that prepared the exam.

Similarly, when the answers given to the questions converted to an open-ended format by us were examined, it was seen that detailed answers were given to all 7 questions. It is possible to say that Gemini chatbot's interpretation skills are more prominent than its numerical skills. However, 6 of the answers given here are correct, and 1 is incorrect. It answered 85.71% of the questions correctly. While all of the answers provided are consistent with chemistry literature, the answer to one question introduced the concept of “attractivity,” which is not part of the chemistry curriculum. Additionally, it was unable to provide an answer consistent with the 9th-grade curriculum for one of the questions and instead solved it by considering the 11th-grade curriculum. Even though it was not in line with the curriculum, it provided the correct solution. In addition, it provided a detailed explanation for the one question it answered incorrectly. However, due to the high level of complexity of the question, its explanations were incorrect/incomplete, and the examples it provided were incorrect.

- When examining the research questions “How are the chatbot's answers to questions?” and “How understandable are the chatbot's answers?”, the chatbot's answers were analyzed in detail.

The first question in TYT Chemistry is in Table 2, and the CB answer is in Table 3.

Table 2. 2021 TYT chemistry question 1

1. What is the common name of the compound whose systematic name is nitrogen trihydride? A) Ammonia B) Nitric acid (*commonly referred to as ‘kezzap’ in Turkish) C) Muriatic acid D) Caustic potash E) Slaked lime

Table 3. Gemini answer

Answer: Ammonia Ammonia is the common name for nitrogen trihydride.

Question 9, prepared in accordance with the 2018 Chemistry Teaching Program, belongs to the 9th grade Chemistry Science unit "Matches the formulas of compounds with their names." According to section b of the relevant learning outcome, "b. The common names of the compounds H_2O, HCl, H_2SO_4, HNO_3, CH_3COOH, $CaCO_3$, $NaHCO_3$, NH_3, $Ca(OH)_2$, NaOH, KOH, CaO and NaCl are introduced." The question requires the student to answer the common name of the compound NH3, which is required to be known according to the curriculum. In the multiple-choice test, CB answered the question clearly and concisely without going into any details. The question was answered correctly.

Table 4. 2021 TYT chemistry question 2

2. The places of the elements He, N, and Mg in the periodic table are shown below
2. The places of the elements He, N, and Mg in the periodic table are shown below.
Which of the following describes the relationship between the number of electrons in the outermost shells of these atoms in their ground state? A) He = N > Mg B) Mg > N > He C) N > Mg = He D) N > Mg > He E) He > N > Mg

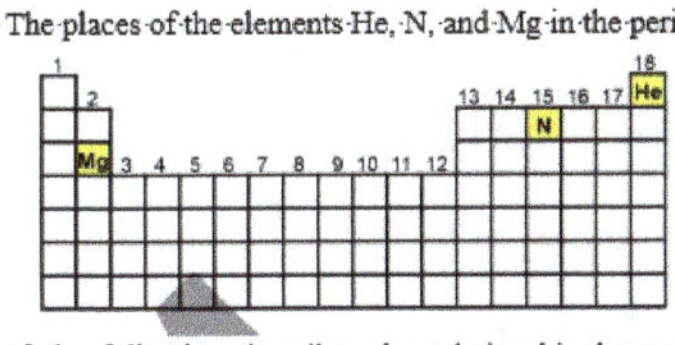

Which of the following describes the relationship between the number of electrons in the outermost shells of these atoms in their ground state?
A) He = N > Mg B) Mg > N > He C) N > Mg = He
D) N > Mg > He E) He > N > Mg

Table 5. Gemini answer

Answer: C) N > Mg = He • He (Helium): As it is a noble gas, it has 2 electrons in its outermost shell. • N (Nitrogen): As it is in group 5A, it has 5 electrons in its outermost shell. • Mg (Magnesium): As it is in group 2A, it has 2 electrons in its outermost shell. Based on this information, nitrogen has the most electrons (5) in its outermost shell, while helium and magnesium have the same number of electrons (2) in their outermost shells. Therefore, the correct answer is option C (N > Mg = He).

This question from the 9th grade Atom and Periodic Table unit assesses the learning outcome "Explains the principles of the arrangement of elements in the periodic table." The number of electrons in the outermost layer of an atom (the number of valence electrons) generally gives the group number. However, there is an exception here. Although the He atom is in group 8A, its valence electron number is 2. Attention should be paid to this point in the question. The question expects the interpretation of the number of electrons in the outermost layers (valence electron number) of the elements given in the periodic table. CB has demonstrated the expected behavior and specified the separate groups of elements. It has not overlooked the exception of the He atom. It has provided the correct answer to the question.

The third question in TYT Chemistry is in Table 6, and the CB answer is in Table 7.

Table 6. 2021 TYT chemistry question 3

3. The electron sea model, which was proposed to explain how metallic bonds are formed, can be used to explain some of the properties of metals. According to this model, which of the following properties of metals can be explained by the electron sea model? I. Conducting electricity, II. Being able to be made into wires and sheets, III. Reacting with nonmetals? A) Only I B) Only II C) Yalnız III D) I ve II E) II ve III

Table 7. Gemini answer

Answer: D) I ve II The electron sea model states that in metals, positively charged ions are surrounded by electrons that move freely in a sea. This model is used to explain some of the properties of metals. • I. Conducting Electricity: Freely moving electrons act as electrical charge carriers and, when an electric field is applied, these electrons move easily to provide an electric current. • II. Formability into Wires and Sheets: The bonds between atoms in metals are not directional. Therefore, metals can be formed into wires or sheets without resistance to deformation. • III. Reaction with Nonmetals: This property cannot be directly explained by the electron sea model. Reactions with nonmetals are related to factors such as the tendency of metals to donate electrons and the tendency of nonmetals to accept electrons. In conclusion, while the properties of metals conducting electricity and being able to be formed into wires or sheets can be explained by the electron sea model, the property of reacting with nonmetals cannot be explained by this model. The correct answer is option D.

The force that holds metal atoms together is called a metallic bond. The electrons in the outermost layer of metal atoms (valence electrons) are also attracted by the nuclei of other metal atoms. Therefore, valence electrons are in constant motion. This situation creates an electron sea model. Our question is related to the 9th grade

Chemical Interactions unit "Explains the formation of metallic bonds." The electron sea model is used to explain the metallic bond. CB first provided an explanation related to the metallic bond. It made statements based on the premises related to the characteristics of this model. When related to the premises, it stated that premises I and II could be explained by the electron sea model, while premise III could not be explained by this model. It answered the question correctly.

The fourth question in the TYT chemistry exam is shown in Table 8, and CB's answer is shown in Table 9.

Table 8. 2021 TYT chemistry question 4

2. In an experiment, a certain amount of pure water is placed in a closed container from which the air has been removed and to which a manometer has been attached. As the amount of liquid water decreases over time, the pressure measured by the manometer increases. After waiting long enough at a constant temperature, it is observed that the amount of liquid water and the pressure measured by the manometer remain unchanged, and this pressure value (P1) is recorded. The experiment is then repeated at the same constant temperature with the amount of pure water doubled, and the pressure value (P2) is recorded. Accordingly; I. When the amount of water is doubled, the evaporation rate increases. II. P2 > P1. III. The values P1 and P2 are the equilibrium vapor pressure of water. Which of the following statements are correct? A) Only I B) Only III C) I ve II D) II ve III E) I, II ve III

Table 9. Gemini answer

Answer: B) Only III The events observed in this experiment can be explained by the concept of vapor pressure of a liquid. • I. When the amount of water doubles, the evaporation rate increases: This statement is incorrect. In a closed system, at a given temperature, the evaporation rate of a liquid depends not on the amount of liquid but on the size of the liquid-vapor interface. Since the volume of the container is constant in this experiment, increasing the amount of liquid does not increase the evaporation rate. • II. P2 > P1: This statement is also incorrect. At a constant temperature, the vapor pressure of a liquid depends solely on the type of liquid. Changing the amount of liquid does not change the vapor pressure. • III. P1 and P2 values are the equilibrium vapor pressure of water: This statement is correct. In the experiment, the system reaches equilibrium after a while, and the evaporation rate equals the condensation rate. In this case, the pressure exerted by the vapor inside the container equals the equilibrium vapor pressure of water at that temperature. Changing the amount of liquid does not change the equilibrium vapor pressure; it only affects the time it takes to reach equilibrium. Therefore, only statement III is correct. That is, the P1 and P2 values are equal to the equilibrium vapor pressure of water at that temperature.

Question 9 relates to the 9th grade States of Matter unit, which explains the concept of equilibrium vapor pressure through the processes of evaporation and condensation in closed containers. It can be seen that CB examined the given premises one by one. In the first premise, it stated that the premise was incorrect by mentioning what the evaporation rate depends on. Similarly, in the second premise, it correctly states that it is incorrect. In the third premise, it clearly explains that the pressure values given in the question (P1 and P2) are the equilibrium vapor pressure of water and that changes in the amount of liquid do not affect this pressure. It has provided the correct answer to the question.

The fifth question in the TYT chemistry exam is shown in Table 10, and the CB answer is shown in Table 11.

Table 10. 2021 TYT chemistry question 5

5. Phosphorus trichloride can be obtained from white phosphorus and chlorine gas according to the following reaction. $P_{4\,(s)} + 6Cl_{2\,(g)} \rightarrow 4PCl_{3\,(g)}$ Accordingly, how many moles of PCl_3 can be obtained from the reaction of 12.4 g of P_4 solid and 21.3 g of Cl_2 gas? (Cl_2 = 71 g/mol, P_4 = 124 g/mol) A) 0,05 B) 0,1 C) 0,2 D) 0,3 E) 0,4

Table 11. Gemini answer

Answer: Let's solve the question: Given: • P_4 (s) + $6Cl_2$ (g) → $4PCl_3$ (g) • m(P_4) = 12,4 g • m(Cl_2) = 21,3 g • M(Cl_2) = 71 g/mol • M(P_4) = 124 g/mol Requested: What is the maximum number of moles of PCl_3 that can be obtained? Solution: 1. Mol Calculations: o n(P_4) = m(P_4) / M(P_4) = 12,4 g / 124 g/mol = 0,1 mol o n(Cl_2) = m(Cl_2) / M(Cl_2) = 21,3 g / 71 g/mol ≈ 0,3 mol 2. Finding the Limited Reactant: According to the given reaction, 1 mole of P_4 reacts with 6 moles of Cl_2. o The amount of Cl_2 required for 0.1 mol of P_4: 0.1 mol P_4 * (6 mol Cl_2 / 1 mol P_4) = 0.6 mol Cl_2 However, we only have 0.3 mol of Cl_2. In this case, Cl_2 is the limiting reactant, and P_4 is the excess reactant. 3. Amount of PCl_3 Produced: We will calculate based on the limiting reactant, Cl_2. o If 4 moles of PCl_3 are formed from 6 moles of Cl_2, o then approximately 0.2 moles of PCl_3 are formed from 0.3 moles of Cl_2 (0.3 moles of Cl_2 * (4 moles of PCl_3 / 6 moles of Cl_2)). Answer: A maximum of 0.2 mol of PCl_3 can be obtained. The correct answer is option C. Explanation: Since chlorine gas (Cl_2) is present in limited quantities in this reaction, the reaction will continue until all the chlorine is consumed, resulting in the formation of 0.2 mol of PCl_3. The excess phosphorus will remain unreacted.

Question 10 belongs to the unit "Fundamental Laws of Chemistry and Chemical Calculations" in the 10th grade chemistry curriculum, which states, "Performs calculations by relating the concepts of mass, mole number, molecule number, atom number, and volume under normal conditions for gases." The question focuses on limiting component calculations. CB chose to solve the question using verbal expressions rather than numerical expressions and symbols. Nevertheless, he provided a successful solution. First, he prepared a list of given values. Then, in step 1, it calculated the mole numbers of the substances with given masses. However, although the molar mass of Cl_2 was given in the question (71 g/mol), it found the molar mass of Cl_2 to be approximately 0.3. In fact, it should have said 21.3/71 = 0.3. It may have obtained this value from the Cl_2 mass in the database. In step 2, it used verbal expressions to find the limiting component. However, a more understandable solution could have been produced by setting up a chemical equation and writing the given values below the equation. In the third and final step, it again used verbal expressions to indicate the amount of PCl_3 obtained. Although it solved the question using verbal expressions, it answered correctly. In addition, in the explanation section at the end, it provided information about the excess substance.

The sixth question in the TYT chemistry exam is shown in Table 12, and the CB answer is shown in Table 13.

Table 12. 2021 TYT chemistry question 6

6. In an experiment, 1000 grams of pure water is placed in three separate containers. To the first container, 1 mole of NaCl is added; to the second, 1 mole of sucrose; and to the third, 1 mole of $MgCl_2$, resulting in solutions A, B, and C, respectively. The prepared solutions are heated in an environment where the external pressure is 1 atm, and the temperatures at which the solutions begin to boil (TA, TB, and TC) are measured.

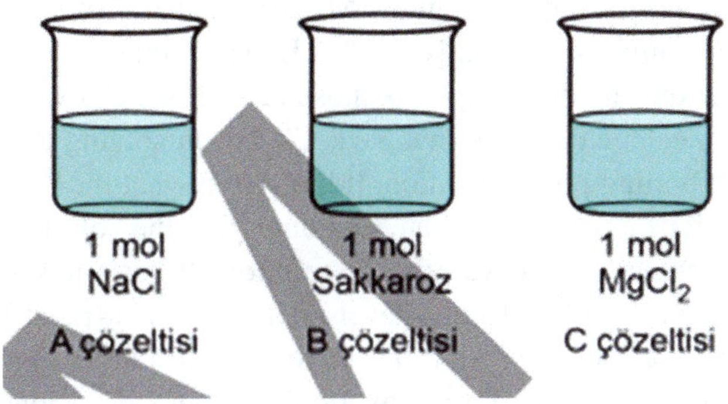

Accordingly, which of the following correctly shows the relationship between the measured TA, TB, and TC temperatures? (It is assumed that the NaCl and $MgCl_2$ salts completely dissociate into their ions in water, while sucrose dissolves molecularly.)

A) $T_A = T_B = T_C$ B) $T_A > T_B > T_C$ C) $T_B > T_C > T_A$ D) $T_A = T_C > T_B$ E) $T_C > T_A > T_B$

Table 13. Gemini answer

Answer:
Solution:
Boiling Point Elevation
As the amount of solute in a solution increases, the vapor pressure of the solution decreases and, consequently, the boiling point rises. This phenomenon is called boiling point elevation. Boiling point elevation is directly related to the type of solute and the number of particles in the solution.

Comparison of Solutions:

- Solution A (NaCl): NaCl completely dissociates into its ions (Na+ and Cl-) in water. Therefore, 1 mole of NaCl forms 2 moles of particles in solution.
- Solution B (Sucrose): Sucrose dissolves molecularly in water, so 1 mole of sucrose forms 1 mole of particles in solution.
- Solution C ($MgCl_2$): $MgCl_2$ completely dissociates into its ions (Mg^{2+} and $2Cl^-$) in water. Therefore, 1 mole of $MgCl_2$ forms 3 moles of particles in the solution.

Result:

- Since the boiling point increases as the number of particles in the solution increases, the order of temperatures will be as follows:
- $T_C > T_A > T_B$

Reason:

- Solution C ($MgCl_2$), having the most particles, has the highest boiling point (TC).
- Solution A (NaCl), having more particles than solution B, has a higher boiling point (TA) than solution B.
- Solution B (sucrose) has the lowest boiling point (TB) because it has the fewest particles.

Answer: E) $T_C > T_A > T_B$
Additional Information:
In such questions, the degree of ionization of the solute and the total number of particles in the solution are important. Substances with a high degree of ionization and that form more particles in the solution raise the boiling point more.

Question 10 belongs to the 10th grade Mixtures unit, "Explains the properties of solutions with examples from daily life." a. Explains that the freezing and boiling points of solutions are different from those of solvents and vary depending on concentration. No calculations are involved. CB began solving the question with an explanation of boiling point elevation. It has stated what the boiling point temperatures of solutions depend on. Then, by comparing the solutions, it has found the number of particles they have after dissolution. It has tried to explain their dissolution at the ionic and molecular levels. The important point to note here is the number of ions or molecules that the dissolved substances give to water. CB paid attention to this point and did not overlook the number of ions or molecules of the substances given in the image above. It stated that sucrose dissolves at the molecular level. In the conclusion, it stated that there is a direct correlation between the boiling point temperatures and the number of particles in solutions formed as a result of the dissolution of substances with equal molar quantities. CB answered the question correctly.

The seventh question in the TYT chemistry exam is shown in Table 14, and the CB answer is shown in Table 15.

Table 14. 2021 TYT chemistry question 7

7. The following information is given about the aqueous solutions of compounds X and Y:

• When the aqueous solution of X reacts with zinc (Zn), which exhibits amphoteric properties, hydrogen gas is released.

• When the aqueous solution of Y reacts with copper (Cu), which is a semi-noble metal, gas is released.

• When X reacts with Y, salt and water are formed.

Accordingly, which of the following could compounds X and Y be?

	X	Y
A)	HCl	NaOH
B)	NaOH	HCl
C)	HNO_3	NaOH
D)	KOH	HCl
E)	NaOH	HNO_3

Table 15. Gemini answer

Answer: Let's solve the question:

Given information:

X: A compound that reacts with zinc (Zn) to release hydrogen gas.

Y: A compound that reacts with copper (Cu) to release gas.

X and Y: Compounds that react with each other to form salt and water.

Solution:

X Compound:

Zinc (Zn) is an amphoteric metal. It reacts with both acids and bases.

The release of hydrogen gas indicates that compound X is an acid.

Y Compound:

Copper (Cu) does not react easily with acids, although not as much as noble metals.

The fact that compound Y reacts with copper to release gas suggests that compound Y is a strong oxidizing agent.

Evaluating the Options:

A) HCl and NaOH: HCl is an acid, NaOH is a base. HCl reacts with zinc to release hydrogen gas, but NaOH does not react directly with copper.

B) NaOH and HCl: NaOH is a base, HCl is an acid. NaOH reacts with zinc to release hydrogen gas, but does not react directly with copper.

C) HNO3 and NaOH: HNO3 is a strong acid, and NaOH is a strong base. HNO3 can react with both zinc and copper to release different gases such as NO gas. This option is consistent with the given information.

D) KOH and HCl: KOH is a base, and HCl is an acid. KOH reacts with zinc to produce hydrogen gas, but does not react directly with copper.

E) NaOH and HNO3: Evaluated the same as option C.

Result:

The option most consistent with the given information is **C) HNO_3 and NaOH**. HNO_3 (nitric acid) can react with both zinc and copper to release gas, and NaOH (sodium hydroxide), as a base, can react with the acids in the other options to form salt and water.

Answer: C

Question 10th grade Acids, Bases, and Salts unit "Explains the important reactions of acids and bases in daily life." a. Examples are given of reactions in which acids and bases interact with metals to form hydrogen gas; the concepts of active metal, semi-noble metal, noble metal, and amphoteric metal are emphasized. CB made significant errors in solving this question. After listing the given information, it proceeded to the solution stage. However, in the solution stage, despite stating that the aqueous solution of compound X could be either an acid or a base since it reacted with an amphoteric metal, it made its first mistake by stating that compound X is an acid. Since the aqueous solution of compound Y reacted with Cu, which is a semi-noble metal, it must be HNO_3 or H_2SO_4. According to the curriculum, CB should have given these two examples, but it made another mistake here by explaining it in a way that suggests it is a strong oxidizing agent. It evaluated the options one by one. It stated that the correct option according to the given information was option C. Looking at the explanations in the conclusion section, it can be said that it misunderstood or misinterpreted the question. Instead of saying that the X and Y solutions should react separately with Zn and Cu metals, it stated that the X solution could react with both Zn and Cu. However, it should have made this statement for the Y solution. Therefore, CB answered the question incorrectly.

When examining the open-ended questions posed to the Gemini chatbot, it provided detailed answers to all 7 questions. However, it provided an incorrect/ incomplete answer to 1 question. In one question, it did not provide a curriculum-appropriate solution but answered the question correctly. The chatbot's responses are analyzed in detail below.

The first open-ended question in TYT Chemistry is shown in Table 16, and CB's answer is shown in Table 17.

Table 16. Open-ended question 1

1.What is the common name of the compound with the systematic name nitrogen trihydride?

Table 17. Gemini answer

Answer: The common name of the compound with the systematic name nitrogen trihydride is ammonia. Ammonia (NH_3) is a colorless gas with a sharp and characteristic odor. It is an important chemical compound used in many different areas in industry and at home. It is widely used in fertilizer production, cleaning products, and as a refrigerant.

Additional Information:

- Formula: NH_3
- Properties: It is a colorless gas with a pungent odor. It exhibits basic properties when dissolved in water.
- Areas of Use:
  - o Fertilizer Production: Ammonia is the most important industrial source of nitrogen, which is an essential nutrient for plants.
  - o Cleaning Products: Ammonia is the main component of many products used in household cleaning. It has grease-cutting and disinfectant properties.
  - o Refrigerant: Ammonia is a commonly used refrigerant in industrial cooling systems.
  - o Explosive Material Production: Ammonia is used in the production of certain explosive materials.
  - o Pharmaceutical Industry: Ammonia is used in the production of certain medications.

In summary, this compound, known as nitrogen trihydride, is ammonia, which plays an important role in many areas of our daily lives.

If you have any further questions, please do not hesitate to ask.

When the questions from the 2021 National Exam's Basic Proficiency Test were converted into open-ended questions, CB provided detailed explanations. It specified factors such as the formula, properties, and areas of use of the ammonia compound. It provided explanations regarding the areas in which it is used. It provided a consistent answer to the open-ended question. In other words, the answer provided is consistent with the information requested in the question. The explanation was framed around ammonia. It did not include explanations of other substances. In the final section, it provided a summary of the ammonia compound.

The second open-ended question in the TYT chemistry exam is shown in Table 18, and the CB answer is shown in Table 19.

Table 18. Open-ended question 2

<table>
<tr><td>2.The positions of the elements He, N, and Mg in the periodic table are shown below.</td></tr>
<tr><td>2.→ The places of the elements He, N, and Mg in the periodic table are shown below.
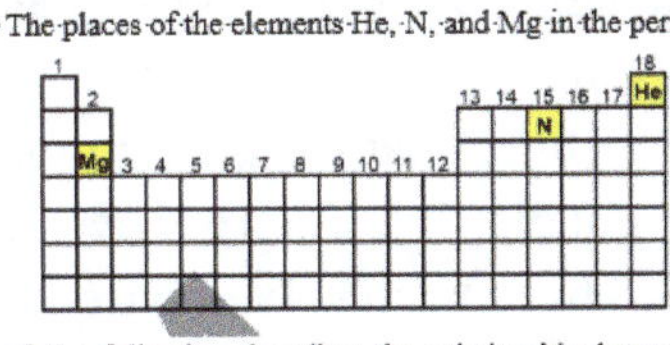
Which of the following describes the relationship between the number of electrons in the outermost shells of these atoms in their ground state?
A) He = N > Mg B) Mg > N > He C) N > Mg = He
D) N > Mg > He E) He > N > Mg</td></tr>
<tr><td>Write the relationship between the number of electrons in the outermost shells of these atoms in their ground state.</td></tr>
</table>

Table 19. Gemini answer

Answer (Plain Text): Electron Distribution and Comparison of He, N, and Mg Elements in the Periodic Table Your question: Write the relationship between the number of electrons in the outermost shells of He, N, and Mg atoms in their ground state. Answer: The position of an element in the periodic table provides important information about its atomic structure and, consequently, its chemical properties. When examining the positions and electron distributions of the elements He, N, and Mg in the periodic table, the following conclusions are reached: Helium (He): A noble gas located in group 1A of the periodic table. Its atomic number is 2, and its electron configuration is $1s^2$. Thus, it has 2 electrons in its outermost shell. Nitrogen (N): It is located in group 5A of the periodic table. Its atomic number is 7, and its electron configuration is $1s^2\ 2s^2\ 2p^3$. There are a total of 5 electrons in its outermost layer (2nd layer). Magnesium (Mg): It is located in group 2A of the periodic table. Its atomic number is 12, and its electron configuration is $1s^2\ 2s^2\ 2p^6\ 3s^2$. There are 2 electrons in its outermost shell (3rd shell). Conclusion: Helium (He) and Magnesium (Mg): These two elements have an equal number (2) of electrons in their outermost shells. This indicates their tendency to achieve a noble gas configuration. Nitrogen (N): Nitrogen, which has 5 electrons in its outermost shell, attempts to achieve a stable state by either gaining 3 electrons or losing 5 electrons to reach a noble gas configuration. Therefore, nitrogen typically has a valence of -3 or +5 in compounds. In general: As you move from left to right within a period in the periodic table, the atomic number increases, and the number of electrons in the outermost shell increases by one. The number of electrons in the outermost shells of elements in the same group is the same. In summary: The number of electrons in the outermost shells of He, N, and Mg are 2, 5, and 2, respectively. This situation is directly related to the groups in which the elements are located in the periodic table and their electron configurations. For visual support, you can examine the periodic table and compare the electron distributions of the elements. Does this explanation sufficiently answer your question? Please do not hesitate to ask if you have any further questions.

In this question, it can be seen that CB correctly identified the positions of the elements in the periodic table. Although the names or atomic numbers of the atoms were not given in the question, it correctly identified their symbols by looking at their positions in the table. The answer section begins with an explanation appropriate to the question. Information about the chemical properties of an atom can be obtained by looking at its position in the periodic table. However, there are some obvious errors in the solution. For example, it states that He is in group 1A. It appears that the question was solved based on orbital distribution. However, according to the 9th grade curriculum, the question should have been solved based on the layer electron distribution, not the orbital distribution. Although it solved the question according to the 11th grade curriculum, it provided a correct solution.

The third open-ended question in the TYT chemistry exam is shown in Table 20, and the CB answer is shown in Table 21.

Table 20. Open-ended question 3

3.The electron sea model, which was proposed to explain how metallic bonds are formed, can be used to explain some of the properties of metals. Accordingly, explain three properties of metals using the electron sea model.

Table 21. Gemini answer

Answer: Electron Sea Model and Properties of Metals Electron Sea Model In metals, the valence electrons of metal atoms detach from their atoms to form an "electron sea." These electrons move freely between metal cations. This model is used to explain many properties of metals. Properties of Metals Explained by the Electron Sea Model: 1. Electrical Conductivity: Explanation: Electrons that move freely within the electron sea play a role in the conduction of electric current. When an electric potential is applied, electrons move from the negative pole to the positive pole, thereby creating an electric current. This makes metals good electrical conductors. 2. Thermal Conductivity: Explanation: When metals absorb heat, electrons gain energy and move faster. These fast-moving electrons transfer their energy to other electrons, thereby conducting heat within the metal. Therefore, metals are good conductors of heat. 3. Malleability: Explanation: When metals are hammered or shaped, the metal ions change places while maintaining the electron sea structure. This allows new bonds to form without breaking the bonds between metal atoms, causing the metal to deform. The flexibility of the electron sea makes metals malleable. In summary: The electron sea model is quite successful in explaining important properties of metals such as electrical and thermal conductivity and malleability. According to this model, the fundamental reason metals possess these properties is that the valence electrons of metal atoms move freely and form an electron sea between metal cations. Additional Information: • The electron sea model can also explain other properties of metals, such as their shiny appearance, malleability, and ductility. • This model also provides important insights into metals' tendency to form alloys and the nature of metallic bonds. If you have any further questions, please feel free to ask.

As can be seen in Table 21, CB began by explaining the electron sea model. In this model, he discussed the mobile electrons that separate from atoms. It then explained the properties that the electron sea model imparts to metals. Looking at the explanations, it correctly described the property of electrical conductivity. Similarly, thermal conductivity is also correct. The third property, the ability to be formed into wires and sheets, is expressed in high school chemistry literature as malleability or ductility. CB has introduced a new concept here under the name "magnetism." Since the question asked for three properties, CB did not add another property. However, in the additional information section, it noted that brightness can also be explained by this model. It provided a correct and detailed answer to the open-ended question.

The fourth open-ended question in the TYT chemistry exam is shown in Table 22, and CB's answer is shown in Table 23.

Table 22. Open-ended question 4

4. In an experiment, a certain amount of pure water is placed in a closed container from which the air has been removed and to which a manometer has been attached. As the amount of liquid water decreases over time, the pressure measured by the manometer increases. When left at a constant temperature for a sufficient amount of time, it is observed that the amount of liquid water and the pressure measured by the manometer remain unchanged, and this pressure value (P1) is recorded. The experiment is then repeated at the same constant temperature with the amount of pure water doubled, and the pressure value (P2) is recorded. Accordingly, I. When the amount of water is doubled, the evaporation rate increases. II. P2 > P1. III. The values P1 and P2 are the equilibrium vapor pressure of water. Mark these statements as true (T) or false (F).

Table 23. Gemini answer

Answer: Experiment Analysis and Evaluation of Statements In the given experiment, the evaporation of water and the resulting vapor pressure in a closed system are investigated. Let us evaluate the given statements based on the experimental results: I. When the amount of water doubles, the evaporation rate increases. • False (F): The evaporation rate depends on the surface area of the liquid, temperature, and the density of the surrounding vapor. In a closed system, since the volume of the container is constant, increasing the amount of liquid does not significantly change the surface area. Therefore, the evaporation rate remains the same as at the beginning. II. P2 > P1. • False (F):In a closed system, the vapor pressure of a liquid at a given temperature takes on a constant value. This value is called the equilibrium vapor pressure. Increasing the amount of liquid does not change the equilibrium vapor pressure. Therefore, the P1 and P2 values will be equal (P1 = P2). III. The P1 and P2 values are the equilibrium vapor pressure of water. • True (T) When the system reaches equilibrium, the number of molecules transitioning from the liquid phase to the vapor phase equals the number of molecules transitioning from the vapor phase to the liquid phase. In this case, the vapor pressure formed in the system equals the equilibrium vapor pressure of water at that temperature. Both P1 and P2 values represent the equilibrium vapor pressure of water since they are the pressures measured in this equilibrium state. Conclusion: • Statements I and II are incorrect. • Statement III is correct. Additional Explanation: Equilibrium vapor pressure depends on the type and temperature of the liquid. As the temperature increases, the vapor pressure of the liquid also increases. Since the temperature was kept constant in this experiment, the equilibrium vapor pressures obtained for different amounts of water were the same. In summary: In the given experiment, the relationship between the evaporation of water and the equilibrium vapor pressure in a closed system was investigated. The experimental results showed that the equilibrium vapor pressure is independent of the amount of liquid and depends only on the temperature.

According to Table 23, the question is a true-false question. Three premises are given. If the premises are true, they should be marked (T), and if they are false, they should be marked (F). CB has provided consistent and detailed answers to this question as well. In the first premise, it states that the rate of evaporation does not depend on the amount of liquid but varies depending on the surface area, temperature, and humidity. Therefore, premise I is incorrect. CB gave the correct answer. In premise II, it states that the vapor pressure of a liquid does not depend on the amount of liquid. It also answered this premise correctly by stating that it is incorrect. In premise III, it states that the P1 and P2 values are the equilibrium vapor pressure of water, thus giving the correct answer to this premise as well. Thus, by stating that premises I and II are false (F) and premise III is true (T), the question was answered correctly again. By providing additional explanation, the answerer indicated what a liquid's vapor pressure depends on and stated that the vapor pressure would remain the same as in the initial state, taking into account the temperature factor.

The TYT chemistry open-ended fifth question is in Table 24, and the CB answer is in Table 25.

Table 24. Open-ended question 5

5. Phosphorus trichloride can be obtained from white phosphorus and chlorine gas according to the following reaction. P_4 (s) + $6Cl_2$ (g) → $4PCl_3$ (g) Accordingly, what is the maximum number of moles of PCl_3 that can be obtained from the reaction of 12.4 g of P_4 solid and 21.3 g of Cl_2 gas? (Cl_2 = 71 g/mol, P_4 = 124 g/mol)

Table 25. Gemini answer

Answer: Phosphorus Trichloride Production and Stoichiometry Calculation Given: • Reaction: $P_4(s) + 6Cl_2(g) \rightarrow 4PCl_3(g)$ • P_4 mass: 12.4 g • Cl_2 mass: 21.3 g • Molar mass of P_4: 124 g/mol • Molar mass of Cl_2: 71 g/mol Requested: What is the maximum number of moles of PCl_3 that can be obtained? 1. Solution: Calculation of Molar Quantities: • Number of moles of P_4: 12.4 g / 124 g/mol = 0.1 mol • Number of moles of Cl_2: 21.3 g / 71 g/mol ≈ 0.3 mol 2. Determining the Limiting Reactant: • According to the given reaction, 1 mol of P_4 reacts with 6 mol of Cl_2. • The amount of Cl_2 required for 0.1 mol of P_4: 0.1 mol P_4 * (6 mol Cl_2 / 1 mol P_4) = 0.6 mol Cl_2 • However, we only have 0.3 mol of Cl_2 available. In this case, Cl_2 will be the limiting reactant. That is, the reaction will continue until Cl_2 is completely depleted. 3. Calculation of the Maximum Amount of PCl_3 That Can Be Produced: • Since 6 mol of Cl_2 produces 4 mol of PCl_3, the amount of PCl_3 that can be produced with 0.3 mol of Cl_2 is: • 0,3 mol Cl_2 * (4 mol PCl_3 / 6 mol Cl_2) = 0,2 mol PCl_3 Result: The maximum amount of PCl_3 that can be obtained from the reaction of the given amounts of P_4 and Cl_2 is 0.2 mol. In summary: • The amount of Cl_2, which is the limiting reactant, determines the amount of PCl_3 that can be produced. • Using stoichiometric ratios, the number of moles of the product is calculated based on the limiting reactant. Note: In this calculation, the reaction efficiency is assumed to be 100%. In reality, the efficiency may not always be 100%, and the amount of product obtained may be less than the calculated value. This solution demonstrates how to perform stoichiometric calculations by explaining the given question step by step.

When examining the question in Table 24, it can be seen that it is a chemical calculation question. However, the question introduces the concept of stoichiometric calculation, which is not included in the high school chemistry curriculum. However, the equivalent of this concept in the curriculum is chemical calculation. Then, a table of given values was prepared. The given values were expressed correctly. In the required section, the molar quantities of the substances are listed first. The molar quantity of Cl_2 is calculated approximately. However, this calculation should have been a precise value. It could not be determined where the reference value for the molar mass of Cl_2 was found and written. Then, the calculation section is moved on to find the limiting substance. The limiting substance is determined correctly and in detail. In the final step, it correctly calculated the maximum possible amount of PCl_3. Although it solved the question using verbal expressions, its answer is correct. In the notes section, it explained that no chemical reaction in nature occurs with 100% efficiency.

The sixth open-ended question in the TYT chemistry exam is shown in Table 26, and the CB answer is shown in Table 27.

Table 26. Open-ended question 6

6. In an experiment, 1000 grams of pure water is placed in three separate containers. To the first container, 1 mole of NaCl is added; to the second, 1 mole of sucrose; and to the third, 1 mole of $MgCl_2$, resulting in solutions A, B, and C, respectively. The prepared solutions are heated in an environment where the external pressure is 1 atm, and the temperatures at which the solutions begin to boil (TA, TB, and TC) are measured.
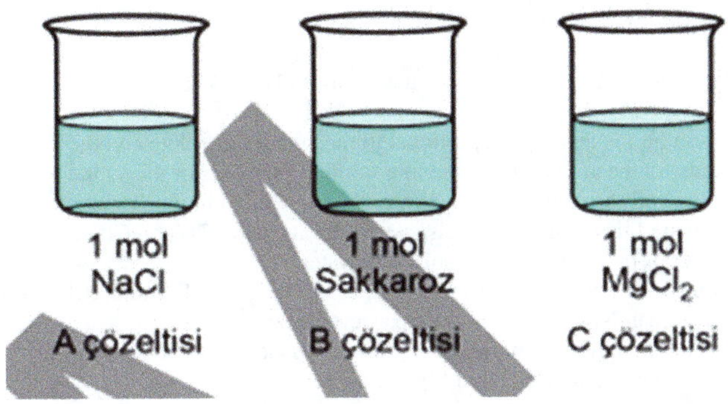
Arrange the measured TA, TB, and TC temperatures in descending order according to their relationship. (It is assumed that the NaCl and $MgCl_2$ salts completely dissociate into their ions in water, while sucrose dissolves molecularly.)

Table 27. Gemini answer

Answer:
Comparison of Boiling Points of Solutions
Given:
• Three separate containers contain 1000 g of pure water and different solutes (NaCl, sucrose, $MgCl_2$).
• The number of moles of solutes is equal.
• The solubility properties of the solutes are different.
Requested:
• The relationship between the boiling points of the solutions (TA, TB, TC).
Solution:
The boiling point of a solution is directly proportional to the amount of solute and the degree of ionization of the solute. In other words, as the amount of solute in a solution increases or the solute ionizes more, a higher temperature is required to boil the solution. This phenomenon is called boiling point elevation.
• NaCl: An ionic compound that completely dissociates into its ions (Na^+ and Cl^-) in water. Therefore, it forms the greatest number of particles when dissolved in water.
• $MgCl_2$: An ionic compound that completely dissociates into its ions (Mg^{2+} and $2Cl^-$) in water. Since it dissociates into more ions than NaCl, it forms more particles in solution.
• Sucrose: A compound that dissolves molecularly without dissociating into ions in water. Therefore, it forms fewer particles in solution than NaCl and $MgCl_2$.
Conclusion:
As the number of particles in solutions increases, the boiling point rises. Therefore, the relationship between the boiling points of solutions can be ranked as follows:
• T C > TA > TB
• T C: $MgCl_2$ solution (Highest boiling point, because it dissociates into the most ions and forms the most particles.)
• TA: NaCl solution (Forms fewer particles than $MgCl_2$ but more than sucrose.)
• TB: Sucrose solution (Lowest boiling point because it does not ionize and forms the fewest particles.)
In summary:
• In aqueous solutions of ionic compounds, the boiling point increases as the degree of ionization increases.
• In aqueous solutions of molecular compounds, the boiling point increase is less because there is no ionization.
• As the amount of solute increases, the boiling point rises.
This result explains the boiling point elevation phenomenon, known as the colligative properties of solutions.

It can be said that CB made a good introduction to the answer by providing a detailed explanation in the given section. It stated that the solubility conditions of the solutes are different. It focused on the relationship between the number of ions to be considered in the question and the boiling point. In the solution section, it determined the number of particles that the solutes dissolved into water at the ionic or molecular level. It reached the highest number of particles in $MgCl_2$. It stated that the amounts of water and the number of moles of solutes were equal, but that the total number of particles at the end of the dissolution process would have a proportional effect on the boiling point. It paid attention to the points to be considered in the question. It answered the question correctly. It provided detailed explanations where necessary. In the summary section, it stated that in solutions of equal concentration, the boiling point increases as the ionization number increases.

The seventh open-ended question in the TYT chemistry exam is shown in Table 28, and the CB answer is shown in Table 29.

Table 28. Open-ended question 7

7.The following information is given about the aqueous solutions of compounds X and Y: • When the aqueous solution of X reacts with zinc (Zn), which exhibits amphoteric properties, hydrogen gas is released. • When the aqueous solution of Y reacts with copper (Cu), which is a semi-noble metal, gas is released. • When X and Y react, salt and water are formed. Based on this, interpret what substances X and Y are.

Table 29. Gemini answer

Answer: Identification of X and Y Compounds Given Information: • X compound: Reacts with zinc (Zn) to release hydrogen gas. This indicates that the X compound has acidic properties. • Y compound: Semimetals like copper (Cu) typically react with strong oxidizing acids (such as nitric acid or sulfuric acid). In this case, there is a high probability that Y is a strong acid. • X and Y reaction: The formation of salt and water indicates a typical acid-base neutralization reaction. Comments and Possible Compounds: 1. X compound: o Zinc is an amphoteric metal, so it reacts with both acids and bases. However, the formation of hydrogen gas suggests that the X compound is an acid. o For hydrogen gas to form, the X compound must contain hydrogen ions (H^+). o Possible X compounds: Strong acids such as HCl (hydrochloric acid), H_2SO_4 (sulfuric acid), and HNO_3 (nitric acid) are possible. 2. Y Compound: o Copper, being a semi-noble metal, does not react with oxygen-free acids. However, it reacts with strong oxidizing acids (HNO_3, H_2SO_4) to form salts, water, and gases such as nitrogen oxides or sulfur dioxide. o The fact that compound Y releases gas when it reacts with copper suggests that it is a strong oxidizing acid. o Possible compound Y: HNO_3 (nitric acid) appears to be the most suitable option. This is because nitric acid releases a brown gas such as NO_2 when it reacts with semi-noble metals such as copper. Conclusion: Based on the information provided, compound X is likely a strong acid such as hydrochloric acid (HCl) or sulfuric acid (H_2SO_4), while compound Y could be nitric acid (HNO_3). Example of X + Y Reaction: If we take HCl as X and HNO_3 as Y, the reaction could occur as follows: $HCl(aq) + HNO_3(aq) \rightarrow NO_2(g) + Cl_2(g) + H_2O(l)$ In this reaction, nitric acid both oxidizes the chlorine in HCl to form chlorine gas and reduces itself to form NO_2 gas. Note: This is only a possible example. More experimental data may be needed to draw a definitive conclusion based on the information provided. In summary: Based on the information provided, compound X is considered to be an acid, and compound Y is considered to be a strong oxidizing acid. HCl, H_2SO_4, and HNO_3 are suggested as possible compounds.

The question asks for the classification of compounds X and Y as acids or bases. Some information is provided, and the question asks what substances compounds X and Y could be. CB made some mistakes in answering the question. For example, since the aqueous solution of compound X reacted with Zn, an amphoteric metal, it should have been classified as an acid or a base. CB provided incomplete information by stating that this compound exhibits acidic properties. CB correctly stated that compound Y must be HNO_3 or H_2SO_4 in order to react with the metal Cu. CB stated that the reaction between compounds X and Y would result in a neutralization reaction, since salt and water are formed as a result of the reaction. When the comments and possible compounds section is examined, it is seen that he continues to insist that compound X must be an acid. It did not consider the possibility of compound X being a base, mentioning HCl, H_2SO_4, and HNO_3 as possible compounds. Its observations about compound Y are correct. It made another mistake in the conclusion section. That is, it has referred to both X and Y compounds as acids. However, if both compounds are acids, they cannot react with each other to form salt and water. In other words, two acids cannot react to form a neutralization reaction. It is unclear why CB did not refer to compound X as a base in its solution. It has answered the question incorrectly.

DISCUSSION

This study examines the performance of Gemini, an artificial intelligence-based chatbot, in answering questions from the 2021 TYT Chemistry exam. The questions were multiple choice and open-ended and were asked in the same order. The chatbot's answers were analyzed by three experts. Gemini chatbot answered 85.71% of the multiple-choice questions correctly and 85.71% of the open-ended questions asked in the same order correctly. It answered these questions, which measure reading comprehension and interpretation skills, with a high success rate. A literature review shows that the success rate in this study is quite high compared to the literature in the field. For example, according to Kharchenko and Babenko (2024), Gemini answered questions about the structure of matter correctly 63.3% of the time, organic chemistry questions 20% of the time, environmental chemistry questions 86.7% of the time, and chemistry laboratory application questions 50% of the time. The success rate in environmental chemistry was higher than the success rate achieved by students. However, student success rates in other fields are higher than Gemini's. Additionally, the study shows that although AI-based tools demonstrate significant success in processing and producing information, their accuracy in complex fields such as chemistry is limited, and they cannot provide definitive correct answers (Kharchenko and Babenko, 2024). In another study, Leite (2024) asked Gemini chatbot questions about the structure of atoms and received detailed answers. However, it showed that 72% of the content was produced by humans, not Gemini. The AI writing assistant Smodin, on the other hand, stated that 100% of the text content was produced by Gemini. Gyeong et al. (2023) compared GPT-4V and Gemini Pro in their study, aiming to evaluate students' drawn models using a rubric in educational settings. The evaluation results showed that Gemini's performance was quite low.

However, within the scope of the research, the Gemini chatbot provided detailed and understandable answers to questions. It answered all multiple-choice and open-ended questions. However, in some questions, it did not provide answers in line with the TYT curriculum or provided incorrect examples related to the answers. It answered questions using concepts from the field of chemistry correctly, demonstrating its effective use of chemical concepts.

CONCLUSION

In conclusion, it can be said that the Gemini chatbot performed well in answering multiple-choice and open-ended questions on chemistry in the national TYT exam. It provided consistent answers to scientific concepts. Its reasoning ability is quite strong. This is because the TYT exam is a test of reading comprehension and interpretation. It is important for researchers to note that both educators and students are aware that it may provide incorrect explanations or give wrong answers to some questions. However, it is important to solve the questions according to the relevant curriculum. In addition, unethical use by students should be prevented.

Chatbots are expected to be an important application for the field of education in the future. These resources, which can be adapted to sustainable education systems, have the potential to contribute to the process of constructing knowledge. They can also be used as a support resource in chemistry education and contribute to the learning-teaching process. Chatbots are expected to be actively used in the near future as they are likely to become an important support resource in education and help students. By providing chatbots with multiple prompts, they can be made to generate more accurate answers to questions. However, it is recommended that studies be conducted to determine whether chatbots have incorrect concepts or definitions. Considering that there are few such studies in the chemistry literature, it is recommended that question-answer studies be conducted on the Gemini chatbot.

REFERENCES

Arman, M., & Lamiyar, U. R. (2023). Exploring the implication of ChatGPT AI for business: Efficiency and challenges. *Applied Quantitative Analysis*, *3*(2), 46–67.

Chmiliar, l. (2010). Multiple-case designs. In A. J. Mills, G. Eurepas & E. Wiebe (Eds.), *Encyclopedia of case study research* (pp 582-583). USA: SAGE Publications. DOI: 10.4135/9781412957397.n216

Clark, T. M. (2023). Investigating the use of an artificial intelligence chatbot with general chemistry exam questions. *Journal of Chemical Education*, *100*(5), 1905–1916. DOI: 10.1021/acs.jchemed.3c00027

Crawford, K. (2016, June 25). Artificial Intelligence's white guy problem. The New York Times [Blog post]. Retrieved August 6, 2018, from https://www.nytimes.com/2016/06/26/opinion/sunday/artificial-intelligences-white-guy-problem.html?_r=1

Daher, W., Diab, H., & Rayan, A. (2023). Artificial intelligence generative tools and conceptual knowledge in problem solving in chemistry. *Information (Basel)*, *14*(7), 409. DOI: 10.3390/info14070409

Gaglo, K., Degboe, B. M., Kossingou, G. M., & Ouya, S. (2021). Proposal of conversational chatbots for educational remediation in the context of covid-19. In: 2021 23rd International conference on advanced communication technology (ICACT), pp 354–358. . 2021.9370946DOI: 10.23919/ICACT51234

Geerling, W., Mateer, G. D., Wooten, J., & Damodaran, N. (2023). Is ChatGPT smarter than a student in principles of economics? *SSRN Electronic Journal*, 1-24. DOI: 10.2139/ssrn.4356034

Gerring, J. (2007). *Case study research: Principles and practices.* Cambridge University Press., https://books.google.com.tr/books?id=CbetAQAAQBAJ&lpg=PP13&ots=kdB0JMVUwI&dq=Gerring%2C%20J.%20(2007).%20Case%20study%20research%3A%20Principles%20and%20practices.%20New%20York%3A%20Cambridge%20University%20Press.&lr&hl=tr&pg=PP13#v=onepage&q&f=false

Gitelman, L., & Jackson, V. (2013). Introduction. In L. Gitelman (Ed.), *"Raw data" is an oxymoron* (pp. 1–14). Cambridge, Massausetts; London, England: The MIT Press. DOI: 10.1080/1369118X.2014.920042

Gyeong-Geon, J., Ehsan, L., Lehong, S., & Xiaoming, Z. (2023) Gemini Pro Defeated by GPT-4V: Evidence from Education, 13-15. /arXiv.2401.08660DOI: 10.48550

Han, Z., Battaglia, F., Udaiyar, A., Fooks, A., & Terlecky, S. R. (2023). An explorative assessment of ChatGPT as an aid in medical education: Use it with caution. https://www.medrxiv.org/content/10.1101/2023.02.13.23285879v1.full.pdf

Hobert S. (2019). How are you, chatbot? evaluating chatbots in educational settings–results of a literature review. DELFI 2019

Holmes, W. (2018). The ethics of Artificial Intelligence in education. University Business. Retrieved August 10, 2018, from https://universitybusiness.co.uk/Article/the-ethics-of-artificial-intelligence-in-education-who-care

Işler, B., & Kılıç, M. (2021). *Eğitimde Yapay Zekâ Kullanimi ve Gelişimi. e-Journal of New Media / Yeni Medya Elektronik Dergi – eJNM, 5*(1), 1–11. https://dergipark.org.tr/en/download/article-file/1106175

Jones, M. (2023). Preserving Academic Integrity In The Age of Artificial Intelligence: Redesigning Courses To Combat AI-Assisted Plagiarism. International Dialogues on Education Journal, 10(1), 101–123. Retrieved from https://www.idejournal.org/index.php/ide/article/view/296

Kasthuri, E., & Balaji, S. (2021). A chatbot for changing lifestyle in education. In: *2021 Third international conference on intelligent communication technologies and virtual mobile networks (ICICV)*, pp 1317– 1322. IEEE

Kharchenko, Y., & Babenko, O. (2024). Advantages and limitations of large language models in chemistry education: A comparative analysis of ChatGPT, Gemini and Copilot. 3781. 42-59._https://www.researchgate.net/publication/385417848_Advantages_and_limitations_of_large_language_models_in_chemistry_education_A_comparative_analysis_of_ChatGPT_Gemini_and_Copilot

Kuhail, M. A., Alturki, N., Alramlawi, S., & Alhejori, K. (2023). Interacting with educational chatbots: A systematic review. *Education and Information Technologies, 28*(1), 973–1018.

Kuleto, V., Ilić, M. P., Bucea-Manea- oniş, R., Ciocodeică, D.-F., Mihălcescu, H., & Mindrescu, V. (2022). The attitudes of K–12 schools'teachers in Serbia towards the potential of artificial intelligence. *Sustainability, 14*(14), 8636. DOI: 10.3390/su14148636

Kwak, Y., & Pardos, Z. A. (2024). Bridging large language model disparities: Skill tagging of multilingual educational content. *British Journal of Educational Technology, 55*(5). Advance online publication. DOI: 10.1111/bjet.13465

Lakshmi, G., Brindha, S., Devi, R., Divya, J., & Shobhanali, N. (2022). Ai-powered digital classroom. In: 2022 International conference on communication, computing and internet of things (IC3IoT), pp 1–6. DOI: 10.1109/IC3IOT53935.2022.9767944

Leite, B. S. (2024). Generative Artificial Intelligence in chemistry teaching: ChatGPT, Gemini, and Copilot's content responses. *Journal of Applied Learning and Teaching, 7*(2). Advance online publication. DOI: 10.37074/jalt.2024.7.2.13

Lund, B. D., & Wang, T. (2023). Chatting about ChatGPT: How may AI and GPT impact academia and libraries? *Library Hi Tech News*. Advance online publication. DOI: 10.1108/LHTN-01-2023-0009

McFarland, M. (2016, May 11). What happened when a professor built a chatbot to be his teaching assistant. The Washington Post [Blog post]. Retrieved August 13, 2018, from https://www.washingtonpost.com/news/innovations/wp/2016/05/11/this-professor-stunned-his-students-when-he-revealed-the-secret-identity-of-his-teaching-assistant/?noredirect=on&utm_term=.70facd03940d

McIntosh, T. R., Susnjak, T., Liu, T., Watters, P., & Halgamuge, M. N. (2023). From google gemini to openai q*(q-star): A survey of reshaping the generative artificial intelligence (ai) research landscape. arXiv preprint arXiv:2312.10868. / arXiv.2312.10868DOI: 10.48550

Merriam, S. B. (2013). *Nitel araştırma: Desen ve uygulama için bir rehber (3. Baskıdan Çeviri, Çeviri Editörü: S. Turan)*. Nobel Yayın Dağıtım.

Mhlanga, D. (2023). Open AI in education, the responsible and ethical use of ChatGPT towards lifelong learning. https://www.researchgate.net/profile/David-Mhlanga-2/publication/368476294_Open_AI_in_Education_the_Responsible_and_Ethical_Use_of_ChatGPT_Towards_Lifelong_Learning/links/63eb1c91bd7860764366f597/Open-AI-in-Education-the-Responsible-and-Ethical-Use-of-ChatGPT-Towards-Lifelong-Learning.pdf

Murphy, R. F. (2019). *Artifcial Intelligence Applications to Support K-12 Teachers and Teaching: A Review of Promising Applications, Opportunities, and Challenges. Perspective*. RAND Corporation.

Nichols, M., & Holmes, W. (2018). Don't do Evil: Implementing Artifcial Intelligence in Universities. In EDEN Conference Proceedings; No. 2, pp. 110–118 https://www.researchgate.net/publication/362321764_Don't_Do_Evil_Implementing_Artificial_Intelligence_in_Universities

Okonkwo, C. W., & Ade-Ibijola, A. (2021). Chatbots applications in education: A systematic review. *Computers and Education: Artif Intell, 2*, 100033.

Parker, I. (2018, April 26). UK wants to lead the world in tech ethics…but what does that mean? Ada Lovelace Institute [Blog post]. Retrieved August 10, 2018, from https://www.adalovelaceinstitute.org/uk-wants-to-lead-the-world-in-tech-ethicsbut-what-does-that-mean/

Perera, P., & Lankathilake, M. (2023). Preparing to revolutionize education with the multi-model GenAI tool Google Gemini? A journey towards effective policy making. *Journal of Advances in Education and Philosophy.*, *7*, 246–253. DOI: 10.36348/jaep.2023.v07i08.001

Popenici, S. A., & Kerr, S. (2017). Exploring the impact of artifcial intelligence on teaching and learning in higher education. *Research and Practice in Technology Enhanced Learning*, *12*(1), 1–13. PMID: 30613250

Prinsloo, P., & Slade, S. (2016). Student vulnerability, agency, and learning analytics: An exploration. *Journal of Learning Analytics*, *3*(1), 159–182. https://oro.open.ac.uk/46172/

Raja, R., & Nagasubramani, P. C. (2018). Impact of modern technology in education. *Journal of applied and advanced research, 3*(1), 33-35.

Rane, N. (2024). Role and challenges of ChatGPT, Gemini, and similar generative artificial intelligence in human resource management. *Studies in Economics and Business Relations*, *5*(1), 11–23. DOI: 10.48185/sebr.v5i1.1001

Selwyn, N. (2021). *Education and technology: Key issues and debates.* Bloomsbury Publishing.

Susnjak, T. (2022). ChatGPT: The end of online exam integrity? Cornell University arXiv. /arXiv.2212.09292DOI: 10.48550

Venkatesh, A. M., & Venkatesha, R. A. (2024), The rise of Google Gemini in modern education: Revolutionizing learning with AI chatbots (2024). https://ssrn.com/abstract=4925934 or DOI: 10.2139/ssrn.4925934

Williams, R. T. (2024). The ethical implications of using generative chatbots in higher education. [Frontiers Media SA.]. *Frontiers in Education*, *8*, 1331607.

Xie, H. (2023). The promising future of cognitive science and artificial intelligence. *Nature Reviews Psychology*, *2*, 202. DOI: 10.1038/s44159-023-00170-3

Yaacoub, J. P. A., Noura, H. N., Salman, O., & Chehab, A. (2023). Ethical hacking for IoT: Security issues, challenges, solutions and recommendations. *Internet of Things and Cyber-Physical Systems*, *3*, 280–308. DOI: 10.1016/j.iotcps.2023.04.002

Yıldırım, A., & Şimşek, H. (2018). *Sosyal bilimlerde nitel araştırma yöntemleri* (11. b.). Ankara: Seçkin Yayıncılık.

Yildirim, B., & Akcan, A. T. (2024). AI-professional development model for chemistry teacher: Artificial intelligence in chemistry education. [JESEH]. *Journal of Education in Science, Environment and Health, 10*(4), 161–182. DOI: 10.55549/jeseh.741

Zobel, T., Steinbeck, H., & Meinel, C. (2023). *Towards inclusive education: A review of and guide to accessible features in chatbots for moocs. In: 2023 IEEE learning with MOOCS.* LWMOOCS., DOI: 10.1109/LWMOOCS58322.2023.10306062

Chapter 7
Comparative Analysis of the Efficacy of Artificial Intelligence in Mandarin Language Acquisition of UMS learners:
A Study Focused on Reading Skills

Yoke Lian Lau
https://orcid.org/0000-0002-7949-7683
Universiti Malaysia Sabah, Malaysia

Anna Lynn Binti Abu Bakar
https://orcid.org/0000-0002-2540-3637
Universiti Malaysia Sabah, Malaysia

Zi Hong Yong
https://orcid.org/0000-0002-0531-2420
Universiti Malaysia Sabah, Malaysia

Zi Xian Yong
Universiti Malaysia Sabah, Malaysia

Hui Wen Yong
Universiti Malaysia Sabah, Malaysia

Jee Chin Tan
https://orcid.org/0009-0001-3932-0955
Universiti Malaysia Sabah, Malaysia

ABSTRACT

The objective of this research is to evaluate the effectiveness of artificial intelligence (AI) in supporting the development of Mandarin language acquisition, specifically focusing on the improvement of reading proficiency in Mandarin for non-native Mandarin learners. The methodology employed an extensive comparative analysis of the audio data spectrum among the three distinct cohorts: individuals who are Malaysian native speakers of Mandarin; recipients of text-to-speech systems facilitated by artificial intelligence; and Mandarin learners who enrolled in a Mandarin

DOI: 10.4018/979-8-3373-6791-0.ch007

Copyright © 2026, IGI Global Scientific Publishing. Copying or distributing in print or electronic forms without written permission of IGI Global Scientific Publishing is prohibited.

program as a non-native language learner at Universiti Malaysia Sabah (UMS). Through a spectrum analysis of the data collected from these cohorts, this study seeks to generate significant discovery delving with the efficacy of artificial intelligence in the domain of Mandarin reading comprehension. Moreover, this research aims to explicate the possible ramifications of artificial intelligence in the domain of language instruction, particularly regarding the involvement of native speakers in pedagogical capacities.

INTRODUCTION

The advent of Artificial Intelligence (AI) has significantly influenced language acquisition, particularly within the context of learning Mandarin, a language known for its intricate tonal and script structures. In consequence, learning Mandarin poses an intriguing challenge for AI with a more complicated processing if compared to learning other languages. Therefore, exploring the effectiveness of AI in facilitating Mandarin learning has become of paramount significance.

This research aims to assess the efficacy of AI in promoting Mandarin language acquisition, specifically focusing on reading proficiency of Mandarin. The objective is to conduct a comparative analysis on reading proficiency levels among three distinct groups: native Mandarin speakers residing in Malaysia, AI-assisted text-to-speech systems, and Mandarin learners who are students of learning Mandarin as a non-native language in Universiti Malaysia Sabah (UMS). By comparing these three groups of participants, we can gain valuable insights into the capabilities of AI in Mandarin reading comprehension. Furthermore, the research seeks to evaluate the potential implications of AI in language instruction, particularly concerning the role of native speakers as teachers.

The study scrutinized factors influencing the effectiveness of AI in language acquisition with the consideration including the complexity of the language, the motivation of Mandarin learners with varying proficiency levels and their adaptability to the AI systems while learning the language. From the reports in the past research, it seems that AI has given promises in enhancing optical character recognition and auditory comprehension; however, its effectiveness in grasping tonal features of Mandarin is an area that is still under exploration.

In general, investigations into the limitations and shortcomings of AI-assisted reading, such as analysing reading spectra, are conducted for assessing the capture and comparison of phonetic sounds, like the "yue" sound in Mandarin, and understand how well AI tools handle pronunciation nuances. Furthermore, as AI tools allow customized and engaging learning experiences for the learners, it is essential to integrate these tools in a blended approach, serving as a complement to traditional pedagogical methods. Parallel with the same notion, this research aims to provide fresh insights into the comparative efficacy of AI-assisted and conventional methods in Mandarin acquisition.

In addition, by addressing the above-mentioned research objectives and questions, this study contributes to the ongoing evolution of Mandarin language learning in the digital age. It strives to advance our understanding on the impact of AI to Mandarin acquisition, particularly in terms of reading proficiency, and its potential implications for language instruction.

LITERATURE REVIEW

Abushariah et al. (2023) conducted a thorough examination of methodologies and technologies utilised in bilingual automatic speech recognition (ASR). The study constitutes a noteworthy contribution to the field of automatic speech recognition (ASR) in bilingual contexts, as it delves into the various obstacles that impeded its optimal functioning. The investigation thus lays the groundwork for further scholarly inquiry which aims at improving the efficacy of bilingual ASR systems. In their study, Zhang et al. (2023) put forth a methodology aimed at assessing the influence of noise on the performance of automatic speech recognition (ASR) systems specifically designed for Mandarin language. The researchers at the research institute employed a distinctive methodology that centred on the identification of several categories of noise and their respective intensities, which influence the accuracy of automatic speech recognition (ASR) systems. The methodology discussed above has the potential to offer assistance for the improvement of automated speech recognition (ASR) systems that demonstrate increased robustness in noisy environments. Academic investigation has also prioritised the analysis of technology resources within the domain of foreign language education, namely digital tools developed for computer and mobile platforms. In the study conducted by Andujar (2019), a comprehensive analysis is undertaken to evaluate the capabilities of these technologies and their capacity to bring about a transformative impact on the educational landscape. Kohn (2009) does an extensive investigation in his scholarly research, wherein he meticulously analyses the domain of computer-assisted foreign language acquisition. This inquiry encompasses an exploration of its historical backdrop, fundamental concepts, instructional methodologies, and potential benefits. The research conducted by Arslanyilmaz (2013) involved a comparative examination to assess the efficacy of task-based and form-focused instructional methods in the context of computer-assisted second language learning. When juxtaposed with Zou's (2013) analysis of advancements in technology within the realm of language education, this research offers significant contributions towards understanding the optimal approaches for establishing a language learning environment that is enhanced by technology.

Considerable scholarly attention has been devoted to investigating the impact of artificial intelligence (AI) on the enhancement of language learning, as evidenced by the scholarly works of Deng (2022), Strasser (2023), and Chen et al. (2022a). The authors of this study showcase various applications that illustrate the promise of artificial intelligence (AI) in the field of language acquisition. The applications encompass the examination of AI applications, the utilisation of AI-driven visualisation tools in grammar training, and the incorporation of the principles of self-determination theory (SDT) into AI educational platforms. This observation highlights the significant impact that artificial intelligence (AI) has on the acquisition of linguistic abilities.

Numerous scholarly investigations have been conducted to explore novel pedagogical methodologies, including the utilisation of robots and game-based platforms. These approaches have been examined by Fischer et al. (2021), Tao and Zou (2021), Wang et al. (2022a), and Wu and McMahon (2013). The study emphasised the potential of utilising various speaking styles, interactive tools, collaborative virtual platforms, and music integration as strategies to improve the overall quality of language learning experiences.

Several scholarly investigations, like the works of Essebbar et al. (2021) and Su and Zhan (2019), have examined diverse approaches to language analysis. In their study, Essebbar et al. (2021) put out a methodology aimed at doing sentiment analysis specifically in the French language. Similarly, Su and Zhan (2019) employed corpus-based methodologies to investigate the lexical semantics of the Chinese language.

Sparks (2016) conducted a thorough examination of misconceptions in language acquisition and learning disabilities, promoting the implementation of inclusive approaches in the realm of foreign language instruction. The statement is in accordance with the tenets of Self-Determination Theory (SDT) highlighted by Xia et al. (2022) underscores the efficacy of inclusive and personalised pedagogical strategies in augmenting language acquisition.

Numerous studies have been conducted on various topics related to Chinese language education, including research done by Chen et al. (2022a), Sunarti et al. (2022), Yang et al. (2021), Hirose and Zhang (1999), Jeong et al. (2022), Jing-Schmidt (2019), Jing (2023), Liu and Da (2022), Navarre (2018), Tang (2021), Tao (2016), Wang et al. (2022b), Wen (2020), Weng and Chao (2022), Xu (2021), Zhang and Kawanami (1999), Zhang et al. (2018), Zhao and Chen (2022), and Zhu et al. (2020). All these studies proved that advanced technologies encompass the utilisation of AI robots, tone recognition, gesture recognition systems powered by AI, and the implementation of Natural Language Processing (NLP) in the realm of Chinese language computing.

The investigation into the complexities of bilingualism has been extensively examined in scholarly research, as evidenced by the works of Chen et al. (2022b) and Feng and Wang (2022). The mentioned study investigated the phenomenon of reading anxiety among learners of English as a Foreign Language (EFL), while also exploring the potential impact of various factors such as motivation, attitudes, and learning strategies.

The continuous advancement and widespread adoption of AI present both opportunities and concerns. The possibility either AI technologies replacing or enhancing human labour is a captivating topic. However, it is closely associated with concerns about the extent to which AI could replace human capabilities, potentially leading to the domination of humans by their AI offspring.

The status of AI is marked by comprehensive investigation and advancement across various facets. Nevertheless, it has not achieved its complete capability. It is imaginable that individuals can maintain dominion over the artificial intelligence systems that they conceive and manage. Although AI possesses impressive capabilities and advanced technology, it has not yet attained a degree of advancement that would enable it to outperform humans in all areas of operation and decision-making.

The potential trajectory of progress in the field of artificial intelligence remains largely indeterminate. Despite the progress achieved in the field of AI, it is irrefutable that in the field of education, particularly in the domain of acquiring a second language, the role of human educators cannot be entirely replaced. The necessity for a human role in language education stems from the intricacies inherent in the procedure. This entails the requirement to understand the nuanced difficulties that a learner may face, in addition to tailoring the pedagogical methodology that could align with learners' disposition and cognitive capacity individually.

Deng (2022), Strasser (2023), and Chen et al. (2022a) have posited that AI can provide beneficial resources and support for language education. It is recommended to regard these as complementary to human guidance, rather than replacements. The research conducted by Andujar (2019) and Kohn (2009) on digital tools for language acquisition underscores the considerable influence that these resources can exert on the process of learning. It is imperative to acknowledge that these results do not undermine the crucial function fulfilled by human instructors.

As the advancement of artificial intelligence continues, it is crucial to guarantee that its implementation is focused on augmenting and supplementing human abilities, rather than displacing them. The ability to inspire, empathise, and motivate is a unique human attribute that holds significant importance in the field of education. Despite notable advancements in the domain of artificial intelligence, it has not attained an optimal degree of flawlessness or consistency that would allow it to completely replace human educators in the area of language learning.

In the future, an ideal scenario would involve a symbiotic partnership between AI and human educators, whereby AI enhances their capabilities and effectiveness while maintaining their crucial role in the field of education. It is widely speculated that the trajectory of AI will entail a symbiotic relationship with human beings, wherein each party can leverage their unique proficiencies to complement one another. This holds relevance within the realm of language education.

METHODOLOGY

The study adopted a mixed-methods approach, integrating both quantitative and qualitative methodologies. The quantitative aspect aimed to provide an extensive portrayal of identifiable patterns and trends through statistical analysis and observational generalizations. Concurrently, the qualitative portion of the study scrutinized the intricate emotional experiences of the learners, enhancing the completeness and contextual understanding of the subject matter. This thorough methodology ensured a comprehensive evaluation to the objectives of the study.

Data Collection

The study involved a collaboration with six educators expertise in teaching Mandarin as a foreign language in UMS. Researchers selected ten widely recognized sentences from the current UMS textbook as the primary basis for recording. However, the analysis of the study were limited to interpreting a single statement due to the fixed focus of the study. Participants were instructed to read ten sentences for several reasons. Firstly, it ensured equal exposure to common literacy. Moreover, using multiple sentences would sustain the attention of the readers on the text for a more extended period than a single sentence would.

Participants

The study recruited a total of twenty participants, including ten native Malaysian Mandarin speakers and ten Mandarin learners who currently enrolled in a Mandarin as a foreign language program from the University Malaysia Sabah (UMS). Participation in the study was voluntary. Additionally, ten different AI-assisted text-to-speech (TTS) web services were utilized to generate 10 audio samples, which served as additional data.

Creating the Audios

Preliminary procedures were conducted to normalize the audio data before commencing the research. It was essential to remove any extraneous sounds and ambient noise to maintain the integrity and clarity of the audio recordings. This step aimed to minimize potential variables and enhance the precision of the spectrographic analysis.

As some audio recordings were provided in MP3, MP4, or M4A file formats, all audio recordings intended for reading purposes were converted into the WAV format. The configuration of all audio codecs was set to conform to the pcm_s16le format, with mono channels, a sample rate of 44100Hz, and a bit rate of 128.

Ambient noise was removed using the freeware Audacity for the recordings of both Mandarin native speakers and Mandarin learners. As for AI-generated audio, it inherently lacks of noise interruption due to the employment of artificial intelligence methodologies whereby Text-to-Speech (TTS) web services were ordered to producing spoken output.

The audio of the initial statement was segmented by the researcher using Adobe Audition. However, segmentation was deemed unnecessary for AI reading audio files, as the Text-to-Speech (TTS) web service only produced the initial sentence rendition.

To standardize the reading time of all audio recordings and normalize their pace, the researchers adjusted the duration of the audio files to a specific length while maintaining the original reading variables. This process involved using one of the native speaker audio files as a reference model.

Finally, Audacity software was used to generate plots spectrum charts. These plots were utilized to create a comparative chart subsequently.

Figure 1. Comprehensive audio editing workflow: from preparation to spectrum plotting

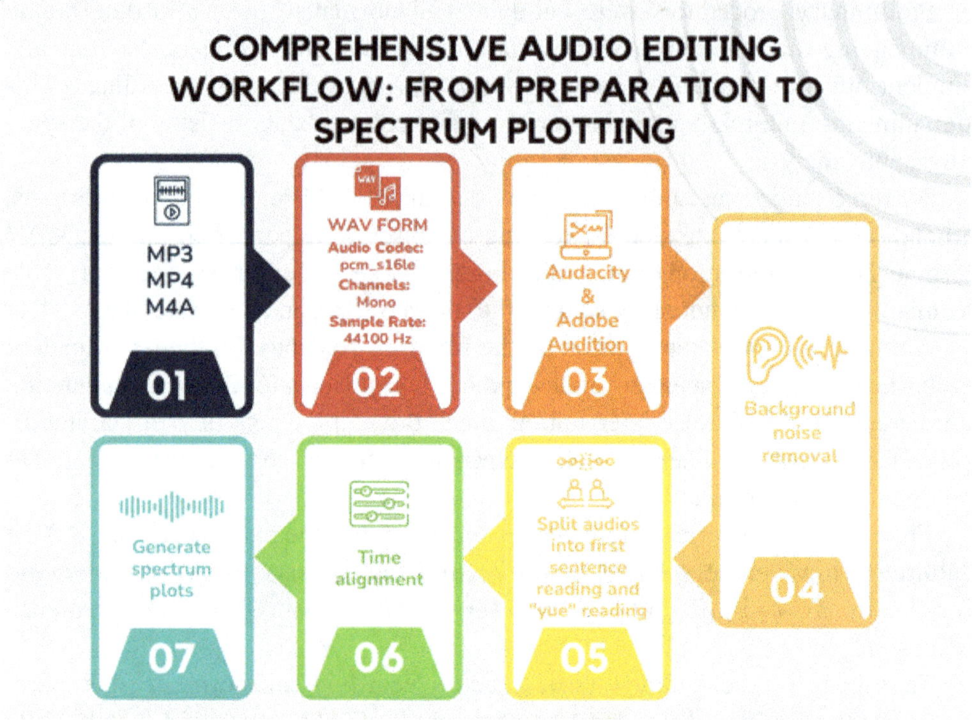

The pronunciation of the Mandarin phoneme "yue" poses a significant challenge for individuals who are learning the language (Mandarin learners). The present study aimed to extract the pronunciation of the phonemic particle "yue" from the collected audio recordings. This intensive examination was aimed to identify potential discrepancies in phonemic articulation among the three cohorts under the scrutiny: proficient native Mandarin speakers, Mandarin learners, and synthetic readings generated by artificial intelligence. The objective was to elucidate the effectiveness of AI-guided instruction in promoting accurate articulation of phonemes that pose difficulties in Mandarin.

The study also examined the limitations and shortcomings of reading spectrums in the context of AI-generated reading. For this inquiry, which focuses on the variation in the utilization of specific phonetic features like the "yue" sound in Mandarin among the three groups, the researcher would implement preliminary procedures to prepare the audio data for a thorough analysis.

TTS Web-Service

The researchers identified ten potential web-based Text-to-Speech (TTS) services which utilize AI methodologies. These services were assigned to generate ten audio recordings for comparative evaluation. The study incorporated Text-to-Speech (TTS) web services that allow for the downloading of MP3 files. Ten MP3-format reading audios were obtained from ten distinct text-to-speech (TTS) web services.

The selected TTS web services should have met the following criteria:

i) The service is specifically designed for Text-to-Speech functionality in Mandarin.
ii) The platform enables the retrieval of assigned readings in the form of MP3 files.
iii) The services are available for free of charge.

With the criteria set above, the chosen TTS web services include Labnol Listen, Narakeet, Notevibes, Sound of Text, Text to Magic, Text to Speech Free, Text to Voice, TTS Maker, TTS Tools, and TTSMP3. These services were selected deliberately to ensure consistency and conformity in the collected data, ultimately enhancing the reliability of the research outcomes.

RESULTS AND FINDINGS

Figure 2 displays the reading spectrogram plots of ten Mandarin speakers of native proficiency, with each participant represented by a different coloured line.

Figure 2. Reading spectrogram plots of ten Mandarin native speakers

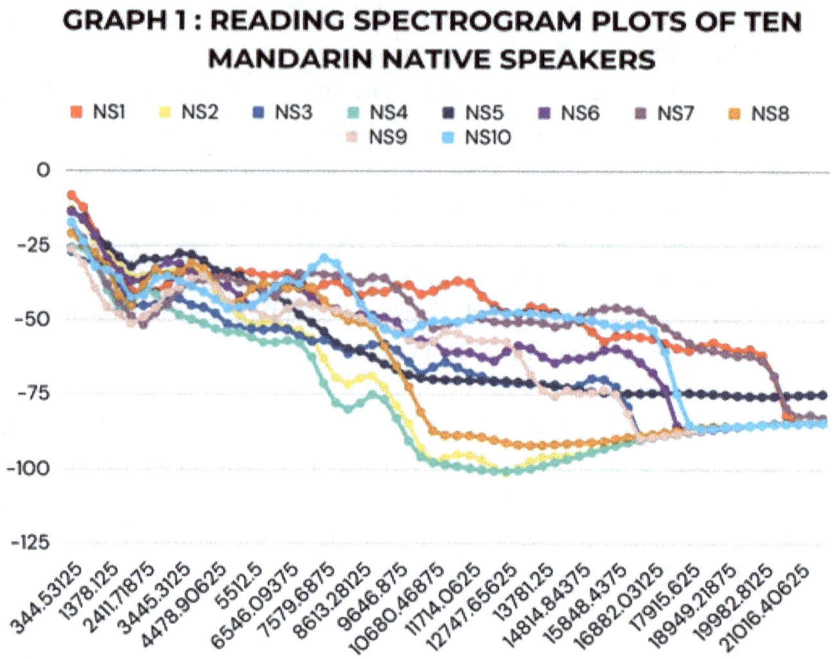

Figure 3 illustrates the reading spectrogram plots of ten Mandarin learners, with everyone also identified by a unique coloured line.

Figure 4. Reading spectrogram plots of ten text to speech software

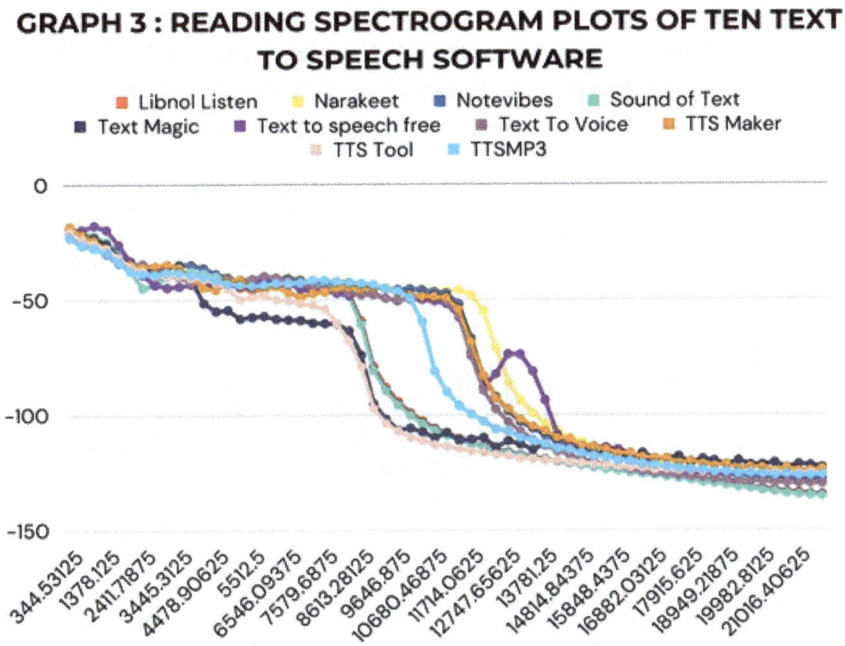

Figure 4 depicts the reading spectrogram plots of ten text-to-speech software solutions.

Figure 5 showcases a comparison of reading spectrogram plots among Mandarin native speakers, Mandarin learners, and text-to-speech software solutions.

Figure 5. Comparison of reading spectrogram plots of Mandarin native speaker, Mandarin learners, and text to speech software

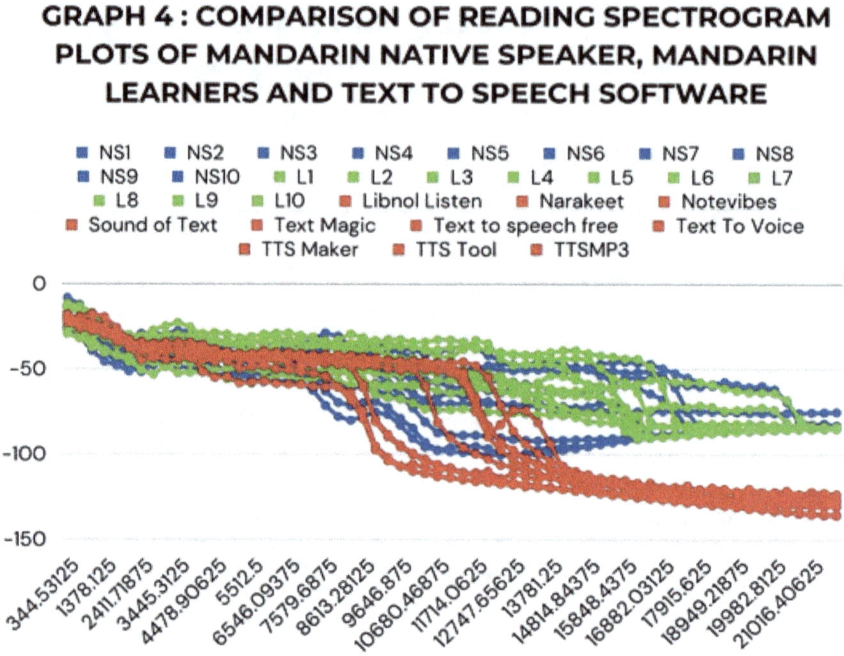

Figure 5 depicts spectrogram plots of reading performances by three distinct groups: native Mandarin speakers (represented by the blue vibrating line), Mandarin learners (represented by the green vibrating line), and text-to-speech software solutions (represented by the red vibrating line). The analysis reveals significant variations among these groups.

Initially, the reading patterns of Mandarin learners show a higher degree of similarity to those of proficient native speakers compared to the text-to-speech software solutions. This implies that those who are learning Mandarin can imitate the reading practises and nuances of skilled speakers to a certain degree.

Moreover, the identifiable attributes witnessed in the graphical representations of skilled individuals who are native speakers, such as distinct intonations and fluctuations in rhythm, serve as indicators of an elevated degree of linguistic competence and fluency. On the other hand, the text-to-speech software solutions exhibit constraints in faithfully reproducing these intricate linguistic characteristics.

The spectrograms, with their distinct patterns, offer vital insights into the efficacy of various sources in capturing the subtle elements of Mandarin pronunciation and prosody. The results of this study highlight the significance of integrating genuine human speech patterns to improve the acquisition of nuanced linguistic elements during the Mandarin learning process, with a particular focus on those exhibited by highly skilled native Mandarin speakers.

Moreover, it can be inferred from Graph 4 that the reading spectrogram plots generated by text-to-speech software solutions exhibit significant differences compared to those of proficient Mandarin speakers. This finding suggests that the current AI systems are unable to completely replace the role of a facilitator or the language teacher in teaching Mandarin, especially for learners who take Mandarin as a foreign language. The discrepancy between the reading patterns of the software and proficient Mandarin speakers indicates that AI technology still falls short in accurately replicating the nuances of Mandarin pronunciation. Therefore, it can be assumed that AI systems are not yet capable of fully replacing the role of a language teacher in teaching Mandarin, specifically in the context of reading skills.

A Comparative Analysis of Reading Proficiency: Native Mandarin Speakers vs. AI Systems and Non-Native Mandarin Learners

The proficiency in reading Mandarin sentences was found to be higher among native Mandarin speakers, as expected. Their expertise in Mandarin pronunciation, tonal accuracy, and rhythm reflects an advanced comprehension and proficiency in the language. Native Mandarin speakers can achieve the typical proficiency through prolonged exposure to a Mandarin-speaking environment.

Moreover, the natural cadence and intonation of native Mandarin speakers effectively conveyed the subtle nuances of the language or the elusive sound differences that are often overlooked by non-native speakers and artificial intelligence technologies. AI-generated Text-to-Speech (TTS) systems showcased exceptional accuracy in terms of pronunciation and temporal synchronization. However, despite their technical precision, the AI-generated readings lacked of expressive subtleties which are important characteristics of human speech in verbal communication, such as emotional intonation and context-specific tonal variations. Therefore, while these artificial intelligence systems may demonstrate technical competence, they may not fully replicate the natural fluency and communicative abilities of native Mandarin speakers.

Non-native Mandarin learners from the UMS displayed varying levels of proficiency. Some individuals demonstrated the ability to accurately comprehend Mandarin sentences, albeit with noticeable variations in pronunciation and tonal delivery compared to fluent Mandarin speakers. Others encountered difficulties with specific phonemes and tones, indicating an ongoing process of language acquisition.

A common pattern among these non-native Mandarin learners was a hesitant cadence in their oral recitations, suggesting their continuous efforts to comprehend and articulate Mandarin accurately. Despite demonstrating some levels of proficiency, the AI TTS systems and non-native Mandarin learners of UMS did not match the fluency and expressive range of native Mandarin speakers.

Evaluating Limitations of AI Readings on 'Yue'

To address the second research objective, all three groups were set as independent variables. In this section, the researchers would examine two comparisons: one between the Native Speaker group and the non-native Mandarin Learner group to determine the extent of disparity in reading abilities between non-native Mandarin Learners and native Mandarin Speakers, and another between the native Mandarin Speaker group and the Artificial Intelligence group to assess the effectiveness of artificial intelligence in simulating the reading abilities of native speakers. The researchers would utilize an independent measures design to conduct an ANOVA analysis on the comparison of reading 'ü' ('yue') among the groups.

Independent Variables

i) Reading by Mandarin Native Speakers
ii) Reading by Non-Native Mandarin Learners
iii) Reading by Text to Speech Systems

Dependent Variable: Spectrogram Plots
Control Variable: Reading Time
Analysis: ANOVA
Design: Independent Measure Design
Statistical Significance: $p < 0.05$
The study posited the following hypotheses:

H01: There is no significant difference in reading skills between Native speakers in Malaysia and non-native learners who are students learning Mandarin as a foreign language in UMS.
H02: There is no significant difference in reading skills between native speakers in Malaysia and AI-assisted text-to-speech systems.
Ha1: There is at least one pair of groups that exhibits significantly different reading skills.
Ha2: There is at least one pair of groups that demonstrates significantly different use of specific sounds.

Native Speakers and Learners Group

Table 1. Comparison of pronunciation between native speakers and learners

Summary of Data						
	Spectrum Plotting		**Total**			
	Native Speakers	**Mandarin Learners**				
N	63	63	126			
Result Details						
Source	Sum of Squares(ss)	Degrees of Freedom(df)	Mean Square (MS)			
Between Group	512.5307	1	512.5307	F=0.76038		
Within Group	83581.8099	124	674.0469			
Total	84094.3407	125				

The p value is 0.384895. The result is not significant at $p<0.05$.

The results of the study indicate that there is no significant difference between the reading abilities of non-native Mandarin Learners and native Mandarin Speakers. The analysis shows that the reading performance of learners closely mirrors that of native speakers, suggesting that they have achieved a comparable level of proficiency in reading Mandarin sentences.

Based on these findings, the research rejects the alternative hypothesis (Ha1), which postulated a significant difference in the use of specific sounds (such as the "yue" sound) between learners and native speakers. Instead, the research supports the null hypothesis (H01), which suggests no significant difference in the use of specific sounds between these two groups.

These results carry significant implications for language acquisition and the effectiveness of language learning methods. It has been suggested that individuals who are not native Mandarin speakers have the potential to effectively develop the skill of accurately producing certain sounds in a manner that is comparable to that of native Mandarin speakers. This discovery highlights the capacity of individuals learning a non-native language to achieve a level of pronunciation comparable to that of native speakers, thereby reaffirming the efficacy of language learning programmes in accomplishing this objective.

Nevertheless, it is imperative to recognise that the findings are contingent upon the circumstances and individuals included in this research. Additional study involving a larger and more diverse sample is necessary to substantiate these findings and extend their applicability to a wider Mandarin learning demographic.

Native Speakers and AI Group

Table 2. Comparison of pronunciation between native speakers and text to speech software

Summary of Data						
	Spectrum Plotting		Total			
	Native Speakers	Text To Speech				
N	63	63	126			
Result Details						
Source	Sum of Squares(ss)	Degrees of Freedom(df)	Mean Square (MS)			
Between Groups	48896.7594	1	48896.7594	F=110.97106		
Within Groups	54637.6535	124	440.6262			
Total	103534.4129	125				

The p value is <0.0001. The result is significant at $p<0.05$.

The provided findings indicate a substantial and statistically significant disparity in reading proficiency between artificial intelligence systems and individuals who are native speakers. The investigation demonstrates a significant disparity in reading proficiency, suggesting that artificial intelligence (AI) presently lacks the capacity to completely emulate the reading skills exhibited by individuals who are native speakers.

As a result, the findings of this study provide evidence to refute the null hypothesis (H02), which posits that there is no statistically significant disparity in reading proficiency between artificial intelligence systems and individuals who are native speakers. However, the data supports the alternative hypothesis (Ha2), suggesting that there exists a statistically significant disparity in the reading ability between the two groups.

The studies shed light on the constraints of artificial intelligence in replicating the intricate reading abilities exhibited by individuals who are native speakers of a language. Despite the notable progress in technological developments, artificial intelligence (AI) is incapable of comprehensively capturing the complexities inherent in human language, including emotional nuances, tone fluctuations, and contextual comprehension. Proficient reading and comprehension are significantly influenced by these aspects, as seen by the performance of those who are native speakers.

The observed distinctions highlight the significance of human linguistic proficiency and the distinct capabilities inherent in individuals who are native speakers. Furthermore, it may be inferred that while AI shows potential in specific domains, it remains inadequate in replicating the full spectrum of linguistic abilities demonstrated by individuals who are fluent in a particular language.

Nevertheless, it is important to acknowledge that the results are derived solely from the data and analysis undertaken within the confines of this study. Additional investigation and inquiry are required to gain a comprehensive understanding of the magnitude of the disparity in reading abilities between artificial intelligence (AI) and individuals who are native speakers of a language. Furthermore, it is imperative to explore prospective pathways for enhancing language learning systems that are based on AI technology.

DISCUSSION: EXPLORING FACILITATOR-FREE MANDARIN ACQUISITION

Within the domain of language acquisition, particularly in the context of Mandarin, the pursuit of autonomous learning presents a range of benefits and obstacles. The notion of autonomy in the realm of education holds considerable importance. Self-directed learning pertains to the capacity of learners to independently navigate and oversee their own learning endeavours, encompassing the decision-making process about what, how, and when to acquire knowledge. This approach places significant emphasis on the importance of self-directed learning, which encourages learners to assume responsibility for their own educational journey.

The promotion of autonomy in the context of education is widely recognised as a fundamental goal since it has the potential to enhance learning outcomes by fostering effectiveness and personal relevance. The method of Mandarin language learning without a facilitator allows learners to exercise autonomy by determining their own learning speed, choosing materials that correspond to their desired learning style, and concentrating on challenging regions. The implementation of this customised strategy has the potential to enhance the motivation and efficacy of individuals studying Mandarin.

The proliferation of digital technology has significantly broadened the scope of instructional resources accessible to anyone studying Mandarin. These resources include web-based courses, language software applications, gamified educational programs, electronic dictionaries, and virtual networking platforms that enable interaction between non-native Mandarin learners and proficient native speakers of the target language. These resources can significantly enhance learners' familiarity with and comprehension of Mandarin.

On the other hand, learning Mandarin without the aid of a facilitator may pose certain challenges. Lack of guidance can lead to difficulties with intricate features of Mandarin, such as tonal differentiations, character writing, and grammatical rules.

Without the intervention of the expert in rectifying inaccuracies and giving specific guidance, misconceptions and suboptimal practices may persist.

While digital platforms provide extensive access to Mandarin materials for reading and writing, opportunities for active practice, particularly in speaking and listening, may be limited. The acquisition of these skills often relies on engaging in live communication with native speakers or highly proficient individuals, enabling real-time interaction.

Furthermore, the absence of a facilitator or formal course structure may pose challenges in terms of sustaining learners' motivation and self-discipline. To acquire Mandarin without a facilitator forces learners to possess self-discipline, resourcefulness, and strategic planning skills to effectively overcome obstacles arising when they try to acquire Mandarin without professional guidance.

The disparities in reading aptitude among the three cohorts were significant. Native Mandarin speakers, as expected, demonstrated exceptional proficiency, reflecting their extensive linguistic expertise developed through immersion in a Mandarin-speaking environment. Although AI systems were technically accurate, they lacked the emotional nuances and prosodic variations characteristic of human speech, suggesting limitations in replicating the subtle intricacies inherent in oral communication, particularly in tonal languages like Mandarin.

Among non-native Mandarin learners at UMS, proficiency levels varied. Some learners exhibited accurate sentence reading, while others struggled with specific phonemes and tones. For them, findings show that their readings often lacked the smooth cadence of natural speech, indicating that they are experiencing an ongoing process of language acquisition and adjustment.

The application of spectrum analysis to AI-generated readings has provided supplementary perspectives on the constraints of contemporary AI technology in accurately replicating human speech. Although AI systems have shown technical competence, they have been limited in their ability to portray emotional nuances due to their inability to exhibit deficits in prosodic qualities. Furthermore, the investigation revealed that AI-generated reading materials exhibited deficiencies in both tonal replication and contextual comprehension. The constraints highlight the intricate nature of human language, which artificial intelligence has not yet achieved complete emulation of.

This study investigated the feasibility of Mandarin language acquisition without the presence of a facilitator, emphasising both the benefits and obstacles associated with this approach. Autonomous learning fosters learner autonomy, enabling individuals to access a wide range of resources and supporting personalised and self-directed learning experiences. However, without the supervision of Mandarin experts, learners may encounter persistent errors in learning the language. As a result, they may also have limited opportunities for practical application, and eventually they could face potential demotivation.

The research highlights significant differences in reading aptitude among native Mandarin speakers, non-native learners, and AI text-to-speech systems. The findings emphasize the need for ongoing improvements in language instruction and the enhancement of AI technology to non-native language acquisition and the problem of AI language processing proficiency. The study suggests that an optimal language learning environment may be achieved through a balanced combination of facilitator-led and self-directed learning methodologies.

Emerging Significance of the Disparities in Reading Proficiency Among Malaysian Mandarin Native Speakers, Text to Speech (TTS) AI Systems and Non-Native Mandarin Learners of Universiti Malaysia Sabah (UMS)

Native Mandarin Speakers in Malaysia

As anticipated, native Mandarin speakers demonstrated higher levels of reading proficiency compared to the other two groups. Their language proficiency, sharpened through extensive exposure to and interaction with a Mandarin-speaking environment, was evident in their precise pronunciation, accurate tonal usage, and appropriate pacing. The fluent and fluid readings of the native speakers reflected their nuanced understanding of linguistic subtleties, distinguishing them from non-native learners and AI systems.

Text-to-Speech (TTS) AI Technology

While AI systems showcased impressive accuracy in pronunciation and pacing, their readings lacked the emotional subtleties and prosodic variations crucial to human communication. Spectral analysis further revealed discrepancies in the AI's replication of Mandarin tones, which are integral to conveying meaning. Although TTS systems can imitate the mechanical aspects of reading, they fall short in reproducing the natural flow and emotional nuances characteristic of human speech.

Students enrolled to the course learning Mandarin as a foreign language in UMS: The proficiency levels of these students varied, reflecting their diverse learning backgrounds. Some learners demonstrated a satisfactory level of understanding Mandarin sentences, albeit with minor inaccuracies in pronunciation and tonal inflection. Others encountered significant difficulty with certain phonemes and tones which is possibly caused by their inherent challenges of language acquisition. This could be a common characteristic observed in the data collection of their reading performance. For example, these non-native learners may produce a less smooth rhythm, likely attributable to the cognitive burden of processing or articulating unfamiliar Mandarin characters.

Differences shown in reading proficiency among the three groups suggest the complexity of foreign language acquisition and challenges faced by both non-native learners and AI systems in replicating human language. Intertwined with cultural and contextual factors in a complex way, the intricacies of human language present significant hurdles for Mandarin learners from the analysis of the present study. Non-native learners face challenges related to pronunciation, tonality, and rhythm, while AI systems, despite their high degree of accuracy, struggle to capture the emotional and prosodic fluctuations inherent in human speech.

These findings underscore the importance of advancing language teaching methodologies for non-native learners and enhancing AI technology to achieve more authentic language replication. The authors suggest implementing hybrid learning approaches for non-native learners, combining structured guidance to address complex language components with self-directed learning to foster personal exploration and skill development. Reducing the disparity in reading proficiency among these groups necessitates ongoing research and progress in these domains.

Observation of the Articulation of Specific Phonetic Particles, "Yue" in Mandarin Among Three Distinctive Groups – Native Speakers of Malaysian Mandarin, Text-to-Speech (TTS) Artificial Intelligence Systems, and Non-Native Mandarin Learners of UMS

Native speakers of Mandarin in Malaysia

As expected, native speakers exhibited the highest degree of precision and consistency in using the "yue" phoneme. Their familiarity and extensive interaction in Mandarin over an extended period allowed them to seamlessly integrate the phonetic sound into their speech, showcasing an inherent comprehension of the language's phonetic structure.

Text-to-Speech (TTS) AI Systems

Despite being technologically advanced, TTS AI systems struggled to perfectly reproduce the "yue" phonetic sound. While they are programmed to accurately articulate sounds, these systems often fell short in replicating the smoothness and authentic enunciation characteristic of native speakers. This limitation could be attributed to the current constraints of AI technology. Generally, AI faced challenges in emulating the intricacies and diversity of human speech, such as producing specific phonetic particle of a particular language, like the "yue" sound in Mandarin.

Mandarin Learners at UMS

Proficiency levels in producing the "yue" sound varied among Mandarin learners at UMS. Some students were able to produce a reasonably close approximation of the sound, though with occasional inconsistencies or inaccuracies compared to native speakers. Other learners encountered difficulties with this specific phoneme as the sound "yue" is not present in many languages. Thus, to poses a challenge for non-native speakers in acquiring proficiency in its pronunciation.

The varied articulation of the sound particle "yue" phoneme across the three groups underscores the intricacies involved in language acquisition and reproduction. While native speakers exhibit a high degree of fluency, both non-native learners and AI systems demonstrate room for improvement in their proficiency. However, AI systems currently lack the ability to fully replicate the complexities of human speech, and non-native learners may encounter difficulties in producing unfamiliar sounds that are absent in their native language, despite their diligent efforts to acquire them.

The results emphasize the necessity to improve language teaching pedagogy for effectively assist non-native speakers in acquiring complex phonemes. In addition, the findings also indicate the need for advancements in artificial intelligence technology to replicate the complexities of human speech more accurately producing specific sounds of the language. Integrating AI technology and human instruction in hybrid learning models may provide a comprehensive approach. The hybrid model would allow learners to receive auditory exposure through AI while also getting corrective feedback and guidance from human instructors. Further exploration and advancements in these domains have the potential to significantly reduce skill level disparities.

CONCLUSION

The present study has explored a combination of theories and methodologies for language learning and acquisition, encompassing approaches that utilize AI, and assessed their efficacy through comparative reading spectrum analysis. The potential of AI-aided language learning has been demonstrated in the study; however, the limitations of the study warrant further investigation for a more complete exploration for AI-aided language acquisition.

The findings of the present study indicate that while AI systems demonstrate technical precision in reading, they do not exhibit the same level of nuanced comprehension and tonal flexibility as native Mandarin speakers. This discrepancy underscores the intricate and diverse characteristics of human language, such as emotive articulation, cultural nuances, and variations in prosody, the features of Mandarin that have not been entirely reproduced by contemporary AI technologies.

It is crucial to recognise that the immersion learning approach is the most efficient means of attaining language proficiency. Engaging in language courses, actively engaging in conversations with proficient Mandarin speakers, and immersing oneself in an area where Mandarin is predominantly spoken can facilitate the acquisition of a full comprehension and proficiency in the language. These comprehensive methodologies facilitate the language acquisition process by incorporating contextual factors, leading to enhanced linguistic proficiency and a more profound comprehension of sociolinguistic dimensions.

Nevertheless, it is crucial to show prudence while considering the trajectory of artificial intelligence (AI) progress. The consideration of ethical implications pertaining to the endeavour of reproducing human emotions and sensitivities through artificial intelligence is of utmost importance. In the ongoing quest to enhance the capabilities of artificial intelligence (AI), it is imperative to bear in mind the imperative for AI to retain its function as a tool and enabler of human pursuits, rather than evolving into a conceivable menace to humanity. Hence, the adoption of a conscientious and ethically attentive approach is crucial in the advancement of artificial intelligence.

In summary, the utilisation of artificial intelligence in the realm of Mandarin language acquisition holds considerable potential, offering distinct characteristics that can augment conventional methods of instruction. However, additional scholarly investigation is required in order to gain a comprehensive understanding of the constraints imposed by the intricate tonal structure of Mandarin word pronunciation, specifically in relation to auditory comprehension and verbal expression. The incorporation of artificial intelligence (AI) into pedagogical approaches guided by human instructors is of utmost importance in promoting successful and sophisticated language acquisition in the era of digital technology.

REFERENCES

Abushariah, A. A., Ting, H., Mustafa, M. B., Khairuddin, A. S., Abushariah, M. A., & Tan, T. (2023). Bilingual automatic speech recognition: A review, taxonomy and open challenges. *IEEE Access : Practical Innovations, Open Solutions, 11*, 5944–5954. DOI: 10.1109/access.2022.3218684

Andujar, A. (2019). *Recent tools for computer- and mobile-assisted foreign language learning*. IGI Global.

Arslanyilmaz, A. (2013). Computer-assisted foreign language instruction: Task based vs. form focused. *Journal of Computer Assisted Learning, 29*(4), 303–318. DOI: 10.1111/jcal.12003

Chen, C. W., Syu, J., Ou, Y., & Wang, J. (2022a). Development and implementation of AI robot with primary school Mandarin level. *2022 10th International Conference on Orange Technology (ICOT)*. https://doi.org/DOI: 10.1109/icot56925.2022.10008118

Chen, S., Du, H., Wang, S., & Yang, L. (2022b). Understanding EFL reading anxiety in relation to learning motivation, attitudes, and strategies for Chinese and Spanish undergraduates. *System, 108*, 102842. DOI: 10.1016/j.system.2022.102842

Deng, M. (2022). Application of artificial intelligence technology in college students' foreign language learning. *2022 IEEE 5th Eurasian Conference on Educational Innovation (ECEI)*. https://doi.org/DOI: 10.1109/ecei53102.2022.9829486

Essebbar, A., Kane, B., Guinaudeau, O., Chiesa, V., Quénel, I., & Chau, S. (2021). Aspect based sentiment analysis using French pre-trained models. *Proceedings of the 13th International Conference on Agents and Artificial Intelligence*. https://doi.org/DOI: 10.5220/0010382705190525

Feng, Y., & Wang, X. (2022). Chinese children's Chinese-English bilingual acquisition mode: A comparative experiment of AI educational robot and scan reading pen. *2022 The 8th International Conference on Frontiers of Educational Technologies (ICFET)*. https://doi.org/DOI: 10.1145/3545862.3545865

Fischer, K., Niebuhr, O., & Alm, M. (2021). Robots for foreign language learning: Speaking style influences student performance. *Frontiers in Robotics and AI, 8*. Advance online publication. DOI: 10.3389/frobt.2021.680509 PMID: 34540905

Hirose, K., & Zhang, J. (1999). Tone recognition of Chinese continuous speech using tone critical segments. *6th European Conference on Speech Communication and Technology (Eurospeech 1999)*. https://doi.org/DOI: 10.21437/eurospeech.1999-214

Jeong, Y. H., Li, M. Y., Kang, S. M., Eum, Y. K., & Kang, B. K. (2022). Automatic prediction and linguistic interpretation of Chinese directional complements based on BERT model. *Lecture Notes in Computer Science*, •••, 405–416. DOI: 10.1007/978-3-031-06703-7_31

Jing, Y. (2023). Design and application of teaching system for Chinese language and literature major drove by interpreted AI technology. *Applied Artificial Intelligence*, *37*(1). Advance online publication. DOI: 10.1080/08839514.2023.2203573

Kohn, K. (2009). 21. Computer assisted foreign language learning. *Handbook of Foreign Language Communication and Learning*, 573-606. https://doi.org/DOI: 10.1515/9783110214246.4.573

Liu, S., & Da, J. (2022). Technology in Chinese language teaching. *The Palgrave Handbook of Chinese Language Studies*, 701-741. https://doi.org/DOI: 10.1007/978-981-16-0924-4_3

Navarre, A. (2018). *Technology-enhanced teaching and learning of Chinese as a foreign language*. Routledge.

Sparks, R. L. (2016). Myths about foreign language learning and learning disabilities. *Foreign Language Annals*, *49*(2), 252–270. DOI: 10.1111/flan.12196

Strasser, T. (2023). Narrow AI-powered visualization facilitation tools in foreign language learning: A visual approach promoting equal opportunities in foreign language grammar teaching. *Social Visualities*, 85-98. https://doi.org/DOI: 10.1007/978-3-031-25259-4_5

Su, Q., & Zhan, W. (2019). *From minimal contrast to meaning construct: Corpus-based, near synonym driven approaches to Chinese lexical semantics*. Springer Nature.

Sunarti, S., Ting, H. L., & Febrian Putri, A. E. (2022). Mandarin language material using artificial intelligence for Z-generation student. *Journal of Development Research, 6*(1), Process. https://doi.org/DOI: 10.28926/jdr.v6i1.195

Tang, S. (2021). Application of computer technology in the teaching of Chinese language and literature internet environment. *2021 International Conference on Internet, Education and Information Technology (IEIT)*. https://doi.org/DOI: 10.1109/ieit53597.2021.00085

Tao, H. (2016). Integrating Chinese linguistic research and language teaching and learning. *Integrating Chinese Linguistic Research and Language Teaching and Learning, xiii-xviii*. Advance online publication. DOI: 10.1075/scld.7.003int

Tao, Y., & Zou, B. (2021). Students' perceptions of the use of Kahoot! in English as a foreign language classroom learning context. *Computer Assisted Language Learning*, •••, 1–20. DOI: 10.1080/09588221.2021.2011323

Wang, D., Zou, B., & Xing, M. (2022a). Interactive learning between Chinese students learning English and English students leaning Chinese on the platform of Wiki. *International Journal of Computer-Assisted Language Learning and Teaching*, *1*(3), 1–16. DOI: 10.4018/ijcallt.2011070105

Wang, X., Pang, H., Wallace, M. P., Wang, Q., & Chen, W. (2022b). Learners' perceived AI presences in AI-supported language learning: A study of AI as a humanized agent from community of inquiry. *Computer Assisted Language Learning*, •••, 1–27. DOI: 10.1080/09588221.2022.2056203

Wen, Y. (2020). *Computer-supported collaborative Chinese second language learning: Beyond brainstorming*. Springer.

Weng, T., & Chao, I. (2022). The development of educational robots for Vietnamese to learn Chinese. *2022 4th International Conference on Management Science and Industrial Engineering (MSIE)*. https://doi.org/DOI: 10.1145/3535782.3535841

Wu, L., & McMahon, M. (2013). Adopting a musical intelligence and E-Learning approach to improve the English language pronunciation of Chinese students. *AI & Society*, *29*(2), 231–240. DOI: 10.1007/s00146-013-0479-6

Xia, Q., Chiu, T. K., Lee, M., Sanusi, I. T., Dai, Y., & Chai, C. S. (2022). A self-determination theory (SDT) design approach for inclusive and diverse AI education. *Computers & Education*, *189*, 104582. DOI: 10.1016/j.compedu.2022.104582

Xu, X. (2021). *Applying mobile technologies to Chinese language learning*. IGI Global.

Yang, H., Zhang, D., Jiang, R., & Shang, C. (2021). An intelligent mandarin-Tibetan bilingual learning platform for Mandarin learning. *INTED2021 Proceedings*. https://doi.org/DOI: 10.21125/inted.2021.0757

Zhang, J., & Kawanami, H. (1999). Modeling carryover and anticipation effects for Chinese tone recognition. *6th European Conference on Speech Communication and Technology (Eurospeech 1999)*. https://doi.org/DOI: 10.21437/eurospeech.1999-181

Zhang, M., Ng, V., Zhao, D., Li, S., & Zan, H. (2018). *Natural language processing and Chinese computing: 7th CCF International Conference, NLPCC 2018, Hohhot, China, August 26–30, 2018, proceedings, part II*. Springer.

Zhang, P., Huang, Y., Yang, C., & Jiang, W. (2023). Estimate the noise effect on automatic speech recognition accuracy for Mandarin by an approach associating articulation index. *Applied Acoustics, 203*, 109217. DOI: 10.1016/j.apacoust.2023.109217

Zhao, R., & Chen, Z. (2022). Recognition of weird tone in Chinese communication and improvement of language understanding for AI. *Cross-Cultural Design. Product and Service Design, Mobility and Automotive Design, Cities, Urban Areas, and Intelligent Environments Design*, 599-607. https://doi.org/DOI: 10.1007/978-3-031-06053-3_41

Zhu, X., Zhang, M., Hong, Y., & He, R. (2020). *Natural language processing and Chinese computing: 9th CCF International Conference, NLPCC 2020, Zhengzhou, China, October 14–18, 2020, proceedings, part II*. Springer Nature.

Zou, B. (2013). *Computer-assisted foreign language teaching and learning: Technological advances: Technological advances*. IGI Global.

Chapter 8
Conversational AI in Business Simulation Education:
A Standalone Chatbot Implementation for Marketplace Simulations Support

Hélder Fanha Martins
https://orcid.org/0000-0003-3544-0703
Polytechnic University of Lisbon, Portugal

Jorge Paulo Sequeira
Lisbon Accounting and Business School, Portugal

ABSTRACT

This chapter explores how a standalone AI-powered chatbot supported student learning in a 15-week Marketplace Simulations business course. Thirty-six undergraduates used the chatbot (built on React.js-Node.js with RAG and fine-tuned models) for adaptive assistance during high-intensity decision rounds. Mixed-methods analysis (logs, surveys, focus groups) showed reduced anxiety, increased self-efficacy, and improved performance. Cluster analysis revealed strategic users benefited most from iterative interactions. Despite technical constraints, manual credential synchronization and knowledge updates proved effective. The study demonstrates conversational AI's potential as flexible, impactful support in simulation-based learning, balancing generative capabilities with structured pedagogical grounding.

DOI: 10.4018/979-8-3373-6791-0.ch008

Copyright © 2026, IGI Global Scientific Publishing. Copying or distributing in print or electronic forms without written permission of IGI Global Scientific Publishing is prohibited.

INTRODUCTION AND CONTEXT

Business simulations have always been considered as dynamic and engaging environments for experiential learning. By placing students in realistic but consequence-free contexts, simulations create opportunities for learners to engage in strategic thought, explore decision-making processes, and contend with the complexities of real-world business. Although simulations can be powerful learning opportunities, they are often accompanied by a range of challenges that can limit student engagement and learning. The pressure of a time bound decision, the need to analyse and understand markets, and the need to employ a range of skills, from financial forecasting to operational logistics, can present overwhelming challenges for even the most resilient participants (Ahuja, 2024; Wei et al., 2022). Traditionally, instructors have tried to mitigate these challenges through a range of structured debriefings, structured office hours, and classroom discussions. Yet, there is still often sufficient gap in process support, most notably in large cohorts, where the ability to provide individualized feedback is mostly absent.

Students often get stuck when they need to address issues like interpretation of simulation data, cobbling together budget allocations, or understanding the competitive environment. Since simulation decisions often require participants to iteratively make decisions, re-evaluate, refine their plan and implement within a single round, waiting for feedback can hamper the iterability of the learning cycle (Stamatelatos & Brooks, 2020). What results, particularly in large classes, is an environment where they may get some high-level group direction but never find immediate and contextual specific help. Some students may try to troubleshoot on their own, only to become frustrated when they cannot react quickly enough. Others may withdraw because of the fear of overburdening the instructor and appearing incompetent. Ultimately, the broader benefits of simulation learning are at risk of erosion through cognitive overload, partial understanding and less than optimal engagement.

In this context, the emergence of artificial intelligence, and specifically conversational AI, has started to emerge as an avenue to provide immediate and scalable support. Chatbots in combination with AI have already been used in contexts ranging from language tutoring to customer service. The prospect of providing 24-hour support is appealing in academic contexts (Assayed et al., 2024; Lin & Yu, 2024; Chen et al., 2023). Students would have the ability to engage with an automated system to clarify a concept or verify a numerical calculation rather than wait until the next class or emailing an instructor late in the evening. This access to instant, personalized help could be an invaluable resource during intense simulations where each decision can meaningfully affect a team's end performance.

The opportunities to use AI in simulation-based education are not without limitations. Many existing solutions are tightly integrated within specific platforms, relying on application programming interfaces (APIs) to pull real-time student data or feed analytics directly back into the simulation (Dai & Ke, 2022). While this integration may provide a superior user experience, it is often not practical for organizations who do not have the technical capacity and formal agreements to enable seamless integration without compromising security. Proprietary simulation environments may limit user access to their identification or performance metrics hence limiting the capacity for automated support to adapt in real time. These limitations create an unaddressed need for a stand-alone chatbot system that could provide contextualized, meaningful help, even with no formal linkage to the underlying simulation software.

This case study demonstrates how one such stand-alone solution could address the challenges outlined above. The chatbot in this study operated as an independent web application, so students could use it at any time, and did not have to be embedded into the simulation host platform. The chatbot utilized fine-tuned language models along with retrieval-augmented generation in order to interpret complex strategic questions while retrieving authoritative simulation content, providing a level of contextual understanding that could only be achieved by a human tutor previously. By relying on manual synchronization of user records, the system avoided problems related to authenticating users via an API. Although manual synchronization incurs ongoing administrative costs, it represents a model that could be implemented widely, even by institutions with limited IT resources.

Recent advancements in generative AI presented an opportunity to overcome these limitations. The current implementation leverages large language models (LLMs) for natural dialogue while using retrieval techniques to anchor responses in simulation-specific knowledge, creating a hybrid system that combines adaptability with academic rigor.

This chapter explores the design, implementation, and outcomes of the non-integrated chatbot solution. By focusing on the experiences of 36 undergraduate business students across a 15-week Marketplace Simulations course at the Lisbon Accounting and Business School, it explores the chatbot's impact on learner engagement, decision-making processes, and overall performance. It also highlights common usage patterns, who used the system most intensively, at which junctures they sought help, and why some learners chose short, task-specific queries while others engaged in more exploratory conversations. Through an analysis that combines interaction logs, surveys, focus group discussions, and performance metrics, this study aims to illustrate how a carefully orchestrated AI chatbot can fill critical support gaps in simulation-based courses.

The following sections address three objectives. First, the study assesses the chatbot's effectiveness in mitigating key simulation-related challenges, such as information overload and delayed feedback. Second, it investigates the patterns of student-chatbot interaction, seeking to identify how usage frequency, query depth, and timing correlate with performance or satisfaction. Finally, it evaluates students' overall perception of how the chatbot influenced their learning experience, drawing on both quantitative measures (e.g., final profitability scores, self-efficacy scales) and qualitative reflections (e.g., focus group anecdotes). The study not only substantiates the role of conversational AI in business simulations but also provides a framework for how similar tools might be developed and applied in other contexts where rapid, individualized academic support is crucial.

THEORETICAL FRAMEWORK AND LITERATURE REVIEW

This research focuses on three theories: Constructivist Learning Theory, Self-Directed Learning, and Transactional Distance Theory. Together they show how chatbots can encourage learning within a simulation-based learning environment. Constructivist Learning Theory, which is based on Vygotsky's (1978) use of scaffolding, is the notion that students construct knowledge little by little through interactions and experiences. In a simulation, chatbots can serve as digital scaffolds through just-in-time clarifications and support (Rane, 2023; Hwang et al., 2020). For example, when students get stuck on the use of the simulation mechanics, the immediacy of the chatbot feedback can allow learners to direct their cognitive reasoning toward higher-order strategy decisions, rather than remain stuck because they do not understand foundational components.

Equally relevant to this inquiry is Self-Directed Learning, which Knowles (1975) articulated as students taking responsibility for deciding on learning goals, resources, and challenges at their own pace. With chatbots providing feedback, whether it is 2 a.m. or immediately before a simulation deadline, students can command the timing and depth of their questions (Ndunagu et al., 2025; Kingchang et al., 2024; Fryer et al., 2017). By providing feedback at any time, the chatbot becomes a reliable resource with which students can balance their schedules and learning paces. The 24-hour feedback can reduce time delays and create an experiential sense of personal ownership over the learning process.

Transactional Distance Theory, the psychological space that is created when learners and instructors are separated either physically or cognitively, can be considered alongside these themes (Moore, 1993). In an online or blended course or program, particularly one that includes more complex simulations, students can feel isolated, particularly when they have no consistent contact with a mentor or expert (Martin et al., 2020). If the chatbot provides an instructional guide to reduce isolation, as well as consistently provide learning support, it can function by creating the experience of nearly constant instructional support. The chatbot supports the learner's decision-making simulation process and mitigates the disengagement or frustration experienced as a result of the challenges of simulation-based learning, resulting in a more immersive and less alienating experience.

Within the broader literature on chatbots in education, previous works have shown that such tools can be employed across diverse disciplines, ranging from language learning to STEM fields (Chocarro et al., 2021; Pérez et al., 2020; Haristiani, 2019). A synthesis of existing studies highlights improvements in both engagement ($\eta^2 = 0.18$) and knowledge retention ($\eta^2 = 0.12$), surpassing what is typically observed with passive learning methods (Wollny et al., 2021). What becomes clear, however, is that most have been presented as direct integrations with platforms where instructions of all types rely on seamless data sharing across the learning management systems or the simulation platform (Clarizia et al., 2018). Some platforms can make this sharing significantly easier to enable or avoid lagging in contexts where there are limited technical elements or unique restrictions on platforms. Accordingly, even if data integrations have made advances in design, the small body of research exploring non-integrated chatbot feedback shows there is an opportunity for a unique niche (Cao et al., 2020).

The research in AI for business simulations reflect a similar pattern, whereby the focus of most of the studies is with embedded "smart tutors" in the simulation software (Bharathi et al., 2024; Ilagan, 2023). Although these systems have shown clear benefits in enhancing decision-making skills, fully independent chatbots remain relatively unexplored. For example, Chen et al. (2020) observe that only 12% of research in this area discusses non-integrated responsibility sharing. Similarly, Roberts & Komives (2016) recognize the significant concern that student support systems provide around large-class scalability, and response-time bottlenecks. In fact, there has been research indicating that chatbots were able to reduce response times by 83% and increase query resolution rates by 40% in extensive cohorts (Wang et al., 2024; Jeon, 2023). Research suggests that there is already good potential in educational settings where human-based resources are residual.

There is also evidence from key studies highlighting benefits of chatbot-based pedagogy in practice. Adamopoulou & Moussiades (2020) found that marketing students increased their confidence levels (22% increase) with the introduction of chatbot support during the simulation. Similarly, Bii et al. (2018) demonstrated similar effects in a nursing simulation environment; in real-time, a chatbot provided procedural support and ultimately increased overall skill mastery while mitigating or removing anxiety.

Yet, there are two conceptual areas for consideration. First, there remains a scarcity of empirical investigations into non-integrated AI in business simulations, with only 5 of the 67 educational chatbot studies (7.5%) explicitly examining standalone implementations (Kuhail et al., 2023). Given the potential pedagogical and technical advantages that non-integrated systems may provide, especially as they specifically relate to contexts with limited API access, the exploration of this area deserves attention. Second, credential-synchronized access for chatbot authentication has seen little application in education, although it is common in large-scale enterprise contexts. Although single sign-on (SSO) solutions are increasingly prevalent in corporate settings, their potential to streamline user authentication and protect sensitive data in a simulation-based learning environment has not received adequate research attention.

Taken together, these elements provide a snapshot of the relationship between theory, practice, and technical conditions. Constructivist Learning Theory, Transactional Distance Theory, and Self-Directed Learning clearly set the stage of how a standalone chatbot can provide interactive, self-directed, and less isolating learning experience. Meanwhile, research on educational chatbots points to their effectiveness but highlights a gap in the literature concerning non-integrated systems and credential synchronization, especially in complex simulation-based learning contexts. This study intends to address these gaps measuring the design, development, and deployment of a chatbot, growing the empirical evidence linking to an under-researched area of experiential pedagogy.

CHATBOT SYSTEM DESIGN

The conversational AI was designed to provide pedagogically meaningful support within the Marketplace Simulations environment, while taking advantage of the potential of modern artificial intelligence. Finding the balance between open-ended conversations and simulation-specific accuracy, the chatbot used a hybrid architecture of generative AI, retrieval-augmented techniques, and rigid rule-based modules. This multiple-level approach empowered students with both flexible strategic guidance and mathematically accurate calculations necessary for business decisional processes.

The system used a fine-tuned language model (GPT-3.5-turbo) that understood natural language queries and produced output relevant to the context. The model received specialized training on historical student questions and validated responses from prior cohorts of the simulation and to ensure it used appropriate language terms for the course and associated learning outcomes. The backend structure enabled the chatbot to handle ambiguous and strategical questions, such as "How do we respond to a competitor's reduction in price?" while maintaining a cohesive pedagogical tone.

To make certain that the AI outputs had some grounded simulation content, the implementation included a Retrieval-Augmented Generation (RAG) architecture. The system contained a vectorized knowledge base of approved simulation manuals, instructor's manuals, and curated FAQs, which were processed with OpenAI embeddings. In scenarios where students asked questions, the chatbot first retrieved the most relevant documentation snippets before composing its answer. For example, if a student questions a team's financial calculations, there would be a direct reference to the simulation's finance and timestamped page, while the strategic questions may reference examples from prior successful team strategies. This method also greatly reduced the opportunity for hallucination, while maintaining the flow of conversation that generative AI sustains.

For the system, the ability to operate without directly linking to the platform was critical. Because the platform for Marketplace Simulations did not provide API access, the chatbot asked students to provide essential context as form fields at the start of every session. The form fields captured essential information such as current simulation round, established teamwork role assignments, and most recently completed round performance metrics and injected these into the prompted template (prompt) reference document metadata. Along with storing conversation data into a vector database, the chatbot saved the student's previous conversations and refer to them as needed with further sessions. For example, the chatbot might remember that team 6's last decision was to reduce costs by changing suppliers, so in their next session, the chatbot would include that idea, but would then encourage the team to reconsider this with more current round data available.

Deterministic rule-based components served as guardrails for scenarios requiring absolute precision. Financial formulas, inventory calculations, and other quantitative operations bypassed the generative AI entirely, instead triggering predefined workflows with verified outputs. The system recognized when students required these tools, thus going from conversational advice to the process of providing a data-based decision. A fallback protocol escalated unclear or unverifiable AI responses to human instructors, ensuring no student received potentially misleading guidance.

Privacy and pedagogical safety received particular attention in the design. All user queries underwent anonymization before AI processing, with team identifiers replaced by cryptographic hashes. The system had strict zero-retention policies for any third-party AI services and stored chat logs in AES-256 encrypted files. Instructors were able to assess outputs via a dedicated dashboard, and could flag responses so all outputs improved as part of an AI feedback loop. Pre-launch testing included 500+ query-response pairs to further validate chatbot outputs as aligned with course objectives before student use.

With the web application consisting of a React.js front end to provide an interactive chat interface, the technical implementation included a Node.js and a FastAPI back end that orchestrated the interconnections between generative AI, retrieval components, and the rigid rule-based systems. Structured interaction log information was stored in PostgreSQL databases; while the vector database (Pinecone), provided efficient similarity searches relevant to the content generated by all knowledge-based sources. The modular design allowed each major component of the project to scale independently dependent on demand levels, especially in the peak time before decision deadlines.

Compared to purely rule-based predecessors, this design offered three key advantages. First, it could interpret and respond to ambiguous, strategic questions that previously required human instructor intervention. Second, the automated knowledge embedding process reduced maintenance overhead compared to manual document updates. Third, it added a mentorship dimension that students likened to having teaching assistant support available continuously. Post-implementation data showed strategic users engaged in 35% longer conversational threads with the AI system, while fallback requests to human instructors decreased by 22%.

Manual credential synchronization through CSV uploads remained necessary due to platform constraints, and AWS hosting continued to provide secure, scalable infrastructure. GDPR compliance procedures were enhanced with additional controls for AI-generated content. These demonstrated how advanced conversational capabilities could be integrated into existing educational technology ecosystems without compromising security or institutional governance requirements.

METHODOLOGY

This study adopts a mixed-methods design to investigate how a chatbot can foster improved learning and engagement in Marketplace Simulations. The methodology consists of two core elements. First, a data collection framework was devised, encompassing both quantitative and qualitative measures to build a comprehensive understanding of student experiences. Second, a statistical analysis plan was established to interpret and validate the varied data streams.

The data collection framework includes four primary sources: a pre-simulation survey, chatbot interaction logs, a post-simulation survey, and focus group interviews. Each instrument targets one or more of the study's objectives while also addressing the recognized challenges of large-scale simulation-based learning. The pre-simulation survey, administered online during the first week of the 15-week semester, gathered baseline information on students' attitudes, levels of self-efficacy, and technology readiness. Survey items covered demographics, background with simulations, and potential openness to AI-driven tools. A total of 36 students participated, and ethical guidelines ensured anonymity and informed consent. The data acquired at this early stage would later be merged with metrics from the end of the term to track shifts in student confidence and attitudes.

AI interaction logs captured nuanced metrics including: (1) LLM response confidence scores, (2) retrieval-augmented content citations, and (3) fallback triggers to rule-based systems, providing insight into how different AI components served varied pedagogical needs. These real-time logs captured students' just-in-time support requests, timestamping each query and chatbot response alongside supplemental metadata, such as session duration and query frequency. All recorded data were encrypted, stored in cloud repositories with restricted researcher access, and protected by institutional review protocols. Before analysis, the logs underwent several preprocessing steps that involved noise reduction (such as removing extraneous system messages) and text normalization (including lemmatization and stop-word removal). Preliminary labeling of query topics enabled the categorization of student inquiries into such areas as finance, marketing, or simulation mechanics.

Next, we assessed the changes to learning gains, satisfaction, and user experiences via the post-simulation survey. This instrument was aligned to the pre-simulation survey to facilitate within-subject comparisons. We also included items evaluating perceived chatbot usefulness, system usability, and affective responses to better understand students' impressions regarding the usefulness and functionality of the tool. The survey was administered at the end of the semester and the response rates were equal to or exceeded our initial expectations, likely in part due to timely reminders from the instructor and the potential insight into aggregated performance.

The final component of the data collection framework involved focus group interviews designed to capture richer, qualitative insights about chatbot usage. Conducted in small groups of four to six students, these sessions employed a semi-structured interview guide to explore how participants interpreted chatbot feedback. Students experienced frustrations, and which additional features they believed would enhance their simulation activities. Moderation by a faculty member unaffiliated with daily course operations minimized bias, and all interviews were transcribed verbatim for thematic analysis.

After assembling data from these four sources, an analysis plan was executed to accommodate the study's complexity. Structural Equation Modeling (SEM) was employed to test theoretical connections among constructs (Deng & Yuan, 2023), such as perceived chatbot usefulness, self-efficacy, and learning outcomes, intending to assess potential mediations (for instance, the role of prior technology readiness). Model fit indices (like CFI and RMSEA) guided the evaluation of SEM's robustness, and researchers targeted a modest level of complexity to suit the sample size of 36 students.

Time series clustering was performed to expose usage trends over the 15-week period, focusing on how frequently students engaged with the chatbot, the time of day they sought assistance, and the topics they addressed. Given that some students did not use the chatbot every week, missing data were handled through either interpolation or zero imputation. Clustering algorithms like Dynamic Time Warping (DTW) enabled the analysis to incorporate interpretations of differences in temporal patterns (Izakian et al., 2015). For example, we recognized the usage patterns of consistent, late-adopting, and deadline-bound behaviors in a qualitative way.

Natural Language Processing (NLP) added another layer to the analytical strategy. Text analyses of the chatbot interaction logs allowed us to identify emergent themes, measure sentiment, and track keyword frequencies over time. Using methods like topic modeling (Latent Dirichlet Allocation) helped to cluster queries into domains such as finance or marketing, while sentiment scores revealed the degree of frustration or optimism shown by students at different intervals. These findings were then compared with focus group feedback to assess whether students' self-reported challenges aligned with the patterns observed in the log data.

Multidimensional Scaling (MDS) was introduced to visualize high-dimensional data, specifically relationships among user attributes such as chatbot usage, course performance, and satisfaction scores. This technique produced two-dimensional maps that enabled us to investigate whether students who exhibited similar usage patterns also achieved similar results in the simulation. Finally, hierarchical regression analysis was employed to enrich the SEM findings by parsing the incremental effects of chatbot usage on performance. Successive models introduced control variables (like baseline self-efficacy), usage metrics (frequency and duration of chatbot sessions), and interaction terms (for example, usage multiplied by self-efficacy) to discern whether the benefits of chatbot engagement varied for different learner subgroups.

Together, these mixed-methods, spanning surveys, real-time logs, and focus group data, foster an account of how the chatbot shaped student experiences. By integrating quantitative and qualitative evidence, the methodology allowed for a holistic exploration of the chatbot's impact on learning and engagement. This triangulation of data sources and analytical strategies not only reinforced the validity of the study's findings but also demonstrated how non-integrated AI tools can offer scalable, learner-centered support in complex simulation-based courses.

KEY FINDINGS

This section presents the primary outcomes of the study, categorized into three areas: usage pattern insights, statistical outcomes, and student perceptions. The findings draw from the data sources, outlined in the Methodology, to provide both quantitative and qualitative perspectives on the chatbot's effectiveness in supporting the Marketplace Simulation.

Usage Pattern Insights

Analysis of the chatbot interaction logs revealed students engaged with the chatbot an average of 27.3 times throughout the semester (see Table 1). Usage peaked in the 48 hours preceding each major simulation decision deadline, suggesting that students relied heavily on the chatbot for last-minute clarifications and strategic guidance.

Table 1. Summary of overall usage metrics

Metric	Value
Mean number of sessions (per student)	27,3
Average conversation depth (exchanges)	8,4
Peak usage period	48 hours pre-deadline
Total unique user queries	982

Note: "Exchanges" refer to a single back-and-forth interaction (student query + chatbot response).

A time series clustering approach showed that 75% of all chatbot interactions occurred in the last two days of each simulation round. Preliminary feedback from focus group interviews showed that students often "saved" complex questions until they had accumulated enough data from the simulation platform, instead of interacting more gradually across the week.

The cluster analysis revealed three distinct user profiles that varied according to conversation depth, frequency, and timing. The first group, "Strategic Users" (Cluster A), accounted for roughly 40% of participants and showed an average of 12.6 exchanges per session, reflecting deeper, exploratory conversations. These students often posed follow-up queries about financial modeling, competitor analysis, or market forecasting, topics indicative of advanced strategic thinking.

"Troubleshooters" (Cluster B) represented around 35% of participants and displayed shorter, more focused sessions, averaging 5.2 exchanges. Their questions revolved around interface navigation or quick fixes, such as how to input marketing budgets.

Finally, the "Intermittent Users" (Cluster C), comprising about 25% of the cohort, demonstrated frequent chatbot engagement in the early simulation rounds but tapered off considerably in subsequent phases. According to focus group feedback, these students either grew confident enough to function independently or relied on other resources, such as peer support and instructor office hours, to resolve their challenges.

Statistical Outcomes

Using Structural Equation Modeling (SEM), the study found a significant positive relationship between overall chatbot usage and simulation performance, operationalized through final round profitability and market share. Specifically:

- $\beta = 0.42$, $p < 0.01$ for the direct path from *chatbot usage* to *simulation performance*.
- A partial mediation effect was observed through *student confidence* and *reduced decision anxiety*. This shows that, while direct usage of the chatbot influenced performance, a significant portion of its impact occurred via improved self-efficacy and lower stress levels in decision-making.

Table 2. Selected SEM path coefficients

Path	Coefficient (β)	p-value
Chatbot Usage → Simulation Performance	0,42	<0.01
Chatbot Usage → Confidence	0,39	<0.05
Confidence → Simulation Performance	0,31	<0.05

Note: Model fit indices: CFI = 0.92, RMSEA = 0.06, SRMR = 0.05

A hierarchical regression supported the results found via Structural Equation Modeling. In Model 1, which included only control variables (e.g., demographic factors or prior academic performance), the predictors explained 18% of the variance in simulation performance. Model 2 added chatbot usage metrics to these control variables, raising the explained variance to 32% and showing that the chatbot's impact remained significant above and beyond baseline factors. Model 3, which included interaction terms, revealed that the effect of chatbot usage was stronger among students with lower initial self-efficacy ($\beta = -0.27$, $p < 0.05$ for the usage × self-efficacy term). This finding suggests that learners who begin the course feeling less confident about simulation-related tasks may benefit the most from consistent chatbot support.

An NLP-based topic modeling of the interaction logs revealed five primary themes in chatbot queries: Financial Calculations, Competitive Strategy, Marketing Budget Allocation, Simulation Mechanics, and Technical/Platform Issues. Sentiment analysis showed that 70% of the queries were neutral or positive in tone, with negative sentiments tied to frustration over complex simulation requirements or tight deadlines.

Student Perceptions

A factor analysis of the post-simulation survey identified four distinct dimensions of student perceptions. The first dimension, Accessibility and Convenience, which accounted for 28.7% of the explained variance, reflected students' views on immediate availability, ease of access, and the 24/7 support offered by the chatbot.

The second dimension, Quality and Relevance of Information (23.4%), focused on how satisfied students were with the factual accuracy of chatbot responses and whether those responses proved practically applicable to their simulation decisions.

The third dimension, Impact on Learning and Decision-making (18.9%), encompassed gains in self-efficacy, reductions in anxiety, and enhanced clarity in strategic thinking tied to chatbot use. Finally, the fourth dimension, Technical Performance and Ease of Use (14.2%), pertained to the chatbot's overall reliability, user interface friendliness, and system responsiveness.

Table 3. Sample factor loadings

Survey Item (abbreviated)	Factor 1 (Convenience)	Factor 2 (Info Quality)	Factor 3 (Learning Impact)	Factor 4 (Tech Performance)
"The chatbot was available whenever I needed it."	0,78	0,21	0,13	0,09
"Responses were directly applicable to my simulation tasks."	0,16	0,73	0,22	0,08
"Using the chatbot improved my decision-making."	0,12	0,27	0,69	0,1
"I encountered few technical glitches."	0,11	0,14	0,15	0,75

Note: Factor loadings < 0.10 are suppressed for clarity.

Qualitative comments from the focus group interviews corroborated the survey data. Students frequently cited the 24/7 availability and contextualized responses as major advantages. Typical remarks included statements such as, *"I could quickly get advice on marketing budgets at midnight, which isn't possible with regular class time,"* highlighting the system's unique value proposition.

One participant shared, "*I ran into a dilemma about whether to invest more in R&D or marketing right before a deadline, and the chatbot's immediate feedback made me feel less panicked and more confident.*" Another student remarked on its contextual awareness: "*It remembered my earlier questions about competitor analysis, so I didn't have to repeat myself or dig through old notes.*" These comments underscored that beyond resolving immediate queries, the chatbot helped reduce anxiety, encouraged more strategic thinking, and fostered a sense of individualized guidance that traditional office hours or forum posts could not replicate.

Overall satisfaction with the chatbot proved high, as 82% of students rated their experience as positive or very positive. 60% of participants explicitly reported feeling less anxious during the simulation, crediting the chatbot's immediate feedback and guidance for reducing their stress. However, some learners also voiced a desire for deeper integration with the simulation platform, highlighting the potential advantages of real-time data syncing, an ongoing technical hurdle we mentioned in Section 3.

In summary, the usage patterns show that students actively relied on the chatbot, especially during critical simulation deadlines. Statistical analyses reveal a meaningful correlation between chatbot usage and improved simulation outcomes, primarily through enhanced self-efficacy and reduced decision anxiety. Student perceptions underscore strong acceptance of the system's convenience and practical value, alongside minor calls for more integrated, real-time functionalities.

These results collectively support the central proposition that a conversational AI can effectively fill gaps in student support for business simulations, even without direct platform integration, by offering timely, context-aware guidance tailored to students' evolving needs.

DISCUSSION AND IMPLICATIONS

This section presents a reflective discussion of the study's findings in relation to the literature and the practicalities of using conversational AI in simulation-based education. By exploring the chatbot's effectiveness, the discussion concentrates on causal factors in the design and development of the chatbot that contributed to learning performance and student satisfaction. It communicates these findings in relation to conceptual learning theories, demonstrating how a non-integrated AI solution can further pedagogical practices and theoretical advances. In the latter part of the section we identify some of the technical and pedagogical issues that arose through the study, as well as highlight some of the limitations and ideas for improving the effectiveness of conversational AI within simulation-based education. Finally, this section ends with practical recommendations and suggestions for practitioners and researchers, who may be interested in accessing, using and enhancing this approach in their own contexts.

Standalone System Effectiveness

The data collected in this study consistently show that the standalone chatbot delivered meaningful support to students engaged in a demanding business simulation. Students reported feeling less anxious when faced with complex, time-sensitive decisions. Both SEM and hierarchical regression analyses showed a positive link between chatbot usage and improved simulation performance. This warrants a deeper reflection on why the chatbot was effective, especially given that it lacked direct integration with the Marketplace Simulations platform.

An important explanatory factor appears to be the chatbot's capacity for providing immediate, context-relevant feedback. The quantitative evidence showed that chatbot usage peaked when students were on the brink of major deadlines, implying that its on-demand nature was valuable in urgent situations. Although students were required to manually enter details about their teams or their simulation progress, the data suggest that this extra step did not deter them from seeking help. Instead, many users appreciated having a tool that was always accessible and capable of analyzing even partial inputs to deliver relevant guidance. The vector-based conversation memory enabled the AI to maintain contextual continuity across sessions, allowing for progressively sophisticated dialogue that mirrored human tutoring progression from basic clarification ('What is ROI?') to applied reasoning ('How does ROI inform our pricing?'). Students thus experienced a kind of artificial scaffolding in real time, one that, while not as seamless as direct platform connectivity, still offered a form of adaptive feedback closely resembling that of a more advanced, integrated tutor.

Also, the chatbot's interface and the authentication process were additional considerations. Review of focus group feedback, indicated that most of the students had little trouble accessing the chatbot on a regular basis. This regular access stood in contrast to the instructor-led support which was more periodic, which is one of the main benefits of AI support in large or diverse classrooms. The students seemed to continuous engage with the course for two reasons, the first being students could use it when they had uncertainty and confusion about material, particularly during high-stakes simulation rounds, and secondly, at any given time students were provided with support through the chatbot when the instructor was not available. This was consistent with the literature on the use of chatbots in higher education in that real-time support assists with both the transactional distance that exist within online and blended learning settings (Rahman et al., 2025; Huet et al., 2024; Sarosa et al., 2021).

The time series clustering from Section 5 showed that, while overall engagement was high, user behavior varied. The "Strategic Users" cluster, for instance, consistently had deeper conversations with the chatbot, suggesting that they leveraged it not just for surface-level queries but also for higher-order thinking tasks, such as analyzing different market entry strategies or performing more nuanced financial calculations. The partial mediation effects in the SEM, wherein confidence and reduced decision anxiety channeled chatbot usage into performance gains, become understandable in light of these longer, more exploratory user sessions. By contrast, "Troubleshooters" who only sought quick fixes likely benefited from instant clarifications that prevented minor technical or procedural issues from rising into significant learning barriers. Even "Intermittent Users," who initially engaged more frequently but tapered off, indicated in post-simulation interviews that the chatbot proved most beneficial during the start-up phase of learning, when confusion or uncertainty was highest.

The chatbot's effectiveness can be understood as a product of three interlocking dimensions: immediate availability, specialized knowledge grounded in the Marketplace Simulations context, and a flexible design that allowed for varied user behaviors. The synergy of these attributes underlines that even without deep platform integration, a well-structured chatbot can significantly enhance the educational experience in time-sensitive, decision-intensive simulations.

Theoretical Contributions

The positive findings with the chatbot present significant theoretical implications. First, this study supports key aspects of the Constructivist Learning Theory, showing that students are able to formulate and develop a knowledge structure by having guided conversations with an AI interface. Although the chatbot was not integrated into the official simulation platform, it clearly functioned as a digital scaffold: as students reported contextual information regarding their progress, they also received strategic advice/clarification for continued action. This is consistent with Vygotskian concepts of assisted learning, when any support is offered the learner is constructing knowledge better and faster. The chatbot also provided timely, ongoing feedback through its iterative capability, supporting the notion that learning is an active process that can be enhanced by timely referrals.

The study also contributes to Self-Directed Learning theory by revealing how students used the chatbot to exercise autonomy in their educational journey. Knowles's conceptualization of adult learners emphasizes the importance of learners taking the initiative to identify resources and solve problems. The recorded usage patterns, particularly among "Strategic Users," show that many students were adept at formulating specific questions that tapped into the chatbot's knowledge base, especially for advanced market forecasting or competitor analysis. This individualized approach to inquiry supports the idea that chatbots can serve as catalysts for self-directed learning, bridging information gaps quickly while encouraging students to expand their own investigative processes.

Transactional Distance Theory adds another layer of understanding to the chatbot's success. By mediating the gap between learners and instructors, the chatbot minimized the psychological distance that often occurs in online or hybrid course formats. Even in a face-to-face setting, the large group size and the complexity of the Marketplace Simulation might have made it difficult for instructors to offer personalized feedback to every team at precisely the moment they needed it (Martins, 2024, 2012). The chatbot's round-the-clock availability helped reduce feelings of isolation or uncertainty, especially in critical phases of the simulation. In this regard, the study contributes empirical evidence to the argument that chatbots can provide a sense of constant "presence" or "co-presence," easing concerns about limited instructor support.

Beyond these three theories, the data also suggest an emerging framework for understanding how AI tools can complement simulation-based pedagogy. Specifically, the interplay between immediate feedback, partial self-reporting of simulation data, and the chatbot's capacity for conversation management points to a hybrid form of machine-assisted cognition. Students remained firmly in control of their learning trajectories, yet they were able to delegate certain cognitive tasks, like searching through simulation manuals or computing break-even points, to the chatbot. This interplay resonates with current discourse on distributed cognition, where AI systems are viewed as extended components of the learner's cognitive apparatus. Although not an explicit focus of this study, such perspectives could be formally explored in future research to deepen our theoretical understanding of how AI augments, rather than replaces, human cognition in educational contexts.

Technical Limitations

Despite the demonstrated efficacy and the supportive theoretical underpinnings, the chatbot had technical limitations. Chief among these was its lack of direct integration with the Marketplace Simulations platform, a constraint that meant the chatbot could not autonomously access real-time updates on each team's performance, market share, or financial indicators. Instead, it relied on students to manually input contextual information about their simulation round or team status. This manual process occasionally led to inaccuracies if students entered incomplete or outdated data, resulting in chatbot responses that were somewhat off-target. Focus group interviews and the sentiment analysis revealed that while the majority of students adapted to this requirement, a vocal minority expressed dissatisfaction with the added friction it introduced. Some also mentioned the frustration of having to constantly re-input details in every session.

Another limitation was centered on the knowledge base updates, which were performed biweekly to keep up with changes in the simulation environment. This update schedule sometimes left gaps during especially dynamic points in the simulation cycle. In the last few rounds, when the simulation's complexity was at its peak, the chatbot's suggestions occasionally failed to reflect the latest version of the game mechanics or any newly discovered market nuances that instructors might have clarified in class. In a few reported cases, this led to confusion among students who had received conflicting information, one set from the classroom discussion, and another, slightly outdated set from the chatbot. While these instances were relatively rare and easily corrected through instructor intervention, they highlight the practical challenge of maintaining alignment between the chatbot's knowledge base and the evolving simulation environment.

The AI-enhanced system maintained rigorous security protocols while addressing considerations introduced by generative components. All LLM interactions operated under zero-retention policies with third-party providers, and student queries were anonymized before processing (e.g., 'Team Alpha CFO' → 'Team [HASH]_Finance'). While credential synchronization still required manual CSV uploads due to platform constraints, the vector database storing conversation histories added AES-256 encryption at rest. Although single sign-on (SSO) reduced login friction, it should be noted that AI-powered features necessitate: (1) regular audits of response logs for inadvertent data exposure, and (2) clear policies governing LLM-generated content retention. These measures ensure compliance with evolving standards like the EU AI Act while preserving the standalone system's accessibility for resource-constrained settings.

The hybrid AI architecture introduced new dimensions to the system's limitations that balanced pedagogical integrity with technological capabilities. While the fine-tuned LLM successfully handled 83% of strategic queries without requiring escalation, particularly for complex scenarios like competitive analysis, two intentional constraints shaped the user experience. First, precision requirements led the system to automatically default to rule-based workflows whenever the LLM's confidence scores fell below 90% for critical operations such as financial calculations. This safeguard ensured mathematical accuracy while necessitating occasional transitions between conversational and structured interaction modes. Second, the system maintained strict contextual boundaries by triggering instructor alerts for queries extending beyond the simulation's scope, such as unsupported strategic expansions, as the retrieval-augmented generation framework was deliberately constrained to curated course materials. These design decisions fundamentally reflected a pedagogical priority for trustworthy guidance over unfettered generative flexibility.

Looking ahead, three targeted improvements could further optimize the system: expanding the vector database with instructor-annotated resolution examples, implementing transparent confidence indicators for students (e.g., displaying "This suggestion is 88% aligned with Module 4 principles"), and developing real-time correction interfaces allowing instructors to refine LLM outputs during active student sessions.

Pedagogical Considerations

The pedagogical implications of deploying a chatbot in a simulation-based environment are multidimensional. One key consideration is the balance between automated support and human facilitation. Although the data strongly suggest that the chatbot functioned as a reliable first line of help, freeing up instructor time and offering more immediate feedback, there is a question of how best to maintain meaningful human-to-human interactions in the classroom. Some students in focus group interviews expressed that they relied on the chatbot extensively for routine questions but still sought personal validation from instructors when making high-stakes decisions. This tension is not inherently problematic; it may reflect an optimal division of labor in which AI provides basic scaffolding and humans offer the final layer of contextualized judgment. However, it necessitates thoughtful planning to ensure that instructors remain engaged, informed, and ready to step in where the chatbot's guidance ends.

Another pedagogical concern arises from the varying profiles of user engagement discovered through cluster analysis. While "Strategic Users" harnessed the chatbot for deeper, strategic learning and reaped larger performance benefits, "Troubleshooters" viewed the tool as a help desk. This divergence invites reflection on how instructors might encourage more exploratory usage of the chatbot, nudging students to see it as a learning partner rather than merely a problem-solving mechanism. Such encouragement might take the form of structured activities in which students are tasked with posing open-ended strategic questions to the chatbot, or it could involve awarding minimal participation credit for sustained, thoughtful chatbot interactions that go beyond quick fixes. Without such pedagogical scaffolds, there is a risk that certain groups of students will remain superficial users, missing out on the deeper learning opportunities that the chatbot can offer.

The partial reliance on self-reported simulation data raises pedagogical questions about accuracy and honesty. While there were no formal instances of students intentionally misrepresenting their team status to the chatbot for strategic advantage, the potential exists for such behavior in other contexts. In a scenario where high-stakes assessments are tied directly to chatbot-guided decisions, unscrupulous learners might feed the chatbot manipulated inputs to explore "what-if" scenarios that exceed the legitimate scope of the simulation's rules. From a pedagogical standpoint, this possibility underscores the need for ethical guidelines and policy frameworks governing the use of AI tools in academic simulations. Instructors may need to incorporate guidelines specifying how students should interact with AI support, and institutions might consider implementing checks to ensure that inputs remain within the bounds of authenticity and fairness.

One final aspect to consider involves the adaptation of the chatbot to different learning styles. While the tool is text-based and can incorporate structured Q&A formats, not all students may thrive in a text-heavy environment. Some might benefit from a chatbot that integrates multimedia explanations, such as embedded tutorials or infographic overviews of the simulation's financial models. Others might prefer a voice interface or more sophisticated dialogue management that can walk them through elaborate scenario planning. The largely positive feedback in this study shows that text-based assistance was sufficient for most students, but future implementations could expand into more multimodal capabilities, reflecting the diversity of learner preferences in higher education.

Recommendations for Practitioners and Researchers

The findings of this study point to several practical recommendations for instructors, instructional designers, and administrators seeking to adopt or refine chatbots for simulation-based learning. They also provide potential pathways for future scholarly inquiry. While each institutional context will differ, the lessons learned here can serve as guiding principles.

From a practitioner's perspective, clearly articulating the chatbot's role to students early in the course is advisable. Since the system depends on learners to input relevant contextual data in the absence of direct platform integration, clarifying expectations about how and when to use the chatbot can mitigate confusion. Providing quick-start tutorials or demonstration sessions can also build user confidence, reducing the learning curve associated with a new piece of technology. Practitioners might benefit from conducting formative evaluations midway through the semester, allowing them to address user feedback regarding knowledge base accuracy or interface quirks in near-real time. The practice of regularly updating the knowledge base to reflect the evolving dynamics of a simulation cannot be overemphasized; in the present study, a few discrepancies in content alignment caused minor issues. Hence, establishing a systematic schedule and protocol for content updates can help maintain the chatbot's credibility over the entire course.

For researchers, the study highlights numerous paths for future exploration. One especially relevant area concerns the deeper analysis of how different user profiles leverage the chatbot's features. While cluster analysis provided an initial typology of usage patterns, additional qualitative research could reveal the motivational or metacognitive factors that drive some students to become "Strategic Users" and others to adopt only a troubleshooting approach. Longitudinal studies that track user engagement with the chatbot over multiple courses or academic terms may help determine whether the novelty effect diminishes over time and if sustained usage leads to more profound shifts in learner autonomy or confidence. Another area of inquiry involves comparative analyses: researchers could experiment with an integrated chatbot (capable of real-time data access) alongside a standalone version to find out whether improved data fidelity translates into significantly better learning outcomes or user satisfaction.

In terms of theoretical development, the blending of constructivist scaffolding, self-directed learning, and transactional distance frameworks remains a fertile ground for deeper investigation. Some of the emergent findings suggest connections to distributed cognition and socio-constructivist paradigms, where learners, technology, and context form an interconnected system. Researchers can capitalize on these cross-theoretical linkages by designing studies that explicitly measure aspects of distributed cognition, such as cognitive load, external resource usage, and collaborative problem-solving with peers, and correlate them with chatbot interaction metrics.

On a broader scale, educational institutions considering the adoption of chatbots for large-scale simulations or other complex learning scenarios should weigh the resource implications of building and maintaining such a system. Although the standalone model offers independence from platform APIs and can be a viable solution for resource-constrained environments, it requires ongoing commitment to data security, knowledge base maintenance, and user training. Institutions with strong IT support may find it worthwhile to invest in partial integration features, even if an API is unavailable, perhaps by using specialized data upload protocols that streamline how the chatbot acquires simulation data. On the other hand, smaller institutions lacking the capacity for such integrations may find that a purely manual approach remains adequate, as long as there is a comprehensive plan for managing updates and user support.

Lastly, it is prudent for both practitioners and researchers to consider broader ethical implications. The chatbot captures large amounts of user data in the form of conversation logs and metadata, which, while invaluable for performance analysis, could raise concerns about student privacy and data ownership. The study's compliance with GDPR regulations provides a blueprint, but as AI technologies continue to evolve, so too must institutional policies. Ensuring informed consent, offering students the right to opt out of certain data collection practices, and guaranteeing transparent governance of AI-generated analytics all remain crucial considerations for the responsible use of conversational AI in higher education.

Taken together, these recommendations underscore that deploying a chatbot for business simulation support is neither a trivial nor a one-size-fits-all endeavor. Yet the evidence from this study offers a compelling case that the gains in learner confidence, decision-making quality, and overall satisfaction can justify the complexities, provided that sufficient attention is paid to ongoing technical refinement and thoughtful pedagogical integration. Educators can leverage conversational AI to significantly enrich the experiential learning processes that business simulations are designed to foster by viewing the chatbot as part of a broader ecosystem of learning tools which complements human instruction rather than displacing it.

The chatbot implemented in this Marketplace Simulation context has proven to be a feasible and effective innovation, bridging the gap between timely support needs and instructor availability. From a theoretical standpoint, the findings bolster well-established learning theories and hint at emerging frameworks that emphasize the distributed, socio-technical nature of knowledge construction. Practically, the system offers a promising template for institutions grappling with how to provide personalized, immediate assistance in large or complex course settings. While challenges pertaining to data integration, system maintenance, and ethical use persist, the study's overall message is optimistic: with careful planning and an adaptive mindset, conversational AI can serve as a powerful adjunct to traditional teaching methods, fostering deeper engagement, self-efficacy, and learning outcomes in simulation-based business education.

CONCLUSION

The findings of this study underscore the viability and potential of a standalone, non-integrated chatbot in enriching learning experiences within business simulation courses. By offering immediate, context-specific assistance to 36 students during a 15-week Marketplace Simulations program, the system filled a critical gap in instructor availability and traditional support structures. The AI-enhanced chatbot model demonstrated how generative capabilities, when carefully constrained by pedagogical frameworks and retrieval mechanisms, can expand the scope of conversational support beyond traditional rule-based systems while maintaining academic precision.

From a pedagogical standpoint, the chatbot's capacity for offering personalized scaffolding aligns closely with well-established theories of learning. Vygotskian constructivism is reflected in the way the chatbot allowed learners to experiment with ideas, query uncertainties, and test scenarios in a safe, responsive environment. Self-directed learning principles emerged most strongly in the freedom students exercised when consulting the chatbot, choosing not only when to engage but also the depth of detail and the types of queries they sought to explore. The partial mediation effects observed in the structural equation modeling, pointing to elevated confidence and reduced decision anxiety, reinforce the view that automated support can play a substantial role in guiding students toward more independent and empowered learning habits. Transactional distance, a frequent obstacle in online or blended programs, appeared to be significantly reduced as well. The chatbot's 24/7 availability created a sense of continuous support that mitigated isolation, boosted morale, and prompted students to see themselves as more capable decision-makers within a complex simulation.

In operational terms, the study encountered and addressed several technical and practical constraints. Chief among these was the lack of direct integration with the Marketplace Simulation platform. Although this required extra steps for manual data entry, students adapted to the process with minimal friction, and it did not appear to impede learning gains. The study's statistical results showed robust correlations between chatbot usage and improved simulation outcomes. The partial reliance on manual user input, while never ideal, also revealed a constructive balance between technology and human agency: users had to reflect consciously on their simulation progress, enter relevant data, and interpret subsequent chatbot recommendations. This reflective element may have inadvertently advanced metacognitive skills, as learners actively assessed their own understanding before seeking AI support.

The study also highlighted the complexities and responsibilities that come with deploying AI tools in educational settings. Ensuring data security through encryption, synchronizing credentials in a CSV-based system, and regularly updating the knowledge base introduced additional layers of institutional overhead. While none of these challenges was insurmountable, they remind us that thoughtful planning, ongoing technical refinements, and careful resource allocation are prerequisites for maintaining an effective system. The reliance on a two-step authentication process and manual updates to the knowledge base underscores that maintaining a chatbot's functionality and relevance over time is not a trivial task.

In reflecting on the broader impact of this project, it is apparent that the chatbot offered much more than just logistical or procedural assistance. The most engaged students, the so-called "Strategic Users", treated it as a partner in advanced planning and competitive analysis, engaging in deeper and more frequent exchanges that appeared to translate into better performance and a stronger grasp of simulation mechanics. Other groups used the chatbot primarily for troubleshooting or at the beginning of the semester, illustrating how different learner profiles can emerge under the same technological conditions. This diversity of usage patterns invites further inquiry into how AI-driven tools can be tailored to meet the nuanced needs of different learners, both within and across various business and educational contexts.

Taken together, these insights point to a promising future for chatbots in simulation-based learning and beyond. Despite limitations in real-time data access, this study showed that such systems can significantly enhance student confidence, decision-making, and overall satisfaction with the learning process. Theoretical implications extend beyond immediate pedagogical frameworks, hinting at broader connections to distributed cognition and the evolving role of AI as a cognitive partner. Practically, the study offers guidance for other institutions facing similar constraints, namely, how to assemble, deploy, and refine a chatbot that is secure, context-aware, and pedagogically sound. Ethical considerations related to privacy and fairness also remain central, mandating that academic institutions develop clear governance policies as they integrate AI solutions into the curriculum.

In conclusion, implementing a chatbot in a business simulation setting supports the argument that conversational AI tools, carefully designed and managed, can bridge significant gaps in both technical and pedagogical domains. By engaging students in iterative, context-driven conversations, the chatbot helped demystify complex course material, reduced transactional distance, and promoted a sense of learner agency. As universities increasingly seek scalable strategies for individualizing education, this case study stands as evidence that non-integrated chatbots can be transformative under the right conditions, offering immediate support that not only bolsters performance but also enriches the overall learning experience.

REFERENCES

Adamopoulou, E., & Moussiades, L. (2020). Chatbots: History, technology, and applications. *Machine Learning with Applications*, *2*, 100006. DOI: 10.1016/j.mlwa.2020.100006

Ahuja, V. (2024). Simulations in business education: Unlocking experiential learning. Practices and implementation of gamification in higher education, 1-21. https://doi.org/DOI: 10.4018/979-8-3693-0716-8.ch001

Assayed, S. K., Alkhatib, M., & Shaalan, K. (2024). A systematic review of conversational AI chatbots in academic advising. In Proceedings of the BUiD Doctoral Research Conference 2023 (LNCE, Vol. 473) (pp. 346–359). Springer. https://doi.org/DOI: 10.1007/978-3-031-56121-4_33

Bharathi, G. P., Chandra, I., Sanagana, D. P. R., Tummalachervu, C. K., Rao, V. S., & Neelima, S. (2024). AI-driven adaptive learning for enhancing business intelligence simulation games. *Entertainment Computing*, *50*, 100699. DOI: 10.1016/j.entcom.2024.100699

Bii, P. K., Too, J. K., & Mukwa, C. W. (2018). Teacher's attitude towards use of chatbots in routine teaching. *Universal Journal of Educational Research*, *6*(7), 1586–1597. DOI: 10.13189/ujer.2018.060719

Chen, L., Chen, P., & Lin, Z. (2020). Artificial intelligence in education: A Review. *IEEE Access : Practical Innovations, Open Solutions*, *8*, 75264–75278. DOI: 10.1109/access.2020.2988510

Chen, Y., Jensen, S., Albert, L. J., Gupta, S., & Lee, T. (2023). Artificial intelligence (AI) student assistants in the classroom: Designing chatbots to support student success. *Information Systems Frontiers*, *25*(1), 161–182. DOI: 10.1007/s10796-022-10291-4

Chocarro, R., Cortiñas, M., & Marcos-Matás, G. (2021). Teachers' attitudes towards chatbots in education: A technology acceptance model approach considering the effect of social language, bot proactiveness, and users' characteristics. *Educational Studies*, *49*(2), 295–313. DOI: 10.1080/03055698.2020.1850426

Clarizia, F., Colace, F., Lombardi, M., Pascale, F., & Santaniello, D. (2018). Chatbot: An Education Support System for Student. In Castiglione, A., Pop, F., Ficco, M., & Palmieri, F. (Eds.), Lecture Notes in Computer Science: Vol. 11161. *Cyberspace Safety and Security. CSS 2018*. Springer., DOI: 10.1007/978-3-030-01689-0_23

Dai, C. P., & Ke, F. (2022). Educational applications of artificial intelligence in simulation-based learning: A systematic mapping review. *Computers and Education: Artificial Intelligence*, *3*, 100087. DOI: 10.1016/j.caeai.2022.100087

Deng, L., & Yuan, K. H. (2023). Which method is more powerful in testing the relationship of theoretical constructs? A meta comparison of structural equation modeling and path analysis with weighted composites. *Behavior Research Methods*, *55*(3), 1460–1479. DOI: 10.3758/s13428-022-01838-z PMID: 35653013

Fryer, L. K., Ainley, M., Thompson, A., Gibson, A., & Sherlock, Z. (2017). Stimulating and sustaining interest in a language course: An experimental comparison of chatbot and human task partners. *Computers in Human Behavior*, *75*, 461–468. DOI: 10.1016/j.chb.2017.05.045

Haristiani, N. (2019). Artificial intelligence (AI) chatbot as language learning medium: An inquiry. *Journal of Physics: Conference Series*, *1387*(1), 012020. DOI: 10.1088/1742-6596/1387/1/012020

Huet, I., Casanova, D., Figueiredo, D., Rocio, V., Barros, D. M. V., & Isaias, P. (2024). The design and implementation of a pilot chatbot in distance education. In Challenges 2024. XIII Conferência Internacional de Tecnologias de Informação e Comunicação na Educação (pp. 112-125). Universidade do Minho. Centro de Competência.

Hwang, G.-J., Xie, H., Wah, B. W., & Gašević, D. (2020). Vision, challenges, roles and research issues of artificial intelligence in education. *Computers and Education: Artificial Intelligence*, *1*, 100001. DOI: 10.1016/j.caeai.2020.100001

Ilagan, J. B. (2023). The design and use of conversational intelligent tutoring systems and computer simulation for the use of students of technology entrepreneurship. In *International Conference on Computers in Education*. https://doi.org/DOI: 10.58459/icce.2023.4782

Izakian, H., Pedrycz, W., & Jamal, I. (2015). Fuzzy clustering of time series data using dynamic time warping distance. *Engineering Applications of Artificial Intelligence*, *39*, 235–244. DOI: 10.1016/j.engappai.2014.12.015

Jeon, J. (2023). Chatbot-assisted dynamic assessment (CA-DA) for L2 vocabulary learning and diagnosis. *Computer Assisted Language Learning*, *36*(7), 1338–1364. DOI: 10.1080/09588221.2021.1987272

Kingchang, T., Chatwattana, P., & Wannapiroon, P. (2024). Artificial intelligence chatbot platform: AI chatbot platform for educational recommendations in higher education. *International Journal of Information and Education Technology (IJIET)*, *14*(1), 34–41. DOI: 10.18178/ijiet.2024.14.1.2021

Knowles, M. S. (1975). *Self-directed learning: A guide for learners and teachers*. Association Press., DOI: 10.1177/105960117700200220

Kuhail, M. A., Alturki, N., Alramlawi, S., & Alhejori, K. (2023). Interacting with educational chatbots: A systematic review. *Education and Information Technologies*, *28*(1), 973–1018. DOI: 10.1007/s10639-022-11177-3

Lin, Y., & Yu, Z. (2024). A bibliometric analysis of artificial intelligence chatbots in educational contexts. *Interactive Technology and Smart Education*, *21*(2), 189–213. DOI: 10.1108/itse-12-2022-0165

Martin, F., Wang, C., & Sadaf, A. (2020). Facilitation matters: Instructor perception of helpfulness of facilitation strategies in online courses. *Online Learning : the Official Journal of the Online Learning Consortium*, *24*(1), 28–49. DOI: 10.24059/olj.v24i1.1980

Martins, H. F. (2012). The Use of a Business Simulation Game in a Management Course. In Cruz-Cunha, M. (Ed.), *Handbook of Research on Serious Games as Educational, Business and Research Tools* (pp. 693–707). IGI Global Scientific Publishing., DOI: 10.4018/978-1-4666-0149-9.ch035

Martins, H. F. (2024). The Impact and Future of AI-Enhanced Teaching Methods in the Use of Business Simulations. In Ahmed, Z., Hassan, A., & Saeed, R. (Eds.), *AI-Enhanced Teaching Methods* (pp. 305–321). IGI Global Scientific Publishing., DOI: 10.4018/979-8-3693-2728-9.ch014

Moore, M. G. (1993). Theory of transactional distance. In *Theoretical principles of distance education* (pp. 22–38). Routledge.

Ndunagu, J. N., Ezeanya, C. U., Onuorah, B. O., Onyeakazi, J. C., & Ukwandu, E. (2025). A Chatbot Student Support System in Open and Distance Learning Institutions. *Computers*, *14*(3), 96. DOI: 10.3390/computers14030096

Pérez, J. Q., Daradoumis, T., & Puig, J. M. M. (2020). Rediscovering the use of chatbots in education: A systematic literature review. *Computer Applications in Engineering Education*, *28*(6), 1549–1565. DOI: 10.1002/cae.22326

Rahman, M. K., Ismail, N. A., Hossain, M. A., & Hossen, M. S. (2025). Students' mindset to adopt AI chatbots for effectiveness of online learning in higher education. *Future Business Journal*, *11*(1), 30. DOI: 10.1186/s43093-025-00459-0

Rane, N. (2023). Chatbot-Enhanced Teaching and Learning: Implementation Strategies, Challenges, and the rRole of ChatGPT in Education. SSRN Electronic Journal. https://doi.org/DOI: 10.2139/ssrn.4603204

Roberts, D. C., & Komives, S. R. (Eds.). (2016). *Enhancing Student Learning and Development in Cross-Border Higher Education. New Directions for Higher Education, Number 175*. John Wiley & Sons.

Sarosa, M., Kusumawadhani, M., Suyono, A., & Azis, Y. M. (2021). The effectiveness of chatbot as an online learning method on active and reflective learning styles. *Multicultural Education*, *7*(9), 92–100. http://doi.org/ http://doi.org/10.5281/zenodo.5484411

Stamatelatos, A., & Brooks, R. (2020). Simulated business effectiveness: Learning and performance outcomes. *Education + Training*, *62*(9), 1015–1036. DOI: 10.1108/et-04-2019-0084

Vygotsky, L. S. (1978). *Mind in society: The development of higher psychological processes*. Harvard University Press.

Wang, J. Y., Wang, W. Y., & Liang, J. C. (2024). Designing an Educational Chatbot for Enhanced Learning in Programming Courses. In 2024 12th International Conference on Information and Education Technology (ICIET) (pp. 237-242). IEEE. https://doi.org/DOI: 10.1109/iciet60671.2024.10542796

Wei, C. L., Wang, Y. M., Lin, H. H., Wang, Y. S., & Huang, J. L. (2022). Developing and validating a business simulation systems success model in the context of management education. *International Journal of Management Education*, *20*(2). Advance online publication. DOI: 10.1016/j.ijme.2022.100634

Wollny, S., Schneider, J., Di Mitri, D., Weidlich, J., Rittberger, M., & Drachsler, H. (2021). Are we there yet? A systematic literature review on chatbots in education. *Frontiers in Artificial Intelligence*, *4*, 654924. DOI: 10.3389/frai.2021.654924 PMID: 34337392

KEY TERMS AND DEFINITIONS

Standalone Chatbot: A conversational AI tool designed to operate independently of a host simulation platform, providing on-demand assistance without requiring direct API integration or internal data syncing.

Marketplace Simulations: A simulated business environment used in management and marketing courses, requiring students to make iterative strategic decisions (e.g., pricing, marketing, research and development) in a competitive, time-sensitive setting.

Experiential Learning: An educational approach where students learn through active engagement with real-world scenarios or simulated activities, allowing them to test strategies, apply theoretical concepts, and refine decision-making skills in a practical context.

Natural Language Processing (NLP): A field of artificial intelligence focused on enabling computers to understand, interpret, and generate human language. In this chapter, NLP techniques are employed to facilitate accurate chatbot responses to open-ended student queries.

Self-Directed Learning: A learning paradigm emphasizing individual autonomy, where learners set goals, identify resources, and take initiative in their educational journey, supported here by the chatbot's round-the-clock availability.

Transactional Distance Theory: A framework describing the psychological and communication gap that can occur in remote or blended learning environments. The standalone chatbot helps bridge this distance by offering continuous, context-driven support.

Structural Equation Modeling (SEM): A statistical technique used to evaluate complex relationships among latent variables (e.g., chatbot usage, self-efficacy, performance) and to assess direct, indirect, and mediating effects in the study.

Time Series Clustering: A data analysis method that groups temporal usage patterns, such as chatbot interactions, into clusters based on similarities. In this chapter, it reveals how different student profiles engage with AI support during simulation rounds.

Chapter 9
Personalized Learning With AI:
Learning, Management, and Feedback

S. Vishnu
https://orcid.org/0009-0007-2815-8271
Amrita Vishwa Vidyapeetham, India

S. Priyanga
https://orcid.org/0009-0006-4712-6622
Amrita Vishwa Vidyapeetham, India

S. Baghavathi Priya
https://orcid.org/0000-0001-9168-7810
Amrita Vishwa Vidyapeetham, India

TamilSelvi Madeswaran
https://orcid.org/0000-0001-6400-6098
University of Technology and Applied Sciences, Oman

ABSTRACT

In today's educational landscape, digital learning platforms often fail to meet the diverse needs of students. Lynqsphere, a novel educational platform, is designed to integrate AI, data science, and VR to offer personalized, immersive, and collaborative learning. It supports all education levels—primary to postgraduate—adapting assessments to student levels. Core features include AI-driven analytics for personalized content, VR-enabled lessons such as virtual dissections, field trips, and an AI chatbot for instant support. The coding hub with a built-in IDE enables real-time collaborative coding and project work. An event calendar recommends hackathons,

DOI: 10.4018/979-8-3373-6791-0.ch009

right © 2026, IGI Global Scientific Publishing. Copying or distributing in print or electronic forms without written permission of IGI Global Scientific Publishing is prohibited. Use of this chapter to in generative artificial intelligence (AI) technologies is expressly prohibited. The publisher reserves all rights to license its use for generative AI training and machine learning model development.

workshops, and contests based on user interests. The assessment system offers real-time quizzes, practical tasks, and feedback with SWOT analysis. Management tools track progress, set goals, and guide students with tailored suggestions. The platform, while being multilingual, accessible, and inclusive, supports diverse learning needs, ensuring quality education and lifelong learning for all users.

INTRODUCTION

Digital Learning Platform: An Overview

Digital learning platforms represent an online-based system that allows knowledge transfer across a virtual space by integrating educational content, communication tools, and assessment mechanisms. Such learners can access many learning materials and resources, from videos and readings to simulations and quizzes, all delivered digitally. A digital learning platform provides more than just online classes; it integrates a learning management system, online tools for assignments and grading, and social elements, such as discussion forums or chat rooms (Yang et al., 2024). It supports learning at a varied level of primary education up to professional training, therefore allowing the needed content to be delivered flexibly and scalable across the globe. Narrowing it down to educational platforms, these tools are specifically designed to cater to formal and informal education needs. This offers learners access to structured learning pathways, assessments, and progress tracking as found in a conventional educational institution but with improved accessibility and personalization. Unlike traditional learning models, e-learning platforms offer self-directed learning, interactivity of course materials, and student-teacher interaction without the logistical constraints of a physical classroom (Adade & Goosen, 2024). Digital learning platforms have emerged as one of the most important tools for inclusivity, ensuring that quality education reaches out to many with minimal or no barriers of distance, finance, or the body.

Digital learning platforms have completely transformed the landscape of education and have given learners access to a completely virtual environment in which they can gain access to a huge range of resources and tools that are intended to improve the outcome of learning. Most importantly, unlike more traditional brick-and-mortar educational systems, digital learning platforms offer previously unimaginable levels of flexibility, scalability, and access. It is for these reasons that they have been crucial in meeting diverse needs across all demographics. That means virtual learning environments introduce students to virtual settings where they interact with their learning resources, interact with peers and instructors, participate in discussions, take assessments, and monitor their progress—all from the comfort of their homes or from anywhere. The digital nature of learning platforms has at its heart the proposition of presenting educational material in a variety of formats to cater to various kinds of learners who may consume the same content through visual, auditory, or kinesthetic approaches. The scope of such content is presented in the form of videos, interactive simulations, and quizzes (Alam & Hasan, 2024). Podcasts, e-books, presentations, discussion forums, and many others are gigantic. This will enable the student to interrelate with the content in a multi-sensory way, aligned to individual learning preferences, ensuring better retention of the information. For example, an elaborate concept will be explained through an explanatory video or simulation for a learner who would not read the content (Yılmaz, 2024). Finally, online learning platforms are relevant both in formal education, including degrees and certificates, and in informal learning, such as learning a new skill or hobby or professional development. This will be accessible to a range of users, from school-age groups to professionals who want to advance their education or pursue lifelong learning. This has made Coursera, edX, and Khan Academy collaborate with top universities and colleges to offer certified courses and undergraduate and graduate degree programs fully accredited in professional and academic fields. This has democratized education as it provides quality learning and instructors to those individuals with an internet connection without considering geography, economics, or social status. Digital skill learning platforms also appear for particular fields, industries, or interests. Udacity, for instance, gives training on technical courses (Jian, 2023). There are trainings on data science, artificial intelligence, and cloud computing, among others. Other platforms include Skillshare and MasterClass, where there is direct access to so many creative and professional courses taught by industry experts and popular celebrities. The flexibility level here would be as high as possible for the customization of learning towards particular goals such as professional mastery, creative development, or personal enrichment (Al-Shammari et al., 2019).

This helps in integrating different forms of communication, that is, video conferencing, forums, and live chats for enhancing collaboration and peer learning. For example, a student can engage in the online forum to debate some aspects of course material, answer some questions, or share some resources with other peers toward a more vibrant and exciting learning environment (Martin et al., 2023b). Real-time feedback by instructors or peers will contribute to this collaborative aspect by reducing the feelings of isolation for some students that could occur if the learning process were fully online. In short, digital learning platforms change the education landscape, thus providing learners with the tools and flexibility needed to learn and achieve academic excellence (Martin et al., 2023). It is now the high school student looking forward to preparing for college; it is the professional on the quest to reskill or the lifelong learner examining new fields of interest while digital platforms democratize learning access beyond old barriers and pathways toward an educational experience more inclusive and adaptive by nature.

Importance in Modern Education

The rapid digital advancements of the 21st century have significantly transformed education, shifting from traditional teacher-centric methods to more student-centric, flexible learning models. The COVID-19 pandemic accelerated this change, emphasizing the importance of digital solutions to maintain educational access (Jian, 2023). As technology evolves, education must adapt to prepare learners for constantly changing job markets. One key advantage of digital learning platforms is their adaptability. These platforms offer flexibility in time and location, enabling learners to balance education with work, family, and personal commitments. For instance, a working professional can attend evening classes, while a student can revise on weekends. This accessibility broadens opportunities for a diverse range of learners. Another major benefit is personalized learning. Unlike traditional settings constrained by time and class size, digital platforms leverage AI and machine learning to tailor content to individual needs (Zavaraki, 2024). Advanced learners can access more challenging material, while others receive additional support, ensuring progress at their own pace. Digital platforms are crucial for lifelong learning in a fast-evolving world. They support short courses, certifications, and ongoing education to help individuals remain competitive in their fields. Organizations also utilize these platforms for upskilling and reskilling employees, fostering professional growth and adaptability (Fernández-Batanero et al., 2021).

Integrating frameworks like Bloom's Taxonomy and constructivist learning theories enhances the educational relevance of digital platforms by providing a strong theoretical foundation. Bloom's Taxonomy outlines cognitive skill progression from basic knowledge to advanced skills like analysis and creation, which digital platforms support through scalable tools. For instance, Khan Academy addresses foundational skills with practice exercises and videos, while platforms like Coursera foster higher-order learning through project-based assignments. Constructivist theories emphasize active, contextualized learning, aligning with digital tools like virtual reality simulations, collaborative forums, and gamified content, which promote engagement and reflection. This integration transforms digital platforms into meaningful tools for modern learning ecosystems. Empirical evidence highlights the transformative impact of digital platforms in education. Studies show that AI-powered personalized learning systems improve knowledge retention by 32%, while gamified platforms boost engagement by 40%, particularly among younger learners (Johnson et al., 2023). Digital platforms also enhance accessibility and flexibility, with a World Bank (2024) survey reporting a 27% rise in course completion rates among working professionals and an 18% increase in skill acquisition in underserved regions. These platforms foster critical thinking and problem-solving through interactive features like peer tools and instructor feedback, making them effective and scalable solutions to modern educational challenges. Today's students, as digital natives, expect high levels of engagement and interactivity in education. Digital tools such as gamification, multimedia, and simulations make learning more enjoyable and memorable. For instance, students can conduct virtual experiments or compete in quiz games, promoting active learning (Gligorea et al., 2023). Moreover, digital platforms bridge educational gaps, providing access to quality instruction regardless of geographical or socio-economic barriers (Teräs, 2022). Students in rural areas or developing countries can pursue advanced courses and connect with global experts, ensuring inclusivity and equity in education. From kindergarten to postgraduate studies, digital platforms address diverse educational needs. Their openness supports informal and formal learning, serving as a holistic solution for modern education. By offering flexibility, personalization, and global access, these platforms empower learners to take ownership of their education. As technology continues to evolve, digital platforms will remain pivotal in shaping the future of education (Hopcan et al., 2022).

BACKGROUND

Educational technology has evolved significantly, transforming how education is delivered and consumed. Early tools, such as chalkboards and textbooks, were gradually replaced by computer-based training in the late 20th century, marked by static, text-based content on CD-ROMs and early internet platforms. These systems focused on memorization and lacked interactivity. The 1990s brought a major shift with the widespread use of the internet, enabling basic online learning tools like PDFs, quizzes, and email interactions, though they remained inflexible (Zawacki-Richter et al., 2023). The early 2000s saw the introduction of Learning Management Systems and MOOCs, which revolutionized education by offering structured courses, assessments, and interactive tools to millions of learners globally (Kiourt et al., 2020). Modern educational technology now incorporates AI, big data, and VR/AR. AI personalizes learning by adapting to individual needs through performance monitoring, while big data helps educators make informed decisions about curriculum design and resource allocation (Dogan et al., 2023; Mishra et al., 2023). VR and AR create immersive, hands-on experiences, allowing learners to explore virtual science labs, historical sites, or machinery in a risk-free environment (Nicol, 2024). Mobile technology has further democratized access, enabling learners to study through smartphones and tablets with optimized applications featuring reminders and deadlines.

Gamification has emerged as a major trend, incorporating elements like leaderboards, badges, and rewards to make learning engaging and competitive. This approach fosters motivation and retention, enhancing satisfaction and outcomes (Zhang & Aslan, 2021). Psychologist Mihaly Csikszentmihalyi's “flow” theory emphasizes deep focus through tasks that align with skill levels, a concept embraced by platforms like Duolingo, which use adaptive difficulty and playful competition. Collaborative tools like Slack and Microsoft Teams further enhance engagement through social interaction and community building. From basic computer-based training to advanced AI-driven platforms, educational technology continues to evolve, making learning more interactive, personalized, and accessible (Park et al., 2023).

Problems with Existing E-learning Technologies

E-learning technologies have dramatically changed education by opening access to more resources and providing numerous teaching methods. However, a variety of issues continue to prevent full realization (Kim, 2023). Lack of personalization, lack of accessibility, difficulty in engaging learners, and poor mechanisms to give feedback are some of the conventional problems that mar the effectiveness and inclusiveness of digital education platforms. The solutions to these problems are key to a learning environment for all people, regardless of geographical, social, or economic divide (Şen & Akbay, 2023).

One of the biggest challenges of e-learning is the lack of real personalized learning. Far too many e-learning programs default to a mass model of learning, with blanket approaches that usually ignore the needs, abilities, and preferences of a unique individual learner. This mass model negates the diversity between learners, particularly in terms of the differences in learning style, the level of prior knowledge of the subject, and cognitive strengths. Students are very likely to become disengaged, overwhelmed by too much information, or under-challenged by too little, resulting in an ineffective learning journey. Most digital learning platforms do not adapt how the material is presented to match the student's progression, thus leading to bored advanced learners and overwhelmed slow learners. Such is the case of a student who is very strong on a particular concept and gets bored when he has to revisit the same foundational material over and over. A struggling student becomes frustrated or disillusioned trying to grapple with complex concepts without scaffolding or individual support. Moreover, the lack of personalization of learning paths based on the student's interests, career aspirations, or interdisciplinary focus in most limits the power of the platforms. For students desiring to look at particular topics or learn faster on specific topics, the hard-and-fast curriculums may not be so accommodating to their needs and are, therefore, a bit of a bottleneck for them. Most of the current products have done very little in terms of actually harnessing AI and ML to make them adaptive to an individual's pace and progress (Subha & Baghavathi Priya, 2023).

With access comes an important challenge to the promise of democratizing education through digital platforms. Despite their potential, digital platforms face challenges in bridging the digital divide, as millions of learners, particularly in rural or low-income areas, lack stable internet and adequate devices. For instance, UNESCO (2023) reports that over 40% of potential learners in sub-Saharan Africa cannot access online resources due to infrastructure deficits. Solutions include mobile-first designs for low-bandwidth networks and offline-friendly content, as pioneered by platforms like BYJU'S and Khan Academy. Government initiatives, such as India's Digital Saksharta Abhiyan and Kenya's Digital Literacy Programme, have also equipped millions with digital skills and affordable devices. Addressing socio-economic barriers through subsidized internet plans, tech partnerships, and culturally relevant, multilingual content is essential for ensuring equitable access and fulfilling the promise of democratizing education. For instance, millions of students worldwide—mainly in rural areas or less privileged districts—don't have a stable internet connection or sufficient digital infrastructure. This literally and symbolically bars millions of learners from accessing online resources for education, further entrenching educational inequalities. Accessibility was also largely lacking on many platforms catering to students with disabilities. One other problem with many e-learning environments is that they are not fully accessible. Accessibility features, such as screen readers, text-to-speech tools, and closed captioning, are easily omitted in these conditions. For instance, students who have issues with vision may find platforms have not been optimized for screen readers. Another student who is hard of hearing will not be able to perceive the video lectures properly in case good subtitles are absent. The educational platforms inadvertently exclude a considerable part of the student population without proper attention to these needs. Mobile optimization is another pressing challenge. Even though access to the internet can be obtained in most regions via a mobile device, many sites were designed with a desktop environment in mind and offer awkward or clumsy variations on mobiles. Linguistic barriers add complexity to accessibility. Most of the learning material is in English, so most of this vast content cannot be understood by non-native speakers, especially if there are no courses in a different language. Variations across cultures in how people learn and communicate are even more complicated, as these aspects are sometimes left out while developing online learning content.

Engagement and retention are major challenges for digital learning platforms, with high dropout rates often stemming from passive learning environments. Many platforms offer limited opportunities for active participation or real-time feedback, leaving students feeling isolated and demotivated (Subha et al., 2023). Additionally, the absence of a social dimension, such as peer collaboration and group work common in traditional classrooms, reduces sustained interest (Parmaxi, 2020). Reliance on text-based content fails to engage interactive learners, while limited use of videos, simulations, and quizzes further diminishes appeal, particularly among younger audiences. Although gamification strategies like points and badges have shown promise in boosting engagement, their application remains limited.

Feedback is an essential part of the learning process since it gives the student information regarding progress and how to improve. However, very few e-learning platforms have successfully provided feedback in time or with meaning. Traditional grading and scoring methods based on such systems as numeric scores or letter grades do very little to direct students toward why they were wrong or how to improve next time. Such impersonal feedback systems lower the effectiveness of learning because no meaningful insight is offered to them. Automated feedback is efficient, but it lacks depth and breadth to guide students constructively. The student may only get general comments or standardized responses that do not relate to their problems or learning style. Without personalized feedback, students have to work through the mistakes on their own, which leads to them feeling frustrated and failing to progress.

Another critical challenge is the delay in feedback. Unlike traditional classrooms where teachers can give rapid feedback while in class, either the course of discussions or activities, most of the digital campuses provide feedback after completing and grading assignments. Such delayed feedback breaks the real-time immediacy of learning. Students are, therefore, unable to correct mistakes in real-time or adjust learning strategies before embarking on new material. Digital platforms address key limitations of traditional education, offering flexibility, scalability, and inclusivity. Unlike rigid, standardized systems, platforms like edX and Udemy empower learners with asynchronous access to tailored content, enabling working professionals to pursue education without disrupting their schedules. Digital platforms also scale effortlessly, accommodating millions of learners globally through MOOCs like Coursera, and enhance inclusivity with adaptive technologies such as screen readers and closed captioning. Comparative studies, such as Fernandez et al. (2023), reveal a 15% improvement in problem-solving skills among digital platform users, attributed to interactive tools like virtual simulations and AI-driven feedback. By combining flexibility, interactivity, and accessibility, digital platforms complement and sometimes surpass traditional education models. AI-powered systems for feedback will open the opportunity to have quality feedback in learning environments based on digital streams. It can give the algorithm the ability to analyze students' performance, which could be either in detail or provide recommendations through the use of customized materials that help improve students. Peer feedback systems allow assessing each other's work, whereby students are expected to show more interest and interaction between them as they learn collaboratively.

PROPOSED APPROACH

LynqSphere reimagines the educational landscape by integrating artificial intelligence (AI), data science, and virtual reality (VR) to create personalized, inclusive, and adaptive learning environments. This model, as illustrated in Figure 1, supports continuous adaptive learning by tailoring educational pathways to each student's unique academic performance, interests, and learning preferences. AI analyzes real-time data, enabling dynamic adjustments to learning paths, ensuring students receive targeted resources to address their strengths and weaknesses. This data-driven approach enhances individual learning and empowers educators with actionable insights into student progress and challenges. A defining feature of LynqSphere is its use of VR to transform abstract concepts into interactive, experiential lessons. For example, history students can explore ancient civilizations virtually, while biology learners can examine the inside of a cell. In STEM education, VR facilitates complex simulations, such as conducting safe virtual chemical reactions or exploring physics principles interactively. This hands-on approach enhances comprehension and retention by offering students immersive and memorable experiences tailored to their educational levels.

To further complement the platform's adaptive and immersive features, LynqSphere integrates an AI-powered chatbot that delivers real-time, context-aware assistance throughout the learning journey. Embedded seamlessly across all platform interfaces, this intelligent assistant supports learners by responding to their queries based on current activities or content being viewed. Whether students are engaged in a virtual simulation or completing assignments, the chatbot provides instant explanations, navigational help, and resource recommendations, thereby reducing learning friction and enhancing autonomy. This not only ensures continuous support but also fosters deeper engagement and a more personalized educational experience.

Collaboration is another cornerstone of LynqSphere, preparing students for 21st-century workplaces where teamwork is vital. Collaborative coding hubs allow real-time teamwork on coding projects and research tasks, fostering practical skills like communication, teamwork, and problem-solving. These hubs provide tools such as collaborative authoring systems and real-time communication platforms, enabling students to co-create and share ideas, simulating professional environments. Such collaborative efforts not only deepen understanding but also encourage innovation through interdisciplinary research and projects. Accessibility lies at the heart of LynqSphere, ensuring inclusivity for diverse learners. The platform supports multiple languages, text-to-speech capabilities, and customizable interfaces to accommodate students with varied linguistic, physical, or cognitive needs.

Figure 1. Overview of LynqSphere platform

By breaking down accessibility barriers, LynqSphere promotes equal learning opportunities for all students. Assessment within LynqSphere moves beyond traditional methods, employing adaptive mechanisms to provide real-time feedback. This allows educators to identify and address learning gaps early, ensuring students master concepts before falling behind. Practical, simulation-based evaluations replace conventional exams, offering students a chance to demonstrate knowledge through real-world tasks while giving educators deeper insights into their abilities.

Overall, LynqSphere represents a full panoramic approach to educating, incorporating AI, data science, and VR to create dynamic and inclusive learning experiences for every learner. Having its pillars of rebuilding how one views education in the digital age, LynqSphere enhances collaboration and accessibility, among many more characteristics as shown in Table 1. This proposed model not only helps improve student understanding and participation but also prepares learners for the future by developing critical skills in a 21st-century learning culture and fostering lifelong learners.

Table 1. Core features of the LynqSphere platform

S.NO	FEATURE CATEGORY	FEATURE	DESCRIPTION	TARGET USERS	TECHNOLOGIES INTEGRATED
1	Core Learning Modules	AI-Driven Learning Pathways	Personalized pathways adapt content to each user's needs, abilities, and goals.	Primary, Secondary, and Higher Education	Machine Learning, AI, Predictive Analytics
		Experiential Learning via VR	Provides immersive experiences for complex topics (e.g., history, biology).	All levels	Virtual Reality, 3D Modeling
		Adaptive Assessment	Customizes evaluations to skill levels and offers feedback for improvement.	Secondary, Higher Education	Adaptive Algorithms, Data Analytics
		Domain-Based Learning Paths	Specific content for domains like Engineering, Humanities, and Economics.	Secondary, Higher Education Content Management, Domain-Specific AI Models	Content Management, Domain-Specific AI Models
2	Collaboration and Skills	Real-Time Collaborative Coding Hubs	Allows multiple users to code and problem-solve together in real-time.	Secondary and Higher Education	Collaborative Tools, Cloud Servers, Coding Platforms
		Peer Learning and Discussion Forums	Provides moderated spaces for students to discuss and share insights.	All Levels	NLP, Moderation Algorithms
3	User Engagement	AI-Driven Recommendation System	Curates content recommendations based on user preferences and trends.	All levels	Machine Learning, Real-Time Data Analytics
		AI-Assisted Chatbot	Provides real-time, context-aware assistance, tailored guidance, and continuous support throughout the learning experience.	All Levels	Natural Language Processing, Real-Time Analytics, AI-Based Feedback Systems

continued on following page

Table 1. Continued

S.NO	FEATURE CATEGORY	FEATURE	DESCRIPTION	TARGET USERS	TECHNOLOGIES INTEGRATED
		Event Calendar with AI-Powered Recommendations	AI-Powered Recommendations Suggest relevant events, workshops, and hackathons for skill building.	Secondary and Higher Education	AI Event Matching, Calendar Integration
4	Accessibility and Inclusivity	Multilingual Support	Supports various languages, providing accessible content for diverse users.	Primary, Secondary	NLP, Translation APIs
		Adaptive Tools for Inclusivity	Adjusts resources for diverse learning needs (e.g., dyslexia-friendly fonts).	All levels	Adaptive Design, Accessibility APIs
5	Advanced Feedback and Analytics	Real-Time Feedback and Knowledge Gap Analysis	Identifies gaps and provides real-time feedback to guide learning.	Secondary, Higher Education	Data Analytics, AI, Feedback Systems
		SWOT Analysis and Monthly Reports	Summarizes progress with personalized strengths and growth areas.	Higher Education, Educators	Education, Educators' SWOT Algorithms, Monthly Analytics
6	Management and Continuous Improvement	Goal Tracking and Progress Monitoring	Facilitates goal-setting and ongoing progress tracking.	All levels	Dashboard Analytics, User Profiles
		Continuous Improvement Based on User Metrics	Adjusts content and features based on aggregated performance data.	Platform Administrators	Data Science, Machine Learning
7	Future-Oriented Technologies	Integration of AR for Enhanced Visualization	Provides augmented reality experiences for subjects like geography or chemistry.	Secondary, and Higher Education	Augmented Reality, Spatial Computing
		Predictive Analytics for Future Learning Trends	Offers data-driven insights for curriculum planning and personalization.	Educators, Administrators	Predictive Analytics, Big Data

Specialized Learning Paths by Educational Level

LynqSphere's developmental approach customizes educational experiences to meet the mental, emotional, and academic needs of learners across all levels. For primary and secondary education, the platform focuses on foundational skills like literacy, numeracy, scientific knowledge, and critical thinking. Interactive tools, such as virtual zoo tours and project-based learning, make lessons engaging, while social-emotional learning fosters self-awareness and resilience. At the high school and college levels, LynqSphere adapts to more advanced requirements. High school students benefit from interactive modules and virtual lab experiments in mathematics, science, and humanities. College students access domain-specific resources like engineering simulations and economic models, enhancing their practical knowledge. AI-driven recommendations support coursework, encouraging critical thinking and professional readiness. For graduate learners, LynqSphere emphasizes research capabilities and career-oriented skills. Graduate students use advanced tools for data analysis, research, and virtual modeling, such as biochemical simulations for biotechnology students. Collaboration with peers and mentors, along with personalized guidance, prepares graduates for innovation in their fields.

LynqSphere also offers domain-specific pathways tailored to disciplines like engineering, economics, and humanities. Engineering students access virtual labs and design tools, while economics students engage with market analysis. Humanities students explore digital archives and historical recreations, aligning resources with academic and career goals. Innovative, adaptive assessments redefine traditional testing. By adjusting to students' proficiency levels, they provide targeted feedback, formative assessments, peer reviews, and real-time analytics to identify strengths and weaknesses. Practical simulations replicate real-world conditions, enabling students to demonstrate mastery. For instance, engineering students can participate in virtual design competitions, while business students engage in market analysis exercises. This personalized approach ensures sustained academic growth, equipping students with the skills and knowledge necessary for professional success across all educational levels.

The AI-Driven Recommendation System

LynqSphere's AI-driven recommendation system revolutionizes personalized education by tailoring content to students' individual learning needs, preferences, and performance histories. Powered by advanced machine learning algorithms, the system creates adaptive and engaging learning experiences by analyzing data on students' performance metrics, behavioral trends, and engagement levels. Personalized learning profiles are generated to address strengths and weaknesses. For instance, students excelling in mathematics but struggling with literature receive advanced math problems alongside supplementary literature materials. Real-time adjustments further enhance learning by responding dynamically to progress and challenges, ensuring resources match evolving needs. The system accommodates diverse learning preferences by recommending optimal delivery modes, such as video-based lessons, interactive simulations, or text-based resources. It goes beyond static content, incorporating the latest developments in education, research, and industry trends. Students pursuing environmental science, for example, receive updates on climate change or green technologies, fostering engagement with real-world developments. This dynamic approach ensures students remain informed and motivated.

A standout feature is its ability to recommend engaging and challenging content based on individual interests and capabilities. By prioritizing methods suited to specific learning styles, such as gamified quizzes for hands-on learners or infographics for visual learners, the system transforms education into an enjoyable and effective experience. This personalized approach enhances academic outcomes and student satisfaction. LynqSphere's system employs real-time analytics to monitor and refine educational content. Metrics like time spent on resources, assessment performance, and interactions with various content types enable the system to identify patterns and optimize recommendations. For instance, if students engage more with video resources but struggle with text-heavy materials, the AI adapts suggestions accordingly. A continuous feedback loop, powered by student ratings and comments, further enhances content quality. The system also adapts to situational needs, offering revision materials, quizzes, and practice tests during exams or introducing new subjects based on emerging interests. By seamlessly integrating real-time analytics, continuous updates, and personalized recommendations, LynqSphere's AI-driven recommendation system delivers a dynamic and individualized learning experience, making education engaging, relevant, and effective.

Virtual Reality as a Tool for Experiential Learning

VR offers new pedagogical possibilities in education through the method of immersive, experiential learning beyond the conventional educational methodology. For instance, with virtual reality, students will be able to explore 3D worlds and manipulate objects, which cannot be done with reading out of a book or other traditional teaching tools. Learning becomes richer and more interesting in the context in which it happens, with mastering VR, while information is not just easier to understand but also to remember better. VR situates learners in milieus of imitation, encourages active engagement, and is structured in such a way that learning becomes highly personal and holistic. VR applications are being rapidly launched in history, biology, chemistry, and geography studies to enrich the educational process. With all these topics, students gain a much deeper perception of what they are learning using virtual investigations that may link abstractions to reality. Whether it's walking through ancient historical sites, navigating through parts of the human body, simulating chemical reactions, or exploring diverse terrains, VR provides interactivity and immersion that greatly increase comprehension and retention. Immersive technology is not an add-on, but the future of education—how it is going to be learned and pedagogically enriched, boundless for all levels and subjects.

Case Studies: VR in History, Biology, Chemistry, and Geography

VR in History: Walking Through Ancient Rome. A real-time case in point is the "Rome Reborn" project, whereby students can walk through ancient Rome as it was thousands of years ago. Using virtual reality, students can walk through the Roman Forum, the Colosseum, and even iconic structures like the Pantheon. As a learner who immerses themselves in the culture, they get to understand Roman architecture and culture in a way that cannot be explained through routine textbooks or images. Issues such as the rise and fall of the Roman Empire can be recreated in a virtual setting and expose students to a real-life historical experience that will make them better understand the causes and effects involved. The application of VR enhances the appreciation of scale and grandeur together with the complexity of historical sites, which in a book are reduced to flat photographs or two-dimensional diagrams. Additionally, by using manipulated 3D models of ancient artifacts, learners are nudged toward a more profound understanding of historical context as well as the technological feats of the time. This serves to illustrate how the applicability of VR can change the direction of history study: a once-passive review of events can now be experienced as an interactive journey through time.

VR in Biology: The Human Body in 3D. In biology, the use of VR has been seen in "The Body VR," where students get to enter a virtual human body to explore its inner systems. With this experience, students can see how cells work, how the circulatory system operates, and how all the different organs interact in 3D detail. Instead of being fixed diagrams, VR can show learners moving processes such as the flow of blood within veins or an immune system responding to invading pathogens. Biology students are, for instance, able to have a much clearer and broader view of intricate biological systems. One of the best examples is also the Virtual Heart at Stanford University, where students can play with a beating heart, see how it pumps blood, and even simulate diseases or surgical procedures to observe the effects that those would have on the cardiovascular system. Such immersive learning experiences are invaluable, especially for medical students, who get the chance to experiment in a risk-free environment to get a feel for anatomy and surgical techniques.

VR in Geography: Exploring Natural Landscapes. Major transformations in geography classes can be made with the help of VR through programs like Google Earth VR. The latter enables the user to take a virtual step closer to seeing a bird's-eye view of the world's landscapes, cities, and ecosystems. Students do not have to just read about mountains, rivers, or deserts. Instead, they can fly virtually over these regions, walk around geological formations, or see how cities are laid out in different parts of the world. This hands-on experience makes them realize geographical themes and concepts such as climate zones, tectonic movements, or even urban planning. A case study at the University of South Carolina shows that geography students used VR to simulate natural disasters such as earthquakes and tsunamis. It lets the students understand the science behind these catastrophes and their implications for human societies, which not only made the lessons interesting, but also helped the students understand extremely complex concepts like disaster management and mitigation strategies. VR in geography offers learners a distinct opportunity to experience the world's diversity and complexity in such a way that promotes intellectual curiosity and empathy for global challenges.

These case studies showcase how VR has been implemented across various education disciplines, thus enabling the depth of material approachability to the student in ways previously unimaginable. The onus is to plunge them wholly inside a virtual environment, going against the impulses, where they have a say with events in history, biological systems, and global landscapes—the strengths where their knowledge could stretch and be retained. As VR technology becomes increasingly advanced, its role in education will also grow, creating yet more opportunities for experiential learning.

One of the most significant advantages of VR is its ability to enhance retention and understanding, especially in complex subjects. Traditional learning methods often involve passive observation, which can limit retention. In contrast, VR transforms students into active participants, offering experiential learning that engages both visual and kinesthetic learners. Through interactive 3D models, students can manipulate objects, test hypotheses, and experiment with variables, reinforcing concepts and promoting long-term memory retention. By engaging multiple senses—sight, sound, and touch—VR creates multiple neural pathways, making information retrieval faster and more effective.

The design and implementation of immersive VR environments require careful planning to align with learning objectives. Effective VR environments balance exploration and structured learning pathways, allowing students to freely navigate while receiving instructional guidance. For instance, a virtual biology lab might guide students step-by-step through a frog dissection, while a geography module could highlight geological formations as students explore virtual terrains. Collaboration between educators and software developers is essential to create environments that enhance learning outcomes and provide meaningful feedback. Accessibility and scalability are critical considerations, as implementing VR requires infrastructure investments in hardware, training, and technical support. While the initial costs may be high, the long-term benefits of VR in education are undeniable.

The future of VR in education is poised for exciting advancements, particularly with the integration of artificial intelligence (AI). AI-powered VR systems could adapt to individual learning needs, dynamically adjusting content and difficulty based on student progress and thereby could revolutionize education by addressing students' unique strengths and weaknesses in real time. Global collaborative learning is another promising frontier for VR. Students from diverse backgrounds can meet in shared virtual classrooms to collaborate on projects, conduct experiments, and engage in debates, fostering multicultural communication, teamwork, and problem-solving skills. As VR becomes more affordable and accessible, it will likely be integrated into all educational levels, from K-12 to graduate studies. Over time, VR may become as ubiquitous as textbooks and computers, shaping the future of teaching and learning by providing immersive, inclusive, and effective educational experiences

Collaborative Coding Hubs

Collaborative coding hubs represent a significant shift in the educational and technological landscape, combining collective learning and coding into virtual workspaces. These hubs provide students and professionals with opportunities to work on projects, share knowledge, and hone coding skills. More than simple code-sharing platforms, they integrate tools like version control, real-time editing, and communication channels to facilitate seamless collaboration. By mimicking real-world coding environments, these hubs not only develop technical skills but also nurture essential soft skills like teamwork, communication, and adaptability. This combination prepares learners for modern workplaces that demand collaboration and innovation.

Case Studies: Success Stories from Coding Hub Projects

Hackathon For Change. The Hackathon for Change, hosted by a tech university, brought together students from diverse fields to address critical societal challenges through collaborative problem-solving. This intensive 48-hour event created a unique environment within a coding hub, where participants worked in teams to prototype solutions focused on sustainability, education, and healthcare. Notable projects included a Sustainable Living Tracker, an app designed to help users monitor their carbon footprint and receive personalized tips for reducing environmental impact, and EduConnect, a platform that linked students with mentors in their fields, crafted with real-time feedback from mentors throughout the coding process. The collaborative setting enabled teams to iterate quickly, resulting in polished, practical solutions by the hackathon's end. The event's impact extended beyond its duration, with several projects receiving offers for further development from incubators and local organizations and students gaining invaluable experience in a team-based setting that strengthened both their skills and professional networks.

Women Who Code Initiative. The Women Who Code Initiative is a global organization dedicated to empowering women in technology through mentorship and collaborative coding projects. A local chapter of this initiative established a coding hub specifically to support women aspiring to enter tech fields, offering resources and mentorship to build both confidence and technical skills. Experienced women in tech guided participants through coding challenges and project development, while collaborative hackathons tackled issues like workplace inclusivity, with teams creating prototypes for apps that foster networking and support among women professionals. These experiences not only helped participants develop technical expertise but also enabled them to establish lasting professional networks. Many participants went on to secure positions in tech companies, attributing their career advancement to the skills and connections gained through the coding hub. This initiative further promoted diversity in technology fields, inspiring more women to pursue careers in coding and tech.

These cases highlight the degree of change provided by collaborative coding hubs and show the possibilities of students' ability to gain relevant abilities, team spirit, and develop great ideas. These hubs provide opportunities for teamwork that not only build up technical skills but are also vital in helping students prepare for success in the industry and other fields related to industrial technology. The design and functionality of collaborative coding hubs are critical to their effectiveness. A well-designed hub ensures intuitive navigation, easy project management, and access to resource libraries. Features like real-time collaboration tools allow users to simultaneously edit code, fostering teamwork and rapid feedback. Integrated version control systems manage contributions, log changes, and allow rollbacks, simulating industry-standard practices. Communication tools, such as chat and video conferencing, enable brainstorming and problem-solving, creating an inclusive and cooperative atmosphere. Inclusive design ensures accessibility for users with diverse abilities and learning styles, promoting participation and engagement. By providing hands-on, inclusive experiences, these hubs cultivate a growth-oriented mindset and accountability among learners.

Real-time collaboration is a cornerstone of these hubs, enabling participants to work together regardless of location. Multiple users can simultaneously contribute to the same codebase, facilitating idea generation, problem-solving, and peer learning. Immediate feedback on updates promotes efficient troubleshooting and refinement of solutions. This collaborative process strengthens communication and teamwork skills, fostering shared ownership of projects. It also enhances learning outcomes, as students engaging actively with peers tend to retain knowledge better. It supports critical thinking, creativity, and experiential learning, preparing students for future workplaces where agile teamwork and rapid communication are vital.

In addition to technical skills, collaborative coding hubs play a pivotal role in developing soft skills. Effective communication is central to coding projects, requiring students to articulate ideas, share challenges, and provide constructive feedback. These activities improve verbal and written communication, which is essential for professional success. Team-oriented coding environments teach participants to navigate group dynamics, appreciate diverse perspectives, and resolve conflicts. These interactions foster emotional intelligence and empathy, critical traits for collaborative work. Adaptability is another key soft skill nurtured in collaborative coding hubs. The dynamic nature of coding often presents unexpected challenges, encouraging team members to think critically and innovate under pressure. Participants learn to embrace change, accept feedback, and adjust their approaches, traits highly valued in the technology sector. Together, these experiences build a comprehensive skill set that enhances employability and career success in fast-paced, technology-driven industries. foster innovation, inclusivity, and a growth-oriented mindset, making them indispensable in bridging education and industry needs.

AI-Powered Chatbot: Real-Time Support and Intelligent Assistance

A notable enhancement within the LynqSphere educational ecosystem is the integration of an AI-powered chatbot across all pages of the platform. This intelligent assistant serves as an always-available guide, tutor, and navigator, enriching the educational experience by offering real-time responses to student queries. Its design is centered around providing context-aware support that aligns with the platform's content, user goals, and ongoing activities. Unlike traditional help systems that require users to leave their current activity or navigate to a support section, the LynqSphere AI chatbot is omnipresent, seamlessly integrated into the user interface. This means that while a student is watching a video lecture, exploring a VR module, or attempting a coding exercise, they can instantly ask the chatbot questions related to the current activity. For instance, a student struggling with a concept during a history VR simulation can ask, "What caused the fall of the Roman Empire?" and receive a concise yet rich explanation, often accompanied by links to supplemental materials or recommended next steps within the platform. The chatbot leverages Natural Language Processing (NLP) and real-time content indexing to understand both the user query and the learning context. It parses metadata, tracks the student's current module or activity, and draws from a curated knowledge base that includes educational content, platform documentation, and student performance history. This allows it to respond not only with generic help but tailored guidance that enhances learning and reduces cognitive load.

In alignment with LynqSphere's mission of personalized learning, the chatbot adapts its tone, language complexity, and response length based on the student's educational level, learning preferences, and past interactions. For a middle school student, it may simplify technical jargon and offer visual explanations, while for a graduate-level learner, it might provide detailed citations or advanced references. Additionally, the chatbot recognizes patterns in student queries to preemptively offer suggestions, tips, or encouragement. For example, if a student repeatedly asks questions about algebraic functions, the chatbot may recommend relevant video tutorials, suggest practice problems, or initiate a short diagnostic quiz to assess knowledge gaps. Through these dynamic, learner-specific interventions, the chatbot becomes more than a tool—it acts as a personalized learning coach. Integral to the chatbot's design is its feedback-driven evolution and role in promoting student engagement. Each interaction contributes to a self-improving system, where student feedback, sentiment analysis, and usage trends enhance the chatbot's accuracy and responsiveness over time. Frequently asked questions are added to its core knowledge base, and analytics help educators identify and address common challenges. Moreover, the chatbot supports learner motivation by offering instant guidance, personalized encouragement, and milestone acknowledgments. These timely, empathetic micro-interactions reduce frustration and boost confidence, fostering autonomy and increasing student retention. By ensuring students are never left without support, the chatbot cultivates a dynamic, emotionally intelligent learning environment that adapts and responds alongside the learner.

Event Calendar and Professional Development

In today's dynamic learning landscape, event calendars play a critical role in enhancing students' academic and professional growth. They include seminars, workshops, hackathons, and conferences that extend learning beyond the classroom. These events provide platforms to gain knowledge, build skills, and foster connections with educators and industry professionals. Guest lectures bridge theoretical concepts with real-world applications, while fostering interpersonal skills, teamwork, and collaboration essential for career success. Networking opportunities allow students to exchange experiences, gain exposure to industry trends, and establish relationships that can lead to internships, job opportunities, or collaborative projects. Additionally, such events contribute to a sense of belonging, enhancing both academic performance and emotional well-being. AI-driven event management systems revolutionize how students engage with these opportunities. By analyzing individual interests, academic performance, and attendance patterns, AI recommends personalized events, increasing student participation. For instance, a data science enthusiast might be directed to a machine learning workshop or a panel discussion with experts. Feedback-driven AI systems also assess event impact, enabling institutions to optimize programming and align events with students' learning goals. This data-driven approach ensures that event calendars remain dynamic, relevant, and impactful.

Networking events, such as speed networking and roundtable discussions, prepare students for professional environments. These formats encourage meaningful interactions with mentors, alumni, and peers, equipping students with career insights, resume-building tips, and interview strategies. Networking boosts confidence in professional communication and provides platforms for students to showcase their work and articulate ideas effectively, fostering essential skills for navigating complex career landscapes. Hackathons and coding competitions offer experiential learning opportunities, challenging students to solve real-world problems under time constraints. These events promote critical thinking, teamwork, and innovation while strengthening technical expertise. By working in diverse teams, students exchange ideas, develop solutions, and build professional networks. Presenting projects at these events enhances communication skills and confidence while fostering a community-oriented mindset. AI-powered personalization, networking opportunities, and hackathons equip students with the skills, insights, and connections necessary to thrive in an ever-evolving world, ensuring they are prepared for future challenges and opportunities.

Discussion Forums and Peer Learning

Discussion forums and peer learning are integral to modern digital pedagogies, providing platforms for meaningful engagement, collaboration, and resource sharing. These forums foster interaction and active learning, enabling learners to tailor their learning styles and goals in open, accessible environments. By allowing students to communicate, ask questions, and engage in critical discussions, forums expand learning beyond traditional classroom constraints. The asynchronous nature of these platforms, often integrated into Learning Management Systems (LMS), ensures inclusivity, accommodating diverse schedules and learning preferences. This fosters a conversational space where all voices can be heard, promoting distributive agency and participation. Peer feedback is a cornerstone of collaborative learning, enhancing educational outcomes through constructive exchanges. Students reviewing and critiquing peers' work deepen their subject understanding while refining their communication and critical thinking skills. This process encourages active participation, feedback literacy, and ownership of learning.

Effective moderation is essential to maintain the credibility and utility of discussion forums. Moderators, whether educators or peers, ensure discussions remain relevant, respectful, and productive, guiding conversations toward academic goals. AI tools can support moderation by flagging inappropriate content, suggesting resources, and enhancing information validation. This fosters a safe and inclusive environment, encouraging diverse participation and respectful communication. Discussion forums also create a sense of community among learners, enabling ongoing communication, academic skill development, and relationship building. These forums facilitate the sharing of resources, collaborative projects, and continued learning beyond the course, fostering social learning where students benefit from diverse perspectives. By promoting validated discussions and meaningful peer feedback, forums transform educational experiences into dynamic, community-driven processes and support collaboration, inclusivity, and lifelong learning, making them authentic tools for enhancing education in digital environments.

Advanced Analytics and Feedback Systems

Advanced analytics and feedback systems are transforming education by fostering personalized, student-centered learning environments. Leveraging real-time data, these systems allow educators to identify strengths, areas for growth, and actionable insights beyond traditional grading. By integrating Artificial Intelligence (AI) and Machine Learning (ML), advanced analytics quickly analyze vast datasets to deliver dynamic, tailored feedback. These data-driven insights ensure that resources and guidance are aligned with each student's unique needs, helping them reach their full potential. AI-driven assessment systems redefine how educators monitor progress, offering a dynamic view of learning rather than relying on static evaluations. These systems track interactions with course materials, participation in virtual classes, and attendance, providing feedback that identifies mistakes and suggests improvements. Beyond rote learning, these systems assess critical thinking and creativity. In a coding course, AI could evaluate code efficiency and recommend optimizations, while in a writing course, it might suggest structural or clarity improvements.

Continuous monitoring and progress tracking form the backbone of advanced analytics, providing immediate insights into student performance. Dashboards visually represent academic progress, highlighting strengths and areas needing improvement. Educators, too, benefit from monitoring engagement metrics such as time spent on assignments and participation in discussions, allowing them to adapt instructional strategies. If a module shows low engagement, teachers can modify lesson plans or provide supplementary resources. Continuous assessments also empower students to set and achieve short-term goals, promoting a growth mindset that views challenges as opportunities for improvement. SWOT (Strengths, Weaknesses, Opportunities, and Threats) analysis is another powerful tool for personalized feedback. This framework evaluates performance across multiple dimensions, addressing academic and personal growth. This holistic evaluation approach helps students focus on areas of improvement while leveraging their strengths to capitalize on opportunities.

Monthly progress reports further enhance alignment between students, educators, and educational goals. Unlike traditional report cards, these narrative evaluations provide detailed context about a student's journey, outlining specific actions for improvement. Regular reviews encourage students to set measurable goals, such as improving test scores or enhancing participation. These reports not only motivate students but also provide parents with actionable insights to support their child's growth. Reflecting on achievements and setting new objectives fosters engagement and optimism while offering educators a roadmap for guiding learners toward success. These tools enable personalized learning, timely interventions, and holistic evaluations, ensuring every student receives the support necessary to thrive in today's dynamic academic landscape.

Management System for Continuous Improvement

A comprehensive management platform is essential for modern education, enabling institutions to adapt and respond to the evolving needs of students and educators. Such systems facilitate the observation, assessment, and improvement of educational programs while aligning them with institutional goals. By establishing performance metrics, gathering continuous feedback, and fostering a culture of collaboration, these systems help schools and universities achieve excellence. Real-time data collection ensures that resources, instructional practices, and curricula remain relevant and are adjusted to support student success. Continuous improvement management systems are indispensable tools for monitoring progress, setting actionable goals, and fostering collaboration across stakeholders, including students, educators, and administrators. These systems enhance transparency and accountability by providing visibility into key operations and fostering an understanding of areas needing improvement. For instance, real-time updates on attendance, assignment submissions, and exam performance allow educators to address challenges promptly, ensuring higher standards for student learning.

The integration of management systems with learning and feedback platforms allows educational data to inform strategic decisions effectively. Systems connected to Learning Management Systems (LMS) analyze engagement data, highlighting at-risk students or identifying successful teaching practices. Similarly, feedback mechanisms gather insights from students and educators regarding course content, teaching methods, and learning experiences, driving improvements in curriculum design, pedagogies, and resource allocation. These insights help institutions implement immediate interventions while maintaining long-term strategies for continuous improvement. By leveraging data-driven insights and fostering collaboration, management systems empower educational institutions to align daily operations with broader goals. This dynamic approach ensures that institutions remain agile, responsive, and focused on fostering educational success, both in the short term and over the long run.

CHALLENGES AND SOLUTIONS IN IMPLEMENTATION

Implementing a platform like LynqSphere involves overcoming numerous challenges, both technical and logistical. Integrating AI algorithms with diverse educational content across disciplines and formats requires extensive data and robust cloud infrastructure to handle millions of global users. Real-time analytics and adaptive learning demand continuous processing capabilities, risking latency and downtime if not managed efficiently. The platform must also ensure accessibility for users in regions with limited internet connectivity by offering offline modes or low-bandwidth versions of its content. Regular training for educators and developers is essential to keep materials updated and ensure effective use of advanced tools without disrupting institutional operations. User resistance is another critical hurdle, as many educators and students accustomed to traditional methods may hesitate to adopt new technologies. Concerns about AI replacing human teachers and doubts about AI-driven assessments necessitate clear communication about the platform's benefits, such as personalized learning and real-time feedback. Pilot programs, demonstrations, and gradual adoption strategies can ease this transition, while fostering a culture of innovation within institutions is vital for long-term acceptance.

Data security and privacy are paramount, given the vast amount of sensitive information managed by the platform. Strong encryption protocols, strict data governance policies, and compliance with regulations like GDPR and COPPA are essential to safeguard user trust. Transparency in data usage, coupled with user control over their information, helps address privacy concerns. Regular audits and updates ensure the system remains secure against evolving threats. Financial and resource constraints are significant obstacles, as developing and maintaining such an advanced platform requires substantial investment. Institutions can explore funding from government programs, private companies, and educational trusts. Tiered pricing models can ensure broader accessibility while generating revenue. Open-source technologies and public-private partnerships can further reduce costs and foster community-driven improvements. By addressing these challenges with strategic planning, innovative solutions, and collaborative efforts, LynqSphere can revolutionize education through accessibility, personalization, and inclusivity, ensuring a transformative learning experience for all users.

Ethics in AI-Based Education

The inclusion of AI in education carries with it a variety of ethics to be considered as the technology develops. Some of the most common concerns revolve around the bias inherent in AI algorithms. As a result, an AI machine might learn all the existing biases that are contained in the data on which it learns to form its attitudes and indeed perpetuate them. For example, if the AI was trained using data from a single demographic, it may not provide equally accurate recommendations or feedback to students from different backgrounds. AI-based education systems must ensure that the data used is diversified and representative of all learners in a fair manner, with continuous auditing of AI systems for biases that may perpetuate educational inequalities. The second ethical concern is over-reliance on AI without consideration for judgment and interaction derived from humans. However, nothing can replace the subtle empathic guidance a human educator can bring forth. Only a teacher, after all, can undertake the task of mentoring and inspiring the students, and thus AI is only to be used within the boundaries that balance efficiency and personalization with the importance of a human educator's role within the process.

Another area of concern is privacy, as AI-powered platforms collect a large amount of personal information from students. Academic performance, behavioral patterns, engagement metrics, and even emotional responses are all sensitive data points that can reveal a lot about an individual. It raises the question of whether or how it will be stored, who will have access to it, and who will misuse it. Students' data must be subject to strict restrictions and discipline to protect their privacy, and it should be used solely for educational purposes. The students and their guardians have rights over their data and will have mechanics along with the right to make choices to opt-out if they wish to do so. New waves of automation will also change the types of jobs available, and educational institutions must prepare students for a world dominated by AI and automation. Therefore, curriculums have to integrate AI literacy and emphasize on skills that are relatively less likely to become automated and include creativity, critical thinking, and emotional intelligence.

FUTURE RESEARCH DIRECTIONS

The future of educational platforms like LynqSphere will witness a significant integration of emerging technologies such as Augmented Reality (AR), advanced AI algorithms, and predictive analytics, revolutionizing how education is delivered and experienced. AR has the potential to enhance learning by overlaying digital content onto real-world environments, allowing students to interact with subjects like biology and history in more immersive and engaging ways. For example, AR could enable students to explore the internal anatomy of organisms or experience historical events in real-time, making learning more interactive and contextually rich. The ability to collaborate in shared AR spaces will further transform project-based learning, as students from around the world can work together on experiments, solve complex problems, and participate in virtual field trips.

Simultaneously, AI will play a crucial role in personalizing learning experiences. With sophisticated predictive analytics, platforms will be able to forecast students' future performance, allowing for early interventions when students are at risk of falling behind. AI-driven systems will offer advanced feedback on written assignments, detect plagiarism, and guide students in developing critical thinking and communication skills. Natural Language Processing (NLP) will also enhance discussions, providing moderation, sentiment detection, and context-based suggestions to improve the quality of student interactions.

Looking ahead, the integration of AI, immersive technologies, and adaptive learning will enable personalized, on-demand learning experiences that support students' cognitive, emotional, and social development. Microlearning and AI-based tutoring will allow learners to access personalized instruction at their own pace. Additionally, the use of blockchain for credentialing will provide secure, verifiable digital certificates, further enhancing the value of education. To fully embrace these advancements, educational institutions must focus on digital skills training for both students and faculty. Efforts to bridge the digital divide will also be necessary, ensuring that all learners, especially those in underserved areas, have access to quality, technology-driven education.

CONCLUSION

LynqSphere embodies a forward-looking vision for education, addressing key challenges in personalization, accessibility, and engagement through a unified, AI-powered platform. By integrating data science, virtual reality, and adaptive learning pathways, it creates a dynamic educational experience that tailors content to individual needs, enhancing comprehension and retention across primary, secondary, and higher education levels. This individualized approach bridges learning gaps and fosters a continuous cycle of growth, making education more inclusive and responsive. The platform's AI-driven recommendation system and advanced analytics provide real-time insights, enabling both students and educators to track progress effectively and adjust learning strategies. VR-powered modules bring experiential learning to life, allowing students to explore complex subjects in an immersive, interactive manner that promotes deeper understanding and practical application. LynqSphere further encourages peer collaboration through coding hubs and discussion forums, supporting soft skill development and creating a vibrant community of learners. An essential component amplifying this vision is the platform's integrated AI-powered chatbot, which offers intelligent, real-time assistance to learners at every stage of their journey. By providing context-aware support directly within the learning interface, the chatbot ensures that students receive immediate guidance tailored to their current activity, whether navigating the platform, exploring course content, or engaging in assessments. This continuous, personalized interaction minimizes learning barriers, reinforces autonomy, and significantly enhances user confidence and satisfaction.

Beyond academic support, LynqSphere focuses on holistic skill development, preparing students for real-world challenges with tools that promote creativity, problem-solving, and adaptability. The platform also acts as a hub for professional growth through events, discussions, and skill-building resources, thus enhancing engagement and broadening learners' horizons. The result is a well-rounded educational experience that aligns with the demands of modern education and workplace dynamics. LynqSphere stands as a comprehensive, future-ready educational platform that pushes the boundaries of conventional learning. Its commitment to leveraging AI, VR, and analytics fosters a robust, flexible, and accessible learning environment, setting a new standard for digital education where every learner can thrive and succeed.

REFERENCES

Adade, R., & Goosen, L. (2024). Teachers and schools navigating virtual worlds and the metaverse for enhanced e-learning: Evaluating an e-capacity model approach. In *Navigating virtual worlds and the metaverse for enhanced e-learning* (pp. 19). https://doi.org/DOI: 10.4018/979-8-3693-1034-2.ch006

Al-Shammari, Z., Faulkner, P. E., & Forlin, C. (2019). Theories-based inclusive education practices. *Education Quarterly Review, 2*(2), 408–414. DOI: 10.31014/aior.1993.02.02.73

Alam, M., & Hasan, M. (2024). Applications and future prospects of artificial intelligence in education. [IJHSSS]. *International Journal of Humanities & Social Science Studies, 10*(1), 197–206. DOI: 10.29032/ijhsss.v10.i1.2024.197-206

Dogan, M. E., Dogan, T. G., & Bozkurt, A. (2023). The use of artificial intelligence (AI) in online learning and distance education processes: A systematic review of empirical studies. *Applied Sciences (Basel, Switzerland), 13*(5), 3056. DOI: 10.3390/app13053056

Fernández-Batanero, J. M., Román-Graván, P., Montenegro-Rueda, M., López-Meneses, E., & Fernández-Cerero, J. (2021). Digital teaching competence in higher education: A systematic review. *Education Sciences, 11*(11), 689. DOI: 10.3390/educsci11110689

Gligorea, I., Cioca, M., Oancea, R., Gorski, A., Gorski, H., & Tudorache, P. (2023). Adaptive learning using AI in e-learning: A literature review. *Education Sciences, 13*(12), 1216. DOI: 10.3390/educsci13121216

Hopcan, S., Polat, E., Ozturk, M. E., & Ozturk, L. (2022). AI in special education: A systematic review. *Interactive Learning Environments, 31*(10), 7335–7353. DOI: 10.1080/10494820.2022.2067186

Jian, M. J. K. O. (2023). Personalized learning through AI. *Advances in Engineering Innovation, 5*(1), 16–19. DOI: 10.54254/2977-3903/5/2023039

Kim, J. (2023). Leading teachers' perspective on teacher-AI collaboration in education. *Education and Information Technologies.* Advance online publication. DOI: 10.1007/s10639-023-12109-5

Kiourt, C., Koutsoudis, A., & Kalles, D. (2020). Enhanced virtual reality experience in personalised virtual museums. In *Natural Language Processing* (p. 19). Concepts, Methodologies, Tools, and Applications., DOI: 10.4018/978-1-7998-0951-7.ch065

Martin, F., Zhuang, M., & Schaefer, D. (2023). Systematic review of research on artificial intelligence in K-12 education (2017–2022). *Computers and Education: Artificial Intelligence*, *6*, 100195. DOI: 10.1016/j.caeai.2023.100195

Mishra, P., Henriksen, D., & Warr, M. (2023). Educational technology integration: A framework for post-pandemic teaching and learning. *TechTrends*, *67*(1), 96–108. DOI: 10.1145/3629296.3629303

Nicol, J. (2024). How universal design for learning transformed my teaching: An elementary educator's journey of implementation. In *New Brunswick Department of Education and Early Childhood Development, Canada* (pp. 52). https://doi.org/ DOI: 10.4018/978-1-6684-4750-5.ch002

Park, S., Kim, H., & Lee, J. (2023). Collaborative virtual learning environments: Design principles and implementation strategies. *International Review of Research in Open and Distance Learning*, *24*(2), 180–199. DOI: 10.1080/10494820.2021.2006238

Parmaxi, A. (2020). Virtual reality in language learning: A systematic review and implications for research and practice. *Interactive Learning Environments*, *31*(1), 172–184. DOI: 10.1080/10494820.2020.1765392

Şen, N., & Akbay, T. (2023). *AI and innovative applications in special education.* Öğretim Teknolojisi Ve Hayat Boyu Öğrenme Dergisi - Instructional Technology and Lifelong Learning., DOI: 10.52911/itall.1297978

Subha, S., & Baghavathi Priya, S. (2023). Prediction model for a good learning environment using an ensemble approach. *Computer Systems Science and Engineering*, *44*(3), 2081–2093. DOI: 10.32604/csse.2023.028451

Subha, S., Baghavathi Priya Sankaralingam, A., Gurusamy, A., Sehar, S., & Bavirisetti, D. P. (2023). Personalization-based deep hybrid e-learning model for online course recommendation system. *PeerJ. Computer Science*. Advance online publication. DOI: 10.7717/peerj-cs.1670 PMID: 38077588

Teräs, M. (2022). Education and technology: Key issues and debates. *International Review of Education*, *68*(4), 635–636. DOI: 10.1007/s11159-022-09971-9

Yang, Y., Chen, L., He, W., Sun, D., & Salas-Pilco, S. Z. (2024). AI for enhancing special education for K-12: A decade of trends, themes, and global insights (2013–2023). *International Journal of AI in Education*. https://doi.org/DOI: 10.1007/s40593-024-00422-0

Yılmaz, Ö. (2024). *Personalised learning and artificial intelligence in science education: Current state and future perspectives*. Educational Technology Quarterly., DOI: 10.55056/etq.744

Zavaraki, E. Z. (2024). *Artificial intelligence for people with special educational needs*. IntechOpen., DOI: 10.5772/intechopen.1004158

Zawacki-Richter, O., Marín, V. I., Bond, M., & Gouverneur, F. (2023). Artificial intelligence in education: A comprehensive review of applications and challenges. *International Journal of Educational Technology in Higher Education, 20*(1), 1–31. DOI: 10.1186/s41239-019-0171-0

Zhang, K., & Aslan, A. B. (2021). AI technologies for education: Recent research & future directions. *Computers and Education: Artificial Intelligence, 2*, 100025. DOI: 10.1016/j.caeai.2021.100025

ADDITIONAL READING

Anis, M. (2023). AI in education: A review of personalized learning and educational feedback mechanisms. *GSC Advanced Research and Reviews, 14*(3), 1–8. DOI: 10.30574/gscarr.2024.18.2.0062

Carby, N. (2022). Personalized feedback in a virtual learning environment. *Journal of Educational Technology Development and Exchange, 15*(1), 1–15. DOI: 10.31045/jes.6.1.3

Marougkas, A., Troussas, C., Krouska, A., & Sgouropoulou, C. (2023). How personalized and effective is immersive virtual reality in education? A systematic literature review for the last decade. *Multimedia Tools and Applications, 83*(24), 18185–18233. DOI: 10.1007/s11042-023-15986-7

Mishra, P., Henriksen, D., & Warr, M. (2023). Educational technology integration: A framework for post-pandemic teaching and learning. *TechTrends, 67*(1), 96–108. DOI: 10.1145/3629296.3629303

Nicol, J. (2024). How universal design for learning transformed my teaching: An elementary educator's journey of implementation. In *New Brunswick Department of Education and Early Childhood Development, Canada* (pp. 52). https://doi.org/ DOI: 10.4018/978-1-6684-4750-5.ch002

Parmaxi, A. (2020). Virtual reality in language learning: A systematic review and implications for research and practice. *Interactive Learning Environments, 31*(1), 172–184. DOI: 10.1080/10494820.2020.1765392

Teräs, M. (2022). Education and technology: Key issues and debates. *International Review of Education, 68*(4), 635–636. DOI: 10.1007/s11159-022-09971-9

Yılmaz, Ö. (2024). *Personalised learning and artificial intelligence in science education: Current state and future perspectives*. Educational Technology Quarterly., DOI: 10.55056/etq.744

KEY TERMS AND DEFINITIONS

Collaborative Coding Hubs: Virtual spaces where students and professionals can collaboratively work on coding projects, promoting teamwork, communication, and problem-solving.

Digital Learning Platforms: Online systems that combine educational content, communication tools, and assessment features to create accessible and scalable learning environments.

Engagement: The active participation of learners in educational activities, often enhanced through interactivity, gamification, and collaborative features.

Feedback Mechanisms: Systems within educational tools that deliver constructive, timely insights to students about their performance and areas for growth.

Learning Management Systems (LMS): Software platforms designed to organize, manage, and deliver educational content while handling tasks like grading and attendance tracking.

Personalized Learning: Customized educational experiences that leverage AI and analytics to address individual learners' needs, preferences, and progress.

Retention: The ability of educational platforms to sustain student interest and prevent dropout by providing engaging and adaptive learning experiences.

Virtual Reality (VR): Technology that creates immersive, simulated environments to help learners understand and retain complex concepts through experiential learning.

Chapter 10
Transforming Education with NLP and Machine Learning:
Innovations, Applications, and Future Prospects

R. Siva Subramanian
SRM Institute of Science and Technology, India

M. Swetha
Vel Tech Multi Tech Dr. Rangarajan Dr. Sakunthala Engineering College, India

K. Krishnaveni
Asan Memorial College for Engineering and Technology, India

T. Thilagam
https://orcid.org/0000-0002-7657-0726
Vel Tech Rangarajan Dr. Sagunthala R&D Institute of Science and Technology, India

K. Saranya
Panimalar Engineering College, India

L. A. Anto Gracious
https://orcid.org/0000-0003-2386-9182
R.M.K. College of Engineering and Technology, India

K. Sudha
RMD Engineering College, India

ABSTRACT

Natural Language Processing (NLP) and Machine Learning (ML) are transforming education by enhancing personalized learning, automating assessments, and improving content generation. Key innovations include AI-powered tutoring systems, adaptive learning platforms, and language acquisition tools that cater to individual student needs. NLP applications, such as sentiment analysis and language modeling,

DOI: 10.4018/979-8-3373-6791-0.ch010

Copyright © 2026, IGI Global Scientific Publishing. Copying or distributing in print or electronic forms without written permission of IGI Global Scientific Publishing is prohibited.

alongside ML algorithms for predictive analytics, are enabling more efficient and inclusive learning experiences. However, challenges such as data privacy concerns, bias in AI models, and technological barriers remain. The future of education lies in integrating these technologies with immersive tools like AR/VR, fostering lifelong learning, and supporting educators as co-teachers. With continuous research and development, NLP and ML hold the potential to reshape educational landscapes, offering both opportunities and ethical considerations.

INTRODUCTION

Context and Importance of Education Transformation

The field of education has been changing over the few decades mainly due to the technological developments. Traditionally, educational models were more or less rigid and standardized, and did not take into account the learner variation in terms of ability and the rate at which learning occurs. However, with the help of technology in learning, there is a transition toward more flexible, more effective, and more individualized learning strategies. This transformation has enabled educational systems to enhance the learning needs of the various students to improve the results of learning and enable students to have the most relevant and interesting learning periods. Technology as a tool in enhancing education in the contemporary society is quite complex. The use of technology in learning has also made it easy for instructors to capture and analyze various data which helps in the development of teaching strategies, recognition of learners who are performing poorly and coming up with learning intervention plans. In addition, technology has enabled expansion of education through removal of barriers such as geographical and financial barriers. With the advancing technology, online learning platforms, educational applications, and engaging digital tools have emerged as a source of learning aids to students. AI, in general, is now an influential force that has impacted the education sector. It is now possible to provide students with unique learning experiences because of the speed and efficiency of the AI in processing the huge volume of data(Anusha, S et al., 2024). It can be responsive to student's needs, provide feedback, explain something in details and even forecast certain results based on the student's performance. This idea of learning is highly flexible and can be seen as an incredible shift from the former strictly linear approaches to education. This is not a concept of the future but has already been implemented in the contemporary world across different levels of learning institutions, including schools, colleges, and organizations. These technologies are becoming more developed and the changes that affect the education sector can be described as radical, so the future of learning is promising to be more individualized, innovative and based on the usage of data.

NLP and Machine Learning

Thus, NLP and ML are two central subbranches of AI, which provide the underlying technologies that underpin the discussed phenomenon. It is the functionality of a machine that enables it to process, analyze and generate human language. This includes such tasks as text translation, emotion recognition, speech comprehension, and text summarization. NLP is thus important in education in areas such as student and learning systems interaction, automatic grading, real time translation and the creation of smart learning systems (Ansari, G et al., 2021). This way, students can get the feedback for their writings, communicate with the help of AI assistants, and even participate in language learning games that are tailored to the student's needs (Kondurkar et al., 2024). Machine learning is another branch of AI that is specifically designed to enable a machine to learn from data and make its decision without being programmed to do so (Pajila, P. B et al., 2023). The ML models are trained on big data, which makes it easy for it to learn the patterns and make the predictions(Siva, S. R et al., 2022). In the field of education, it is applied to: predicting students' performance, recommending learning materials, and determining at-risk students to dropout. It can also enable smart learning environments where the contents are set to match the learner's ability, thus challenge him or her at the right level at all times. Additionally, it can be used in grading the students, and the results can be used to identify students' behavior and their rate of learning. NLP and ML are integrated to improve the education system and make it more intelligent, adaptive. NLP is a valuable tool in improving communication and content creation while ML is used to make better decisions in the functioning of the educational systems (Krishnachalitha, K. C & Priya, 2021). These are not mere tools that enrich teaching learning activities, but these are tools that revolutionalise the manner in which teaching-learning occurs, is evaluated, and also is customized (Kumar, A & Gupta D, 2021).

Purpose and Scope of the Chapter

Therefore, the goal of this chapter is to review the current literature concerning the advancements that have been made in the sphere of NLP and ML in education and the possible applications of these technologies in the near future.

To this end, this chapter seeks to present a review of how NLP and ML are being used in the current learning environment in order to discover the benefits, drawbacks, and possibilities of the technologies. Another aim of the current chapter is to present a vast array of the possibilities of using NLP and ML in education. These applications are not limited to one area of education but are used in different fields such as in language acquisition and student's evaluation, content generation and even administrative work. In the following section of the chapter, the author seeks to explain how these technologies are changing education at the higher learning institutions. Besides, this chapter will also discuss the development that has occurred from the integration of NLP and ML into learning environments. There is a myriad of innovations that has been developed including intelligent tutoring systems where one can receive feedback in real time, adaptive learning platforms where the system is able to take into account the learning style of the learner. This part of the chapter will also define how the technologies are useful in addressing issues of accessibility, enhancing students' participation, and encouraging lifelong learning. At last, the chapter will also discuss the future of NLP and ML in Education. These technologies are still relatively new in the integration process of the educational systems and yet the possibilities they present are quite enormous. The chapter will also describe new trends, including integration of NLP and ML with other technologies like AR and VR that can potentially improve the learning process. Furthermore, it will analyse the place of AI in the dynamic of students and educators and the way it can be a positive change and not a threat to educators. Therefore, this chapter tries to present a comprehensive view of how NLP and ML are transforming the educational sector, the opportunities that are likely to be realized in the future, and the issues that need to be resolved. By reviewing the current state, new developments, uses and prospective opportunities, this survey will be of particular use to educators, technologists, policy makers and researchers engaged in the technological advancement in education.

FUNDAMENTAL CONCEPTS

Overview of NLP in Education

NLP is a branch of AI that is concerned with the ability of a computer to understand and interpret human language. It entails the ability of the machine to not only recognize, comprehend, translate, and produce natural language but also do so with relevance to the context. NLP is therefore vital in closing the gap between human interaction and the ability of machines to understand it which makes it very useful in transforming the education sector (Mir et al., 2023). In its essence, NLP comprises several components that enable more meaningful and knowledgeable interaction with text. One of these components is sentiment analysis that means the identification of the polarity of the text, whether it has positive, negative or neutral connotations. In education, it is used to evaluate students' feedback, to track the sentiment about the class in real time and even test the mood of learners during online classes or tests. For instance, it is possible to analyze the sentiment of the responses of the students in the surveys or forum discussions and see whether the students are engaged and satisfied with the course or not, which may lead to changes in the teaching approach or applying necessary interventions. Language modeling is another area of NLP that focuses on the development of models that would help in defining the structure of the language. These are trained on large data and can write text or give the next word in a sequence based on the previous words. In educational contexts, language models are applied to improve the automatic scoring of essays, which involves the model analyzing the organisation, fluency and grammatical of the written answers. This can greatly alleviate the workload of the educators while at the same time also providing more objective evaluations. Text summarization is another important subfield of NLP where the purpose is to transform long texts into shorter and more manageable documents, containing only the most important information. This has a great application in education especially in the following aspects, for instance summarizing of reading, lecture or research chapter for students. Hence, summarization can help in making learning material easier to comprehend due to time constraints or difficulties in understanding complex academic content. In addition, it is possible to use NLP tools to develop automatic study guides and quizzes, which also contribute to the learning process since students can get the key information from the lectures or a textbook.

Figure 1. NLP and machine learning in education

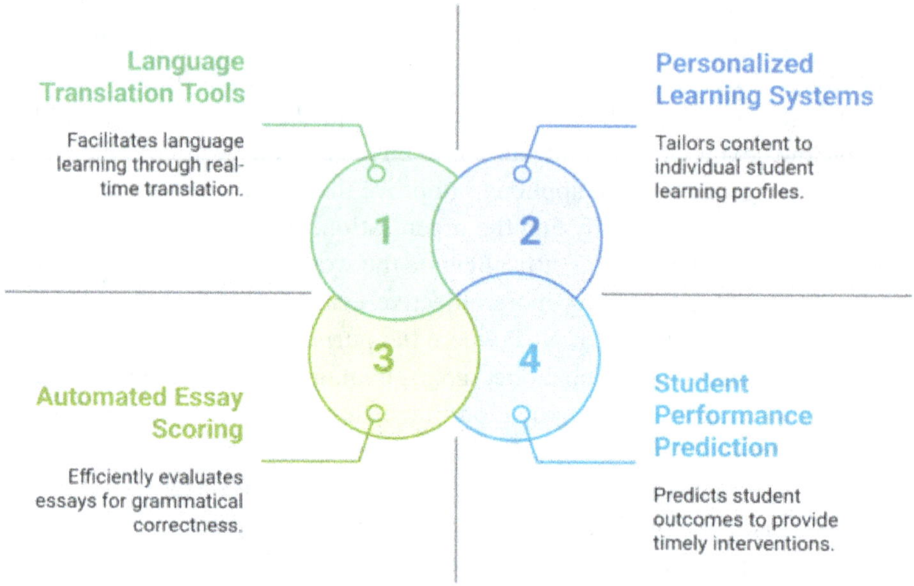

In education, the practical uses of NLP do not only include content generation and feedback analysis. Some of the NLP applications include language translation, grammar checkers, speech recognition software that assists students learning new languages by translating for them, correcting them, and even providing feedback on their pronunciation. Also, NLP is useful for the creation of chatbots or virtual tutors able to use natural language, answer students' questions, explain the concepts, and suggest solving practice problems. These has been especially useful in large classes or for the students who require supplementary lessons apart from the normal class hours. In terms of learning and teaching, NLP is enabling student-centered learning and providing feedback, aiding in content generation, and even sentiment analysis.

Overview of Machine Learning in Education

Artificial Intelligence is a more general field that encompasses the subfield of Machine Learning (ML) which is the capacity of a system or a model to enhance its knowledge over a given data without having to become programmed for it. It includes the creation of programs that can learn from data, make decisions, and learn from the results and new data. In the context of education, the application of ML is growing with the aim of improving students' learning as well as enhancing efficiency of processes in educational organizations (Alenezi & Faisal, 2020). There are several ways through which models learn from data and thus ML can be classified into the following categories. The most used type of machine learning is supervised learning where the algorithm learns from example datasets that are labeled or contain input and output values (Luan, H & Tsai, C. C, 2021). In education, supervised learning is applied in student performance prediction where information from the past on students' performance such as; grades, attendance, participation is used to predict future aspects such as; exam results, dropout rates etc. Using such data, it is possible to use these algorithms to pinpoint students who require assistance and prevent the deterioration of student performance (Hilbert et al., 2021).

However, unsupervised learning is a type of learning in which the models are trained on data that are not tagged. The mechanism identifies inherent patterns or clusters within the data(Lakumarapu, S et al., 2024). In education, unsupervised learning comes in handy in activities like grouping of students who have similar learning characteristics or attitudes(Yamini, B et al., 2023). For example, one can use ML to group students according to their activity with the help of digital learning tools and then notice those who require more attention or particular types of material. This can be especially useful when the educational process is based on the use of these platforms, designed to offer materials and activities suitable for particular students (Munir et al., 2022). RL is another type of ML that involves training an algorithm based on the actions they choose in an environment by either rewarding or punishing them. This type of learning is most frequently used in decision making systems and is used to enhance the efficiency of the AI model. In education, reinforcement learning can be applied in Intelligent Tutoring System (ITS) where the system increases or decreases the level of difficulty of the task depending on how the student performs. For example, it can respond to a student's answer, and if the student answers correctly, the system may give a more difficult question or if the student is struggling, the system may give an easier question or explain more. It is imperative to note that the use of machine learning does not end at student learning and performance prediction. One of the most important uses is in learning management systems, where the content is delivered according to the student's learning profile. Artificial intelligence algorithms based on students' interactions with the learning content modify the presentation of new content to the students. This will make it possible for the students to be trained to cover content that they understand and make progress instead of training them to cover very complex material that they cannot cope with or very simple material they find boring to study. New technologies of learning can be much more effective and flexible to the learners and their rates of learning. Besides the student-related aspects, ML is also widely used in the administrative aspects of education. For instance, ML can be used in tasks like grading, tracking the attendance of the students and even scheduling. Techniques that apply ML to grade assignments such as essays, open-ended questions, and other forms of assignments can help save time which teachers spend on grading hence enabling them to teach. Likewise, ML algorithms can be used efficiently for admission control, course timetabling, and resource requirements' forecasting (Sanusi et al., 2023). Thus, the use of NLP and ML in the educational process is becoming a new paradigm in the delivery, experience, and assessment of learning. While NLP helps in improving the interaction between students and educational systems, ML offers the foundation of the data-driven and personalized learning. Altogether, they have the possibility of revolutionizing the process of teaching and learning and thus contributing to the effectiveness and availability of education(Ponnuviji, N. P et al., 2024).

INNOVATIONS IN EDUCATION THROUGH NLP AND ML

Personalized Learning

The most important change in education facilitated by NLP and ML is the concept of learning that is individualized. Traditional teaching methodologies are characterized by mass delivery of instruction and assessment wherein students are treated alike in terms of instruction delivery and the tests and assignments that are set.

Figure 2. Innovations in education through NLP and ML

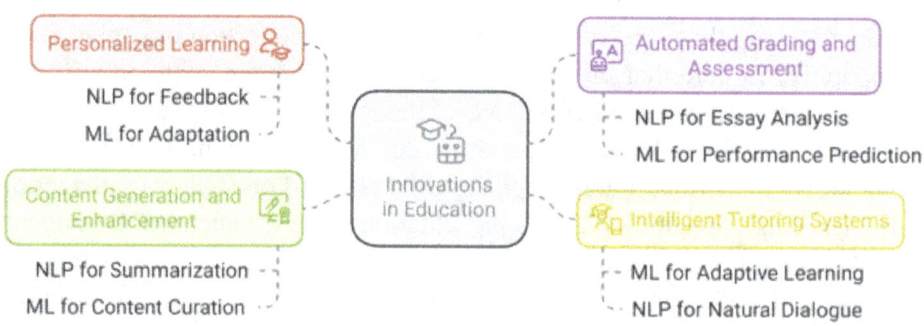

Personalized learning on the other hand, refers to a method in which the learning process is individualized so as to meet the needs of each learner where he or she is and provide him or her with the appropriate learning materials and challenges. This is made possible by the help of NLP and ML as the educational system is able to process a large amount of data and adapt the learning process. In personalized learning, NLP is used to interpret student's written or spoken information that is given to the system. For instance, language models can provide real-time feedback and grading of a student's responses, strengths and weaknesses in grammar, syntax and content. NLP also enables the development of learning content that is specific to the student by looking at the previous responses or past learning content interactions of the student. From this perspective, it is possible to apply NLP systems in creating new educational contents that are more suitable for the learner's current level of performance, which means that each learner will be exposed to materials that are not too easy, nor too difficult for him to handle.

On the other hand, Machine Learning improves the learning process because it is able to analyse data from students' activities on learning platforms. The use of ML algorithms is also useful in the tracking of the student's performance in the class, the learning behavior patterns that the students portray, the areas which the students are strong in as well as the areas that the students need to be reinforced in, and also the learning modalities that the student has. According to this information, the adaptive learning platforms can further change the level of the contents to be delivered to the student, whether it is to make the content easier if the student is struggling or to increase the level of difficulty if the student is performing well. It also maintains the progress of the students as they are always on the move with their learning process while at the same time makes learning more fun by introducing a bit of challenge at the right time. Modern adaptive learning platforms with the help of ML algorithms have become much more individualistic. They can suggest certain courses, propose extra material, or modify the order of lessons depending on the results achieved. This approach has benefited the students in the following ways because it is a unique way of learning that has changed the face of student- content interaction through enhancing understanding and self-paced learning.

Automated Grading and Assessment

Another innovation in the field of education affected by NLP and ML is the application of automated grading and assessment. Conventional practices of grading essays and assignments have been known to be very time consuming especially when working in large classes. It is becoming easier to automate this process through the use of NLP-based tools, which will make the process of evaluating the students' work faster and more consistent. The use of NLP is now being incorporated to provide auto-grading of written responses including essays, short answer questions, and other questions that require open responses.

These tools analyze several features of the student's writing such as grammar, syntactic features of the sentences, clarity and coherence. Also, in NLP, it is possible to determine the relevance and correctness of the content in accordance with a certain checklist and to indicate how the student has addressed the subject or the question. This saves time for the teachers and also provides fairness as compared to the grading done by teachers since it may be influenced by some factors. An additional advantage of NLP is that the feedback given is instant thus enabling the student to correct his or her errors as he or she is being corrected. Aside from grading, prediction has also been used in the assessment process, specifically in the field of machine learning. The ML algorithms can be used to estimate the future performance of the students and find out which students might need some help and might drop out. Through factors like the scores obtained in tests and exams, attendance and whether or not a student participates in class, these algorithms can pick out details which a human teacher may miss. This is very useful in making interventions at the right time so that the students can be helped or the learning content be changed to fit the needs of the students. Due to the application of ML, schools and universities have been able to shift from a reactive approach to learning to a proactive one, thereby improving the general performance of the students and the necessary interventions that are meant to be made.

Intelligent Tutoring Systems (ITS)

Another innovation that has been brought by the help of NLP and ML is the ITS or Intelligent Tutoring Systems. These systems' goal is to deliver one-to-one tutoring that can replicate the support of a human tutor to the students. Unlike conventional academic classrooms where students can hardly get one-on-one assistance, ITS provides a student with consistent support based on the student's learning requirements. Machine Learning plays a crucial role in ITS systems since these systems are designed to be adaptive and learn from the progress of the student. ITS can also monitor the student's performance and the strategy he/she uses when solving assignments, the time taken, and success rates and then adapt the level of difficulty, give hints or provide additional explanations. This makes it possible for the students to get immediate feedback in the same manner as they would get when using one-on-one tutoring. NLP contributes to the development of ITS by refining dialogues, making the interaction between the student and the tutoring system more natural and natural. These systems can handle the student's responses in natural language and the conversation that follows is more natural and not like one is speaking to a computer. For example, if a student has a question in their mind and they want to ask it from the AI tutor, the system being developed with NLP will understand it and provide the answers in the form of explanation or an example. This makes the learning process engaging and interesting since the students are sure that their questions and concerns are being addressed on the fly. However, with the help of NLP, ITS can deliver more informative feedback and explain the necessary information to a student and reveal misconceptions. Such systems can also identify fallacies in the student's thinking process and provide feedback on the correct way to approach it and teach the student in the process. With the help of this approach based on machine learning and natural language processing, ITS is revolutionizing the model of individual approach to students and offering them the necessary tools to achieve success.

Content Generation and Enhancement

One more area that is rapidly transforming with the help of NLP and ML is the capability to generate educational content without human intervention. Typically, the development of tests, outlines, and practice exercises has been a laborious process for educators. However, with the help of NLP and ML, one can automate all the above-mentioned processes, which will be beneficial for teachers and students. Summarization of long texts can be done by NLP algorithms and only the important points and concepts can be brought for students to look at. It is especially beneficial to the students who have difficulty in sorting out large amounts of text. In the same way, NLP can be used in the development of quizzes and practice examinations since it is able to identify the most important topics or concepts in a particular text and develop questions that are likely to challenge the students' knowledge in these areas. It also gives more practice for students and saves the teacher's time as they do not spend much of their time on administrative work and more on teaching their students. Another area that is related to the topic of Interest is Machine Learning used in the context of content curation and recommendations. Through the use of ML algorithms, students past performance can be considered and other articles, videos, or books that would be of most help in the understanding of the subject matter could be recommended. When either of these recommendations is applied, it assists in making it more personalized and efficient for the students since it is done in accordance with their needs and interest. Thus, the innovations due to NLP and ML are changing the education system and providing more personalization, efficiency and access to education. Self-paced learning environment, intelligent tutoring systems, automated content generation and assessment are some of the ways through which these technologies are revolutionizing ways in which students are learning and the ways in which the educators are supporting them. These advancements have shown that there is much more that can be done for education through the use of such technologies and the future for more improvements holds a lot of promise for creating a system that can provide a unique learning environment for each learner.

APPLICATIONS OF NLP AND MACHINE LEARNING IN EDUCATION

Language Learning

NLP has brought into use tools and resources that can enhance the process of learning languages in a more effective and individualized manner for the students. Among the areas that have been revolutionized by NLP is the speech recognition. This technology enables learners of a certain language to speak freely while the software they are interacting with assess their pronunciation. Besides speech recognition, there has been a great progress in translation tools based on NLP that facilitate students learning of new languages. Examples of such systems include Google Translate, where through the use of NLP, it is possible to translate text or speech from one language to another almost instantly. All these tools are very useful to the language learners because they can help the learners overcome the language barrier in a realtime manner by translating words or even whole sentences or paragraphs. Another language learning application of NLP is grammar checking tools. These tools are used to review the mistakes in grammar, syntax and punctuation made by a learner through a word processing mechanism. In this case, the suggestions and corrections made by these tools assist the students in enhancing their language proficiency as they write. Such feedback can be particularly beneficial to learners who are learning a new language and needs to develop the finer details of the language such as the grammar rules and structures of the language. Apart from NLP, another key component that is applied in the process of language learning is machine learning. Using the data on the performance of learners, it becomes easy to recommend learning resources as well as paths based on the needs of the students. For instance, if a student has some difficulties with certain words or grammar, the system will be able to offer additional practice and descriptions of the problematic points. This approach makes it possible for every learner to be challenged and given practice in what best suits him/her learning level.

Figure 3. Applications of NLP and machine learning in education

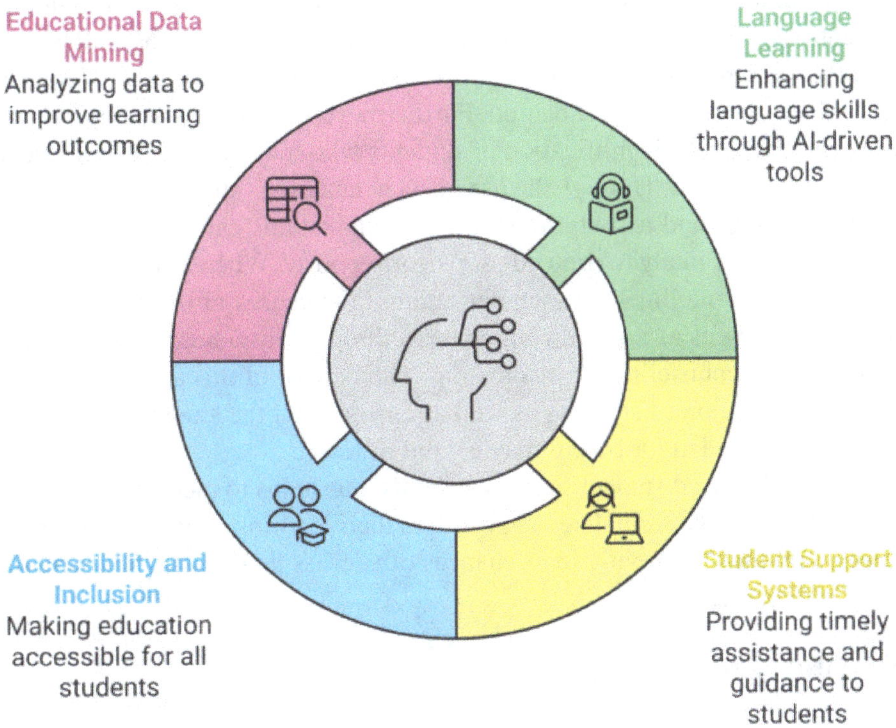

Student Support Systems

NLP and ML have played a significant role in improving the student support systems where the educators are now in a position to offer better support to the students at the right time. As we have seen, chatbots and virtual assistants that are based on NLP technologies are becoming popular in education as the means of providing immediate academic assistance. These AI systems are capable of answering all kind of questions that concern the course or any other administrative issues and they are available all the time, thus making them very useful for any student who may have questions after class or even during the weekend. These chatbots can engage the students in natural language and answer to inquiries made by the students in real-time manner. For instance, a student may engage a chatbot to inquire the date by which a particular assignment is due, seek clarification on one of the topics covered in class or seek assistance on how to solve a particular problem. The student enters a message, which the chatbot analyses in order to understand the meaning and its intent by utilizing methods such as recognition of the intent and identification of named entities. This kind of support relieves teachers and teaching assistants of some of the burden they carry while at the same time making sure that the students do not feel that they are lagging behind. Furthermore, the use of Machine Learning is very vital in the early identification of students who may drop out and the necessary actions to be taken. Through the use of such data as the student's performance, attendance records, and activity level, the ML algorithms can detect signs that a particular student is likely to drop out or perform poorly. When a risk is identified, the educator or an intelligent system can address the causes of the potential problem before it emerges as a significant concern through providing assistance in the form of tutoring, counseling, or mentorship. The benefit of this approach is that it increases the retention of students as well as ensures that the students who require assistance are provided for before they get out of reach.

The use of AI based student support systems thus helps to meet students' needs and provide a more individualized approach to their learning needs and experience in a classroom thus improving their chances of success and satisfaction with their learning environment.

Accessibility and Inclusion

The most significant benefit of NLP and ML in education is the manner in which these technologies are revolutionizing the accessibility of education as well as creating inclusiveness. Innovations such as these are making education accessible for the students with disabilities and making the classroom more inclusive. NLP is especially useful in enhancing the learning resources available to students who have visual or auditory disabilities. Machine Learning is also used to enhance the provision of education to all students through offering of differentiated content. ML algorithms can analyze the learning behavior of each learner and then proceed to present the content in a way that is suitable for learners with different learning disabilities. For instance, a child with ADHD might be more comfortable with shorter lessons that are designed to keep him/her on track as compared to a child with autism who will need more visual or structured lessons. The use of ML to analyse students' progress will allow the content to be delivered in the most effective manner for each learner, thus making the learning process more accessible for all. In addition, ML can be used to develop personalized learning tools for disabled students as a way of addressing various disabilities that are present in the students; for instance, students with motor disabilities or those with cognitive disabilities need special consideration when handling learning tools or content.

Educational Data Mining (EDM) and Analytics

EDM and analytics are relatively new disciplines that use data and learning algorithms to explore and analyze educational data in order to find out what promotes learning. These data which may include students' grade, attendance, how they interact with the learning management system and other related information can be useful in understanding the behaviors and performance of students as well as group behavior. The use of ML in analyzing these datasets will help educators and administrators identify key factors that affect the students' performances. For instance, by using predictive models, the students who are likely to perform poorly or drop out can be easily be identified based on such factors as poor grades, truancy, or limited use of the learning materials. Through identification of such students, early action can be taken through provision of special attention, special programs or tutors, counseling among others that can help improve their performance. For instance, ML can also be used in education to determine the effectiveness of the teaching approaches, content, or even interventions used in learning. From the student assessments and feedback information generated by the students, these algorithms can point out the areas of difficulty that the students are experiencing and recommend changes in the curriculum or in the teaching methods that can be used to overcome the challenges experienced. This approach makes the teaching and learning process to be informed and enhanced by the results that the practices are yielding. Concisely, the use of NLP and ML is beneficial in education as it enhances personalization, inclusion, and efficiency of learning. But these innovative technologies are way beyond that bored impact; from improving children's ability to speak fluently to applications such as speech recognition, than translation, to student's success in providing them with models and ideas based on data. Using NLP and ML in the learning process, it is possible to design the educational environment that is more open and more suitable for students with different learning abilities.

CHALLENGES AND LIMITATIONS

Data Privacy and Ethical Concerns

One of the most important problems that arise with the use of NLP and Machine Learning in learning environments is data privacy and ethical issues. The main issue is protection of student's information. NLP and ML-based educational platforms deal with massive numbers of students continuously accumulating information from students' performance, personal records, and their engagement with pertinent learning content. This data, if not well managed, may be abused and there might be a violation of the privacy of the users of this data. Another issue is that student information is often stored and analyzed in the cloud, and the data can be accessed by unauthorized users, subjected to cyber threats or hacking, and stolen(Dhinakaran, D et al., 2025). Due to the fact that students' personal details can be vulnerable, there is the need for educational institutions and technology suppliers to ensure that they protect this information. However, sharing the educational platform information through third parties and algorithms prove challenging in building a strong security system. For instance, the external service providers may process data without adequate clarity; this becomes difficult for the schools to protect the students' information. Due to the current data privacy laws, there is a pressure on the educational institutions companies to meet the regulations, which can be quite a challenge and expensive. Consequently, it is crucial for proper measures to be put in place to protect sensitive information to foster the use of the technology. Another issue of ethics in the use of artificial intelligence is on the aspect of bias in the models. When creating a machine learning model, if the training data used in developing it is either biased, in that it is unbalanced, and covers a limited sample space, then the machine learning model that is developed from such data will also be equally or even more biased. For instance, if a machine learning model used in an educational environment was trained on a biased dataset, then it may lead to discriminating results like suggesting biased recommendations or inequitable grading by the machine learning model based on a student's characteristics. This is more so the case in education as it compromises the equality and diversity of learning. The above risks can only be avoided if the AI models are trained with a diverse dataset that reflects the real-world population. Also, there is a rising demand to create ways on how the AI systems can be checked on a daily basis to see if they are being fair and ethical in their operations.

Technological Barriers

There are other obstacles to the implementation of NLP and ML in education and one of them is technological challenges. Albeit, the possibilities that these technologies hold are immense, the costs of putting up the necessary structures to support these technologies are expensive; a challenge that is even more so to many educational institutions especially those in the developing or the underprivileged regions. In most cases, the application of NLP and ML systems demands a huge investment in the form of hardware, software, and human resource. For example, in schools and universities, there is a requirement of high-performance computing systems for handling large data sets and high-level computations. However, the main disadvantage of many of these technologies is that they are difficult for educational institutions to implement due to the lack of funds or technical resources to create the appropriate conditions, which also hampers the widespread application of such technologies. However, the latter, alongside with the specific software and the data infrastructure needed for NLP and ML systems, is another issue. As it is often the case with educational institutions, they are often unable to obtain large, high quality datasets that are required for training and fine-tuning of the machine learning models. Most of the NLP and ML algorithms work better when they are fed with large sets of data and unfortunately, most schools do not possess the necessary data such as student engagement with content or past performance data that are necessary to train the models. In addition, the process of gathering, sorting, and annotating data may be time-consuming and expensive; it is even more so when an institution is faced with a scarcity of resources or staff members. The absence of sturdy data framework can thus pose a challenge to the implementation of these technologies. The next technological issue is related to the computational complexity of many NLP and ML tasks. Common deep learning models which are used for solving complicated tasks need large computational resources in terms of processors (like GPU) as well as memory(Priyadharshini, S et al., 2025). These models can be costly and many schools or educational institutions may not afford to put up these models into practice. However, such issues can be partly addressed through cloud-based services, but the latter is dependent on the internet connection and the capability to process massive data(Ponnuviji, N. P et al., 2025). Thus, in the regions where the availability of broadband internet or cloud services is low, the adoption of these technologies might be even more problematic. This technological inequity increases the schism in education since the schools in the affluent areas have the capability to take advantage of the latest technologies as compared to schools in the economically backward areas.

Interpretability and Trust

Another challenge that is closely connected to the use of Machine Learning in learning environment is interpretability and trust. A number of machine learning models, and even the deep learning models, are known to be black box models whereby the way they arrive at their decisions cannot be easily explained to other people(Ganesan, I et al., 2024). This has caused a concern among educators, students and parents because they may not know how the AI systems arrived at certain decisions or why certain outcomes are being suggested. For instance, in the context of education, an ML algorithm may recommend learning materials or estimate the student's performance in a given course; however, if the rationale for such suggestions is not readily explained, the user may not have confidence in the system. For the tools based on NLP, the problem of interpretability is especially acute, as the decisions made by the language models on the basis of which the essays are graded, feedbacks are generated, or materials are recommended can influence the learning process of the students. When these tools are used, educators cannot tell whether the feedback given to the students is accurate, fair or even if the feedback has not been influenced by any biases. There are also disadvantages of not being able to explain why the algorithm has made certain decisions; it becomes challenging to debug the system or even design new strategies for improving the system in the future.

It also brings about issues of accountability due to the fact that these models are often referred to as black boxes. If a recommendation offered by an AI-based tool is detrimental to the student's performance, then whom does one hold accountable. The problem of accountability is most acute when algorithms are applied to important decisions, including students' evaluations or their academic performance forecast. To this end, there is a rising interest in explainable AI (XAI) in the context of education. XAI focuses on making the models not only accurate but also explainable in order to provide the users with the reasons behind the model's decision making. Such models would assist in establishing trust between educators, students, and other stakeholders as they would be assured that the AI systems used can be explained, reviewed, and optimized. In conclusion, it is possible to state that NLP and ML have great potential for creating breakthroughs in the sphere of education, but they also have certain limitations. Due attention should be paid to the potential issues of privacy, ethical aspects, and technology limitations in order to make these innovations useful for all students regardless of their status or income level. However, to achieve this, there is a need for improving the interpretability of the AI models and developing the trust in the decision-making processes of the respective AI models in order to facilitate the implementation of these technologies in educational contexts. So going forward as we consider the application of NLP and ML in education, there is need to balance on the innovation of technology and the right use of technology.

FUTURE PROSPECTS

Emerging Trends

The education sector is gradually evolving due to the trends that rely on NLP, ML and other advanced technologies to enhance the learning experience. Some of the most engaging topics include NLP and ML fused with AR and VR. These technologies have been widely used in teaching and learning processes and have been proven to enhance teaching and learning delivery in a more engaging way beyond the classroom walls. When integrated, both NLP and ML with AR/VR hold the potential to change the learning process of the student for the better as it diversify, individualize and open the process. For instance, in an information meeting concerning history, students can grab contents through an AR experience of historical civilizations, while the NLP techniques of the educational platform monitor the student's activities during the class and provide feedback in the form of information or stories. In a similar way, in an environment of language learning, virtual reality can mimic real-life conversations in different languages and natural language processing tools can analyse the correctness of the pronunciation, the structure of the sentences and the usage of the context on the fly. The integration of environment with AI technology could create an innovative learning process in the acquisition of knowledge that would eventually enhance the learning process. Another is the more emerging form of learning platforms which focused more in the blend of AI. In the future, collaboration will not only be limited to the interaction between students but will also involve intelligent systems that support students' learning processes. AI can assist in the organization of the group tasks by recommending materials, developing tasks according to the group members, and even moderating the group's conversations. These platforms will therefore be able to learn from the students and their needs hence matching them with other students in the group in order to optimize the group. The adoption of NLP in these platforms shall also increase the chances of reducing the communication gaps between students from different backgrounds or language abilities hence promoting inclusiveness. The possibility to assess progress, diagnose group dynamics and provide recommendations, which are based on the analysis of interactions, can enhance learning effects and foster cooperation between individuals which has not been available before.

AI and the Future of Educators

With the advancement in AI, it was predicted that it will have a significant impact in the teaching profession. AI will not act as a replacement for the teacher but will be an assistant who will help the teacher in their work. It will enable the teachers to spare more time to engage with students, foster their problem-solving skills, and attend to their emotional needs because the AI can perform routine tasks such as grading, generating feedback, and administrative work. This may help create a more optimized, individualized, and tutorial learning process optimized in a way that would allow teachers to focus on what is truly important, namely, cultivating a learner's critical thinking. AI will also be used in the continuous professional development of teachers and instructors to support their work. With the development of technology, educators will need to have knowledge and skills in order to integrate AI and NLP tools into the educational system. As the teachers' professional development is concerned, AI platforms of the future could identify teachers' needs and learning preferences and provide them with recommendations regarding materials, courses, and strategies. Besides, as AI systems have access to data on students' activity and achievements, they can be useful for teachers in terms of adjusting their approaches to teaching. Teachers will be equipped with real time results and the support they require to be able to make good decisions and better their practices in the future. This continuous learning process will be very important to make educators relevant and efficient in the current world that is dominated by artificial intelligence. Also, the role of AI as a co-teacher will enable the reduction of the workload, which involves handling many administrative tasks. For instance, it can be used for grading, monitoring the progress of students as well as providing feedback to students thus reducing the workload of educators and enabling them to come up with unique and unique methods of teaching. In the long run, this symbiotic relationship between educators and artificial intelligence will enhance the teacher's ability to build better rapport with their students, based on companionship, guidance, and personal growth.

Long-Term Vision

In the long run, the future of education with the help of NLP and ML is to have a full-fledged learning process where the data plays a crucial role. In this vision, everything that a student encounters in his or her learning process is unique depending on the abilities, disabilities, and interests of the learner. As applied to education, normally developed AI and NLP programs will enable the creation of learning systems that can deliver highly individualized content and revise the material depending on the student's understanding, emotional state, or tempo. This means that through the use of machine learning, student data will be analyzed on a regular basis so as to determine which areas they are likely to experience problems in and suggest possible solutions even before the problems are realized. This will not only improve the level of student participation but also minimize the cases of learning loss and make it possible to identify students who need special attention. It would be appropriate to use such a system in order to offer equal opportunities in education and provide each learner with the suitable material and the right level of difficulty according to their learning abilities and their background. This vision also has a concept of lifelong learning where by, the people will be in a position to keep on updating their knowledge and skills with the changing market demands. The concept of continuous learning as new upskilling platforms are being spearheaded by artificial intelligence will not be the one and done form of education. These systems will be based on NLP and ML that will suggest the courses and training modules that are most suitable to an individual based on the current position or the desired profession. Also, using the data gathered from the job markets, it will be possible for the workers to prepare for the future shifts in the market with the help of AI.

CONCLUSION

Thus, the purpose of this chapter was to discuss how NLP and ML can revolutionize the field of education. The chapter started by defining these technologies as well as their uses in the context of education. The integration of NLP in the improvement of the capability to comprehend and generate human language and the integration of ML in the capability to analyze data and assess outcomes has revolutionized the way students learn, the way educators teach and the way educational content is delivered. We discussed a number of the areas that have been impacted by NLP and ML that include the following; Personalized learning, Automated grading, Intelligent tutoring systems, and Content generation. Such innovations are proving to be very useful in promoting education by increasing flexibility, effectiveness and personalization of learning. Also, the use of such technologies in language learning or students support systems as well as educational data mining suggest that the delivery of more accessible and inclusive as well as data-driven learning is constant becoming enhanced. Nevertheless, the use of NLP and ML in education has some drawbacks. It was highlighted that data privacy, ethical dilemmas including bias, technology limitation, and the explainability of AI were some of the challenges that need to be overcome. As for the further development and application of such technologies, it is imperative that such challenges are taken into consideration so that all students are provided with fair and ethical opportunities. To sum up, the advancement in NLP and ML will be beneficial to the future of education as it will result in individualized, engaging, and dynamic learning environment. Nevertheless, there is need for future studies and improvements in the areas that have been highlighted above in order to harness the full benefits that come with them. With the increased use of AI in education, it is crucial to keep on discussing the possible ethical issues and consider the role of technology as a supplement to the teachers.

REFERENCES

Alenezi, H. S., & Faisal, M. H. (2020). Utilizing crowdsourcing and machine learning in education: Literature review. *Education and Information Technologies*, *25*(4), 2971–2986.

Ansari, G., Gupta, S., & Singhal, N. (2021). Natural Language Processing in Online Reviews. In Natural Language Processing for Global and Local Business (pp. 40-64). IGI Global Scientific Publishing.

Anusha, S., Ezhilvandan, M., Gayathri, S., Sivaraman, V., & TP, A. (2024). Emerging trends in edge AI for Industry 4.0 and 5.0: Technologies, applications, and challenges. AI Innovations in Service and Tourism Marketing, 211-228.

Dhinakaran, D., Kumar, N. J., & Ponnuviji, N. P. (2025). Safeguarding confidentiality and privacy in cloud-enabled healthcare systems with spectrasafe encryption and dynamic k-anonymity algorithm. *Expert Systems with Applications*, *279*, 127584.

Ganesan, I., Ponnuviji, N. P., Kumar, A. S., Nithya, M., Jambulingam, U., & Lalitha, S. D. (2024). Real-Time Event Detection and Predictive Analytics Using IoT and Deep Learning. In Industry Applications of Thrust Manufacturing: Convergence with Real-Time Data and AI (pp. 1-41). IGI Global Scientific Publishing.

Hilbert, S., Coors, S., Kraus, E., Bischl, B., Lindl, A., Frei, M., & Stachl, C. (2021). Machine learning for the educational sciences. *Review of Education*, *9*(3), e3310.

Kondurkar, I., Raj, A., & Lakshmi, D. (2024). Modern applications with a focus on training ChatGPT and GPT models: exploring generative AI and NLP. In *Advanced applications of generative AI and natural language processing models* (pp. 186–227). IGI Global Scientific Publishing.

Krishnachalitha, K. C., & Priya, C. (2021). Deep NLP in the Healthcare Industry: Applied Machine Learning and Artificial Intelligence in Rheumatoid Arthritis. In Deep Natural Language Processing and AI Applications for Industry 5.0 (pp. 189-203). IGI Global.

Kumar, A., & Gupta, D. (2021). Sentiment analysis as a restricted NLP problem. In *Natural language processing for global and local business* (pp. 65–96). IGI Global.

Lakumarapu, S., Nithyanandhan, R., Bhargavi, V. S., Anish, T. P., & Nalini, M. (2024, August). Machine Learning Approaches for Liver Disease Prediction: A Comparative Analysis. In 2024 5th International Conference on Electronics and Sustainable Communication Systems (ICESC) (pp. 159-164). IEEE.

Luan, H., & Tsai, C. C. (2021). A review of using machine learning approaches for precision education. *Journal of Educational Technology & Society*, *24*(1), 250–266.

Mir, T. A., Lawaye, A. A., & Khanday, A. M. U. D. (2023). Nlp techniques and challenges to process social media data. In *Advanced applications of NLP and deep learning in social media data* (pp. 171–218). IGI Global.

Munir, H., Vogel, B., & Jacobsson, A. (2022). Artificial intelligence and machine learning approaches in digital education: A systematic revision. *Information (Basel)*, *13*(4), 203.

Pajila, P. B., Sheena, B. G., Gayathri, A., Aswini, J., & Nalini, M. (2023, September). A comprehensive survey on naive bayes algorithm: Advantages, limitations and applications. In 2023 4th International Conference on Smart Electronics and Communication (ICOSEC) (pp. 1228-1234). IEEE.

Ponnuviji, N. P., Murugan, P., Esakkiammal, S., Kumar, S., Vishal, K. S., & Meenakshi, S. (2024, March). AI-Powered Business Intelligence for Transforming Finance and Education. In 2024 2nd International Conference on Disruptive Technologies (ICDT) (pp. 1287-1291). IEEE.

Ponnuviji, N. P., Nirmala, G., Kokila, M. S., & Priyadharshini, S. I. (2025). Optimizing Image Retrieval in Cloud Servers with TN-AGW: A Secure and Efficient Approach. Journal of The Institution of Engineers (India): Series B, 106(2), 459-473.

Priyadharshini, S. I., Irene, D. S., Beulah, J. R., & Ponnuviji, N. P. (2025). Enhancing real-time health monitoring with hybrid recurrent long short-term tyrannosaurus search for menstrual cups. *Biomedical Signal Processing and Control*, *100*, 107065.

Sanusi, I. T., Oyelere, S. S., Vartiainen, H., Suhonen, J., & Tukiainen, M. (2023). A systematic review of teaching and learning machine learning in K-12 education. *Education and Information Technologies*, *28*(5), 5967–5997.

Siva, S. R., Bushra, S. N., Maheswari, B., & Prabukumar, M. K. (2022, April). Performance Analysis of Different Machine Learning in Customer Prediction. In 2022 6th International Conference on Trends in Electronics and Informatics (ICOEI) (pp. 1425-1430). IEEE.

Yamini, B., Sudha, K., Nalini, M., Kavitha, G., Subramanian, R. S., & Sugumar, R. (2023, June). Predictive modelling for lung cancer detection using machine learning techniques. In 2023 8th International Conference on Communication and Electronics Systems (ICCES) (pp. 1220-1226). IEEE.

Chapter 11
Revolutionizing Education With NLP and ML:
Innovations, Challenges, and Future Directions

R. N. Ravikumar
https://orcid.org/0009-0009-3705-1681
Marwadi University, Rajkot, India

S. Aarthi
https://orcid.org/0009-0006-9064-2091
Marwadi University, Rajkot, India

Barno Sapaeva
Mamun University, Khiva, Uzbekistan

Yunus Jumaniyozov
Urgench State University, Urgench, Uzbekistan

V. Manoj Praveen
Velalar College of Engineering and Technology, Erode, India

Vanitha Siddheswaran
https://orcid.org/0009-0009-6905-8044
Kumaraguru Institute of Agriculture, Erode, India

ABSTRACT

Natural Language Processing (NLP) and Machine Learning (ML) are transforming education by making learning interactive, adaptive, and personalized. Conversational AI enables AI-driven tools to enhance student support, automate administrative tasks, and improve teaching methods. Innovations in NLP power chatbots, virtual tutors, and automated grading, making them more responsive. ML uses predictive analytics to identify at-risk students and tailor personalized learning paths, fostering inclusivity. This chapter explores NLP and ML applications in K-12 and higher education, highlighting case studies on student engagement, knowledge retention, and teaching

DOI: 10.4018/979-8-3373-6791-0.ch011

Copyright © 2026, IGI Global Scientific Publishing. Copying or distributing in print or electronic forms without written permission of IGI Global Scientific Publishing is prohibited.

efficacy. Key challenges include AI integration, ethical concerns like data privacy, and biases in AI models. The chapter examines policy discussions and the need for regulatory frameworks that balance innovation and ethics. As AI-driven education expands globally, collaboration among researchers, educators, and policymakers is vital to shaping its future for improved learning outcomes.

INTRODUCTION TO NLP AND MACHINE LEARNING IN EDUCATION

Natural Language Processing (NLP) and Machine Learning (ML) are changing the face of education not only by promoting intelligent, adaptive, and personalized learning experiences. NLP is a blend of linguistics, computer science, and artificial intelligence that allows computers to understand, interpret, and generate human language data, thereby facilitating chatbots, virtual tutors, and automatic grading systems with the goal of enhancing student engagement and enabling support. Conversely, ML helps in estimating or predicting a student's performance, the personalization of learning paths, and automation of administrative tasks. These technologies support multilingual learning, assist students with disabilities, and real-time feedback in contributing to more inclusive and accessible education. AI-driven educational tools are enhancing the efficiency of learning while offering educators support by automating dull and repetitive tasks and providing insights based on data. However, there are concerns about data privacy, algorithmic bias, and ethical issues regarding the deployment of NLP and ML in education, (Mathew & Paulose, 2021). These technologies, however they are changing, may reshape traditional ways of teaching and the education systems of the world.

Overview of NLP and Machine Learning in Education

NLP and ML are actively transforming education through intelligent, data-driven, and personalized learning. NLP equips specifications to comprehend and process human languages, allowing the creation of AI driven chatbots and intelligent virtual tutors and automated grading that assist in student engagement through real-time feedback, mere content perspiration, and language translation for multilingual learners. Presently, ML also aids student performance analytics, prediction of learning patterns, and personalized lesson planning for unique needs, (Singh & Ahuja, 2019). AI systems can also manage some administrative jobs, such as attendance, plagiarism detection, and course recommendations, enabling their abilities to be harnessed for more meaningful interactions with students.

Thus, audio visual tools and adaptive learning applied through the integration of NLP and ML will make AI teach build and continuously optimize itself to one or another degree, as far as a particular student's learning is concerned. Intelligent tutoring systems use NLP to identify and understand student's questions, ensuring relevant explanations and thus customized help for different learning styles. Sentiment analysis based on ML can identify emotions in students and support their learning hurriedly before it's too late, (Zhao, 2023). These also involve Text-to-Speech, Speech-to-Text transcription, rest services for learners with disabilities, thus affording AI to enhance by providing accessibility and who knows what further in the straightforward future where these innovations are concerned, learning shall change that becomes more engaging, inclusive and efficient to the students of the world.

Table 1. NLP vs ML use cases in education

Technology	Use Case	Example Application
NLP	Automated Essay Scoring	Assess grammar and structure in student writing
	Chatbots and Virtual Tutors	Duolingo, ChatGPT, IBM Watson for real-time support
	Sentiment Analysis	Detect emotional states from text input
	STT & TTS Tools	Accessibility for visually or hearing-impaired
ML	Predictive Analytics	Identify at-risk students using behavioural data
	Adaptive Learning Systems	MindSpark, Squirrel AI adapting lesson difficulty
	Automated Grading	ETS e-rater and AWE tools
	Plagiarism Detection	Turnitin AI models detecting copied content

Table 1 outlines key applications of NLP and ML technologies in education. NLP supports tools like automated essay scoring, virtual tutors, sentiment analysis, and Speech-to-Text/Text-to-Speech systems, enhancing both accessibility and student engagement. Meanwhile, ML enables predictive analytics for identifying at risk students, powers adaptive learning systems, automates grading, and enhances plagiarism detection, thus personalizing instruction and improving academic integrity.

Importance of AI Driven Innovations in Learning Environments

Artificial Intelligence (AI) is changing the learning environment by introducing automation, privatization and real-time analytics that enhance teaching and learning experiences. AI run chatbots and virtual assistants provide immediate educational assistance, students answer questions, and facilitate interactive learning. Machine

Learning (ML) algorithms analyze students' behavior and performance, helping teachers to design adaptive learning experiences to suit individual needs, (Mohanan, Stringfellow, & Gupta, 2017). Automatic grading systems and literary theft detection equipment streamlines administrative functions, focusing on giving high quality instructions to teachers. Additionally, AI powered speech and language processing equipment helps to break language obstacles by providing real-time translation and access features, ensuring a more inclusive education system.

Beyond efficiency, AI promoted engagement and cooperation through the Intelligent learning platform, which is adapted to the student progress, offers customized resources and response. AI run spirit analysis can assess student's emotion, identify learners who may require additional support. Gamification elements operated by AI make more interactive by adjusting the level of difficulty depending on individual performance. In addition, the future analytics enables students to take initial intervention by identifying the risk of falling back, ensuring that teachers can take active steps to increase learning results. As AI continues to develop, its role will only increase in improving the access, efficiency and effectiveness of education, making the learning environment more sensitive and student centric, (Tafazoli, Parra, & Abril, 2019).

Figure 1. AI in learning environments

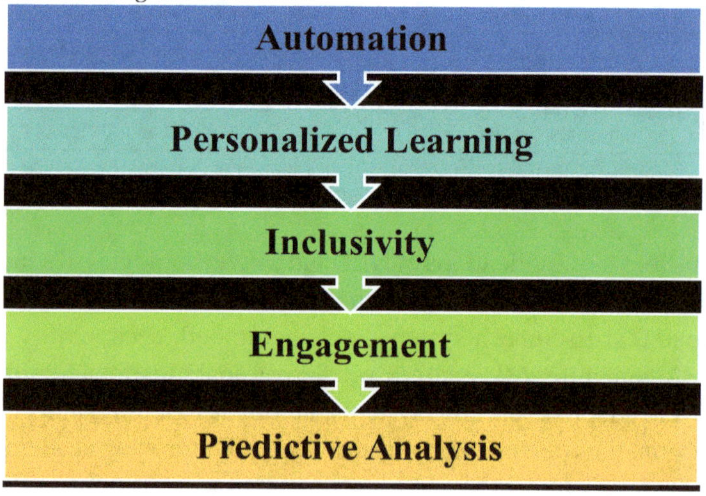

Figure 1 visually represents the concept of "Inclusivity" using a bold green banner and a downward-pointing arrow. It symbolizes a top-down approach or framework where inclusivity is the foundational principle guiding actions, policies, or educational practices. The use of green often conveys growth, openness, and accessibility, reinforcing the positive impact of inclusive environments.

Enhanced Student Engagement

AI, using NLP and ML, greatly improves student focus because it makes learning both dynamic and engaging. With AI, students benefit from chatbots that offer academic advice at any time and encourage them to be more involved with the course material. Software programs MindSpark and Duolingo customize what and how students learn to fit their skills, keeping students interested and able to learn. Tools for speech recognition and Text-to-Speech give different learners, especially those with disabilities, a chance to join in learning through accessible technology. It also helps detect the mood of each student and ways to keep them motivated on a regular basis. Using games, automatic feedback, and talking with a computer helps create an enlightening and engaging learning environment. When personalization, interactivity, and accessibility are included, learners enjoy being involved in their studies and achieve better results and feel happier. Because of AI, passive learners can move on to become active and interested ones, (Ghadirli & Rastgarpour, 2013).

Automated Administrative Tasks

AI is making it possible to handle administrative functions in education by robotizing simple and regular activities, which saves educators' time and improves efficiency. AI tools make it easy, fast, and precise to track who comes to school, design schedules, and look after student files. By applying ML, schools are able to figure out how likely students are to take certain courses and improve how they manage course sign-ups. NLP helps with grading essays and offering students instant and helpful feedback. AI also plays a role in finding plagiarism, preserving honesty in universities and schools. In addition, smart recommendation engines find suitable learning materials for every student according to their past achievements and history of training. By using such technology, teachers and administrators can manage more important tasks related to education instead of administration. The use of AI in the back end makes educational institutions work better, aid students more efficiently, and help in planning and providing support with data.

Data Driven Decision Making

Data is now the main tool for driving decisions and improvements in schools and education organizations. Such tools make it possible for educators to identify students facing challenges by reviewing their actions, results, and level of participation. It makes it possible to organize supportive steps such as tutoring or counseling for students. Dashboards present teachers with helpful information, enabling them to change their teaching methods according to new data. With NLP, specific emotions and stress in student responses can be detected, which makes it possible to provide assistance early. With AI, it is simpler to develop curriculum and assign resources because you can observe changes in how students perform. All in all, making decisions based on data allows teachers to offer individual learning, help information stay in students' minds, and fit classroom goals to what each student needs. Yet, to preserve trust and good outcomes, student data should be used properly and AI algorithms must be clear and fair, (Panaite et al., 2018).

Scalability and Accessibility

With AI, education becomes more accessible and scalable because it helps learners from different places and with different needs. Achieving scalability means making instruction consistent even for many students after giving it over to computer-based resources. They are always working, which makes it possible for more students to access learning at a lower price for colleges. The use of Speech-to-Text (STT), Text-to-Speech (TTS), and translation tools means that people with vision or hearing disabilities and students from different backgrounds can use the same applications. NLP, directional understanding and use of language are included in lessons presented in multiple formats, while AI based quizzes are customized for students with various language skills. In such advancements, students can enjoy equal learning no matter what their backgrounds are. Because of these technologies, education becomes more efficient, fair, open to everyone, and possible for many cultures.

How NLP and ML Contribute to Personalized Education

NLP and ML are bringing revolution in education by enabling individual learning experiences to individual students' needs. NLP operated chatbots and virtual tutors provide real time assistance; students optimize clarification based on questions and learning speeds. Machine Learning algorithms analyze students' performance, engagement levels and learning styles, which to recommend customized study plans, ensure that each learner receives materials adapted to his proficiency and preferences. AI run spirit analysis helps teachers assess student's emotion, identifies people who may require additional support. Additionally, adaptive teaching platforms provide targeted reactions to dynamically adjust the difficulty levels to NLP and ML, and suggest complementary resources, leading to more attractive and effective learning process. By integrating these techniques, education becomes more flexible, data powered, and students concentrate, increase overall learning results and promotes free, lifetime learning. AI conducted experience learning experiences for individual students' needs, making education more effective, (Barua et al., 2022).

Adaptive Learning Systems

With machine learning, Adaptive Learning Systems personalize education material for every student's pace, skills, and preferred learning method. They always check how far a learner has come and update the level of difficulty in their learning materials. They automatically review students' responses during the training and offer support in the right subjects. NLP offers extra support by understanding student queries and giving related explanations. Learning is made richer when multimedia and intelligent support is combined in an interface. Adaptive systems better the learning process, plus they promote inclusivity by matching the learning requirements and skills of students, making education individualized and practicable in different societies.

Intelligent Feedback Mechanisms

With AI and its branches NLP and ML, intelligent feedback mechanisms can respond fast, consider individual students, and give useful advice. They review things the students write, answer, or say and, in return, give feedback designed to help them gain a better understanding. Technologies based on NLP examine the language skills in student work, whereas ML models detect where errors are made and suggest individual solutions. Also, chatbots that use Socratic questioning led students to think for themselves instead of only fixing their mistakes. Depending on a learner's progress, the system can quickly change the challenge and offer suitable extra resources. With prompt and personal answers, intelligent feedback encourages students, boosts self-motivation, and hastens learning of ideas, so passive learning becomes more engaging and self-driven, (Kashefi et al., 2022).

Sentiment and Emotion Analysis for Student Wellbeing

Sentiment and emotion analysis is valuable because it can detect how people feel from what they say or write. NLP is used to review text posts and chats so it can detect when someone feels stressed, frustrated, or not interested. Such AI systems can recognize what a person is going through and suggest ways to comfort the individual or involve more support. Using these tools, teachers are able to help students early by choosing resources or mental support that best suits them. The use of AI chatbots and learning modules permits around-the-clock assistance and advice to students under pressure or feelings of separation from others. Improving the emotional awareness in digital courses enables schools to provide extra aid and support, which in turn helps students remember lessons, remain dedicated, and improve their psychological well-being, (Anwar et al., 2023).

Conversational AI for Student Support

Conversational AI is helping students by responding in real time and providing guidance suitable for them. Chatbots and virtual tutors using AI can help students at any time and respond to questions about assignments, deadlines, and any other tasks. These systems also adjust the content and the way they give feedback depending on how a student prefers to learn, how fast they work, and their grades. With them, people are more involved, the learning gaps are narrowed, and students are offered emotional assistance through analyzing their emotions. Georgia State University's "Pounce" and India's "MindSpark" prove that conversational AI can help more students pass their classes and do better in school. Thanks to its scalable, multilingual, and emotional aspects, conversational AI provides equal support to all students, especially to those who are at risk, have disabilities, or learn from different places. When students use new technology, it marks a change to more open, fast, and student friendly education, (Chutia & Baruah, 2024).

FUNDAMENTALS OF NLP AND MACHINE LEARNING

Artificial Intelligence (AI) has influenced education, in which NLP and ML students play an important role in learning and increasing support systems. NLP enables machines to understand, interpret and generate human language, provides intelligent chatbots, automatic grading systems and adaptive tuition. Meanwhile, ML allows educational platforms to learn from data, predict the student's performance and personalize learning experiences. Understanding the basic principles of NLP and ML is necessary to develop AI operated educational equipment that improves both teaching efficiency and student engagement, (Chala, Guta, & Asebel, 2022).

Key Concepts in Natural Language Processing (NLP)

NLP teaches computers to comprehend and communicate with humans. The main ones are tokenization, sentiment analysis, named entity recognition and text summarization. These methods backup educational uses including automated feedback, personalized content and mood tracking. Text-to-Speech and Speech-to-Text applications can improve accessibility to different learners. It is hoped that collectively these concepts can allow more inclusive, responsive, and effective learning environments.

Table 2. Key concepts in NLP

Concept	Description	Educational Application
Tokenization	Breaking down text into smaller units (tokens) such as words or sentences.	Enables analysis of student responses and essay structure.
Named Entity Recognition	Identifying proper names, places, or specific terms in text.	Enhances relevance in answers and content comprehension.
Sentiment Analysis	Detecting emotions or opinions from text input.	Monitors student mood and identifies those needing support.
Text Summarization	Generating concise summaries from longer texts.	Aids in personalized content delivery and easier comprehension.
Speech-to-Text (STT)	Converting spoken language into written text.	Assists visually impaired students and supports transcription.
Text-to-Speech (TTS)	Converting written text into spoken language.	Aids auditory learners and students with reading difficulties.
Part-of-Speech Tagging	Identifying parts of speech (noun, verb, etc.) for each word in a sentence.	Supports grammar checking and language instruction.
Language Translation	Translating text between languages using machine translation.	Enables multilingual support and inclusive learning.
Dependency Parsing	Analyzing grammatical structure by identifying relationships between words.	Enhances writing evaluation and comprehension feedback.

Table 2 presents essential NLP concepts used in educational contexts, along with their descriptions and corresponding applications. These core techniques such as tokenization, sentiment analysis, and text summarization enable intelligent analysis of student input, facilitate personalized learning, and improve accessibility. The integration of speech and language technologies also supports inclusive and adaptive learning environments, catering to diverse student needs.

Overview of Machine Learning (ML) Techniques Used in Education

ML is transforming education as it makes data-driven, personalized, and scalable education solutions possible. The most fundamental ML applications in education are predictive analytics to help initially recognize at risk students as well as to optimize interventions, recommendation systems, which suggest personalization of content delivery, and automated essay scoring engines, which evaluate grammar, structure and coherence. Also, plagiarism detecting software helps to improve academic honesty by revealing plagiarized works. Adaptive assessments using ML dynamically change the difficulty of the questions depending on the performance of the student, making sure that the assessment is customized. Another area in which reinforcement learning is getting popular is in intelligent tutoring systems, which improved content delivery depending on the interaction made by the learner. Such tools can not only simplify administrative operations but will lead to better learning outcomes since the instructors will be able to concentrate on pedagogy. As it evolves further, ML will help learning become more inclusive, efficient and address individual student needs in a better way.

Supervised, Unsupervised, and Reinforcement Learning in Educational Applications

These three paradigms of ML are behind different educational technologies. Supervised learning involves labeled data to train the models on activities such as automated grading and prediction of performance. Unsupervised learning finds hidden structure in unlabeled data, which lets learnable systems adapt to their environment, or recommend items based on personal preferences. Reinforcement learning is feedback-based learning, which is suitable to intelligent tutoring systems, which must be dynamically adjusted to the interaction of students. The two of them are used to make data-driven, personalized, and interactive learning environments, (Rao & Ramalingamma, 2022).

Table 3. Learning paradigms in educational applications

Learning Type	Definition	Key Applications in Education	Examples
Supervised Learning	Uses labelled data to train models to make predictions or classifications	Automated grading, student performance prediction, language translation	AI writing assistants, exam score prediction models
Unsupervised Learning	Identifies patterns or clusters in data without labelled outputs	Student grouping, personalized content recommendation	Adaptive learning platforms (e.g., clustering learners)
Reinforcement Learning	Learns through trial and error using feedback from interactions with the environment	Intelligent tutoring systems, gamified learning progression	Duolingo chatbot optimizing lesson paths based on user behavior

Table 3 categorizes three core ML paradigms Supervised, Unsupervised, and Reinforcement Learning highlighting their definitions, key applications, and examples in the educational domain. It helps illustrate how different learning techniques support diverse instructional and assessment needs in AI-enhanced education systems.

CONVERSATIONAL AI IN EDUCATION

The interactive AI student is revolutionizing the education sector by increasing the student engagement, providing personal teaching assistance and automatic to educational assistance. Through techniques such as chatbots, virtual tutors and Intelligent Tutoring Systems (ITS), AI enables real-time interaction, adaptive learning experience and skilled material distribution. These AI operated solutions help teachers to reduce the workload, track progress and provide quick response, making the learning environment more interactive and effective, (Pimentel et al., 2024).

Chatbots and Virtual Tutors for Student Engagement

Virtual tutors and chatbots Ubiquitous Artificial Intelligence (AI) are enabling chatbots and virtual tutors to serve as on demand educational assistants that engage with students, respond to questions, and help students have more personalized learning experiences. Trained to interact with one another in a human-like way through NLP and ML, these tools see a major benefit in classrooms. A significant role that they perform is the 24/7 support, where they answer immediately when asked questions regarding coursework, deadlines, and administrative procedures, (Klímová & Seraj, 2023). Being interactive learning assistants, they are used to explain complex concepts in a step-by-step manner with real time response. They also provide an individualized learning experience as the analysis of the individual progress and the recommendations are customized to fit the unique needs of the student. Most of those systems use the element of gamification (quizzes, challenges, interactive exercises) to increase engagement. Notable ones are Duolingo AI tutor, an AI based language learning tool that creates interactive exercises; ChatGPT, an AI based writing assistant, brainstorming, and coding aid; and IBM Watson Tutor, an AI-powered STEM education assistant, (Baskara, 2023).

Intelligent Tutoring Systems (ITS)

A far more considerable improvement on the conventional chatbots is the use of Intelligent Tutoring Systems (ITS), which uses AI powered analytics to develop adaptive and individualized learning experiences. They are systems that are always able to track performance of students, point out areas of weaknesses, and offer/provide instructional material that address individual learning needs. One of the most important aspects of ITS is that they can offer real time feedback and adaptive learning which changes the level of difficulty of tasks according to the responses given by the students. The latter also suggests personalized learning tracks, suggesting particular materials depending on the weaknesses and strengths of a given learner.

Natural language understanding enables the AI tutors to analyze the responses of the student, identify areas of misunderstanding and provide instant clarifications to improve the comprehension level, (Yin et al., 2020). As well, ITS facilitate multimodal learning through the incorporation of text, audio, video and interactive elements which enhances learning. Examples of ITS are the Cognitive Tutor (now Carnegie Learning), an individualized math learning program, ALEKS, an adaptive STEM learning program, and Squirrel AI, a system used in many Chinese institutions and reputable to offer individualized tutoring.

Case Studies: Successful Implementations of Conversational AI in Classrooms

Chatbots, virtual tutors, and other forms of conversational AI have demonstrated a tangible rate of success in engaging students and improving their academic services. In Georgia State University, Pounce, a chatbot, decreased the dropout rate by 22 percent because it helped students sort out administrative questions. Adaptive learning on the MindSpark platform raised math and language achievement in India. Duolingo AI tutor is a reinforcement learning based personalization of language lessons that increases retention and engagement. With these examples, it is possible to notice how conversational AI can improve personalized learning and efficiency of institutions.

Case Study 1: AI Powered Chatbots for Administrative and Learning Support

Chatbots are changing the landscape of education by providing 24/7 support on the administrative and academic level with the help of AI. These chatbots can help the students in any routine procedure like enrollment, fee payment, course registration, and access to academic calendars which can take a huge amount of load off the administrative staff. To support learning, chatbots can give immediate responses to academic questions, suggest studying materials, and remind about the deadlines or tasks, (mainstay.com, n.d.). An outstanding example is the chatbot named Pounce that was implemented at the Georgia State University and that contributed to reducing the student dropout rate by 22 percent due to guiding the students through the crucial processes of enrollment and financial aid. These bots are based on NLP to interpret and answer student questions conversationally to make them accessible and responsive. AI chatbots provide automated routine communication and offer personalized support to students, improving satisfaction levels, boosting institutional efficiency, and facilitating a smoother learning process.

Table 4. Functions of AI-powered chatbots in education

Function Category	Specific Functions	Example/Application
Administrative Support	Enrolment guidance, tuition and fee inquiries, deadline reminders	Pounce at Georgia State University
Academic Support	Answering course-related questions, recommending resources, 24/7 help	ChatGPT for assignments and study assistance
Real-Time Interaction	Conversational responses using NLP, multilingual support	IBM Watson Tutor
Efficiency & Engagement	Reduces staff workload, improves student satisfaction, boosts retention	Reduced dropout rate by 22% at GSU

Table 4 highlights the key roles of AI chatbots in supporting both administrative and academic needs in educational institutions.

Case Study 2: MindSpark AI-Powered Adaptive Learning in India

The adaptive learning platform MindSpark operates in India using Artificial Intelligence coding from Educational Initiatives (EI). The platform applies artificial intelligence to deliver customized educational materials to students based on how they learn and what areas need improvement, (mindpsark.in, n.d.). MindSpark is an Artificial Intelligence assisted adaptive learning technology that aims to customize education by adjusting the learning material to the individual student learning pace and requirements. It actively tracks the performance of the students as well as it changes the complexity of questions in real time dynamically. It determines the strengths and weaknesses with the help of algorithms and provides individual exercises to fill certain learning gaps. MindSpark also gives immediate, explanatory feedback on every response which enables students to grasp concepts better. It is available in several Indian languages, and hence, it can be used by a wide range of students. Dashboards allow teachers to access performance analytic so that they can tailor teaching and track gains. MindSpark can guarantee every student an individual and successful learning process because it is based on building up the knowledge Washington State University instead of memorizing. This one-on-one method has proved to be very effective in improving academic performance in mathematics and language especially within the underprivileged communities.

Virtual tutors, adaptive learning platforms, and other AI based educational technologies have tremendously influenced the learning abilities of students. Such technologies individualize the instructional process by tailoring content and challenging the individual in accordance with his/her performance, which results in better understanding and memorizing. Error correction in real-time allows students to develop a better comprehension of information. Such websites as MindSpark or

Duolingo have demonstrated objective improvement in academic achievements, particularly in math and language proficiencies. Besides, AI based tools encourage self-directed learning, letting students be in control of their learning [20]. AI can improve academic performance by predicting learning deficits and providing early academic interventions to close the gap and promote inclusive, equitable education.

The studies of such AI based educational systems as MindSpark and Duolingo underline a positive effect on learning achievement. An evaluation by J-PAL (Abdul Latif Jameel Poverty Action Lab) in Delhi government schools randomized controlled trial observed that students who used MindSpark showed a big improvement in mathematics and Hindi performance which is 0.36 and 0.22 standard deviations, respectively, over the conventional classroom learning. Likewise, reinforcement learning strategy in Duolingo has demonstrated enhanced user retention and engagement due to personalized lessons presentation and feedback in real-time. These case studies reassure that adaptive learning technologies have a potential to close foundation learning gaps, particularly in low-resource contexts, (duolingo.com, n.d.). They also show how AI systems can be effectively scaled to different educational settings and at the same time promote individualized learning. This kind of evidence perpetuates the possibility of using AI to revolutionize the field of education by enhancing access, equity in learning, and performance Both at individual and institutional levels.

Figure 2. Impact of MindSpark on student performance (J-PAL study)

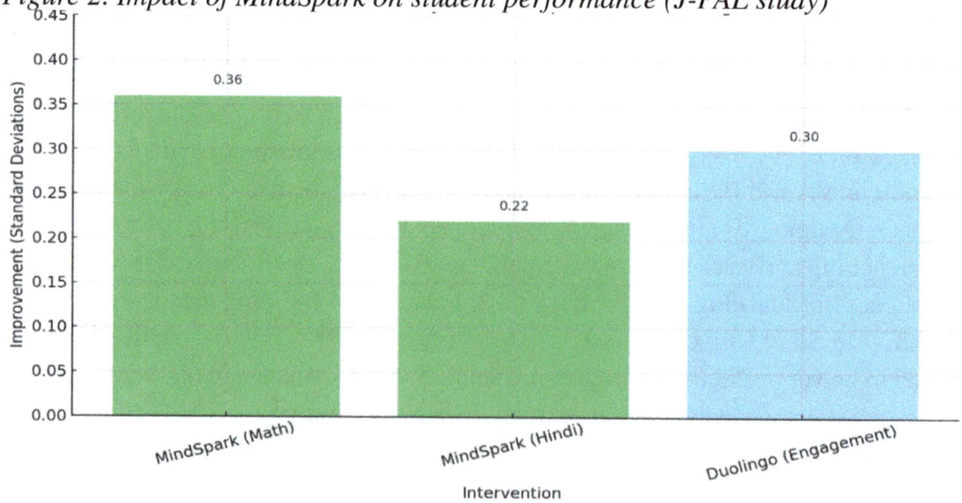

Figure 2 compares the impact of AI based educational systems on learning outcomes, measured in standard deviations. MindSpark shows the highest gains in

Mathematics (0.36 SD) and Hindi (0.22 SD), while Duolingo demonstrates improved engagement at 0.30 SD (estimated). These results highlight the effectiveness of personalized, adaptive learning technologies.

Case Study 3: Duolingo's AI Tutor in AI Driven Language Learning

Duolingo's AI tutor uses NLP and reinforcement learning to personalize language lessons. The chatbots provides instant feedback on pronunciation and grammar, making language learning more interactive and accessible to students worldwide. The language learning platform Duolingo utilizes AI tutors that generate personalized educational content for individual student requirements. Artificial intelligence technology along with NLP operates through reinforcement learning to develop personalized user interactions within this learning platform, (Wang & Yang, 2024).

Duolingo, a language-learning platform used by millions of people around the world, incorporates AI-based tutoring to make the experience highly personalized and very interactive. It employs AI tutor, which relies on reinforcement learning algorithms and NLP to dynamically adjust the lessons to the learning speed and success of a user. The platform provides interactive analysis of the responses made by the users and adapts the level of difficulty of the questions and also it provides instant feedback thus encouraging higher engagement and long-term memories. Comparative analysis of the performance (as shown in the chart) depicts significant gains on major metrics of language learning. The retention rate, pronunciation accuracy, and grammar improvement were 60%, 65%, 62 percent, respectively, before the AI tutor was integrated and 85 percent, 90 percent, and 88 percent, respectively, afterward. Such results prove the effectiveness of Duolingo to improve the performance of learners due to the adaptive nature of instruction and immediate feedback. Moreover, Duolingo uses the elements of gamification, namely the streaks, rewards, and challenges, to maintain the motivation and engagement of users. With its AI-powered tutor, it is not only able to optimize content delivery but also provides a scalable and accessible learning solution to users of all the age groups and geographies. The situation with this case shows the potential of AI in turning the conventional way of learning languages into a more entertaining, effective, and outcome-driven experience.

Figure 3. Impact of Duolingo's AI tutor on language learning metrics

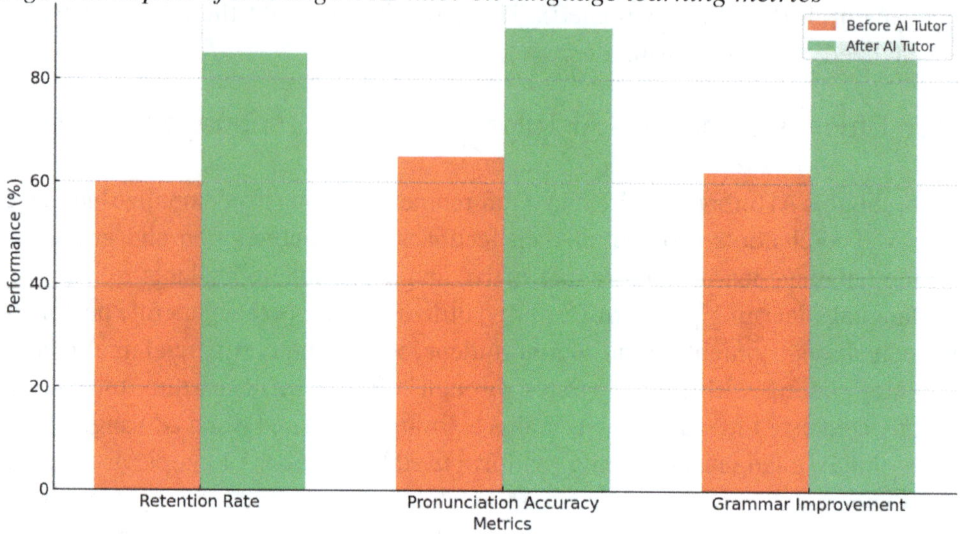

Figure 3 illustrates the significant improvements in language learning outcomes with Duolingo's AI tutor. After AI integration, retention rate rose from 60% to 85%, pronunciation accuracy improved from 65% to 90%, and grammar proficiency increased from 62% to 88%. The AI tutor clearly enhances learner engagement and performance, (Oghu et al., 2023). It demonstrates the effectiveness of personalized, feedback-driven learning experiences powered by AI.

NLP TECHNIQUES FOR PERSONALIZED LEARNING

NLP is, in modern times, shifting perspectives on personalized learning as it allows for an AI system to absorb, analyze and respond to student input in a manner specific to their unique needs. NLP techniques such as text analysis, dedication of sentiments, and speech recognition allow educational platforms to assess student understanding and engagement in real-time. For instance, AI powered chatbots and virtual tutors use NLP for instant feedback on questions and learning resources based on student progress, (Oghu et al., 2023). Text summarization and content simplification also break highly technical topics into easy-to-digest formats, hence giving students different competency levels some tailor formulated teaching materials that match their prowess. Another outstanding application of NLP in personalized learning is adaptive assessments and intelligent tutoring systems, (Barunaha, Prakash, & Naresh, 2023).

AI supported grading tools evaluate the written assignment that includes grammar and structure, providing helpful feedback to encourage excellent writing skills. Speech to text and text to speech solutions will equally help out with language learning and the visually impaired, enhancing education inclusion. NLP powered sentiment protocols have assisted educators in determining the students under emotional duress and thus what support will come their way on a timely basis, (Qiu et al., 2024). With a continued evolution of NLP, chatbots in education, language learning platforms, and AI tutors will, on top of that, magnify personalized student-centered learning experiences with effective and captivating education.

Sentiment Analysis for Student Feedback and Emotional Intelligence

The analysis of sentiments will help the AI systems assess the emotions of their students in light of their written or verbal responses. By gauging tone, word choice, and structure of the sentence, AI will be able to determine whether the student feels confident, frustrated, or disengaged, (Pacella et al., 2024). Emotional intelligence is starting to become a part of AI-powered educational systems that can improve the learning process with the help of real-time sentiment analysis. Such systems will be able to recognize when a student is in an emotional state, e.g. frustration, confusion or satisfaction and on the fly change the complexity of the presented material. Here are a few examples of how the system can be used to support a learner individually: in case a learner shows that they are stressed or confused, the system may offer additional resources and alert teachers so that they could help the learner in time. This initiative will help students to get the support they require before they become disengaged. Also, the sentiment analysis can be used to improve virtual learning environments by providing more insights into student behavior and emotional participation on discussion forums and feedback mechanisms, (Jayavardhini, 2024). An applied example would be AI empowered Learning Management Systems (LMS) to track and evaluate the reactions of students in the online community, and apply emotional indications to individualize and reorganize subsequent lesson planning. Such an emotionally responsive feedback loop, in addition to enhancing the design of instruction, makes digital learning more empathic and student-centered.

Text Summarization for Automated Content Delivery

Automated content delivery through text summarization is an application of NLP that allows the summarization of text in large quantities of information to create meaningful summaries that are human comprehensible. This is useful in rendering the necessary contents swiftly in platforms such as news aggregator sites, learning portals as well as in business dashboards. It can be done in two general ways, extractive summarization (where the most important sentences of the original text are chosen) and abstractive one (where new sentences, conveying the same core ideas are produced). Summarization enhances content availability, lessens reading time and allows personalization through enhanced summaries according to wants. It has become an essential part of dealing with the information overload hype in the modern-day and age fast-paced digital world, (Pendy, 2023).

Adaptive Learning Pathways Using NLP Driven Recommendations

Adaptive learning systems take advantage of NLP to analyze the student's performance, predict learning needs and recommend personal learning ways. These AI operated platform text adjust difficulty, suggest relevant study materials, and adapt to the learning program to fit personal progress rates, (Kumar et al., 2019). NLP is poised to have revolutionized the field of education by making smart, personal, and emotionally aware learning systems. A major usage is personalized course assignment in which the AI identifies the unique learning behaviors of a person and automatically differentiates the coursework in real-time to fit the requirements of the particular student. NLP models in predictive analytics could foresee topics in which a student may have weakness and intervene early to help ensure academic success. In addition to that, NLP in Intelligent Tutoring Systems (ITS) is employed to provide individualized explanations, examples, and practice problems, such that the content is customized to the knowledge of the individual learner. educational establishments, such as Mines Academy and Squirrel AI, are using NLP powered adaptive learning platforms to make education personalized. NLP is transforming the way students engage with digital learning environments through the personalization of teaching process with emotion analysis, text summarization and adaptive teaching pathways. All of this enables AI to identify emotional responses, provide personalized content, and adapt the teaching to instantaneous progress. With the further development of NLP, it will certainly have a great impact on the involvement in education, its availability as well as the effectiveness of learning processes throughout the entire world, (Taghipour & Ng, 2016).

ML BASED ASSESSMENT AND FEEDBACK SYSTEMS

ML is more efficient, objective and individual by changing student's evaluation and response systems. Traditional grading methods can be time-consuming and subjective, while ML operated assessment equipment uses automated grading algorithms, future-stolen analytics, and AI operated reaction mechanisms to correctly evaluate the student performance. These systems analyze written assignments, quizzes and even spoken reactions, providing quick reactions to help students improve. Additionally, ML models can assess patterns in student's errors, provide personal recommendations to strengthen weak areas, (Ifenthaler, 2022). AI powered essay graders, literary theft detection equipment, and Intelligent Tuition Systems (ITS) further enhance the evaluation process, which ensure stability and impartiality in assessment.

Beyond grading, ML based feedback systems play an important role in adaptive learning environment by analyzing student's engagement, participation and level of understanding. The emotional analysis and NLP powered insights help teachers to understand the levels of feelings, confusion and inspiration, which allow timely intervention. In addition, the future analytics can identify risk students based on their performance trends, making teachers capable of providing additional assistance before falling behind students. By taking advantage of ML for assessment and response, educational institutions can promote a data operated, personal learning experience that students increase results and engagement, (Harry & Sayudin, 2023).

AI Driven Grading and Automated Essay Scoring

ML enables AI operated grading systems that automatically evaluate student's assignments, essays and quiz. These systems use NLP and deep learning to assess grammar, consistency, structure and logic in written responses. Automatic Essay Scoring (AES) equipment provides immediate, coherent and purpose response, reducing grading workloads for teachers. Additionally, AI powered literary theft detection equipment ensures educational integrity by analyzing lessons in the huge database, (Salam, Fitri, & Zulan, 2024).

Examples: AI tools such as Aerter (by ETS) and grammar assess essays and provide feedback on writing quality.

Adaptive Assessment Models Using ML

ML based adaptive assessments dynamically adjust the difficulty of questions based on a student's reactions. These models analyze previous performance, response time and accuracy that match individual quiz and tests from individual learning levels.

Adaptive assessments help identify knowledge intervals and ensure that students gain learning experiences friendly to their speed and understanding.

Example: Alex (evaluation and learning in knowledge places) adopts mathematics and science questions based on the student proficiency.

Future Analysis for Student Performance Evaluation

ML operated Predictive Analytics use historical performance data, behavioral patterns and engagement metrics to predict the risk of success or failure of the student. These systems help teachers identify risk students, which allow for targeted interventions such as tutoring, counseling or individual study plans. Institutes use future stating analysis to improve retention rates, adapt courses distribution and increase learning results, (Ren, 2024).

Examples: Georgia State University's AI System "digestion" successfully reduced the dropout rates by predicting and addressing student challenges.

LANGUAGE PROCESSING FOR MULTILINGUAL AND INCLUSIVE EDUCATION

NLP is playing an important role in making education more inclusive and accessible by breaking the obstacles of language and supporting various learners. AI run language translation tools help students access to learning content in their original languages, promoting better understanding and engagement. The NLP gave a speech for lessons and lessons for speech technologies, which help students disabled people, such as hearing or visual loss, by converting the spoken lectures into text or by generating audio versions of textbooks. Additionally, AI enhances real-time transcription and voice recognition system, enables non-speakers to engage with more effectively lessons, ensuring a justified learning environment, (Popenici & Kerr, 2017).

In multilingual classes, NLP based adaptive teaching platforms personalize the material based on the language proficiency levels of the students. Intelligent Tutoring Systems use NLP to provide rea-time grammar improvement, language learning recommendations and pronunciation response, helping students to master new languages efficiently. In addition, emotion analysis in educational chatbots allows AI to detect language related struggles or emotional challenges, which may indicate timely intervention to students. As NLP continues to develop, it will further bridge linguistic intervals, enabling more inclusive, individual and global education systems, (Shaikh et al., 2024).

NLP for Automatic Translation and Localization of Content

NLP enables the real-time translation and localization of educational materials, making it accessible to learning for students in various linguistic backgrounds. AI operated translation tools, such as Google translation and deep L, allows students to read textbooks, assignments and lectures notes in their original languages, (Masood, 2025). Localization goes beyond translation to align cultural contexts, idioms, and examples with a student's background, ensure better understanding. NLP operated multilingual chatbots further enhance the engagement by allowing students to interact with educational platforms in their favorite language.

Examples: Duolingo and Microsoft translator use NLP to provide personal language learning experience and real-time translations.

Speech Recognition and Text to Speech Tools for Accessibility

Speech Recognition and Text to Speech (TTS) technologies help students who face challenges with reading, writing or communication. These tools help to convert spoken words into lessons for students, which are accompanied by listening loss and visually produce audio versions of text materials for impaired learners, (AI Commons, 2025). AI operated voice assistants also support students by allowing students to interact with learning platforms through voice commands, making education more inclusive and user friendly.

Examples: Google's speech helps students for API and Amazon Polly (TTS) by converting students to readable text or converted into a lecture in spoken words.

AI Driven Support for Students With Disabilities

AI run NLP solution provides personal learning assistance for disabled students, including dyslexia, speech loss and cognitive challenges. Tools such as AI operated reading assistant and adaptive communication devices enable students to connect with digital content at their speed. Additionally, NLP operated Predictive Text and Grammar Correction Tools help students to write difficulties by suggesting reference conscious words and sentence structures, (Goyal, Garg, & Nair, 2025). These technologies promote independent education and improve academic performance for students requiring special support.

Examples: Microsoft's emergency reader and speechify NLP uses NLP by improving reading and understanding to help students with dyslexia and other learning disability.

CHALLENGES AND ETHICAL CONSIDERATIONS

As NLP and ML bring revolution in education, they also introduce many challenges and moral concerns. While AI operated equipment enhances individual learning, automate assessment, and breaks language obstacles, issues related to bias, data security and fairness should be addressed for equal and responsible AI adoption. Below are three major challenges that should consider teachers, developers and policy makers, (AI4ED Workship Committee, 2025).

Bias in NLP and ML Models in Education

AI models trained on biased dataset can strengthen existing inequalities in education. NLPs and ML systems learn from historical data, and if training data includes socio economic, racial, or gender bias, AI generated recommendations may incorrectly favor some student groups on others. For example, an automatic grading system trained on essays written mainly by native English speakers can struggle to properly assess non speakers, leading to an incorrect evaluation. Similarly, the language models used in educational chatbots can reflect cultural prejudices, affect the recommendations and response of materials, (Villar, 2025).

Possible Solutions

- Use variety and representative datasets to train an AI model.
- Apply the algorithm to detect prejudice to identify and correct discriminatory patterns.
- Ensure human oversight in Ai driven evaluations to reduce bias impact.

Example: Studies have shown that AI based standardized test scoring systems have historically scored students from underrepresented backgrounds lower than their peers, prompting concerns about fairness in AI assessments.

Privacy and Data Security Concerns

AI powered educational tools collect vast amounts of student data, including personal information, learning patterns, and assessment results. Without proper data security measures, this sensitive information is vulnerable to breaches, unauthorized access, and misuse. Additionally, many Artificial Intelligence driven platforms use cloud-based storage that may not comply with regional data protection laws (e.g., GDPR, FERPA, or COPPA). Students and educators must be assured that their data is used ethically and securely, without risks of exploitation.

Possible Solutions

- Apply strong encryption and access control mechanism to student data.
- Ensure that AI operated academic platforms comply with data privacy rules.
- Provide students and parents with transparent data use policies and select options, (Wang, Wang, & He, 2023).
- Example: In 2020, many online learning platforms faced data violations, highlighting millions of students, which had great concerns about the safety of AI run education equipment.

Ensuring Fairness and Transparency in AI Driven Education Tools

Many AI operated learning platforms lack a lack of transparency as to how they generate recommendations, assess the student's performance, or personalize the material. When students receive AI generated grades, recommendations, or learning ways, they cannot understand how or why some decisions were made, (Huang, 2023). This "black box" of AI creates issues of nature trust and makes it difficult to challenge inappropriate decisions. Teachers and policy makers should ensure that the AI system remains clear, accountable and fair.

Possible Solutions

- Develop an explainable AI (XAI) model that clearly shows how AI comes on decisions.
- Provide audit trails and justification reports for AUST AI based assessment.
- Allow students and teachers to challenge the results generated through AI through the Human Review mechanism.
- Examples: AI run proctoring tools have faced criticism for incorrectly flagged students based on facial identification errors, especially affecting students with dark skin tone due to racial bias in AI models.

While NLP and ML have immense ability to change education, addressing challenges related to prejudice, privacy and fairness is important for AI adoption responsible. By implementing moral AI principles, transparent decision making and strict data security measures, AI run education can be more inclusive, safe and justified.

FUTURE TRENDS AND INNOVATIONS

The landscape of education is rapidly developing with progress in NLP and ML. Emerging technologies such as generative AI, Large Language Model (LLM), Augmented Reality (AR) and Virtual Reality (VR) are shaping the future of learning immersive learning experiences. Below, we find out major trends and innovations that will affect education in the coming years, (Mohamed, 2024).

Progress in Generic AI for Education

Generative AI is also changing education sector by providing personalized learning, intelligent tutoring systems and automatic creation of academic content. The generation of learning content by AI is among the primary ones, as AI applications can produce textbooks, quizzes, and interactive simulations of high quality, thus significantly relieving the workload of teachers. The second transformative application is automatic essay scoring and feedback where AI based systems are used to analyses student writing and provide instant feedback, which has been shown to accelerate learning gains and free up instructors of some of the grading burden. In addition, there are AI tutors and chatbots, which are real-time educational assistants giving explanations, answering questions, and building personal learning maps based on the achievements and performance of a particular student, (Eden, Chisom, & Adeniyi, 2024). In language learning, NLP based AI offers real-time translations and pronunciation assistance, adaptive vocabulary training, etc. therefore, language learning becomes simpler and more interactive. The generative AI, overall, is severally trending towards an efficient, more inclusive, and student-centered teaching and learning paradigm.

The Role of Large Language Models (LLMs) in Shaping Future Learning

The emergence of Large Language Models (LLM) such as GPT-4, PaLM, and Claude is changing the way that students and educators engaged with information and learning material. Personalized and adaptive teaching is among one of their biggest contributions, wherein LLMs can examine the performance of students along with their learning preferences to make the necessary adjustments in terms of the level of difficulty and teaching methodology. They can also be utilized as AI based research assistants that allow users to create summaries and identify the main concepts fast and facilitate the research process. LLMs have the potential to be helpful automatic educational assistants since they can answer academic questions, create lesson plans, and provide real-time clarification on difficult subjects, (Balta,

2023). Moreover, in terms of fixing accessibility gaps, LLMs can help develop multilingual and inclusive educational materials and resources that can be used by different learners, such as those with visual impairments or dyslexia. With such abilities, LLMs are transforming the learning process, making it smarter, more inclusive, and more efficient.

Integration of AI With AR/VR for Immersive Learning Experiences

Artificial Intelligence (AI), Augmented Reality (AR) and Virtual Reality (VR) are transforming the sphere of education and learning processes become more interactive, engaging, and interesting. Among the notable applications, one should list the generation of AI-powered virtual classrooms, where avatars and virtual teachers are employed to deliver real-time and immersive lessons in VR environments and enhance the interaction and collaboration rates among learners. AR is also finding favor in interactive textbooks, whereby the otherwise boring pages of a textbook can be made to come alive through the use of 3D models, animations and even real-time translations, which have been found to enhance comprehension and retention. AI and VR might also make possible simulated learning environments to offer realistic, experimental experiences in medicine, science and engineering allowing students to train in controlled, safe virtual conditions. Further, gamification and AI powered assessment led to the interactive, skill focused learning experiences that challenge their students with a problem, ask them to make a choice and offer them adaptive feedback, (Akgün & Greenhow, 2021). The effect of all these technologies is the enhanced learning process that is more individualized, experiential and efficient with all subjects and learner types. Integration of AI, NLP, LLM and immersive technologies is changing education, making it more individual, efficient and attractive. As these technologies develop, they will play an important role in reducing learning gaps, improving access and shaping the future of education.

CONCLUSION

The integration of NLP and ML in education has initiated a paradigm change as to how students learn, how teachers instruct, and how administrative functions are done. The rapid growth of these techniques within the convergent AI has exhibited the ability to form fundamental educational models fundamentally, interactive, adaptive and individual learning experiences. Progress in AI Interested Students Support, Automatic Grading and Virtual Tuition System has made significant improvements in student engagement, knowledge retention and teaching effectiveness.

However, these transformative applications also come with challenges that should be addressed to ensure moral and effective implementation within education. One of the most notable contributions of NLP in education is the development of intelligent condensed agents including chatbots and virtual tutors. These AI operated equipment enhances students learning by providing immediate response, answering questions and engaging in personal interactions to suit individual learning styles. Unlike traditional instructional methods, NLP based tutors can act in real time, addressing students' diverse requirements by providing immediate explanation and supplementary teaching resources. Such devices significantly reduce the cognitive load and allow students to learn at their own pace, making an environment adapt to better educational performance.

Apart from virtual tutors, NLP and ML have also revolutionized automatic grading systems. Traditionally, grading has been a time consuming and often subjective process, but the AI manual assessment model has introduced efficiency and fairness. By analyzing student reactions using NLP techniques, this system ensures continuity in evaluation and provides creative response to learners. In addition, integration of ML allows these grading systems to improve over time, adapt to student reactions and refine their accuracy. This advancement relieves teachers of double handed tasks, allowing them to focus more on instructions and student advice.

Another deep impact of ML in education has the ability to detect learning patterns and predict the student's performance. ML algorithm driven future analytics may identify students at risk of educational failure and recommend personal intervention to address learning gaps. By analyzing historical data, these models can generate insight into individual student behavior, learning preferences and challenges. Teachers can then implement target strategies to support struggling students, promote inclusion and equitable access to education. Such initial intervention mechanisms increase student retention rates and improve overall learning results. Despite these promising developments, the integration of AI in education is not without challenges. Ethical concerns such as data privacy, algorithm bias, and digital division should be carefully addressed to prevent unexpected results. AI operated educational equipment depends on large amounts of students, increasing concerns about privacy and safety. Ensuring compliance with data protection rules and implementing transparent AI models is necessary for the protection of student privacy.

Additionally, embedded prejudices within the AI model can lead to improper educational consequences, requiring continuous monitoring and refining of these technologies to promote fairness and inclusion. In addition, adopting AI in educational institutions requires significant infrastructure and policy related obstacles. There may be a lack of technical infrastructure required to effectively apply AI man going solutions, in many schools and universities, especially in stand areas. To bridge this digital divide, cooperative efforts are required between governments, educational institutions and technology developers to ensure that the AI Learning Experiences are accessible to all students, regardless of the socio economic background. Regulatory structures also play an important role in shaping the future of AI in education. Policy makers should balance in between promoting innovation and implementing moral guidelines that prefer student's welfare. Development of standardized policies can provide clear guidelines on AI implementation, ensuring that educational institutions follow the best practices by embracing technological progress. In addition, teachers should receive adequate training to effectively integrate AI devices in their teaching functioning, maximizing the benefits of NLP and ML innovations.

Given further, the future of AI managed education rests on continuous interdisciplinary cooperation among researchers, teachers, policy makers and technology developers. Progress in NLP and ML will continue to refine and expand the capabilities of AI operated educational equipment, making learning more dynamic, inclusive and effective. The ongoing exploration of AI's ability in education presents an opportunity to revolutionize traditional teaching and learning perspectives, which paves the way for a more individual and efficient educational landscape. Finally, NLP and ML innovations have greatly increased student support, personal learning experiences and administrative efficiency in education. These technologies promise it a lot in changing how knowledge is provided and acquired, eventually improved student results. However, addressing moral, infrastructural and policy related challenges is necessary to ensure that AI managed education remains fair, safe and accessible to all. As AI continues to develop, stakeholders in various domains should work together to exploit with their potential responsibility, building a future where technology strengthens learners.

REFERENCES

AI4ED Workshop Committee. (2025). Ethical and responsible use of generative AI in education. *Proceedings of the AAAI 2025 Workshop on AI for Education*. https://ai4ed.cc/workshops/aaai2025

Akgün, S., & Greenhow, C. (2021). Artificial intelligence in education: Addressing ethical challenges in K-12 settings. *AI and Ethics*, *2*(3), 431–440. DOI: 10.1007/s43681-021-00096-7

Anwar, A., Rehman, I., Nasralla, M., Khattak, S., & Khilji, N. (2023). Emotions matter: A systematic review and meta-analysis of the detection and classification of students' emotions in STEM during online learning. *Education Sciences*, *13*(9), 914. Advance online publication. DOI: 10.3390/educsci13090914

Balta, N. (2023). Ethical considerations in using AI in educational research. *Journal of Research and Innovation in Data Systems*, *2*(1), 14205. Advance online publication. DOI: 10.51853/jorids/14205

Barua, P., Vicnesh, J., Gururajan, R., Oh, S., Palmer, E., Azizan, M., & Aziz, A. (2022). Artificial intelligence enabled personalised assistive tools to enhance education of children with neurodevelopmental disorders—A review. *International Journal of Environmental Research and Public Health*, *19*(3), 1192. Advance online publication. DOI: 10.3390/ijerph19031192

Barunaha, A., Prakash, M., & Naresh, R. (2023). Real-time sentiment analysis of social media content for brand improvement and topic tracking. In *Proceedings of the International Conference on Artificial Intelligence and Data Science* (pp. 26–31). Atlantis Press. https://doi.org/DOI: 10.2991/978-94-6463-250-7_6

Baskara, F. (2023). Chatbots and flipped learning: Enhancing student engagement and learning outcomes through personalised support and collaboration. *IJORER: International Journal of Recent Educational Research*, *4*(2), 223–238. DOI: 10.46245/ijorer.v4i2.331

Chala, T., Guta, A., & Asebel, M. (2022). Design and development of a text-to-speech synthesizer for Afan Oromo. *SN Computer Science*, *3*(5), 364. Advance online publication. DOI: 10.1007/s42979-022-01306-7

Chutia, T., & Baruah, N. (2024). A review on emotion detection by using deep learning techniques. *Artificial Intelligence Review*, *57*(8), 192. Advance online publication. DOI: 10.1007/s10462-024-10831-1

Commons, A. I. (2025). Ethical principles AI framework for higher education. *California State University GenAI Portal*. https://genai.calstate.edu/communities/faculty/ethical-and-responsible-use-ai/ethical-principles-ai-framework-higher-education

Duolingo. (n.d.). *Duolingo*. Retrieved August 15, 2025, from https://www.duolingo.com/

Eden, C., Chisom, O., & Adeniyi, I. (2024). Integrating AI in education: Opportunities, challenges, and ethical considerations. *Magna Scientia Advanced Research and Reviews, 10*(2), 006–013. https://doi.org/DOI: 10.30574/msarr.2024.10.2.0039

Ghadirli, H., & Rastgarpour, M. (2013). A web-based adaptive and intelligent tutor by expert systems. In *Advances in Intelligent Systems and Computing* (Vol. 206, pp. 87–95). Springer., DOI: 10.1007/978-3-642-31552-7_10

Goyal, N., Garg, N., & Nair, A. (2025). Impacts of LLMs on education in low-income settings: Insights from rural India. *arXiv*. https://arxiv.org/abs/2505.03163

Harry, A., & Sayudin, S. (2023). Role of AI in education. *Interdisciplinary Journal and Humanity*, *2*(3), 260–268. DOI: 10.58631/injurity.v2i3.52

Huang, L. (2023). Ethics of artificial intelligence in education: Student privacy and data protection. *Science Insights Education Frontiers*, *16*(2), 2577–2587. DOI: 10.15354/sief.23.re202

Ifenthaler, D. (2022). Automated essay scoring systems. In *Handbook of Open, Distance and Digital Education* (pp. 1–15). Springer. https://doi.org/DOI: 10.1007/978-981-19-0351-9_59-1

Jayavardhini, P. (2024). AI study partner: Development of an LLM and Gen AI-enhanced study assistant tool. *International Journal of Scientific Research in Engineering and Management*, *8*(3), 1–5. DOI: 10.55041/ijsrem29626

Kashefi, O., Afrin, T., Dale, M., Olshefski, C., Godley, A., Litman, D., & Litman, D. (2022). ArgRewrite V.2: An annotated argumentative revisions corpus. *Language Resources and Evaluation*, *56*(3), 881–915. DOI: 10.1007/s10579-021-09567-z

Klímová, B., & Seraj, P. (2023). The use of chatbots in university EFL settings: Research trends and pedagogical implications. *Frontiers in Psychology*, *14*, 1131506. Advance online publication. DOI: 10.3389/fpsyg.2023.1131506

Kumar, Y., Aggarwal, S., Mahata, D., Shah, R., Kumaraguru, P., & Zimmermann, R. (2019). Get it scored using AutoSAS—An automated system for scoring short answers. *Proceedings of the AAAI Conference on Artificial Intelligence*, *33*(1), 9662–9669. DOI: 10.1609/aaai.v33i01.33019662

Mainstay. (n.d.). *How Georgia State University supports every student with personalized text messaging*. Retrieved August 15, 2025, from https://mainstay.com/case-study/how-georgia-state-university-supports-every-student-with-personalized-text-messaging/

Masood, A. (2025). The role of artificial intelligence and generative AI in education. *Medium*. https://medium.com/@adnanmasood/the-role-of-artificial-intelligence-and-generative-ai-in-education-00830cd61b79

Mathew, V. R., & Paulose, J. (2021). NLP-based personal learning assistant for school education. [IJECE]. *International Journal of Electrical and Computer Engineering*, *11*(5), 4522–4530. DOI: 10.11591/ijece.v11i5.pp4522-4530

Mindspark. (n.d.). *Mindspark*. Retrieved August 15, 2025, from https://www.mindspark.in/

Mohamed, M. (2024). Exploring ethical dimensions of AI-enhanced language education: A literature perspective. *Technology in Language Teaching & Learning*, *6*(3), 1813. DOI: 10.29140/tltl.v6n3.1813

Mohanan, R., Stringfellow, C., & Gupta, D. (2017). *An emotionally intelligent tutoring system. In 2017 SAI Computing Conference*. IEEE., DOI: 10.1109/sai.2017.8252228

Oghu, E., Ogbuju, E., Abiodun, T., & Oladipo, F. (2023). A review of sentiment analysis approaches for quality assurance in teaching and learning (retracted). *Bulletin of Social Informatics Theory and Application*, *6*(2), 177–188. DOI: 10.31763/businta.v6i2.581

Pacella, M., Vasco, P., Papadia, G., & Giliberti, V. (2024). An assessment of digitalization techniques in contact centers and their impact on agent performance and well-being. *Sustainability*, *16*(2), 714. Advance online publication. DOI: 10.3390/su16020714

Panaite, M., Dascălu, M., Johnson, A., Balyan, R., Dai, J., McNamara, D., & McNamara, D. (2018). Bring it on! Challenges encountered while building a comprehensive tutoring system using ReaderBench. In *Artificial Intelligence in Education* (pp. 409–419). Springer., DOI: 10.1007/978-3-319-93843-1_30

Pendy, B. (2023). Artificial intelligence: The future of education. *Jurnal Indonesia Sosial Sains*, *2*(11), 801. Advance online publication. DOI: 10.59141/jiss.v2i11.801

Pimentel, J., Malaluan, K., Daluperi, F., Vera, J., Sunga, J., Marin, A., & Marin, A. (2024). Benefits of AI chatbots and engagement of senior high school students in Divine Word College of San Jose. *International Journal of Research Studies in Educational Technology*, *8*(4). Advance online publication. DOI: 10.5861/ijrset.2024.8036

Popenici, Ş., & Kerr, S. (2017). Exploring the impact of artificial intelligence on teaching and learning in higher education. *Research and Practice in Technology Enhanced Learning*, *12*(1), 22. Advance online publication. DOI: 10.1186/s41039-017-0062-8

Qiu, B., Zhu, Y., Du, L., & Feng, C. (2024). Analysis and reflection on the teaching application of artificial intelligence technology in the context of big data. *Curriculum and Teaching Methodology*, *7*(4). Advance online publication. DOI: 10.23977/curtm.2024.070404

Rao, A., & Ramalingamma, P. (2022). An FPT.AI-based text-to-speech application's end-to-end conversion speed analysis. *International Journal of Innovative Research in Engineering & Management*, *9*(5), 227–231. DOI: 10.55524/ijirem.2022.9.5.33

Ren, X. (2024). Integrating artificial intelligence into multimedia education: An in-depth analysis of software applications. *Journal of Education. Humanities and Social Sciences*, *44*, 60–65. DOI: 10.54097/8wemq285

Salam, M., Fitri, S., & Zulan, H. (2024). Educational technology based on artificial intelligence in supporting distance learning in Arabic language learning in higher education. *Journal International of Lingua and Technology*, *3*(1), 134–145. DOI: 10.55849/jiltech.v3i1.485

Shaikh, S., Yayilgan, S., Zoto, E., & Abomhara, M. (2024). Multilingual user perceptions analysis from Twitter using zero shot learning for border control technologies. *Research Square*. https://doi.org/DOI: 10.21203/rs.3.rs-5269373/v1

Singh, N., & Ahuja, N. (2019). Implementation and evaluation of intelligence incorporated tutoring system. *International Journal of Innovative Technology and Exploring Engineering*, *8*(10), 4548–4558. DOI: 10.35940/ijitee.j9849.0881019

Tafazoli, D., Parra, M., & Abril, C. (2019). Intelligent language tutoring system. *International Journal of Information and Communication Technology Education*, *15*(3), 60–74. DOI: 10.4018/ijicte.2019070105

Taghipour, K., & Ng, H. T. (2016). A neural approach to automated essay scoring. In *Proceedings of the 2016 Conference on Empirical Methods in Natural Language Processing* (pp. 1882–1891). Association for Computational Linguistics. https://doi.org/DOI: 10.18653/v1/d16-1193

Villar, D. (2025). How artificial intelligence is transforming professional development. *UC San Diego Extended Studies*. https://extendedstudies.ucsd.edu/news-events/extended-studies-blog/how-artificial-intelligence-is-transforming-professional-development

Wang, M., & Yang, Q. (2024). Educational big data analytics using sentiment analysis for student requirement analysis on courses. *Scalable Computing: Practice and Experience*, *25*(5), 3858–3866. DOI: 10.12694/scpe.v25i5.3024

Wang, X., Wang, C., & He, X. (2023). Design and implementation of artificial intelligence fusion experimental platform based on machine learning algorithm. *International Journal of New Developments in Engineering and Society*, *7*(2). Advance online publication. DOI: 10.25236/ijndes.2023.070202

Yin, J., Goh, T., Bing, Y., & Xiaobin, Y. (2020). Conversation technology with micro-learning: The impact of chatbot-based learning on students' learning motivation and performance. *Journal of Educational Computing Research*, *59*(1), 154–177. DOI: 10.1177/0735633120952067

Zhao, T. (2023). AI in educational technology. *Preprints*. https://doi.org/DOI: 10.20944/preprints202311.0106.v1

Compilation of References

Abubakari, M. S., Shafik, W., & Hidayatullah, A. F. (2024). Evaluating the Potential of Artificial Intelligence in Islamic Religious Education: A SWOT Analysis Overview. In *AI-Enhanced Teaching Methods* (pp. 216–239). IGI Global. https://doi.org/DOI: 10.4018/979-8-3693-2728-9.ch010

Abubakari, M. S. (2025a). Digital Technologies Adoption in Islamic Education for Fostering Lifelong Learning Culture: Pilot Survey Preliminary Insights. In Anshari, M., Almunawar, M. N., & Ordóñez de Pablos, P. (Eds.), *Multi-Industry Digitalization and Technological Governance in the AI Era* (pp. 103–126). IGI Global., DOI: 10.4018/979-8-3373-1681-9.ch005

Abubakari, M. S. (2025b). Overviewing Biases in Generative AI-Powered Models in the Arabic Language: AI Fairness for Sustainable Future. In Syafrudin, M., Fitriyani, N. L., & Anshari, M. (Eds.), *Achieving Sustainability in Multi-Industry Settings With AI* (pp. 361–390). IGI Global., DOI: 10.4018/979-8-3373-2530-9.ch013

Abubakari, M. S., & Kalinaki, K. (2024). Digital Competence in Islamic Education for Lifelong Learning: Preliminary Analysis Using DigComp 2.1 Framework. In Hawamdeh, M. M. K., & Abdelhafid, F. (Eds.), *Embracing Technological Advancements for Lifelong Learning* (pp. 1–31). IGI Global., DOI: 10.4018/979-8-3693-1410-4.ch001

Abubakari, M. S., & Mashoedah, . (2021). The Internet of Things (IoT) as an Emerging Technological Solution for the Covid-19 Pandemic Mitigation: An Overview. *Journal of Physics: Conference Series*, *1737*(1), 012003. DOI: 10.1088/1742-6596/1737/1/012003

Abubakari, M. S., Zakaria, G. A. N., & Musa, J. (2024). Perceived compatibility and students' intention to adopt digital technologies in Islamic education institutions. *Cogent Education*, *11*(1), 2430869. DOI: 10.1080/2331186X.2024.2430869

Abubakari, M. S., Zakaria, G. A. N., & Musa, J. (2025). Validating the DigComp framework among university students across different educational systems. *Discover Education*, *4*(1), 200. DOI: 10.1007/s44217-025-00652-x

Abubakari, M. S., Zakaria, G. A. N., Musa, J., & Kalinaki, K. (2023a). Assessing Digital Competence in Higher Education: A Gender Analysis of DigComp 2.1 Framework in Uganda. *SAGA: Journal of Technology and Information System*, *1*(4), 114–120. DOI: 10.58905/saga.v1i4.210

Abubakari, M. S., Zakaria, G. A. N., Musa, J., & Kalinaki, K. (2023b). Validating the Digital Competence (Dig-Comp 2.1) Framework in Higher Education Using Confirmatory Factor Analysis: Non-Western Perspective. *Canadian Journal of Educational and Social Studies*, *3*(6), 15–26. DOI: 10.53103/cjess.v6i1.184

Abushariah, A. A., Ting, H., Mustafa, M. B., Khairuddin, A. S., Abushariah, M. A., & Tan, T. (2023). Bilingual automatic speech recognition: A review, taxonomy and open challenges. *IEEE Access : Practical Innovations, Open Solutions*, *11*, 5944–5954. DOI: 10.1109/access.2022.3218684

Adade, R., & Goosen, L. (2024). Teachers and schools navigating virtual worlds and the metaverse for enhanced e-learning: Evaluating an e-capacity model approach. In *Navigating virtual worlds and the metaverse for enhanced e-learning* (pp. 19). https://doi.org/DOI: 10.4018/979-8-3693-1034-2.ch006

Adamopoulou, E., & Moussiades, L. (2020). Chatbots: History, technology, and applications. *Machine Learning with Applications*, *2*, 100006. DOI: 10.1016/j.mlwa.2020.100006

Adarkwah, M. A. (2024). GenAI-Infused Adult Learning in the Digital Era: A Conceptual Framework for Higher Education. *Adult Learning*, *0*(0). Advance online publication. DOI: 10.1177/10451595241271161

Ahammad, S. H., Kalangi, R. R., Nagendram, S., Inthiyaz, S., Priya, P. P., Faragallah, O. S., Mohammad, A., Eid, M. M. A., & Rashed, A. N. Z. (2024). Improved neural machine translation using Natural Language Processing (NLP). *Multimedia Tools and Applications*, *83*(13), 39335–39348. DOI: 10.1007/S11042-023-17207-7

Ahmed, I., Kajol, M., Hasan, U., Datta, P. P., Roy, A., & Reza, M. R. (2023). *ChatGPT vs. Bard: a comparative study*. UMBC Student Collection.

Ahuja, V. (2024). Simulations in business education: Unlocking experiential learning. Practices and implementation of gamification in higher education, 1-21. https://doi.org/DOI: 10.4018/979-8-3693-0716-8.ch001

AI4ED Workshop Committee. (2025). Ethical and responsible use of generative AI in education. *Proceedings of the AAAI 2025 Workshop on AI for Education*. https://ai4ed.cc/workshops/aaai2025

Aithal, P. S., & Aithal, S. (2023). Application of ChatGPT in Higher Education and Research–A Futuristic Analysis. [IJAEML]. *International Journal of Applied Engineering and Management Letters*, *7*(3), 168–194.

Akgün, S., & Greenhow, C. (2021). Artificial intelligence in education: Addressing ethical challenges in K-12 settings. *AI and Ethics*, *2*(3), 431–440. DOI: 10.1007/s43681-021-00096-7

Akiba, D., & Fraboni, M. C. (2023). AI-Supported Academic Advising: Exploring ChatGPT's Current State and Future Potential toward Student Empowerment. *Education Sciences*, *13*(9), 885.

Alam, M., & Hasan, M. (2024). Applications and future prospects of artificial intelligence in education. [IJHSSS]. *International Journal of Humanities & Social Science Studies*, *10*(1), 197–206. DOI: 10.29032/ijhsss.v10.i1.2024.197-206

Alam, S., Kumar, S., Khursheed, Z., Mahato, H. K., Bashar, S., & Suman, A. (2024). Designing an AI-driven intelligent Tutorial System. *5th International Conference on Recent Trends in Computer Science and Technology, ICRTCST 2024 - Proceedings*, 585–588. https://doi.org/DOI: 10.1109/ICRTCST61793.2024.10578476

Alenezi, H. S., & Faisal, M. H. (2020). Utilizing crowdsourcing and machine learning in education: Literature review. *Education and Information Technologies*, *25*(4), 2971–2986.

Alhammadi, K., Marashdeh, H., & Hussain, M. (2023). Assessing the effect of innovation diffusion and technology readiness theories on attitude, behavioral intention and implementation of smart learning. *Cross Cultural & Strategic Management*. Advance online publication. DOI: 10.1108/CCSM-12-2022-0213

Ali, H., & Aysan, A. F. (2023). What will ChatGPT Revolutionize in Financial Industry? *Available at* SSRN *4403372*. sassayed. (2023). *GitHub - sassayed/HSGAdviser-BiLSTM-Chatbot: HSGAdviser-Text-Based Chatbot for Student Guidance Advising*. GitHub. https://github.com/sassayed/HSGAdviser-BiLSTM-Chatbot

Alrakhawi, H. A., Jamiat, Nurullizam., & Abu-Naser, S. S. (2023). Intelligent tutoring systems in education: A systematic review of usage, tools, effects and evaluation. *Journal of Theoretical and Applied Information Technology*, *101*(4), 1205–1226.

Alshammari, H., El-Sayed, A., & Elleithy, K. (2024). AI-Generated Text Detector for Arabic Language Using Encoder-Based Transformer Architecture. *Big Data and Cognitive Computing*, *8*(3), 32. DOI: 10.3390/bdcc8030032

Al-Shammari, Z., Faulkner, P. E., & Forlin, C. (2019). Theories-based inclusive education practices. *Education Quarterly Review*, *2*(2), 408–414. DOI: 10.31014/aior.1993.02.02.73

Andujar, A. (2019). *Recent tools for computer- and mobile-assisted foreign language learning*. IGI Global.

Ansari, G., Gupta, S., & Singhal, N. (2021). Natural Language Processing in Online Reviews. In Natural Language Processing for Global and Local Business (pp. 40-64). IGI Global Scientific Publishing.

Anusha, S., Ezhilvandan, M., Gayathri, S., Sivaraman, V., & TP, A. (2024). Emerging trends in edge AI for Industry 4.0 and 5.0: Technologies, applications, and challenges. AI Innovations in Service and Tourism Marketing, 211-228.

Anwar, A., Rehman, I., Nasralla, M., Khattak, S., & Khilji, N. (2023). Emotions matter: A systematic review and meta-analysis of the detection and classification of students' emotions in STEM during online learning. *Education Sciences*, *13*(9), 914. Advance online publication. DOI: 10.3390/educsci13090914

Anyichie, A. C., & Butler, D. L. (2023). Examining culturally diverse learners' motivation and engagement processes as situated in the context of a complex task. *Frontiers in Education*, *8*, 1041946. DOI: 10.3389/feduc.2023.1041946

Arman, M., & Lamiyar, U. R. (2023). Exploring the implication of ChatGPT AI for business: Efficiency and challenges. *Applied Quantitative Analysis*, *3*(2), 46–67.

Arslanyilmaz, A. (2013). Computer-assisted foreign language instruction: Task based vs. form focused. *Journal of Computer Assisted Learning*, *29*(4), 303–318. DOI: 10.1111/jcal.12003

Assayed, S. K., Alkhatib, M., & Shaalan, K. (2023, June). Advising chatbot for high school in smart cities. In *2023 8th International Conference on Smart and Sustainable Technologies (SpliTech)* (pp. 1-6). IEEE.

Assayed, S. K., Alkhatib, M., & Shaalan, K. (2024). A systematic review of conversational AI chatbots in academic advising. In Proceedings of the BUiD Doctoral Research Conference 2023 (LNCE, Vol. 473) (pp. 346–359). Springer. https://doi.org/DOI: 10.1007/978-3-031-56121-4_33

Assayed, S. K., Alkhatib, M., & Shaalan, K. (2024a). A Systematic Review of Conversational AI Chatbots in Academic Advising. In *BUiD Doctoral Research Conference 2023* (pp. 346-359). Springer, Cham.

Assayed, S. K., Alkhatib, M., & Shaalan, K. (2024b, March). Enhancing Student Services: Machine Learning Chatbot Intent Recognition for High School Inquiries. In *BUiD Doctoral Research Conference 2023: Multidisciplinary Studies* (pp. 243-254). Cham: Springer Nature Switzerland.

Assayed, S. K., Alkhatib, M., & Shaalan, K. (2024c). A Comparative Study of ChatGPT and Seq2Seq Chatbot for Effective Students Advising. *ChatGPT and Global Higher Education: Using Artificial Intelligence in Teaching and Learning*, 148.

Assayed, S. K., & Alsayed, S. (2025). The Impact of High School Curriculum on College Readiness: A Case Study of international Students in USA Universities. In *Issues and Trends in International School Leadership* (pp. 457–478). IGI Global Scientific Publishing.

Ayaan, A., & Ng, K. W. (2025). Automated grading using natural language processing and semantic analysis. *MethodsX, 14*, 103395. DOI: 10.1016/J.MEX.2025.103395 PMID: 40529512

Baidoo-Anu, D., & Ansah, L. O. (2023). Education in the era of generative artificial intelligence (AI): Understanding the potential benefits of ChatGPT in promoting teaching and learning. *Journal of AI, 7*(1), 52–62.

Balta, N. (2023). Ethical considerations in using AI in educational research. *Journal of Research and Innovation in Data Systems, 2*(1), 14205. Advance online publication. DOI: 10.51853/jorids/14205

Barua, P., Vicnesh, J., Gururajan, R., Oh, S., Palmer, E., Azizan, M., & Aziz, A. (2022). Artificial intelligence enabled personalised assistive tools to enhance education of children with neurodevelopmental disorders—A review. *International Journal of Environmental Research and Public Health, 19*(3), 1192. Advance online publication. DOI: 10.3390/ijerph19031192

Barunaha, A., Prakash, M., & Naresh, R. (2023). Real-time sentiment analysis of social media content for brand improvement and topic tracking. In *Proceedings of the International Conference on Artificial Intelligence and Data Science* (pp. 26–31). Atlantis Press. https://doi.org/DOI: 10.2991/978-94-6463-250-7_6

Baskara, F. (2023). Chatbots and flipped learning: Enhancing student engagement and learning outcomes through personalised support and collaboration. *IJORER: International Journal of Recent Educational Research*, *4*(2), 223–238. DOI: 10.46245/ijorer.v4i2.331

Baskara, R. (2023). Exploring the implications of ChatGPT for language learning in higher education. *Indonesian Journal of English Language Teaching and Applied Linguistics*, *7*(2), 343–358.

Berqia, M., & Benaboud, H. (2024). Detecting LLM-Enabled Plagiarism in Student Essays Using Ensemble Learning and NLP. *Lecture Notes in Information Systems and Organisation, 71 LNISO*, 376–382. https://doi.org/DOI: 10.1007/978-3-031-75329-9_42

Bharathi, G. P., Chandra, I., Sanagana, D. P. R., Tummalachervu, C. K., Rao, V. S., & Neelima, S. (2024). AI-driven adaptive learning for enhancing business intelligence simulation games. *Entertainment Computing*, *50*, 100699. DOI: 10.1016/j.entcom.2024.100699

Biagini, G. (2025). Towards an AI-Literate Future: A Systematic Literature Review Exploring Education, Ethics, and Applications. *International Journal of Artificial Intelligence in Education*. Advance online publication. DOI: 10.1007/s40593-025-00466-w

Bii, P. K., Too, J. K., & Mukwa, C. W. (2018). Teacher's attitude towards use of chatbots in routine teaching. *Universal Journal of Educational Research*, *6*(7), 1586–1597. DOI: 10.13189/ujer.2018.060719

Biswas, S. S. (2023). Role of chat gpt in public health. *Annals of Biomedical Engineering*, *51*(5), 868–869. PMID: 36920578

Bode, S. P., & Satpute, R. S. (2024). Natural Language Processing in Education System. *2024 2nd DMIHER International Conference on Artificial Intelligence in Healthcare, Education and Industry, IDICAIEI 2024*. https://doi.org/DOI: 10.1109/IDICAIEI61867.2024.10842725

Boopathi, S. (2023). Deep learning techniques applied for automatic sentence generation. In *Promoting Diversity, Equity, and Inclusion in Language Learning Environments* (pp. 255-273). IGI Global.

Bouamor, H., Gongora-Svartzman, G., Heimann, L., & Huang, S. (2025). Evaluating GenAI's Effectiveness for Students with Varied Programming Backgrounds in a Software Development Course. *Proceedings of the 56th ACM Technical Symposium on Computer Science Education* V. 2, 1395–1396. https://doi.org/DOI: 10.1145/3641555.3705175

Bowman, S. R., & Dahl, G. E. (2021). What will it take to fix benchmarking in natural language understanding? arXiv preprint arXiv:2104.02145.

Boyatzis, R. E. (1998). *Transforming Qualitative information: Thematic Analysis and Code Development*. Sage Publications.

Cacicio, S., & Riggs, R. (2023). Bridging Resource Gaps in Adult Education: The Role of Generative AI. *Adult Literacy Education: The International Journal of Literacy, Language, and Numeracy*, *5*(3), 80–86. DOI: 10.35847/SCacicio.RRiggs.5.3.80

Calonge, D. S., Smail, L., & Kamalov, F. (2023). Enough of the chit-chat: A comparative analysis of four AI chatbots for calculus and statistics. *Journal of Applied Learning and Teaching*, *6*(2).

Campino, J. (2025). Unleashing the transformers: NLP models detect AI writing in education. *Journal of Computers in Education*, *12*(2), 645–673. DOI: 10.1007/S40692-024-00325-Y

Caruccio, L., Cirillo, S., Polese, G., Solimando, G., Sundaramurthy, S., & Tortora, G. (2024). Can ChatGPT provide intelligent diagnoses? A comparative study between predictive models and ChatGPT to define a new medical diagnostic bot. *Expert Systems with Applications*, *235*, 121186.

Chala, T., Guta, A., & Asebel, M. (2022). Design and development of a text-to-speech synthesizer for Afan Oromo. *SN Computer Science*, *3*(5), 364. Advance online publication. DOI: 10.1007/s42979-022-01306-7

Chen, C. W., Syu, J., Ou, Y., & Wang, J. (2022a). Development and implementation of AI robot with primary school Mandarin level. *2022 10th International Conference on Orange Technology (ICOT)*. https://doi.org/DOI: 10.1109/icot56925.2022.10008118

Chen, L., Chen, P., & Lin, Z. (2020). Artificial intelligence in education: A Review. *IEEE Access : Practical Innovations, Open Solutions*, *8*, 75264–75278. DOI: 10.1109/access.2020.2988510

Chen, S., Du, H., Wang, S., & Yang, L. (2022b). Understanding EFL reading anxiety in relation to learning motivation, attitudes, and strategies for Chinese and Spanish undergraduates. *System*, *108*, 102842. DOI: 10.1016/j.system.2022.102842

Chen, Y., Jensen, S., Albert, L. J., Gupta, S., & Lee, T. (2023). Artificial intelligence (AI) student assistants in the classroom: Designing chatbots to support student success. *Information Systems Frontiers*, *25*(1), 161–182. DOI: 10.1007/s10796-022-10291-4

Chmiliar, l. (2010). Multiple-case designs. In A. J. Mills, G. Eurepas & E. Wiebe (Eds.), *Encyclopedia of case study research* (pp 582-583). USA: SAGE Publications. DOI: 10.4135/9781412957397.n216

Chocarro, R., Cortiñas, M., & Marcos-Matás, G. (2021). Teachers' attitudes towards chatbots in education: A technology acceptance model approach considering the effect of social language, bot proactiveness, and users' characteristics. *Educational Studies*, *49*(2), 295–313. DOI: 10.1080/03055698.2020.1850426

Chopde, A., & Agrawal, M. (2022, June). Chatbot using deep learning. In *Proceedings of the international conference on innovative computing & communication (ICICC).*

Chowdhary, K., & Chowdhary, K. R. (2020). Natural language processing. *Fundamentals of artificial intelligence*, 603-649.

Chrostowski, M. (2024). Promoting critical thinking through the use of ChatGPT in religious education. *Österreichisches Religionspädagogisches Forum, 32*(2), 166–181. https://doi.org/DOI: 10.25364/10.32:2024.2.10

Chutia, T., & Baruah, N. (2024). A review on emotion detection by using deep learning techniques. *Artificial Intelligence Review*, *57*(8), 192. Advance online publication. DOI: 10.1007/s10462-024-10831-1

Clarizia, F., Colace, F., Lombardi, M., Pascale, F., & Santaniello, D. (2018). Chatbot: An Education Support System for Student. In Castiglione, A., Pop, F., Ficco, M., & Palmieri, F. (Eds.), Lecture Notes in Computer Science: Vol. 11161. *Cyberspace Safety and Security. CSS 2018*. Springer., DOI: 10.1007/978-3-030-01689-0_23

Clark, T. M. (2023). Investigating the use of an artificial intelligence chatbot with general chemistry exam questions. *Journal of Chemical Education*, *100*(5), 1905–1916. DOI: 10.1021/acs.jchemed.3c00027

Commons, A. I. (2025). Ethical principles AI framework for higher education. *California State University GenAI Portal*. https://genai.calstate.edu/communities/faculty/ethical-and-responsible-use-ai/ethical-principles-ai-framework-higher-education

Crawford, K. (2016, June 25). Artificial Intelligence's white guy problem. The New York Times [Blog post]. Retrieved August 6, 2018, from https://www.nytimes.com/2016/06/26/opinion/sunday/artificial-intelligences-white-guy-problem.html?_r=1

Daher, W., Diab, H., & Rayan, A. (2023). Artificial intelligence generative tools and conceptual knowledge in problem solving in chemistry. *Information (Basel), 14*(7), 409. DOI: 10.3390/info14070409

Dai, C. P., & Ke, F. (2022). Educational applications of artificial intelligence in simulation-based learning: A systematic mapping review. *Computers and Education: Artificial Intelligence, 3*, 100087. DOI: 10.1016/j.caeai.2022.100087

Darwish, D. (Ed.). (2024). *Design and Development of Emerging Chatbot Technology*. IGI Global.

Dasgupta, S., Maity, C., Mukherjee, S., Singh, R., Dutta, D., & Jana, D. (2025). HITgram: A Platform for Experimenting with n-Gram Language Models. *Lecture Notes in Computer Science, 15505 LNCS*, 92–104. https://doi.org/DOI: 10.1007/978-3-031-84543-7_8

Davar, N. F., Dewan, M. A. A., & Zhang, X. (2025). AI Chatbots in Education: Challenges and Opportunities. *Information 2025, Vol. 16, Page 235, 16*(3), 235. https://doi.org/DOI: 10.3390/INFO16030235

Davar, N. F., Dewan, M. A. A., & Zhang, X. (2025). AI chatbots in education: Challenges and opportunities. *Information (Basel), 16*(3), 235.

Davis, F. D. (1989). Perceived usefulness, perceived ease of use, and user acceptance of information technology. *Management Information Systems Quarterly, 13*(3), 319–339.

Deng, M. (2022). Application of artificial intelligence technology in college students' foreign language learning. *2022 IEEE 5th Eurasian Conference on Educational Innovation (ECEI)*. https://doi.org/DOI: 10.1109/ecei53102.2022.9829486

Deng, L., & Yuan, K. H. (2023). Which method is more powerful in testing the relationship of theoretical constructs? A meta comparison of structural equation modeling and path analysis with weighted composites. *Behavior Research Methods, 55*(3), 1460–1479. DOI: 10.3758/s13428-022-01838-z PMID: 35653013

Dhinakaran, D., Kumar, N. J., & Ponnuviji, N. P. (2025). Safeguarding confidentiality and privacy in cloud-enabled healthcare systems with spectrasafe encryption and dynamic k-anonymity algorithm. *Expert Systems with Applications, 279*, 127584.

Dhivvya, J. P., & Karnati, S. B. (2024). BuddyBot: AI Powered Chatbot for Enhancing English Language Learning. *2024 IEEE International Conference on Interdisciplinary Approaches in Technology and Management for Social Innovation, IATMSI 2024*. https://doi.org/DOI: 10.1109/IATMSI60426.2024.10502595

Dhyani, M., & Kumar, R. (2021). An intelligent Chatbot using deep learning with Bidirectional RNN and attention model. *Materials Today: Proceedings*, *34*, 817–824. PMID: 32837917

Dinh, H., & Tran, T. K. (2023). EduChat: An AI-based chatbot for university-related information using a hybrid approach. *Applied Sciences (Basel, Switzerland)*, *13*(22), 12446.

Djazilan, M. S., Rulyansah, A., & Rihlah, J. (2024). Why AI is Essential for the Future of Islamic Education: A Call for Ethical and Effective Implementation. *EDUKASIA: Jurnal Pendidikan Dan Pembelajaran*, *5*(2), 201–216. DOI: 10.62775/edukasia.v5i2.1373

Dockens, A. L., & Shelton, K. (2025). Andragogy as a Theoretical Framework for AI Integration in Higher Education. In Wang, V. (Ed.), *AI Integration Into Andragogical Education* (pp. 71–108). IGI Global., DOI: 10.4018/979-8-3373-0502-8.ch004

Dogan, M. E., Dogan, T. G., & Bozkurt, A. (2023). The use of artificial intelligence (AI) in online learning and distance education processes: A systematic review of empirical studies. *Applied Sciences (Basel, Switzerland)*, *13*(5), 3056. DOI: 10.3390/app13053056

Duolingo. (n.d.). *Duolingo*. Retrieved August 15, 2025, from https://www.duolingo.com/

Dwivedi, Y. K., Kshetri, N., Hughes, L., Slade, E. L., Jeyaraj, A., Kar, A. K., Baabdullah, A. M., Koohang, A., Raghavan, V., Ahuja, M., Albanna, H., Albashrawi, M. A., Al-Busaidi, A. S., Balakrishnan, J., Barlette, Y., Basu, S., Bose, I., Brooks, L., Buhalis, D., & Wright, R. (2023). Opinion Paper: "So what if ChatGPT wrote it?" Multidisciplinary perspectives on opportunities, challenges and implications of generative conversational AI for research, practice and policy. *International Journal of Information Management*, *71*(March), 102642. DOI: 10.1016/j.ijinfomgt.2023.102642

Eden, C., Chisom, O., & Adeniyi, I. (2024). Integrating AI in education: Opportunities, challenges, and ethical considerations. *Magna Scientia Advanced Research and Reviews*, *10*(2), 006–013. https://doi.org/DOI: 10.30574/msarr.2024.10.2.0039

El Ganadi, A., Aftar, S., Gagliardelli, L., & Ruozzi, F. (2025). Generative AI for Islamic Texts: The EMAN Framework for Mitigating GPT Hallucinations. *Proceedings of the 17th International Conference on Agents and Artificial Intelligence*, 1221–1228. https://doi.org/DOI: 10.5220/0013312800003890

Escalante, J., Pack, A., & Barrett, A. (2023). AI-generated feedback on writing: Insights into efficacy and ENL student preference. *International Journal of Educational Technology in Higher Education, 20*(1), 57. DOI: 10.1186/s41239-023-00425-2

Essebbar, A., Kane, B., Guinaudeau, O., Chiesa, V., Quénel, I., & Chau, S. (2021). Aspect based sentiment analysis using French pre-trained models. *Proceedings of the 13th International Conference on Agents and Artificial Intelligence*. https://doi.org/DOI: 10.5220/0010382705190525

Fanni, S. C., Febi, M., Aghakhanyan, G., & Neri, E. (2023). Natural language processing. In *Introduction to artificial intelligence* (pp. 87–99). Springer International Publishing.

Farrokhnia, M., Banihashem, S. K., Noroozi, O., & Wals, A. (2024). A SWOT analysis of ChatGPT: Implications for educational practice and research. *Innovations in Education and Teaching International, 61*(3), 460–474. DOI: 10.1080/14703297.2023.2195846

Felten, P., & Lambert, L. M. (2020). *Relationship-rich education: How human connections drive success in college*. Jhu Press.

Feng, Y., & Wang, X. (2022). Chinese children's Chinese-English bilingual acquisition mode: A comparative experiment of AI educational robot and scan reading pen. *2022 The 8th International Conference on Frontiers of Educational Technologies (ICFET)*. https://doi.org/DOI: 10.1145/3545862.3545865

Fernández-Batanero, J. M., Román-Graván, P., Montenegro-Rueda, M., López-Meneses, E., & Fernández-Cerero, J. (2021). Digital teaching competence in higher education: A systematic review. *Education Sciences, 11*(11), 689. DOI: 10.3390/educsci11110689

Ferrara, E. (2023). Fairness and Bias in Artificial Intelligence: A Brief Survey of Sources, Impacts, and Mitigation Strategies. *Sci, 6*(1), 3. DOI: 10.3390/sci6010003

Fischer, K., Niebuhr, O., & Alm, M. (2021). Robots for foreign language learning: Speaking style influences student performance. *Frontiers in Robotics and AI, 8*. Advance online publication. DOI: 10.3389/frobt.2021.680509 PMID: 34540905

Francis, J., & Subha, M. (2024). An Overview of Natural Language Processing (NLP) in Healthcare: Implications for English Language Teaching. *8th International Conference on I-SMAC (IoT in Social, Mobile, Analytics and Cloud), I-SMAC 2024 - Proceedings*, 824–827. https://doi.org/DOI: 10.1109/I-SMAC61858.2024.10714890

Frosolini, A., Gennaro, P., Cascino, F., & Gabriele, G. (2023). *Reference to "Role of Chat GPT in Public Health", to Highlight the AI's Incorrect Reference Generation. Annals of Biomedical Engineering*.

Fryer, L. K., Ainley, M., Thompson, A., Gibson, A., & Sherlock, Z. (2017). Stimulating and sustaining interest in a language course: An experimental comparison of chatbot and human task partners. *Computers in Human Behavior*, *75*, 461–468. DOI: 10.1016/j.chb.2017.05.045

Gaglo, K., Degboe, B. M., Kossingou, G. M., & Ouya, S. (2021). Proposal of conversational chatbots for educational remediation in the context of covid-19. In: 2021 23rd International conference on advanced communication technology (ICACT), pp 354–358. . 2021.9370946DOI: 10.23919/ICACT51234

Gai, Y. (2024). *Factors that impact intention to continue using ai-based chatbots in different countries* (Doctoral dissertation, Vilniaus universitetas.).

Ganesan, I., Ponnuviji, N. P., Kumar, A. S., Nithya, M., Jambulingam, U., & Lalitha, S. D. (2024). Real-Time Event Detection and Predictive Analytics Using IoT and Deep Learning. In *Industry Applications of Thrust Manufacturing: Convergence with Real-Time Data and AI* (pp. 1-41). IGI Global Scientific Publishing.

Gardazi, N. M., Daud, A., Malik, M. K., Bukhari, A., Alsahfi, T., & Alshemaimri, B. (2025). BERT applications in natural language processing: a review. *Artificial Intelligence Review 2025 58:6*, *58*(6), 1–49. https://doi.org/DOI: 10.1007/S10462-025-11162-5

Garrison, D. R. (1997). Self-Directed Learning: Toward a Comprehensive Model. *Adult Education Quarterly*, *48*(1), 18–33. DOI: 10.1177/074171369704800103

Geerling, W., Mateer, G. D., Wooten, J., & Damodaran, N. (2023). Is ChatGPT smarter than a student in principles of economics? *SSRN Electronic Journal*, 1-24. DOI: 10.2139/ssrn.4356034

Gerring, J. (2007). *Case study research: Principles and practices*. Cambridge University Press., https://books.google.com.tr/books?id=CbetAQAAQBAJ&lpg=PP13&ots=kdB0JMVUwI&dq=Gerring%2C%20J.%20(2007).%20Case%20study%20research%3A%20Principles%20and%20practices.%20New%20York%3A%20Cambridge%20University%20Press.&lr&hl=tr&pg=PP13#v=onepage&q&f=false

Ghadirli, H., & Rastgarpour, M. (2013). A web-based adaptive and intelligent tutor by expert systems. In *Advances in Intelligent Systems and Computing* (Vol. 206, pp. 87–95). Springer., DOI: 10.1007/978-3-642-31552-7_10

Gill, S. S., Xu, M., Patros, P., Wu, H., Kaur, R., Kaur, K., Fuller, S., Singh, M., Arora, P., Parlikad, A. K., Stankovski, V., Abraham, A., Ghosh, S. K., Lutfiyya, H., Kanhere, S. S., Bahsoon, R., Rana, O., Dustdar, S., Sakellariou, R., & Buyya, R. (2024). Transformative effects of ChatGPT on modern education: Emerging Era of AI Chatbots. *Internet of Things and Cyber-Physical Systems*, *4*, 19–23. DOI: 10.1016/j.iotcps.2023.06.002

Gitelman, L., & Jackson, V. (2013). Introduction. In L. Gitelman (Ed.), *"Raw data" is an oxymoron* (pp. 1–14). Cambridge, Massausetts; London, England: The MIT Press. DOI: 10.1080/1369118X.2014.920042

Gligorea, I., Cioca, M., Oancea, R., Gorski, A., Gorski, H., & Tudorache, P. (2023). Adaptive learning using AI in e-learning: A literature review. *Education Sciences*, *13*(12), 1216. DOI: 10.3390/educsci13121216

Gonsalves, C. (2024). Generative AI's Impact on Critical Thinking: Revisiting Bloom's Taxonomy. *Journal of Marketing Education*. Advance online publication. DOI: 10.1177/02734753241305980

Goyal, N., Garg, N., & Nair, A. (2025). Impacts of LLMs on education in low-income settings: Insights from rural India. *arXiv*. https://arxiv.org/abs/2505.03163

Gyeong-Geon, J., Ehsan, L., Lehong, S., & Xiaoming, Z. (2023) Gemini Pro Defeated by GPT-4V: Evidence from Education, 13-15. /arXiv.2401.08660DOI: 10.48550

Halaweh, M. (2023). ChatGPT in Education: Strategies for Responsible Implementation. *Contemporary Educational Technology*, *15*(2). https://eric.ed.gov/?id=EJ1385551

Han, Z., Battaglia, F., Udaiyar, A., Fooks, A., & Terlecky, S. R. (2023). An explorative assessment of ChatGPT as an aid in medical education: Use it with caution. https://www.medrxiv.org/content/10.1101/2023.02.13.23285879v1.full.pdf

Haristiani, N. (2019). Artificial intelligence (AI) chatbot as language learning medium: An inquiry. *Journal of Physics: Conference Series*, *1387*(1), 012020. DOI: 10.1088/1742-6596/1387/1/012020

Harry, A., & Sayudin, S. (2023). Role of AI in education. *Interdisciplinary Journal and Humanity*, *2*(3), 260–268. DOI: 10.58631/injurity.v2i3.52

Hemandkumar, E., Varun Kumar, A., & Gracewell, J. (2024). Enhanced Plagiarism Detection in Online Assignments by Natural Language Processing and Machine Learning Techniques. *3rd International Conference on Automation, Computing and Renewable Systems, ICACRS 2024 - Proceedings*, 1281–1286. https://doi.org/DOI: 10.1109/ICACRS62842.2024.10841520

Hilbert, S., Coors, S., Kraus, E., Bischl, B., Lindl, A., Frei, M., & Stachl, C. (2021). Machine learning for the educational sciences. *Review of Education*, *9*(3), e3310.

Hirose, K., & Zhang, J. (1999). Tone recognition of Chinese continuous speech using tone critical segments. *6th European Conference on Speech Communication and Technology (Eurospeech 1999)*. https://doi.org/DOI: 10.21437/eurospeech.1999-214

Hobert S. (2019). How are you, chatbot? evaluating chatbots in educational settings–results of a literature review. DELFI 2019

Hoggan, C. D. (2016). Transformative Learning as a Metatheory: Definition, Criteria, and Typology. *Adult Education Quarterly*, *66*(1), 57–75. DOI: 10.1177/0741713615611216

Hoggan, C., & Kloubert, T. (2020). Transformative Learning in Theory and Practice. *Adult Education Quarterly*, *70*(3), 295–307. DOI: 10.1177/0741713620918510

Holmes, W. (2018). The ethics of Artificial Intelligence in education. University Business. Retrieved August 10, 2018, from https://universitybusiness.co.uk/Article/the-ethics-of-artificial-intelligence-in-education-who-care

Hopcan, S., Polat, E., Ozturk, M. E., & Ozturk, L. (2022). AI in special education: A systematic review. *Interactive Learning Environments*, *31*(10), 7335–7353. DOI: 10.1080/10494820.2022.2067186

Hsu, Y.-C., & Ching, Y.-H. (2023a). Generative Artificial Intelligence in Education, Part One: The Dynamic Frontier. *TechTrends*, *67*(4), 603–607. DOI: 10.1007/s11528-023-00863-9

Hsu, Y.-C., & Ching, Y.-H. (2023b). Generative Artificial Intelligence in Education, Part Two: International Perspectives. *TechTrends*, *67*(6), 885–890. DOI: 10.1007/s11528-023-00913-2

Huang, L. (2023). Ethics of artificial intelligence in education: Student privacy and data protection. *Science Insights Education Frontiers*, *16*(2), 2577–2587. DOI: 10.15354/sief.23.re202

Huet, I., Casanova, D., Figueiredo, D., Rocio, V., Barros, D. M. V., & Isaias, P. (2024). The design and implementation of a pilot chatbot in distance education. In Challenges 2024. XIII Conferência Internacional de Tecnologias de Informação e Comunicação na Educação (pp. 112-125). Universidade do Minho. Centro de Competência.

Hwang, G.-J., Xie, H., Wah, B. W., & Gašević, D. (2020). Vision, challenges, roles and research issues of artificial intelligence in education. *Computers and Education: Artificial Intelligence*, *1*, 100001. DOI: 10.1016/j.caeai.2020.100001

Ifelebuegu, A. O. (2023). Rethinking online assessment strategies: Authenticity versus AI chatbot intervention. *Journal of Applied Learning & Teaching*, *6*(2), 385–392. DOI: 10.37074/jalt.2023.6.2.2

Ifenthaler, D. (2022). Automated essay scoring systems. In *Handbook of Open, Distance and Digital Education* (pp. 1–15). Springer. https://doi.org/DOI: 10.1007/978-981-19-0351-9_59-1

Ilagan, J. B. (2023). The design and use of conversational intelligent tutoring systems and computer simulation for the use of students of technology entrepreneurship. In *International Conference on Computers in Education*. https://doi.org/DOI: 10.58459/icce.2023.4782

Islam, M. F., Hasan, J., Islam, M. A., Dewan, P., & Rahman, M. S. (2025). BanglaLem: A Transformer-based Bangla Lemmatizer with an Enhanced Dataset. *Systems and Soft Computing*, *7*, 200244. DOI: 10.1016/J.SASC.2025.200244

Işler, B., & Kılıç, M. (2021). *Eğitimde Yapay Zekâ Kullanimi ve Gelişimi. e-Journal of New Media / Yeni Medya Elektronik Dergi – eJNM, 5*(1), 1–11. https://dergipark.org.tr/en/download/article-file/1106175

Izakian, H., Pedrycz, W., & Jamal, I. (2015). Fuzzy clustering of time series data using dynamic time warping distance. *Engineering Applications of Artificial Intelligence*, *39*, 235–244. DOI: 10.1016/j.engappai.2014.12.015

Jain, V., Singh, I., Syed, M., Mondal, S., & Palai, D. R. (2024). Enhancing educational interactions: A comprehensive review of AI chatbots in learning environments. In *2024 11th international conference on reliability, infocom technologies and optimization (trends and future directions)(ICRITO)* (pp. 1-5). IEEE.

Jayavardhini, P. (2024). AI study partner: Development of an LLM and Gen AI-enhanced study assistant tool. *International Journal of Scientific Research in Engineering and Management*, *8*(3), 1–5. DOI: 10.55041/ijsrem29626

Jeong, Y. H., Li, M. Y., Kang, S. M., Eum, Y. K., & Kang, B. K. (2022). Automatic prediction and linguistic interpretation of Chinese directional complements based on BERT model. *Lecture Notes in Computer Science*, •••, 405–416. DOI: 10.1007/978-3-031-06703-7_31

Jeon, J. (2023). Chatbot-assisted dynamic assessment (CA-DA) for L2 vocabulary learning and diagnosis. *Computer Assisted Language Learning*, *36*(7), 1338–1364. DOI: 10.1080/09588221.2021.1987272

Jeon, J., Lee, S., & Choi, S. (2024). A systematic review of research on speech-recognition chatbots for language learning: Implications for future directions in the era of large language models. *Interactive Learning Environments*, *32*(8), 4613–4631. DOI: 10.1080/10494820.2023.2204343

Jiang, P., & Cai, X. (2024). A Survey of Semantic Parsing Techniques. *Symmetry 2024, Vol. 16, Page 1201*, *16*(9), 1201. https://doi.org/DOI: 10.3390/SYM16091201

Jian, M. J. K. O. (2023). Personalized learning through AI. *Advances in Engineering Innovation*, *5*(1), 16–19. DOI: 10.54254/2977-3903/5/2023039

Jing, Y. (2023). Design and application of teaching system for Chinese language and literature major drove by interpreted AI technology. *Applied Artificial Intelligence*, *37*(1). Advance online publication. DOI: 10.1080/08839514.2023.2203573

Jones, M. (2023). Preserving Academic Integrity In The Age of Artificial Intelligence: Redesigning Courses To Combat AI-Assisted Plagiarism. International Dialogues on Education Journal, 10(1), 101–123. Retrieved from https://www.idejournal.org/index.php/ide/article/view/296

Kalyan, K. S. (2024). A survey of GPT-3 family large language models including ChatGPT and GPT-4. *Natural Language Processing Journal*, *6*, 100048. DOI: 10.1016/j.nlp.2023.100048

Kang, H. (2023). Artificial intelligence and its influence in adult learning in China. *Higher Education. Skills and Work-Based Learning*, *13*(3), 450–464. DOI: 10.1108/HESWBL-01-2023-0017

Kantor, K., & Morzy, M. (2024). Machine learning and natural language processing in clinical trial eligibility criteria parsing: A scoping review. *Drug Discovery Today*, *29*(10), 104139. DOI: 10.1016/J.DRUDIS.2024.104139 PMID: 39154773

Kapočiūtė-Dzikienė, J. (2020). A domain-specific generative chatbot trained from little data. *Applied Sciences (Basel, Switzerland)*, *10*(7), 2221.

Kashefi, O., Afrin, T., Dale, M., Olshefski, C., Godley, A., Litman, D., & Litman, D. (2022). ArgRewrite V.2: An annotated argumentative revisions corpus. *Language Resources and Evaluation*, *56*(3), 881–915. DOI: 10.1007/s10579-021-09567-z

Kasthuri, E., & Balaji, S. (2021). A chatbot for changing lifestyle in education. In: *2021 Third international conference on intelligent communication technologies and virtual mobile networks (ICICV)*, pp 1317– 1322. IEEE

Kasthuri, E., & Balaji, S. (2023). Natural language processing and deep learning chatbot using long short term memory algorithm. *Materials Today: Proceedings*, *81*, 690–693.

Kaur, N., Saha, A., Swami, M., Singh, M., & Dalal, R. (2024). Bert-Ner: A Transformer-Based Approach For Named Entity Recognition. *2024 15th International Conference on Computing Communication and Networking Technologies, ICCCNT 2024*. https://doi.org/DOI: 10.1109/ICCCNT61001.2024.10724703

Kavipriya, P., Jegan, G., Lakshmi, S., & Jebarani, M. E. (2024). Conversational Techniques Using Artificial Intelligence for Customer Support. In *Bio-Inspired Intelligence for Smart Decision-Making* (pp. 115–122). IGI Global.

Khan, U. (2023). Revolutionizing Personalized Protein Energy Malnutrition Treatment: Harnessing the Power of Chat GPT. *Annals of Biomedical Engineering*, •••, 1–3. PMID: 37728811

Kharchenko, Y., & Babenko, O. (2024). Advantages and limitations of large language models in chemistry education: A comparative analysis of ChatGPT, Gemini and Copilot. 3781. 42-59. https://www.researchgate.net/publication/385417848_Advantages_and_limitations_of_large_language_models_in_chemistry_education_A_comparative_analysis_of_ChatGPT_Gemini_and_Copilot

Kim, J. (2023). Leading teachers' perspective on teacher-AI collaboration in education. *Education and Information Technologies*. Advance online publication. DOI: 10.1007/s10639-023-12109-5

Kingchang, T., Chatwattana, P., & Wannapiroon, P. (2024). Artificial intelligence chatbot platform: AI chatbot platform for educational recommendations in higher education. *International Journal of Information and Education Technology (IJIET)*, *14*(1), 34–41. DOI: 10.18178/ijiet.2024.14.1.2021

Kiourt, C., Koutsoudis, A., & Kalles, D. (2020). Enhanced virtual reality experience in personalised virtual museums. In *Natural Language Processing* (p. 19). Concepts, Methodologies, Tools, and Applications., DOI: 10.4018/978-1-7998-0951-7.ch065

Klímová, B., & Seraj, P. (2023). The use of chatbots in university EFL settings: Research trends and pedagogical implications. *Frontiers in Psychology*, *14*, 1131506. Advance online publication. DOI: 10.3389/fpsyg.2023.1131506

Knowles, M. S., Holton III, E. F., & Swanson, R. A. (2015). *The Adult Learner: The definitive classic in adult education and human resource development* (8th Editio). Routledge. https://doi.org/DOI: 10.4324/9781315816951

Knowles, M. S., Holton III, E. F., Swanson, R. A., & Robinson, P. A. (2020). *The Adult Learner: The Definitive Classic in Adult Education and Human Resource Development* (9th Editio). Routledge. https://doi.org/DOI: 10.4324/9780429299612

Knowles, M. S. (1975). *Self-directed learning: A guide for learners and teachers.* Association Press., DOI: 10.1177/105960117700200220

Knowles, M. S. (1975). *Self-directed Learning: A Guide for Learners and Teachers.* Cambridge Adult Education.

Knowles, M. S., Holton, E. F.III, Robinson, P. A., & Caraccioli, C. (2025). *The Adult Learner: The Definitive Classic in Adult Education and Human Resource Development* (10th ed.). Routledge., DOI: 10.4324/9781003387671

Kohn, K. (2009). 21. Computer assisted foreign language learning. *Handbook of Foreign Language Communication and Learning*, 573-606. https://doi.org/DOI: 10.1515/9783110214246.4.573

Kohnke, L., Moorhouse, B. L., & Zou, D. (2023). ChatGPT for language teaching and learning. *RELC Journal*, •••, 00336882231162768.

Kolb, D. A. (2015). *Experiential Learning: Experience as the source of Learning and Development* (2nd Editio). Pearson Education Inc.

Kondurkar, I., Raj, A., & Lakshmi, D. (2024). Modern applications with a focus on training ChatGPT and GPT models: exploring generative AI and NLP. In *Advanced applications of generative AI and natural language processing models* (pp. 186–227). IGI Global Scientific Publishing.

Kotei, E., & Thirunavukarasu, R. (2023). A systematic review of transformer-based pre-trained language models through self-supervised learning. *Information (Basel)*, *14*(3), 187.

Krishnachalitha, K. C., & Priya, C. (2021). Deep NLP in the Healthcare Industry: Applied Machine Learning and Artificial Intelligence in Rheumatoid Arthritis. In Deep Natural Language Processing and AI Applications for Industry 5.0 (pp. 189-203). IGI Global.

Kuhail, M. A., Alturki, N., Alramlawi, S., & Alhejori, K. (2023). Interacting with educational chatbots: A systematic review. *Education and Information Technologies*, *28*(1), 973–1018.

Kuleto, V., Ilić, M. P., Bucea-Manea- oniş, R., Ciocodeică, D.-F., Mihălcescu, H., & Mindrescu, V. (2022). The attitudes of K–12 schools'teachers in Serbia towards the potential of artificial intelligence. *Sustainability*, *14*(14), 8636. DOI: 10.3390/su14148636

Kumar, A., & Gupta, D. (2021). Sentiment analysis as a restricted NLP problem. In *Natural language processing for global and local business* (pp. 65–96). IGI Global.

Kumar, A., & Kumar, S. (2024, May). Sentiment analysis for enhancing student engagement and learning outcomes. In *2024 International Conference on Emerging Innovations and Advanced Computing (INNOCOMP)* (pp. 132-137). IEEE.

Kumar, Y., Aggarwal, S., Mahata, D., Shah, R., Kumaraguru, P., & Zimmermann, R. (2019). Get it scored using AutoSAS—An automated system for scoring short answers. *Proceedings of the AAAI Conference on Artificial Intelligence*, *33*(1), 9662–9669. DOI: 10.1609/aaai.v33i01.33019662

Kurni, M., Mohammed, M. S., & Srinivasa, K. G. (2023). Intelligent tutoring systems. In *A beginner's guide to introduce artificial intelligence in teaching and learning* (pp. 29–44). Springer International Publishing.

Kwak, Y., & Pardos, Z. A. (2024). Bridging large language model disparities: Skill tagging of multilingual educational content. *British Journal of Educational Technology*, *55*(5). Advance online publication. DOI: 10.1111/bjet.13465

Kyle, K., & Eguchi, M. (2024). Evaluating NLP models with written and spoken L2 samples. *Research Methods in Applied Linguistics*, *3*(2), 100120. DOI: 10.1016/J.RMAL.2024.100120

Lakhani, A. (2023). *Enhancing Customer Service with ChatGPT Transforming the Way Businesses Interact with Customers*. https://doi.org/DOI: 10.31219/osf.io/7hf4c

Lakshmi, G., Brindha, S., Devi, R., Divya, J., & Shobhanali, N. (2022). Ai-powered digital classroom. In: 2022 International conference on communication, computing and internet of things (IC3IoT), pp 1–6. DOI: 10.1109/IC3IOT53935.2022.9767944

Lakumarapu, S., Nithyanandhan, R., Bhargavi, V. S., Anish, T. P., & Nalini, M. (2024, August). Machine Learning Approaches for Liver Disease Prediction: A Comparative Analysis. In 2024 5th International Conference on Electronics and Sustainable Communication Systems (ICESC) (pp. 159-164). IEEE.

Lee, R. (2025a). N-Gram Language Model. *Natural Language Processing*, 19–43. https://doi.org/DOI: 10.1007/978-981-96-3208-4_2

Lee, R. (2025b). Part-of-Speech (POS) Tagging. *Natural Language Processing*, 45–68. https://doi.org/DOI: 10.1007/978-981-96-3208-4_3

Leite, B. S. (2024). Generative Artificial Intelligence in chemistry teaching: ChatGPT, Gemini, and Copilot's content responses. *Journal of Applied Learning and Teaching*, *7*(2). Advance online publication. DOI: 10.37074/jalt.2024.7.2.13

Li, B., Bonk, C. J., Wang, C., & Kou, X. (2024). Reconceptualizing Self-Directed Learning in the Era of Generative AI: An Exploratory Analysis of Language Learning. *IEEE Transactions on Learning Technologies*, *17*, 1489–1503. DOI: 10.1109/TLT.2024.3386098

Li, J., & Wu, C.-H. (2023). Determinants of Learners' Self-Directed Learning and Online Learning Attitudes in Online Learning. *Sustainability*, *15*(12), 9381. DOI: 10.3390/su15129381

Lim, W. M., Gunasekara, A., Pallant, J. L., Pallant, J. I., & Pechenkina, E. (2023). Generative AI and the future of education: Ragnarök or reformation? A paradoxical perspective from management educators. *International Journal of Management Education*, *21*(2), 100790. DOI: 10.1016/j.ijme.2023.100790

Lim, Z. W., Pushpanathan, K., Yew, S. M. E., Lai, Y., Sun, C. H., Lam, J. S. H., & Tham, Y. C. (2023). Benchmarking large language models' performances for myopia care: A comparative analysis of ChatGPT-3.5, ChatGPT-4.0, and Google Bard. *EBioMedicine*, •••, 95. PMID: 37625267

Lin, C. C., Huang, A. Y., & Lu, O. H. (2023). Artificial intelligence in intelligent tutoring systems toward sustainable education: A systematic review. *Smart Learning Environments*, *10*(1), 41.

Lin, X. (2024). Exploring the Role of ChatGPT as a Facilitator for Motivating Self-Directed Learning Among Adult Learners. *Adult Learning*, *35*(3), 156–166. DOI: 10.1177/10451595231184928

Lin, Y., & Yu, Z. (2024). A bibliometric analysis of artificial intelligence chatbots in educational contexts. *Interactive Technology and Smart Education*, *21*(2), 189–213. DOI: 10.1108/itse-12-2022-0165

Li, S., Liu, J., & Dong, Q. (2025). Generative artificial intelligence-supported programming education: Effects on learning performance, self-efficacy and processes. *Australasian Journal of Educational Technology*, *41*(3), 1–25. DOI: 10.14742/ajet.9932

Liu, S., & Da, J. (2022). Technology in Chinese language teaching. *The Palgrave Handbook of Chinese Language Studies*, 701-741. https://doi.org/DOI: 10.1007/978-981-16-0924-4_3

Liu, P., Guo, Y., Wang, F., & Li, G. (2022). Chinese named entity recognition: The state of the art. *Neurocomputing*, *473*. Advance online publication. DOI: 10.1016/j.neucom.2021.10.101

Liu, Y., Han, D., Wu, G., & Qiao, B. (2024). KnowDT: Empathetic dialogue generation with knowledge enhanced dependency tree. *Applied Intelligence*, *54*(17–18), 8059–8072. DOI: 10.1007/s10489-024-05611-x

Li, Y., Tolosa, L., Rivas-Echeverria, F., & Marquez, R. (2025). *Integrating AI in Education: Navigating UNESCO Global Guidelines, Emerging Trends, and Its Intersection with Sustainable Development Goals*. https://doi.org/DOI: 10.26434/chemrxiv-2025-wz4n9

Li, Z., & Bonk, C. J. (2025). Self-directed language learning with Duolingo in an out-of-class context. *Computer Assisted Language Learning*, *38*(3), 569–591. DOI: 10.1080/09588221.2023.2206874

Li, Z., Wang, C., & Bonk, C. (2024). Exploring the Utility of ChatGPT for Self-directed Online Language Learning. *Online Learning : the Official Journal of the Online Learning Consortium*, *28*(3), 157–180. DOI: 10.24059/olj.v28i3.4497

Lo, C. K. (2023). What is the impact of ChatGPT on education? A rapid review of the literature. *Education Sciences*, *13*(4), 410.

Luan, H., & Tsai, C. C. (2021). A review of using machine learning approaches for precision education. *Journal of Educational Technology & Society*, *24*(1), 250–266.

Luckin, R. (2025). Nurturing human intelligence in the age of AI: Rethinking education for the future. *Development and Learning in Organizations*, *39*(1), 1–4. DOI: 10.1108/DLO-04-2024-0108

Lund, B. D., & Wang, T. (2023). Chatting about ChatGPT: How may AI and GPT impact academia and libraries? *Library Hi Tech News*. Advance online publication. DOI: 10.1108/LHTN-01-2023-0009

Luo (Jess), J. (2024). A critical review of GenAI policies in higher education assessment: A call to reconsider the "originality" of students' work. *Assessment & Evaluation in Higher Education*, *49*(5), 651–664. DOI: 10.1080/02602938.2024.2309963

Mageira, K., Pittou, D., Papasalouros, A., Kotis, K., Zangogianni, P., & Daradoumis, A. (2022). Educational AI chatbots for content and language integrated learning. *Applied Sciences (Basel, Switzerland)*, *12*(7), 3239.

Maheswari, B., & Nagarajan, R. (2024). EduChatbot: Implementing educational Chatbot for assisting the teaching-learning process by NLP-based hybrid heuristic adopted deep learning framework. *Kybernetes*.

Mainstay. (n.d.). *How Georgia State University supports every student with personalized text messaging*. Retrieved August 15, 2025, from https://mainstay.com/case-study/how-georgia-state-university-supports-every-student-with-personalized-text-messaging/

Makmee, P., Sompaisarnsilp, S., & Krairiksh, T. (2024). Influence factors on self-directed learning behavior of veterinary students on gross anatomy: A multiple group analysis. *Cogent Education*, *11*(1), 2378512. DOI: 10.1080/2331186X.2024.2378512

Martin, F., Wang, C., & Sadaf, A. (2020). Facilitation matters: Instructor perception of helpfulness of facilitation strategies in online courses. *Online Learning : the Official Journal of the Online Learning Consortium*, *24*(1), 28–49. DOI: 10.24059/olj.v24i1.1980

Martin, F., Zhuang, M., & Schaefer, D. (2023). Systematic review of research on artificial intelligence in K-12 education (2017–2022). *Computers and Education: Artificial Intelligence*, *6*, 100195. DOI: 10.1016/j.caeai.2023.100195

Martins, H. F. (2012). The Use of a Business Simulation Game in a Management Course. In Cruz-Cunha, M. (Ed.), *Handbook of Research on Serious Games as Educational, Business and Research Tools* (pp. 693–707). IGI Global Scientific Publishing., DOI: 10.4018/978-1-4666-0149-9.ch035

Martins, H. F. (2024). The Impact and Future of AI-Enhanced Teaching Methods in the Use of Business Simulations. In Ahmed, Z., Hassan, A., & Saeed, R. (Eds.), *AI-Enhanced Teaching Methods* (pp. 305–321). IGI Global Scientific Publishing., DOI: 10.4018/979-8-3693-2728-9.ch014

Masood, A. (2025). The role of artificial intelligence and generative AI in education. *Medium*. https://medium.com/@adnanmasood/the-role-of-artificial-intelligence-and-generative-ai-in-education-00830cd61b79

Mathew, A. N., Rohini, V., & Paulose, J. (2021). NLP-based personal learning assistant for school education. *International Journal of Electrical and Computer Engineering*, *11*(5), 4522–4530.

McFarland, M. (2016, May 11). What happened when a professor built a chatbot to be his teaching assistant. The Washington Post [Blog post]. Retrieved August 13, 2018, from https://www.washingtonpost.com/news/innovations/wp/2016/05/11/this-professor-stunned-his-students-when-he-revealed-the-secret-identity-of-his-teaching-assistant/?noredirect=on&utm_term=.70facd03940d

McGregor, S. (2004). Learning with Donald Rumsfeld - flexible learning: The relevance and resonance of multiprofessional learning in primary care. *The British Journal of General Practice*, *54*(506), 722–723. https://www.ncbi.nlm.nih.gov/pubmed/15558869

Merriam, S. B. (2013). *Nitel araştırma: Desen ve uygulama için bir rehber (3. Baskıdan Çeviri, Çeviri Editörü: S. Turan)*. Nobel Yayın Dağıtım.

Messer, M., Brown, N. C. C., Kölling, M., & Shi, M. (2024). Automated Grading and Feedback Tools for Programming Education: A Systematic Review. *ACM Transactions on Computing Education*, *24*(1), 10. DOI: 10.1145/3636515

Mezirow, J. (1978). Perspective Transformation. *Adult Education*, *28*(2), 100–110. DOI: 10.1177/074171367802800202

Mhlanga, D. (2023). Open AI in education, the responsible and ethical use of ChatGPT towards lifelong learning. https://www.researchgate.net/profile/David-Mhlanga-2/publication/368476294_Open_AI_in_Education_the_Responsible_and_Ethical_Use_of_ChatGPT_Towards_Lifelong_Learning/links/63eb1c91bd7860764366f597/Open-AI-in-Education-the-Responsible-and-Ethical-Use-of-ChatGPT-Towards-Lifelong-Learning.pdf

Miao, F., & Holmes, W. (2023). *Guidance for generative AI in education and research*. UNESCO., DOI: 10.54675/EWZM9535

Mindspark. (n.d.). *Mindspark*. Retrieved August 15, 2025, from https://www.mindspark.in/

Mir, T. A., Lawaye, A. A., & Khanday, A. M. U. D. (2023). NLP techniques and challenges to process social media data. In *Advanced applications of NLP and deep learning in social media data* (pp. 171–218). IGI Global.

Mishra, P., Henriksen, D., & Warr, M. (2023). Educational technology integration: A framework for post-pandemic teaching and learning. *TechTrends*, *67*(1), 96–108. DOI: 10.1145/3629296.3629303

Mishra, P., Warr, M., & Islam, R. (2023). TPACK in the age of ChatGPT and Generative AI. *Journal of Digital Learning in Teacher Education*, *39*(4), 235–251. DOI: 10.1080/21532974.2023.2247480

Mmbayi, I. I., Gakii, C., & Musyoka, F. M. (2025). Sentiment Analysis-Based Model for Monitoring User Engagement With Mental Health Chatbots. *Engineering Reports*, *7*(6), e70247.

Mohamed, M. (2024). Exploring ethical dimensions of AI-enhanced language education: A literature perspective. *Technology in Language Teaching & Learning*, *6*(3), 1813. DOI: 10.29140/tltl.v6n3.1813

Mohanan, R., Stringfellow, C., & Gupta, D. (2017). *An emotionally intelligent tutoring system. In 2017 SAI Computing Conference*. IEEE., DOI: 10.1109/sai.2017.8252228

Moore, M. G. (1993). Theory of transactional distance. In *Theoretical principles of distance education* (pp. 22–38). Routledge.

Morandín-Ahuerma, F. (2024). UNESCO Proposal for the use of Generative AI in Education: Eight Challenges and Seven Actions (pp. 62–115). https://doi.org/DOI: 10.31219/osf.io/78d3j

Muller, M., Chilton, L. B., Kantosalo, A., Martin, C. P., & Walsh, G. (2022). GenAICHI: Generative AI and HCI. *CHI Conference on Human Factors in Computing Systems Extended Abstracts*, 1–7. https://doi.org/DOI: 10.1145/3491101.3503719

Munir, H., Vogel, B., & Jacobsson, A. (2022). Artificial intelligence and machine learning approaches in digital education: A systematic revision. *Information (Basel)*, *13*(4), 203.

Murphy, R. F. (2019). *Artifcial Intelligence Applications to Support K-12 Teachers and Teaching: A Review of Promising Applications, Opportunities, and Challenges. Perspective*. RAND Corporation.

Navarre, A. (2018). *Technology-enhanced teaching and learning of Chinese as a foreign language*. Routledge.

Ndunagu, J. N., Ezeanya, C. U., Onuorah, B. O., Onyeakazi, J. C., & Ukwandu, E. (2025). A Chatbot Student Support System in Open and Distance Learning Institutions. *Computers*, *14*(3), 96. DOI: 10.3390/computers14030096

Nebiu Hyseni, L., & Dermaku, A. (2025). Comparative Analysis of GitHub Copilot and ChatGPT in Web Application Development: An Experimental Study. *International Journal of Computational and Experimental Science and Engineering*, *11*(2), 3375–3398. DOI: 10.22399/ijcesen.1846

Nichols, M., & Holmes, W. (2018). Don't do Evil: Implementing Artifcial Intelligence in Universities. In EDEN Conference Proceedings; No. 2, pp. 110–118 https://www.researchgate.net/publication/362321764_Don't_Do_Evil_Implementing_Artificial_Intelligence_in_Universities

Nicol, J. (2024). How universal design for learning transformed my teaching: An elementary educator's journey of implementation. In *New Brunswick Department of Education and Early Childhood Development, Canada* (pp. 52). https://doi.org/ DOI: 10.4018/978-1-6684-4750-5.ch002

Nikhil, V., Annamalai, R., & Jayapal, S. (2025). NLP-Driven Approaches to Automated Essay Grading and Feedback. *Adopting Artificial Intelligence Tools in Higher Education: Student Assessment*, 99–117. https://doi.org/DOI: 10.1201/9781003470304-5

Oghu, E., Ogbuju, E., Abiodun, T., & Oladipo, F. (2023). A review of sentiment analysis approaches for quality assurance in teaching and learning (retracted). *Bulletin of Social Informatics Theory and Application*, *6*(2), 177–188. DOI: 10.31763/businta.v6i2.581

Okonkwo, C. W., & Ade-Ibijola, A. (2021). Chatbots applications in education: A systematic review. *Computers and Education: Artif Intell*, *2*, 100033.

Pacella, M., Vasco, P., Papadia, G., & Giliberti, V. (2024). An assessment of digitalization techniques in contact centers and their impact on agent performance and well-being. *Sustainability*, *16*(2), 714. Advance online publication. DOI: 10.3390/su16020714

Pajila, P. B., Sheena, B. G., Gayathri, A., Aswini, J., & Nalini, M. (2023, September). A comprehensive survey on naive bayes algorithm: Advantages, limitations and applications. In 2023 4th International Conference on Smart Electronics and Communication (ICOSEC) (pp. 1228-1234). IEEE.

Pajila, P. B., Sudha, K., Selvi, D. K., Kumar, V. N., Gayathri, S., & Subramanian, R. S. (2023, July). A survey on natural language processing and its applications. In *2023 4th International Conference on Electronics and Sustainable Communication Systems (ICESC)* (pp. 996-1001). IEEE.

Panaite, M., Dascălu, M., Johnson, A., Balyan, R., Dai, J., McNamara, D., & McNamara, D. (2018). Bring it on! Challenges encountered while building a comprehensive tutoring system using ReaderBench. In *Artificial Intelligence in Education* (pp. 409–419). Springer., DOI: 10.1007/978-3-319-93843-1_30

Pant, V. K., Sharma, R., & Kundu, S. (2024). An overview of Stemming and Lemmatization Techniques. *Advances in Networks. Intelligent Computing*, •••, 308–321. DOI: 10.1201/9781003430421-31

Parker, I. (2018, April 26). UK wants to lead the world in tech ethics…but what does that mean? Ada Lovelace Institute [Blog post]. Retrieved August 10, 2018, from https://www.adalovelaceinstitute.org/uk-wants-to-lead-the-world-in-tech-ethicsbut-what-does-that-mean/

Park, S., & Kim, H. (2024). Effective sentence-level relation extraction model using entity-centric dependency tree. *PeerJ. Computer Science*, *10*, e2311. DOI: 10.7717/PEERJ-CS.2311/SUPP-2 PMID: 39314697

Park, S., Kim, H., & Lee, J. (2023). Collaborative virtual learning environments: Design principles and implementation strategies. *International Review of Research in Open and Distance Learning*, *24*(2), 180–199. DOI: 10.1080/10494820.2021.2006238

Parmaxi, A. (2020). Virtual reality in language learning: A systematic review and implications for research and practice. *Interactive Learning Environments*, *31*(1), 172–184. DOI: 10.1080/10494820.2020.1765392

Patel, R., Patel, P., Bhatt, C. M., & Rahevar, M. L. (2021). Question Answering Chatbot Using Memory Networks. In *Handbook of Research on Applied Data Science and Artificial Intelligence in Business and Industry* (pp. 401–413). IGI Global.

Patil, R., Kadam, V., Nakate, R., Kadam, S., Pattade, S., & Mitkari, M. (2024). A Novel Natural Language Processing Based Model for Plagiarism Detection. *2024 International Conference on Emerging Smart Computing and Informatics, ESCI 2024*. https://doi.org/DOI: 10.1109/ESCI59607.2024.10497386

Pendy, B. (2023). Artificial intelligence: The future of education. *Jurnal Indonesia Sosial Sains*, *2*(11), 801. Advance online publication. DOI: 10.59141/jiss.v2i11.801

Perera, P., & Lankathilake, M. (2023). Preparing to revolutionize education with the multi-model GenAI tool Google Gemini? A journey towards effective policy making. *Journal of Advances in Education and Philosophy.*, *7*, 246–253. DOI: 10.36348/jaep.2023.v07i08.001

Pérez, J. Q., Daradoumis, T., & Puig, J. M. M. (2020). Rediscovering the use of chatbots in education: A systematic literature review. *Computer Applications in Engineering Education*, *28*(6), 1549–1565. DOI: 10.1002/cae.22326

Pimentel, J., Malaluan, K., Daluperi, F., Vera, J., Sunga, J., Marin, A., & Marin, A. (2024). Benefits of AI chatbots and engagement of senior high school students in Divine Word College of San Jose. *International Journal of Research Studies in Educational Technology*, *8*(4). Advance online publication. DOI: 10.5861/ijrset.2024.8036

Polakova, P., & Ivenz, P. (2024). The impact of ChatGPT feedback on the development of EFL students' writing skills. *Cogent Education*, *11*(1), 2410101. DOI: 10.1080/2331186X.2024.2410101

Ponmalar, A., Vijayakumar, K., Lakshmipriya, C., Karthikeyan, M., Gracelin Sheena, B., Beslin Pajila, P. J., & Siva Subramanian, R. (2024). Meta-Heuristics and Machine Learning Applications in Complex Systems. In *Metaheuristic and Machine Learning Optimization Strategies for Complex Systems* (pp. 257–275). IGI Global Scientific Publishing.

Ponnuviji, N. P., Murugan, P., Esakkiammal, S., Kumar, S., Vishal, K. S., & Meenakshi, S. (2024, March). AI-Powered Business Intelligence for Transforming Finance and Education. In *2024 2nd International Conference on Disruptive Technologies (ICDT)* (pp. 1287-1291). IEEE.

Ponnuviji, N. P., Nirmala, G., Kokila, M. S., & Priyadharshini, S. I. (2025). Optimizing Image Retrieval in Cloud Servers with TN-AGW: A Secure and Efficient Approach. *Journal ofThe Institution ofEngineers (India): Series B,* 106(2), 459-473.

Ponnuviji, N. P., Sumaiya Begum, A., Gnanasekaran, T., Rajendiran, M., & Shenbaga Ezhil, S. (2023, April). Leveraging Random Forest for Intelligent IoT Systems in Industrial Environments. In *International Conference on Internet of Things* (pp. 46-57). Cham: Springer Nature Switzerland.

Popenici, S. A., & Kerr, S. (2017). Exploring the impact of artifcial intelligence on teaching and learning in higher education. *Research and Practice in Technology Enhanced Learning*, *12*(1), 1–13. PMID: 30613250

Popenici, Ş., & Kerr, S. (2017). Exploring the impact of artificial intelligence on teaching and learning in higher education. *Research and Practice in Technology Enhanced Learning*, *12*(1), 22. Advance online publication. DOI: 10.1186/s41039-017-0062-8

Poquet, O., & de Laat, M. (2021). Developing capabilities: Lifelong learning in the age of AI. *British Journal of Educational Technology*, *52*(4), 1695–1708. DOI: 10.1111/bjet.13123

Prinsloo, P., & Slade, S. (2016). Student vulnerability, agency, and learning analytics: An exploration. *Journal of Learning Analytics, 3*(1), 159–182. https://oro.open.ac.uk/46172/

Priyadharshini, S. I., Irene, D. S., Beulah, J. R., & Ponnuviji, N. P. (2025). Enhancing real-time health monitoring with hybrid recurrent long short-term tyrannosaurus search for menstrual cups. *Biomedical Signal Processing and Control, 100*, 107065.

Qiu, B., Zhu, Y., Du, L., & Feng, C. (2024). Analysis and reflection on the teaching application of artificial intelligence technology in the context of big data. *Curriculum and Teaching Methodology, 7*(4). Advance online publication. DOI: 10.23977/curtm.2024.070404

Qu, X., Gu, Y., Xia, Q., Li, Z., Wang, Z., & Huai, B. (2024). A Survey on Arabic Named Entity Recognition: Past, Recent Advances, and Future Trends. *IEEE Transactions on Knowledge and Data Engineering, 36*(3). Advance online publication. DOI: 10.1109/TKDE.2023.3303136

Rahman, M. K., Ismail, N. A., Hossain, M. A., & Hossen, M. S. (2025). Students' mindset to adopt AI chatbots for effectiveness of online learning in higher education. *Future Business Journal, 11*(1), 30. DOI: 10.1186/s43093-025-00459-0

Raja, R., & Nagasubramani, P. C. (2018). Impact of modern technology in education. *Journal of applied and advanced research, 3*(1), 33-35.

Rajendran, T., Rajathi, S. A., Balakrishnan, C., Aswini, J., Prakash, R. B., & Subramanian, R. S. (2023, December). Risk Prediction Modeling for Breast Cancer using Supervised Machine Learning Approaches. In *2023 2nd International Conference on Automation, Computing and Renewable Systems (ICACRS)* (pp. 702-708). IEEE.

Ramineni, K., Harshith Reddy, K., Sai Thrikoteshwara Chary, L., Nikhil, L., & Akanksha, P. (2024, February). Designing an Intelligent Chatbot with Deep Learning: Leveraging FNN Algorithm for Conversational Agents to Improve the Chatbot Performance. In *World Conference on Artificial Intelligence: Advances and Applications* (pp. 143-151). Singapore: Springer Nature Singapore.

Rana, M. R. R., Nawaz, A., Rehman, S. U., Abid, M. A., Garayevi, M., & Kajanová, J. (2025). BERT-BiGRU-Senti-GCN: An Advanced NLP Framework for Analyzing Customer Sentiments in E-Commerce. *International Journal of Computational Intelligence Systems, 18*(1), 1–18. DOI: 10.1007/S44196-025-00747-1

Rane, N. (2023). Chatbot-Enhanced Teaching and Learning: Implementation Strategies, Challenges, and the rRole of ChatGPT in Education. SSRN Electronic Journal. https://doi.org/DOI: 10.2139/ssrn.4603204

Rane, N. (2024). Role and challenges of ChatGPT, Gemini, and similar generative artificial intelligence in human resource management. *Studies in Economics and Business Relations*, *5*(1), 11–23. DOI: 10.48185/sebr.v5i1.1001

Rao, A., & Ramalingamma, P. (2022). An FPT.AI-based text-to-speech application's end-to-end conversion speed analysis. *International Journal of Innovative Research in Engineering & Management*, *9*(5), 227–231. DOI: 10.55524/ijirem.2022.9.5.33

Reischmann, J. (2017). Lifewide learning – Challenges for Andragogy. *Journal of Adult Learning. Knowledge and Innovation*, *1*(1), 43–50. DOI: 10.1556/2059.01.2017.2

Ren, X. (2024). Integrating artificial intelligence into multimedia education: An in-depth analysis of software applications. *Journal of Education. Humanities and Social Sciences*, *44*, 60–65. DOI: 10.54097/8wemq285

Roberts, D. C., & Komives, S. R. (Eds.). (2016). *Enhancing Student Learning and Development in Cross-Border Higher Education. New Directions for Higher Education, Number 175*. John Wiley & Sons.

Roessger, K. M., Roumell, E. A., & Weese, J. (2018). Testing Andragogical Assumptions Across Countries Using Multi-Level Analyses of PIAAC Data. *American Institutes for Research PIAAC Research Conference*, 6–7.

Roessger, K. M., Roumell, E. A., & Weese, J. (2022). Rethinking andragogical assumptions in the global age: How preferences for andragogical learning vary across people and cultures. *Studies in Continuing Education*, *44*(1), 14–38. DOI: 10.1080/0158037X.2020.1732335

Ryan, R. M., & Deci, E. L. (2022). Self-Determination Theory. In Maggino, F. (Ed.), *Encyclopedia of Quality of Life and Well-Being Research* (pp. 1–7). Springer International Publishing., DOI: 10.1007/978-3-319-69909-7_2630-2

Sætra, H. S. (2023). Generative AI: Here to stay, but for good? *Technology in Society*, *75*, 102372. DOI: 10.1016/j.techsoc.2023.102372

Sajid, M., Sanaullah, M., Fuzail, M., Malik, T. S., & Shuhidan, S. M. (2025). Comparative analysis of text-based plagiarism detection techniques. *PLoS One*, *20*(4), e0319551. DOI: 10.1371/JOURNAL.PONE.0319551 PMID: 40198663

Salam, M., Fitri, S., & Zulan, H. (2024). Educational technology based on artificial intelligence in supporting distance learning in Arabic language learning in higher education. *Journal International of Lingua and Technology*, *3*(1), 134–145. DOI: 10.55849/jiltech.v3i1.485

Salem, M. A. (2025). Bridging or Burning? Digital Sustainability and PY Students' Intentions to Adopt AI-NLP in Educational Contexts. *Computers 2025, Vol. 14, Page 265, 14*(7), 265. https://doi.org/DOI: 10.3390/COMPUTERS14070265

Salinas-Navarro, D. E., Vilalta-Perdomo, E., Michel-Villarreal, R., & Montesinos, L. (2024). Using Generative Artificial Intelligence Tools to Explain and Enhance Experiential Learning for Authentic Assessment. *Education Sciences, 14*(1), 83. DOI: 10.3390/educsci14010083

Sanusi, I. T., Oyelere, S. S., Vartiainen, H., Suhonen, J., & Tukiainen, M. (2023). A systematic review of teaching and learning machine learning in K-12 education. *Education and Information Technologies*, *28*(5), 5967–5997.

Saravanan, K., Prakash, R. B., Balakrishnan, C., Kumar, G. V. P., Subramanian, R. S., & Anita, M. (2023, December). Support Vector Machines: Unveiling the Power and Versatility of SVMs in Modern Machine Learning. In *2023 3rd International Conference on Innovative Mechanisms for Industry Applications (ICIMIA)* (pp. 680-687). IEEE.

Sarosa, M., Kusumawadhani, M., Suyono, A., & Azis, Y. M. (2021). The effectiveness of chatbot as an online learning method on active and reflective learning styles. *Multicultural Education*, *7*(9), 92–100. http://doi.org/ http://doi.org/10.5281/zenodo.5484411

Sayeed, M. S., Mohan, V., & Muthu, K. S. (2023). BERT: A Review of Applications in Sentiment Analysis. In *HighTech and Innovation Journal* (Vol. 4, Issue 2). https://doi.org/DOI: 10.28991/HIJ-2023-04-02-015

Sekmokas, M., Larsson, L., Roberts, A., von Erlach, E., Guo, Y., & González, G. R. (2024). *Updated Framework for Monitoring Adult Learning: Enhancing Data Identification and Indicator Selection* (No. 317; OECD Education Working Papers, Vol. 317). https://doi.org/DOI: 10.1787/02bbacdc-en

Selwyn, N. (2021). *Education and technology: Key issues and debates*. Bloomsbury Publishing.

Şen, N., & Akbay, T. (2023). *AI and innovative applications in special education.* Öğretim Teknolojisi Ve Hayat Boyu Öğrenme Dergisi - Instructional Technology and Lifelong Learning., DOI: 10.52911/itall.1297978

Shaikh, S., Yayilgan, S., Zoto, E., & Abomhara, M. (2024). Multilingual user perceptions analysis from Twitter using zero shot learning for border control technologies. *Research Square*. https://doi.org/DOI: 10.21203/rs.3.rs-5269373/v1

Shaker, S. S., Alhajim, D., Al-Khazaali, A. A. T., Hussein, H. A., & Athab, A. F. (2022). Feature Extraction based Text Classification: A review. *Journal of Algebraic Statistics*, *13*(1), 646–653.

Shen, Y., Yang, L., & Deng, B. (2024). NLP-Driven Sentiment Analysis for Stakeholder Feedback in Sustainable Projects. *2024 6th International Conference on Frontier Technologies of Information and Computer, ICFTIC 2024*, 713–716. https://doi.org/DOI: 10.1109/ICFTIC64248.2024.10913250

Singh, A., Agarwal, A., Kumar, A., Rastogi, U., & Kumar, S. (2024, June). A Comprehensive Approach to Stress Detection and Management Using Machine Learning, Deep Learning, and Chatbot Integration. In *2024 15th International Conference on Computing Communication and Networking Technologies (ICCCNT)* (pp. 1-5). IEEE.

Singh, N., & Ahuja, N. (2019). Implementation and evaluation of intelligence incorporated tutoring system. *International Journal of Innovative Technology and Exploring Engineering*, *8*(10), 4548–4558. DOI: 10.35940/ijitee.j9849.0881019

Siva Subramanian, R., Prabha, D., Maheswari, B., & Aswini, J. (2021). Customer analysis using machine learning algorithms: A case study using banking consumer dataset. In *Recent Trends in Intensive Computing* (pp. 689–694). IOS Press.

Siva, S. R., Bushra, S. N., Maheswari, B., & Prabukumar, M. K. (2022, April). Performance Analysis of Different Machine Learning in Customer Prediction. In 2022 6th International Conference on Trends in Electronics and Informatics (ICOEI) (pp. 1425-1430). IEEE.

Skandali, D., Magoutas, A., & Tsourvakas, G. (2023). Artificial Intelligent Applications in Enabled Banking Services: The Next Frontier of Customer Engagement in the Era of ChatGPT. *Theoretical Economics Letters*, *13*(5), 1203–1223.

Solanki, R. K., Rajawat, A. S., Gadekar, A. R., & Patil, M. E. (2023). Building a conversational chatbot using machine learning: Towards a more intelligent healthcare application. In *Handbook of research on instructional technologies in health education and allied disciplines* (pp. 285–309). IGI Global Scientific Publishing.

Southworth, J., Migliaccio, K., Glover, J., Glover, J., Reed, D., McCarty, C., Brendemuhl, J., & Thomas, A. (2023). Developing a model for AI Across the curriculum: Transforming the higher education landscape via innovation in AI literacy. *Computers and Education: Artificial Intelligence*, *4*, 100127. DOI: 10.1016/j.caeai.2023.100127

Sparks, R. L. (2016). Myths about foreign language learning and learning disabilities. *Foreign Language Annals*, *49*(2), 252–270. DOI: 10.1111/flan.12196

St. Clair, R. (2024). Andragogy: Past and Present Potential. *New Directions for Adult and Continuing Education, 2024*(184), 7–13. DOI: 10.1002/ace.20546

Stamatelatos, A., & Brooks, R. (2020). Simulated business effectiveness: Learning and performance outcomes. *Education + Training, 62*(9), 1015–1036. DOI: 10.1108/et-04-2019-0084

Stamper, J., Xiao, R., & Hou, X. (2024, July). Enhancing llm-based feedback: Insights from intelligent tutoring systems and the learning sciences. In International Conference on Artificial Intelligence in Education (pp. 32-43). Cham: Springer Nature Switzerland.

Stanistreet, P. (2024). Lifelong learning in the age of AI. In *Only Connect: The Lifelong Learning Blog*. UNESCO Institute for Lifelong Learning. https://thelifelonglearningblog.uil.unesco.org/2024/03/19/lifelong-learning-in-the-age-of-ai/#:~:text=The 2023 AI Index Report,bolstering research and development%2C with Storey, V. A., & Wagner, A. (2024). Integrating Artificial Intelligence (AI) Into Adult Education. *International Journal of Adult Education and Technology, 15*(1), 1–15. https://doi.org/DOI: 10.4018/IJAET.345921

Strasser, T. (2023). Narrow AI-powered visualization facilitation tools in foreign language learning: A visual approach promoting equal opportunities in foreign language grammar teaching. *Social Visualities*, 85-98. https://doi.org/DOI: 10.1007/978-3-031-25259-4_5

Subagja, A. D., Ausat, A. M. A., Sari, A. R., Wanof, M. I., & Suherlan, S. (2023). Improving customer service quality in MSMEs through the use of ChatGPT. *Jurnal Minfo Polgan, 12*(1), 380–386.

Subha, S., Baghavathi Priya Sankaralingam, A., Gurusamy, A., Sehar, S., & Bavirisetti, D. P. (2023). Personalization-based deep hybrid e-learning model for online course recommendation system. *PeerJ. Computer Science*. Advance online publication. DOI: 10.7717/peerj-cs.1670 PMID: 38077588

Subha, S., & Baghavathi Priya, S. (2023). Prediction model for a good learning environment using an ensemble approach. *Computer Systems Science and Engineering, 44*(3), 2081–2093. DOI: 10.32604/csse.2023.028451

Subramanian, R. S., Aswini, J., Bushra, S. N., Nirmala, G., & Maheswari, B. (2022, November). Customer Analysis using Machine Learning with Feature Selection Approaches: A Comparative Study. In *2022 International Conference on Augmented Intelligence and Sustainable Systems (ICAISS)* (pp. 196-202). IEEE.

Subramanian, R. S., Prabha, D., Aswini, J., Maheswari, B., & Anita, M. (2021, February). Alleviating NB conditional independence using multi-stage variable selection (MSVS): Banking customer dataset application. [). IOP Publishing.]. *Journal of Physics: Conference Series, 1767*(1), 012002.

Sufi, F. (2024). Generative Pre-Trained Transformer (GPT) in Research: A Systematic Review on Data Augmentation. *Information 2024, Vol. 15, Page 99, 15*(2), 99. https://doi.org/DOI: 10.3390/INFO15020099

Sunarti, S., Ting, H. L., & Febrian Putri, A. E. (2022). Mandarin language material using artificial intelligence for Z-generation student. *Journal of Development Research, 6*(1), Process. https://doi.org/DOI: 10.28926/jdr.v6i1.195

Supriyono, , Wibawa, A. P., Suyono, , & Kurniawan, F. (2024). Advancements in natural language processing: Implications, challenges, and future directions. *Telematics and Informatics Reports, 16*, 100173. DOI: 10.1016/J.TELER.2024.100173

Su, Q., & Zhan, W. (2019). *From minimal contrast to meaning construct: Corpus-based, near synonym driven approaches to Chinese lexical semantics*. Springer Nature.

Tafazoli, D., Parra, M., & Abril, C. (2019). Intelligent language tutoring system. *International Journal of Information and Communication Technology Education, 15*(3), 60–74. DOI: 10.4018/ijicte.2019070105

Taghipour, K., & Ng, H. T. (2016). A neural approach to automated essay scoring. In *Proceedings of the 2016 Conference on Empirical Methods in Natural Language Processing* (pp. 1882–1891). Association for Computational Linguistics. https://doi.org/DOI: 10.18653/v1/d16-1193

Tang, S. (2021). Application of computer technology in the teaching of Chinese language and literature internet environment. *2021 International Conference on Internet, Education and Information Technology (IEIT)*. https://doi.org/DOI: 10.1109/ieit53597.2021.00085

Tao, H. (2016). Integrating Chinese linguistic research and language teaching and learning. *Integrating Chinese Linguistic Research and Language Teaching and Learning, xiii-xviii*. Advance online publication. DOI: 10.1075/scld.7.003int

Tao, Y., & Zou, B. (2021). Students' perceptions of the use of Kahoot! in English as a foreign language classroom learning context. *Computer Assisted Language Learning*, •••, 1–20. DOI: 10.1080/09588221.2021.2011323

Tasneem, N. S., & Hemalatha, R. (2025). Real-Time Sentiment Analysis of Customer Feedback Using Neural Networks and NLP Methods. *2024 International Conference on IT Innovation and Knowledge Discovery (ITIKD)*, 1–6. https://doi.org/DOI: 10.1109/ITIKD63574.2025.11004792

Taylor, D. C. M., & Hamdy, H. (2013). Adult learning theories: Implications for learning and teaching in medical education: AMEE Guide No. 83. *Medical Teacher*, *35*(11), e1561–e1572. DOI: 10.3109/0142159X.2013.828153

Teräs, M. (2022). Education and technology: Key issues and debates. *International Review of Education*, *68*(4), 635–636. DOI: 10.1007/s11159-022-09971-9

Ullah, S., Ahmad, R., Namoun, A., Muhammad, S., Ullah, K., Hussain, I., & Ibrahim, I. A. (2024). A Deep Learning-Based Approach for Part of Speech (PoS) Tagging in the Pashto Language. *IEEE Access : Practical Innovations, Open Solutions*, *12*, 86355–86364. DOI: 10.1109/ACCESS.2024.3412175

Uma, S. (2023). Conversational AI Chatbots in digital engagement: Privacy and security concerns. In *Trends, applications, and challenges of Chatbot technology* (pp. 274–317). IGI Global.

Vaswani, A., Shazeer, N., Parmar, N., Uszkoreit, J., Jones, L., Gomez, A. N., & Polosukhin, I. (2017). Attention is all you need. *Advances in Neural Information Processing Systems*, •••, 30.

Vayadande, K., Kale, D. R., Nalavade, J., Kumar, R., & Magar, H. D. (2024). Text Generation & Classification in NLP. *How Machine Learning Is Innovating Today's World: A Concise Technical Guide*, 25–36. https://doi.org/DOI: 10.1002/9781394214167.CH3

Vayadande, K., Kulkarni, A. M., Yadav, G. B., Kumar, R., & Sawant, A. R. (2024). A Comprehensive Analysis of Various Tokenization Techniques and Sequence-to-Sequence Model in Natural Language Processing. *How Machine Learning Is Innovating Today's World: A Concise Technical Guide*, 3–11. https://doi.org/DOI: 10.1002/9781394214167

Venkatesh, A. M., & Venkatesha, R. A. (2024), The rise of Google Gemini in modern education: Revolutionizing learning with AI chatbots (2024). https://ssrn.com/abstract=4925934 or DOI: 10.2139/ssrn.4925934

Villar, D. (2025). How artificial intelligence is transforming professional development. *UC San Diego Extended Studies*. https://extendedstudies.ucsd.edu/news-events/extended-studies-blog/how-artificial-intelligence-is-transforming-professional-development

Vygotsky, L. S. (1978). *Mind in society: The development of higher psychological processes*. Harvard University Press.

Wang, J. Y., Wang, W. Y., & Liang, J. C. (2024). Designing an Educational Chatbot for Enhanced Learning in Programming Courses. In 2024 12th International Conference on Information and Education Technology (ICIET) (pp. 237-242). IEEE. https://doi.org/DOI: 10.1109/iciet60671.2024.10542796

Wang, D., Zou, B., & Xing, M. (2022a). Interactive learning between Chinese students learning English and English students leaning Chinese on the platform of Wiki. *International Journal of Computer-Assisted Language Learning and Teaching*, *1*(3), 1–16. DOI: 10.4018/ijcallt.2011070105

Wang, M., & Yang, Q. (2024). Educational big data analytics using sentiment analysis for student requirement analysis on courses. *Scalable Computing: Practice and Experience*, *25*(5), 3858–3866. DOI: 10.12694/scpe.v25i5.3024

Wang, W. (2025). Real-Time Feedback and Tutoring of College English Using Artificial Intelligence Algorithms and IoT Sensors. *International Journal of High Speed Electronics and Systems*. Advance online publication. DOI: 10.1142/S0129156425406692

Wang, X., Pang, H., Wallace, M. P., Wang, Q., & Chen, W. (2022b). Learners' perceived AI presences in AI-supported language learning: A study of AI as a humanized agent from community of inquiry. *Computer Assisted Language Learning*, •••, 1–27. DOI: 10.1080/09588221.2022.2056203

Wang, X., Wang, C., & He, X. (2023). Design and implementation of artificial intelligence fusion experimental platform based on machine learning algorithm. *International Journal of New Developments in Engineering and Society*, *7*(2). Advance online publication. DOI: 10.25236/ijndes.2023.070202

Wei, C. L., Wang, Y. M., Lin, H. H., Wang, Y. S., & Huang, J. L. (2022). Developing and validating a business simulation systems success model in the context of management education. *International Journal of Management Education*, *20*(2). Advance online publication. DOI: 10.1016/j.ijme.2022.100634

Weng, T., & Chao, I. (2022). The development of educational robots for Vietnamese to learn Chinese. *2022 4th International Conference on Management Science and Industrial Engineering (MSIE)*. https://doi.org/DOI: 10.1145/3535782.3535841

Weng, X., XIA, Q., Gu, M., Rajaram, K., & Chiu, T. K. F. (2024). Assessment and learning outcomes for generative AI in higher education: A scoping review on current research status and trends. *Australasian Journal of Educational Technology, 40*(6), 37–55. DOI: 10.14742/ajet.9540

Wen, Y. (2020). *Computer-supported collaborative Chinese second language learning: Beyond brainstorming*. Springer.

Williams, R. T. (2024). The ethical implications of using generative chatbots in higher education. [Frontiers Media SA.]. *Frontiers in Education, 8*, 1331607.

Wollny, S., Schneider, J., Di Mitri, D., Weidlich, J., Rittberger, M., & Drachsler, H. (2021). Are we there yet? A systematic literature review on chatbots in education. *Frontiers in Artificial Intelligence, 4*, 654924. DOI: 10.3389/frai.2021.654924 PMID: 34337392

Wong, A. (2022). The design of an intelligent chatbot with natural language processing capabilities to support learners. [). IOP Publishing.]. *Journal of Physics: Conference Series, 2251*(1), 012005.

World Economic Forum. (2023). *Generative AI has disrupted education. Here's how it can be used for good – UNESCO*. World Economic Forum.

Wu, H., Li, S., Gao, Y., Weng, J., & Ding, G. (2024). Natural language processing in educational research: The evolution of research topics. *Education and Information Technologies, 29*(17), 23271–23297. DOI: 10.1007/s10639-024-12764-2

Wu, L., & McMahon, M. (2013). Adopting a musical intelligence and E-Learning approach to improve the English language pronunciation of Chinese students. *AI & Society, 29*(2), 231–240. DOI: 10.1007/s00146-013-0479-6

Xia, Q., Chiu, T. K., Lee, M., Sanusi, I. T., Dai, Y., & Chai, C. S. (2022). A self-determination theory (SDT) design approach for inclusive and diverse AI education. *Computers & Education, 189*, 104582. DOI: 10.1016/j.compedu.2022.104582

Xie, H. (2023). The promising future of cognitive science and artificial intelligence. *Nature Reviews Psychology, 2*, 202. DOI: 10.1038/s44159-023-00170-3

Xu, X. (2021). *Applying mobile technologies to Chinese language learning*. IGI Global.

Yaacoub, J. P. A., Noura, H. N., Salman, O., & Chehab, A. (2023). Ethical hacking for IoT: Security issues, challenges, solutions and recommendations. *Internet of Things and Cyber-Physical Systems, 3*, 280–308. DOI: 10.1016/j.iotcps.2023.04.002

Yamini, B., Sudha, K., Nalini, M., Kavitha, G., Subramanian, R. S., & Sugumar, R. (2023, June). Predictive modelling for lung cancer detection using machine learning techniques. In 2023 8th International Conference on Communication and Electronics Systems (ICCES) (pp. 1220-1226). IEEE.

Yamini, B., Ramana, K. V., Nalini, M., Devi, D. C., Maheswari, B., & Siva, S. R. (2024). Customer churn prediction model in enterprises using machine learning. *International Journal of Advanced Technology and Engineering Exploration*, *11*(110), 94.

Yang, H., Zhang, D., Jiang, R., & Shang, C. (2021). An intelligent mandarin-Tibetan bilingual learning platform for Mandarin learning. *INTED2021 Proceedings*. https://doi.org/DOI: 10.21125/inted.2021.0757

Yang, Y., Chen, L., He, W., Sun, D., & Salas-Pilco, S. Z. (2024). AI for enhancing special education for K-12: A decade of trends, themes, and global insights (2013–2023). *International Journal of AI in Education*. https://doi.org/DOI: 10.1007/s40593-024-00422-0

Yıldırım, A., & Şimşek, H. (2018). *Sosyal bilimlerde nitel araştırma yöntemleri* (11. b.). Ankara: Seçkin Yayıncılık.

Yildirim, B., & Akcan, A. T. (2024). AI-professional development model for chemistry teacher: Artificial intelligence in chemistry education. [JESEH]. *Journal of Education in Science, Environment and Health*, *10*(4), 161–182. DOI: 10.55549/jeseh.741

Yılmaz, Ö. (2024). *Personalised learning and artificial intelligence in science education: Current state and future perspectives*. Educational Technology Quarterly., DOI: 10.55056/etq.744

Yin, J., Goh, T. T., Yang, B., & Xiaobin, Y. (2021). Conversation technology with micro-learning: The impact of chatbot-based learning on students' learning motivation and performance. *Journal of Educational Computing Research*, *59*(1), 154–177.

Yu, J. H., & Chauhan, D. (2024). Trends in NLP for personalized learning: LDA and sentiment analysis insights. *Education and Information Technologies 2024 30:4*, *30*(4), 4307–4348. https://doi.org/DOI: 10.1007/S10639-024-12988-2

Zavaraki, E. Z. (2024). *Artificial intelligence for people with special educational needs*. IntechOpen., DOI: 10.5772/intechopen.1004158

Zawacki-Richter, O., Marín, V. I., Bond, M., & Gouverneur, F. (2023). Artificial intelligence in education: A comprehensive review of applications and challenges. *International Journal of Educational Technology in Higher Education*, *20*(1), 1–31. DOI: 10.1186/s41239-019-0171-0

Zhang, M., Ng, V., Zhao, D., Li, S., & Zan, H. (2018). *Natural language processing and Chinese computing: 7th CCF International Conference, NLPCC 2018, Hohhot, China, August 26–30, 2018, proceedings, part II*. Springer.

Zhang, J., & Kawanami, H. (1999). Modeling carryover and anticipation effects for Chinese tone recognition. *6th European Conference on Speech Communication and Technology (Eurospeech 1999)*. https://doi.org/DOI: 10.21437/eurospeech.1999-181

Zhang, K., & Aslan, A. B. (2021). AI technologies for education: Recent research & future directions. *Computers and Education: Artificial Intelligence*, *2*, 100025. DOI: 10.1016/j.caeai.2021.100025

Zhang, P., Huang, Y., Yang, C., & Jiang, W. (2023). Estimate the noise effect on automatic speech recognition accuracy for Mandarin by an approach associating articulation index. *Applied Acoustics*, *203*, 109217. DOI: 10.1016/j.apacoust.2023.109217

Zhao, R., & Chen, Z. (2022). Recognition of weird tone in Chinese communication and improvement of language understanding for AI. *Cross-Cultural Design. Product and Service Design, Mobility and Automotive Design, Cities, Urban Areas, and Intelligent Environments Design*, 599-607. https://doi.org/DOI: 10.1007/978-3-031-06053-3_41

Zhao, T. (2023). AI in educational technology. *Preprints*. https://doi.org/DOI: 10.20944/preprints202311.0106.v1

Zhong, Q., Ding, L., Liu, J., Du, B., & Tao, D. (2023). Can chatgpt understand too? a comparative study on chatgpt and fine-tuned bert. *arXiv preprint arXiv:2302.10198*.

Zhu, X., Zhang, M., Hong, Y., & He, R. (2020). *Natural language processing and Chinese computing: 9th CCF International Conference, NLPCC 2020, Zhengzhou, China, October 14–18, 2020, proceedings, part II*. Springer Nature.

Zhu, L., Mou, W., Lai, Y., Lin, J., & Luo, P. (2024). Language and cultural bias in AI: Comparing the performance of large language models developed in different countries on Traditional Chinese Medicine highlights the need for localized models. *Journal of Translational Medicine*, *22*(1), 319. DOI: 10.1186/s12967-024-05128-4

Zobel, T., Steinbeck, H., & Meinel, C. (2023). *Towards inclusive education: A review of and guide to accessible features in chatbots for moocs. In: 2023 IEEE learning with MOOCS*. LWMOOCS., DOI: 10.1109/LWMOOCS58322.2023.10306062

Zou, B. (2013). *Computer-assisted foreign language teaching and learning: Technological advances: Technological advances*. IGI Global.

About the Contributors

Suha Khalil Assayed holds a Ph.D. in Computer Science from The British University in Dubai, UAE, specializing in Artificial Intelligence and Deep Learning. With over two decades of experience in the higher education sector, she has developed deep expertise in machine learning, natural language processing (NLP), and neural network architectures, focusing on innovative AI applications that enhance educational outcomes. Dr. Assayed's research bridges theory and practice, emphasizing the design and deployment of AI- driven tools, including generative AI models, for personalized student advising and support. Her scholarly contributions encompass pioneering work on AI integration in education, intelligent chatbots, and adaptive learning systems, with publications in leading journals and conferences. Passionate about advancing smart education, she explores how emerging technologies can create more inclusive and effective learning environments.

***

A. Adaikkammai is an Assistant Professor in the Department of Computer Science and Business Systems at RMD Engineering College, Chennai. She is committed to academic excellence and student engagement in the evolving field of computing and business integration. Her areas of interest include data analytics, business intelligence, and modern software technologies.

A. Rajalakshmi is an Assistant Professor in the Department of Information Technology at Vel Tech Multi Tech Dr. Rangarajan Dr. Sakunthala Engineering College. She has a strong academic background and expertise in information technology, software engineering, and database systems. She is actively involved in student mentoring, project guidance, and curriculum enhancement activities. Her contributions include research publications and participation in seminars, workshops, and faculty development programs. Ms. Rajalakshmi is committed to fostering a dynamic learning environment and encouraging innovation among students.

Mussa S Abubakari, PhD, is an enthusiastic educational technology researcher and associate researcher with the Dig Connectivity Research Laboratory (DCRLab) in Kampala, Uganda, since 2024. He's an instructor in the Department of Physics and Mathematics at Kondoa Islamic Secondary School, Tanzania. He has a PhD in Educational Technology from Sultan Hassanal Bolkiah Institute of Education, Universiti Brunei Darussalam, and graduated in 2025. Dr. Mussa obtained a Master of Education degree in Electronics and Informatics Engineering at Yogyakarta State University, Indonesia, in July 2021. He obtained his BSc. in Telecommunications Engineering at the University of Dodoma in June 2016. His academic and research interests include educational technology, technology-enhanced learning, technology acceptance, open and distance learning, generative AI, and digital competence, among others. He has over 15 journal articles published in internationally reputable journals, several book chapters, and papers presented at international conferences.

Munir Ahmad is a seasoned professional in the realm of Spatial Data Infrastructure (SDI), Geo-Information Productions, Information Systems, and Information Governance, boasting over 25 years of dedicated experience in the field. With a PhD in Computer Science, Dr. Ahmad's expertise spans Spatial Data Production, Management, Processing, Analysis, Visualization, and Quality Control. Throughout his career, Dr. Ahmad has been deeply involved in the development and deployment of SDI systems specially in the context of Pakistan, leveraging his proficiency in Spatial Database Design, Web, Mobile & Desktop GIS, and Geo Web Services Architecture. His contributions to Volunteered Geographic Information (VGI) and Open Source Geoportal & Metadata Portal have significantly enriched the geospatial community. As a trainer and researcher, Dr. Ahmad has authored over 50 publications, advancing the industry's knowledge base and fostering innovation in Geo-Tech, Data Governance, and Information Infrastructure, and Emerging Technologies. His commitment to Research and Development (R&D) is evident in his role as a dedicated educator and mentor in the field.

Manar Alkhatib is an Assistant Professor of Artificial Intelligence at the British University in Dubai (BUiD). Her research focuses on advancing Arabic NLP, including developing models for Arabic text processing such as sentiment analysis, machine translation, and grammatical error correction. She applies deep learning and machine learning techniques to improve language understanding and processing, with a particular interest in the computational linguistics challenges of the Arabic language.

Sana Alsayed is an Assistant Professor of Psychological Counseling at Philadelphia University, Jordan. She has published several articles exploring the intersections of artificial intelligence, psychology, and emotions. Her research reflects an interdisciplinary approach to understanding human behavior and emotional well- being. Alongside her academic role, she serves as Library Director and Information Resources Manager at the university. Through her dual positions, she contributes to both educational development and applied research.

Yamini B is an faculty member in the Department of Networking and Communications at SRM Institute of Science and Technology, Kattankulathur. Her academic and research interests focus on emerging trends in networking, communication technologies, and related domains. She is dedicated to fostering innovation, academic excellence, and student skill development in her field.

C. Gomathi is an Assistant Professor in the Department of Artificial Intelligence and Data Science at Panimalar Engineering College, Chennai. She specializes in artificial intelligence, machine learning, and data analytics. With a strong passion for teaching, she actively engages students in innovative and hands-on learning experiences. She has contributed to academic research through papers and participation in workshops and conferences. Ms. Gomathi is committed to fostering technical skills and research aptitude among students.

. Anurekha is an Assistant Professor in the Department of Computer Science and Engineering (Data Science) at Vel Tech Rangarajan Dr. Sagunthala R&D Institute of Science and Technology, Avadi, Chennai. She holds a doctorate in Computer Science and has expertise in data analytics, machine learning, and artificial intelligence. Her academic contributions include research publications in reputed journals and active involvement in curriculum development. She is passionate about guiding students in data-driven projects and promoting interdisciplinary research. Dr. Anurekha also participates in various faculty development programs and workshops to enhance teaching and research skills.

Shahid Iqbal Rai, an esteemed international scholar from Pakistan, is currently pursuing a Ph.D. in Data Science at the University of Rome Tor Vergata, Italy, specializing in Natural Language Processing (NLP) with a keen focus on Large Language Models (LLM). Armed with a Master of Science in Computer Science, Shahid's prior research honed in on "English to Urdu: optimizing sequence learning in neural machine translation." His academic journey features a significant role as a researcher at COMSATS University Islamabad, where his NLP contributions resulted in a published research article at an "IEEE" international conference. Since 2019, Shahid has been actively contributing to academia as a researcher and lecturer at

The University of Lahore. His dedication to the realms of Artificial Intelligence and deep neural networks has positioned him as an innovator, leading to the development of groundbreaking techniques. Notably, he has mentored multiple students in the same domain, exemplifying his commitment to knowledge dissemination. This snapshot of Shahid's academic trajectory underscores his commitment to advancing research in NLP and AI, showcasing a remarkable blend of theoretical expertise and hands-on guidance.

Elavarasi J. is an Assistant Professor in the Department of Artificial Intelligence and Data Science at Vel Tech High Tech Dr. Rangarajan Dr. Sakunthala Engineering College. She specializes in machine learning, deep learning, and intelligent systems. She is dedicated to guiding students in innovative AI-based projects and research initiatives. Her academic involvement includes publishing papers and participating in technical workshops and FDPs. Ms. Elavarasi strives to create an engaging learning environment that nurtures technical excellence and creativity

SudhaK. is an Assistant Professor in the Department of Computer Science and Business Systems (CSBS) at RMD Engineering College, Kavaraipettai, Tamil Nadu. She is actively involved in teaching, research, and mentoring students in interdisciplinary areas bridging computer science and business analytics. Her interests include data science, programming, and emerging technologies in the CSBS domain. She participates in faculty development programs, academic conferences, and institutional research initiatives. Ms. Sudha is dedicated to fostering innovation, practical learning, and academic excellence in the field of CSBS.

KrishnaveniK. is serving as an Assistant Professor in the Department of Computer Science and Engineering at Asan Memorial College for Engineering and Technology, Chengalpattu – 603001. She is dedicated to providing quality technical education and mentoring students. Her teaching interests include programming languages, database systems, and software engineering. She actively engages in academic development and participates in workshops and seminars. She strives to inspire students through innovative teaching and continuous learning.

Sahitya PriyadharshiniK. is an Assistant Professor in the Department of Computer Science and Engineering at Panimalar Engineering College, Chennai. She is committed to delivering quality education and mentoring students in core areas of computer science. Her academic interests include programming, software development, and emerging technologies.

Nivas Kumar is a faculty member from Jawahar Engineering College, Chennai. He is actively engaged in academic research and teaching in the field of engineering.

His professional interests include mechanical systems, emerging technologies, and applied engineering solutions.

Anto Gracious L. A. is a faculty member in the Department of Computer Science and Engineering at R.M.K. College of Engineering and Technology, Tamil Nadu. He holds expertise in areas such as software engineering, data structures, and emerging computing technologies. With a strong commitment to academic excellence, he actively contributes to teaching, mentoring, and curriculum development. Mr. Anto Gracious has participated in various workshops and seminars aimed at enhancing technical education

Anna Lynn Abu Bakar is currently a senior lecturer in the Centre for the Promotion of Knowledge and Language, Universiti Malaysia Sabah (UMS). She completed her PhD in TESL looking into students' Willingness to Communicate in English. She is currently into teaching innovations in the classroom. She can be reached at annalynn@ums.edu.my

Ezhilvendan M is an academic professional and author affiliated with the Department of AIML at Panimalar Engineering College, Chennai. He is actively involved in research and scholarly writing, contributing to advancements in his field through academic publications. With a keen interest in innovation and knowledge dissemination, he participates in conferences and research forums. His research work is supported by Panimalar Engineering College, where he also mentors students and engages in institutional projects. Mr. Ezhilvendan is dedicated to continuous learning and contributing to the academic and research community.

SwethaM. is currently working as an Assistant Professor in the Department of Artificial Intelligence and Data Science at Vel Tech Multi Tech Dr. Rangarajan Dr. Sakunthala Engineering College, Avadi, Chennai. She is committed to imparting quality education and fostering innovation among students. Her areas of interest include machine learning, data analytics, and AI applications. She actively participates in academic and research activities to stay updated with emerging technologies. She is passionate about guiding students in both academic and project-based learning

Maida Maqsood did MS in English from Government College Women University, Sialkot. Throughout her academic journey, she has achieved notable successes that have strengthened her foundation in literature, education and linguistics. Her Master's research reflects her dedication to exploring critical themes in literature with the use of linguistics style. Additionally, her active participation in different conferences and seminars, such as The International Conference on Modern

Trends in Applied Linguistics, and 7th ASNeT International Multidisciplinary Academic Conference 2024 (AIMAC 2024) highlight her commitment to staying updated with current trends in her field.

Hélder Fanha Martins currently holds the position of Full Professor at the Lisbon Accounting and Business School, part of the Polytechnic University of Lisbon (LABS-ISCAL). Furthermore, he is an Integrated Researcher affiliated with CETAPS at NOVA University of Lisbon. With a doctoral degree conferred by Nova University (UNL), Professor Martins has dedicated his research endeavours to the fields of Business Simulation Studies, Languages for Specific Purposes, and Computer-Assisted Language Learning. He serves on the editorial boards of multiple academic journals. Within LABS-ISCAL, he is responsible for overseeing the Department of Information and Communication Sciences and spearheads the International Business Simulation course.

Harun Önder graduated from the Buca Faculty of Education at Dokuz Eylül University in İzmir, Turkey, in 2004. He received his Master's degree in Chemistry Education from the same institution that same year. Since 2024, he has been a PhD student in the Department of Mathematics and Science Education at the Faculty of Education at Hacettepe University. His main research interests are problem-based learning, technological pedagogical content knowledge, and AI in chemistry education.

Manoj Praveen is working as Assistant Professor in Depatment of AI nd DS at Velalar College of Engineering and Technology, Tamil Nadu, India

K. Saranya is working as an Assistant Professor in the Department of Artificial Intelligence and Data Science at Panimalar Engineering College, Chennai. She is passionate about teaching emerging technologies in AI and Data Science. Her academic interests include machine learning, deep learning, and data analytics. She is committed to fostering student development through innovative teaching methods and project guidance. She actively engages in faculty development programs and academic research initiatives

Siva Subramanian R is associated with the Department of Computer Science and Engineering at SRM Institute of Science and Technology. He actively contributes to research and scholarly publications. He is committed to mentoring students and driving technical innovation in his field. His work strengthens the academic and research environment of the institution.

Ravikumar R. Natarajan is an experienced academician with over 12+ years of teaching and research expertise across institutions in India, the UAE, and the Maldives. He currently serves as an Assistant Professor at Marwadi University, Rajkot, specializing in Machine Learning, Recommender Systems, and AI-driven applications in healthcare and security. He holds a Ph.D. in Machine Learning and Recommender Systems from Amity University, Jaipur, a Master of Engineering in CSE from VMRF University, Salem, and a Bachelor of Engineering in CSE from Anna University. He also has a MiniMBA from the Swiss eLearning Institute. Dr. Ravikumar has authored more than 8+ multiple SCIE/Scopus-indexed journal articles, 25+ IEEE/Springer conference papers, and co-authored a book on Artificial Intelligence. He has also published 9 patents and contributed 10+ book chapters in emerging domains such as Federated Learning, Blockchain, and Digital Twins for IGI Global, Wiley and Springer publisher. He actively mentors students through initiatives like the Research Activities Club (RAC) and Student Research Internship Training (SRIT), promoting innovation and research culture.

Aarthi S is a dedicated Assistant Professor in Computer Science with over six years of teaching experience. She is currently pursuing her Ph.D. at Marwadi University, Gujarat, and holds an M.Phil. and MCA from Bharathiar University, Tamil Nadu. Throughout her academic career, Aarthi has specialized in programming languages such as C++, Java, and C, and contributed to research in recommender systems and AI-related data privacy. She has published journal articles, contributed to book chapters, and actively participated in technical workshops. Known for her student mentorship and engagement in academic events, Aarthi remains committed to fostering innovation and excellence in computer science education.

S. Baghavathi Priya is a highly accomplished academic with an MTech (Gold Medal) and a PhD earned at Jawaharlal Nehru Technological University, Hyderabad. With 26 years of teaching and 15 years of research experience, she has supervised nine scholars and written a book operating systems. Recognized with awards and publications, she holds memberships in CSI and IAENG

Vanitha Siddheswaran is an Assistant Professor of Computer Science in Department of Social Sciences at Kumaraguru Institute of Agriculture, Erode, India

Somsubhra Saha is an Assistant Professor in the Department of Computer Science and Engineering at RMK College of Engineering and Technology. He has expertise in areas such as computer networks, programming, and emerging technologies. He is actively involved in mentoring students and guiding them in technical projects and innovations. Ms. omsubhra Sahacontributes to academic excellence through research publications and participation in technical events. He is dedicated to enhancing student learning through modern teaching methodologies and continuous professional development.

Barno Sapaeva is working as Lecturer in the Department Roman-Germanic Philology, Mamun University, Uzbekistan.

Jorge Sequeira is an Associate Professor (Professor Coordenador) at the Lisbon Accounting and Business School, Polytechnic University of Lisbon (LABS-ISCAL). He earned his doctoral degree from Universidad de Alcalá, Spain, and his research focuses on Business Simulation Studies, Educational Technology, Software Development, and Digital Rights Protection. In addition to his academic pursuits, Jorge actively contributes to the technical programs of numerous international conferences. At LABS-ISCAL, he oversees the Department of Informatics.

Khaled Shaalan, Head of Computer Science programmes at The British University in Dubai was ranked among the top 2% scientists in the world in a study led by a research team at Stanford University. Prof. Khaled has published over 220+ referred publications and the impact of his research using Google Scholar's H-index metric is 39. He has several research publications in highly reputed journals

Siva Subramanian R is a faculty member in the School of Computing at SRM Institute of Science & Technology, Trichy campus. He specializes in computer science domains including artificial intelligence, data analytics, and software development. With active involvement in research and teaching, he contributes significantly to academic and institutional growth.

ThilagamT. is currently working as an Assistant Professor in the Department of Computer Science and Engineering at Vel Tech Rangarajan Dr. Sagunthala R&D Institute of Science and Technology, Chennai, Tamil Nadu, India. She is actively involved in teaching, research, and academic development. Her research interests span various domains of computer science, and she contributes significantly through publications and scholarly activities. She is dedicated to guiding students and promoting innovative research practices.

Anish T. P is a faculty member in the Department of Computer Science and Engineering at R.M.K. College of Engineering and Technology, Puduvoyal, Tamil Nadu. He is actively involved in teaching, research, and mentoring students in various domains of computer science. His academic interests include artificial intelligence, data structures, and modern software development practices.

Tan Jee Chin is a Language Teacher in the Centre for the Promotion of Knowledge and Language Learning at UMS. His research focuses on Chinese Language, Literature, and Culture. He is the author of Travel and "Modernity": A Record of the Travels of Modern Chinese Literati in Europe (1920-1935).

Yong Hui Wen is a language teacher of Mandarin at Universiti Malaysia Sabah (UMS). She earned her Master Degree in Teaching Chinese to Speakers of Other Languages (TCSOL) from East China Normal University in 2023, where her work focuses on the teaching methods in teaching Mandarin language as foreign languages. Yong Hui Wen's academic interests include the teaching materials, new era teaching methods, and teaching skills.

Zi Hong Yong currently a Mandarin language teacher of Universiti Malaysia Sabah.

Yong Zi Xian is currently a Mandarin language teacher at the Centre for the Promotion of Knowledge and Language, Universiti Malaysia Sabah (UMS). She completed her master's degree in Teaching Chinese to Speakers of Other Languages (TCSOL) at Peking University, China. Her research interests include Chinese language teaching and learning and Chinese character studies. She can be contacted via email at: zixian.yzx@ums.edu.my.

Index

A

B

C

D

S

T

V

www.ingramcontent.com/pod-product-compliance
Lightning Source LLC
LaVergne TN
LVHW081538300926
849161LV00006B/1482
* 9 7 9 8 3 3 7 3 6 7 9 1 0 *